The Practice of Social Work

The Practice of Social Work
Second Edition

Robert W. Klenk

Huron County Mental Health and Mental Retardation Board

Robert M. Ryan

The Ohio State University

Wadsworth Publishing Company, Inc., Belmont, California

Sociology Editor: Steve Rutter

ISBN 0-534-00341-9
L. C. Cat. Card No. 73-91742
Printed in the United States of America

2 3 4 5 6 7 8 9 10—78 77 76 75 74

Preface

In social work, both generalist practitioners and specialists are important. This book attempts to present the generalist approach to social work. "Approach," as used here, implies more than a method. It suggests the use of a variety of methods.

Chapter 1, an overview of the generalist approach, establishes a meaningful conceptual framework for the articles. The framework stresses that a practitioner must know things common to all areas of social work and also know things unique to specific areas. For example, the social worker needs to know how to interview, whether dealing with individuals or organizations. And he needs to know several theories of human behavior to be effective with the individual, the small group, and the large group.

The articles in Chapter 2 stress client self-determination, in which the social worker first learns the client's needs and then suggests a solution. The chapter identifies values, moral commitments, and human rights that social workers should appreciate. The chapter emphasizes that human rights are a legitimate concern for social workers, who should also consider problems of individuals and groups along with the public issues of society.

Chapter 3 focuses on the behavior of individuals, exploring situational factors, role expansion, and systems concepts. Individuals are seen in a wide range of contexts, calling for a variety of approaches. The "social treatment" view is the major thrust of the chapter.

An individual cannot be fully understood apart from his social roles. Chapter 4 examines how an individual functions in a group and identifies principles and models that can be used when dealing with behavioral and organizational change, staff and community development, and social action.

Chapter 5 examines how social services are provided. The major focus is not the community at large but rather social welfare organizations in the community.

The articles in Chapter 6 illustrate the generalist in action and inte-

v

grate concepts from earlier chapters through studies of a broad network of client systems.

Further refinement and development of social work practice must continue to keep pace with individual and social needs and problems. We believe the ideas in this book provide a basis for further evolution of the field.

Our thanks go to the reviewers, who made many helpful suggestions: Theodore Brooks, Texas Women's University; Wynetta Bryant, Rutgers University; Lawrence Grossman, School of Social Policy, SUNY at Buffalo; Vernon R. Hanson, Pacific Lutheran University; LaMoyne Matthews, Morgan State College; and Irving Tebor, California State College at San Diego.

We would also like to acknowledge the contributions of our wives, secretaries, students, and colleagues as well as the Huron County Mental Health–Mental Retardation Board and The Ohio State University School of Social Work. Special thanks go to the true experts on their own needs and problems—the countless clients of social workers.

Contents

Contents

1

General Introduction

Introduction to the
Generalist Approach

The generalist approach to social work practice as it is now defined was developed, for the most part, in the 1960s, from a variety of causes. Among them were: changes in social conditions, and therefore in the kinds of problems brought to social welfare agencies; a more sophisticated understanding of the relationships between man and his environment; and the effect of systems theories on the acquisition of knowledge in social work. Given the basic aim of social work—to enhance social functioning—these developments made it clear that a new kind of social worker was needed, one with the requisite knowledge and skills to work with a variety of situations. The generalist approach to social work practice is a response to that need.

The idea of a generalist approach to social work now appears to be widely accepted within the profession. But the knowledge and skills required by this approach have not yet been organizable in such a way that one can simultaneously understand the parts and the whole. (The *parts* are those individuals, families, groups, formal organizations, or communities that are or might become objects of the worker's interventive efforts. The *whole* is those parts recognized as units in one or more interrelated systems.) Hence, while generalists share the same set of values[1] and constraints as all other social work professionals,[2] and place as much importance upon them, the generalist approach is now preoccupied with the critically important development of practical procedures. (Among the values shared are: client self-determination, individualization, confidentiality, and acceptance; these and other significant values are considered in the following chapters—chiefly in the readings—as are such issues as social control and the role of the client in the social work process.)

In this chapter we will describe the criteria by which the articles that follow were chosen. It was important, for one thing, that they convey in linear form (that is, in sentences, which deal adequately with only one aspect of a thing at a time) the complex simultaneity of the area under study. Because the worker must have a frame of reference that allows simultaneous understanding of many interacting relationships, the literature must be organized to at once make the potential need for intervention recognizable and yet allow for the separate entities to be individually analyzed. Also to be studied are which skills and kinds of knowledge are shared by the generalist and specialist alike, and which are not. These are but a few of the concerns that guided our choice of the material that follows.

In this chapter the social work generalist area of responsibility is described by the *basic framework of human service problem areas* (Figure 1, p. 3).This framework—an alternative to the "disease" model, taken from medicine, that has dominated social work thinking in the past—suggests the breadth of the generalist's activities.

Within the basic framework, the social worker's fundamental rule of measure is the level of functioning manifested by the individual; if the individual is functioning at what is considered less than an adequate level, the causes must be sought and remedied.

The idea of functioning leads logically to that of the *objective.* When the principle of functioning is applied by the generalist worker to a particular individual (or particular individuals) in a particular set of circumstances, the product will likewise be particular: the *objective.* An objective is a product of the goals that have been arrived at by client and worker together. Both client and worker have objectives. The focus here is on worker objectives which allow the generalist to impose order on the resources available once goals have been established with the advice and consent of the client. The objective enables the generalist

---

[1]See Schneiderman's articles in chapters 2 and 6 for a view that is strongly endorsed by the editors.
[2]See Charles S. Levy, "The Value Base of Social Work," *Journal of Education for Social Work* (Winter 1973), pp. 34–42, for a discussion of the relationship of values to social work practice.

Figure 1. Basic Framework of Social Welfare Human Services Problem Areas

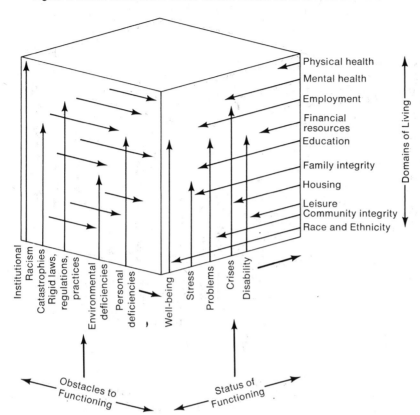

to select and organize activities, from the diverse array of those available, into a potentially effective strategy.

Twelve objectives are enumerated in this chapter; though they are not the entire range of the generalist approach, they illustrate its breadth and are directly related to the basic framework (Figure 1). Each objective demands of a worker certain kinds of knowledge from which skills can be drawn.

In the final section of the chapter, A Model for Practice, the social work process is described. This description will indicate how difficult it is to understand that what seems to be a step by step process is in reality a dynamic interplay of various phases. The section introduces a set of terms that relate this process back to the basic framework and the enumerated objectives. The process is essentially an adaptation of the scientific method—a cyclical process wherein the worker moves back and forth among its various phases as the needs of his client and the joint efforts of client and worker indicate.

Development of a Generalist
Approach

Social work practice today encompasses more alternative models than perhaps at any other point in its history. Many practitioners apply to this diversity an either/or judgment that a given method or combination of methods is sounder than others.[3] However, our judgment is that this diversity is not an either/or question but instead a recognition and response by social workers to our ever-changing social conditions.

The generalist view of social work practice advocated in this text is one of these developments. Although some practitioners and educators see this particular orientation as a return to a turn-of-the-century style of practice,[4] the generalist of today is more sophisticated than his predecessors. This is so because he must deal with a society that is more complex than that of the early 1900s; today's generalist social worker must have the requisite knowledge and skills to intervene in a number of different sizes of systems (individuals, families, groups, and organizations).

In other words, a generalist practitioner begins from a holistic perspective (that is, one that sees the total client) and works toward the satisfaction of that client's total needs.

This philosophy forms the basis for the notion of the *generalist*—the person who plays whatever roles and does whatever activities are necessary for the person or family when the person or family needs them. His concern is the person in need—not specific tasks or techniques or professional prerogatives. He is an aide to the individual or family—not an aide to an agency or to a profession.[5]

We can use a New York City project, Mobilization For Youth (MFY), to illustrate this generalist approach.[6] MFY began with the assumption that because the individual is a product of the interaction between himself and his environment, juvenile delinquency was a product of a number of interacting environmental conditions. The resolution of such a problem called for a worker to be prepared, individually and in concert with other professionals, to work throughout that environment. The workers on this project were expected to work with different sizes of systems (individuals, families, groups, and organizations), and to be able to work with professionals from other disciplines, as there was an

---

[3]See Schwartz, "Private Troubles and Public Issues: One Social Work Job or Two?" in chapter 2 for further discussion of this issue.

[4]See the two articles by Siporin in chapter 3 for further discussion along these lines.

[5]Harold L. McPheeters and Robert M. Ryan, *A Core of Competence For Baccalaureate Social Welfare and Curricular Implications* (Atlanta: Southern Regional Education Board, 1971), p. 22.

[6]Harold H. Weissman is editor of a four-volume series related to this project that has the overall title *The New Social Work* (New York: Association Press, 1969).

early recognition that many of the situations these workers were confronting needed medical, legal, or major organizational interventions that were beyond the knowledge and skill of MFY workers.

The generalist approach to practice is in many respects different from those conceptions of practice that had dominated until recent years. Social casework, social group work, and community organization have been the standard approaches to the direct delivery of services. (Administration and research have long held an important place within social work practice, but the above three methods have been the chief modes of direct delivery of services.) Parts of each of these three approaches are combined within a holistic point of view to produce a distinctly different kind of practitioner: the generalist.

Social casework, perhaps the oldest of the three methods, grew out of early concerns for the poor and sick. Man was viewed from a moral perspective by which poverty or disability were evidence of immorality, whether vice or sloth. This moral explanation of dysfunctioning gave way to a recognition of the impact social conditions had on the individual, only to return with the ascendance of "Social Darwinism" (the application of the theory of "survival of the fittest" to human society). Later, Freudian psychology brought another dramatic change to the social worker's understanding of the individual in relation to his environment. Each of these views premised that the individual was to varying degrees responsible for his own conditions; and the social caseworker endeavored to change individuals in such ways that they would conform to the status quo.

Group work developed in recreational settings, usually in religiously oriented settlement houses. Like the caseworker's, the early group worker's views of the individual had a moral base; but unlike the caseworker, the group worker dealt fundamentally with interaction among individuals. Freudian psychology eventually had a major impact on group work, as the group worker—though he still concentrated on the individual's interactions within the group—became more concerned with the psychology of individual behavior.

As a social work method, community organization grew out of the Charity Organization Society movement; the COS group, concerned with the large number of overlapping services developing in urban areas, had seen the need to coordinate public and private social agencies and to develop standards for them. In addition, a need for financial support moved community organization into fund-raising. Although its workers were influenced by the same views as caseworkers and group workers, community organization practice was influenced more by sociological than by psychological theories.

These are the three major service delivery views that have dominated social work practice theory in recent years; each of these broad areas is a specialization, derived from the specialist's view of man as either an individual, *or* a group, *or* a community. Although none of these areas entirely excludes the others, as may seem to have been implied above, each has minimized the others in practice. As a result, each area has compartmentalized human needs to suit its specialization instead of adapting its practice to human needs. Not one looked at the individual in relation to his total environment.

The generalist's perspective is more holistic than the specialist's. He shares certain basic knowledge with the caseworker *and* the group worker *and* the community organizer, but is not all of these at one time. Instead, according to the system (individual, family, group, organization) with which he were at the moment working, he would manifest the basic characteristics of the specialist who worked exclusively with that type of client—although he would not have that specialist's level of skill and knowledge.

Among the generalist's unique contributions to social work practice is the ability to work with the client's total system as well as with the client himself. For example, the generalist might work with a social planner to identify problems, collect data, and develop policy; or he might intervene with formal organizations to obtain exceptions or changes to policies that prevent clients from realizing their aspirations and/or satisfying unmet needs; or he might mediate, if the need arises, to construct support systems for his client. At the same time, if it is appropriate, the worker might be intervening with the client to teach him either alternative behaviors or how to negotiate the system on his own; or he might be working with the client as a member of a group.

In summary, the social work generalist intervenes when an individual is functioning at a less than desirable level,[7] or when a group is functioning at such a less than desirable level—especially when its individual members are the obstacle, and/or environmental factors obstruct the functioning of these group members.[8] The generalist will also intervene with formal organizations when they do not respond to client needs.[9] None of these targets of the generalist's interventive efforts is a separate area; each is part of the generalist's whole.[10]

Just as the continuous evolution in the rationale of social work practice within the specialties reflected changes in our understanding of man, so does the growing interest in generalist practice. The generalist orientation is not so much a change in emphasis as it is the addition of another dimension to social work practice, one that embodies, through social and general systems theories, changes in our understand-

[7]See chapter 3 for treatment of this topic.
[8]Chapter 4 studies this area.
[9]This topic is treated in chapter 5.
[10]Treated in chapter 6.

ing of the relationships between man and his environment; in our ability to theorize about these relationships; in social welfare programming; and in the responsibilities of social work with respect to these new insights.

The generalist's value premise is holistic. Like the general practitioner in medicine, he is expected to have the basic knowledge of each area of specialization, its basic skills, and the basic values of his profession. Although the breadth of his knowledge, skills, and values might mean that his competence in any area of specialization will be somewhat less than that of the specialist, his very diversity permits his intervention in several different systems, making his area of specialization that of the total person in situation rather than a specific modality of skills and techniques.

The Social Work Generalist

As we have said, the service delivery of a generalist social worker resembles that of the generalist medical practitioner. He has basic knowledge about the individual in relation to his total environment, yet knows the limits of his competency. His set of skills permits him to work with a variety of the more common problems brought to social agencies; to engage in a variety of preventive endeavors; usually to be a competent diagnostician; and to work either one to one with individuals, or with groups, or with selected decision-makers in formal organizations.

The generalist social worker is *not* simultaneously a highly skilled caseworker, who works with the individual to achieve change in that client's behavior; a highly skilled group worker, who works with individuals within a group to achieve change in their behavior; a community organizer or social planner, who is primarily involved with the design and development of programs, organizations, and policies; or an administrator, who is concerned with the structure, organization, and management of a program or agency. Rather, he has the *basic knowledge* and the *basic skills* of each of these areas of specialization, which he uses within a holistic frame of reference. His skill in diagnosis, like that of the medical practitioner, includes a recognition of his own limits of competence; and when the demands of a situation exceed these limits, he would be expected to call on experts for consultation or service delivery. However, even when a specialist is called in, the generalist would tend to retain primary responsibility for services to that client. For example, were the client referred to a family therapist, the generalist might remain involved to insure that the client was obtaining the service he needed and to act as a source of support for the client and the therapist.

Analyzing Social Work
Practice

A Basic Framework

Before we analyze social work practice we must identify a set of *boundaries* within which that practice will be undertaken. One such formulation is presented in Figure 1:[11] the Basic Framework of Social Welfare Human Services Problem Areas graphically illustrates the multidimensional world in which the generalist must intervene if he is to cope with the variety of elements of the systems within which individuals function. The three dimensions of this cube suggest that a number of interrelationships exist among individual needs, forces that impinge on these needs, and the different levels of functioning with respect to each need.[12] It is implicit in this illustration that the social work professional must work with formal organizations as well as with individuals.[13]

The Basic Framework suggests the multiple variables that are related to a client's problems; it also illustrates the breadth of the generalist's scope of practice (which is coextensive with the breadth of responsibility for the whole social work profession). The *domains of living* are the areas of man's basic human needs, which can be infinite in number or contracted to as few as six; for example, health, education, financial resources, employment, and family and community integrity.[14] *Status of functioning* is a continuum on which any given individual may be functioning at a different level for each domain of living, ranging from *well-being* at one end through *stress, problems,* and *crises* to *disability.* *Obstacles to functioning* categorizes those factors in the environment or in the individual that may be impinging upon his or her ability to achieve maximum potential.[15] The continuum extends from individual deficiency at one extreme to natural catastrophe at the other, with such factors as institutional racism, ghettos, poor schools, and inadequate housing implied in the terms "rigid laws and regulations" and "environmental deficiency." Some obstacles to functioning afflict their victims so pervasively that these obstacles almost warrant a dimension of their own. Many of those who are poor or belong to certain ethnic minority groups are forced into an oppressed way of life, because society's values and institutions have, for irrational reasons, identified such groups of persons as dysfunctional. The obstacles to functioning will

---

[11]McPheeters and Ryan, op. cit., p. 15.

[12]The three dimensions of this cube are expanded upon in Appendix A, "Taxonomy of Problem Areas." This taxonomy illustrates the breadth to which these dimensions may be developed.

[13]See page 13 for an example of the use of these concepts with respect to a specific case illustration.

[14]See Appendix A at the end of this chapter for an expansion of these particular domains of living.

[15]See Appendix A at the end of this chapter for an expanded list of these obstacles.

be characteristically great for persons in these groups, and their status of functioning poor, for all or almost all domains of living. Therefore, the social work professional is obligated to work against this kind of value dissonance.[16]

Well-being, definable as a condition in which, by both his own and society's standards, the individual is functioning satisfactorily, makes two points. First, a chief responsibility of social workers is to prevent dysfunctioning; and every other point on this continuum suggests dysfunctioning. Only well-being implies the individual is functioning normally. Well-being also indicates the social worker's preventive role: we have a responsibility to work to maintain that particular state; we must support those social systems that encourage normal functioning, and must work to change those systems that, directly or indirectly, respond to or act upon individuals to produce dysfunctioning.

The second point is that an individual may move in either direction along this continuum. Someone who is dysfunctional in one or more domains of living need not be as dysfunctional in all domains of living. Part of the social worker's rehabilitative task is to build upon the client's strengths and assets for leverage against the dysfunctional aspects. To emphasize pathology and ignore or negate health puts the worker in danger of employing inappropriate techniques to solve a problem. We must be as concerned with an individual's strengths as we have tended to be with his shortcomings.

In summary, the Basic Framework schematizes the system of interacting forces in which a generalist social worker must function; its dimensions illustrate the breadth of his work: the rationale for his work is represented by the *status of functioning* dimension; the targets are suggested by the *obstacles to functioning* dimension; and client considerations are illustrated by the *domains of living* dimension. Although necessarily an oversimplification, this cube illustrates the variety of interrelationships involved in any social welfare problem.

Objectives

The express purpose and sole justification of any interventive act·by a professional social worker is that it will directly or indirectly enhance the social functioning of current or potential clients of social welfare organizations.[17] It is essential that the client participate in defining the kinds of opportunities needed.[18]

Given his primary purpose, the social work generalist must begin with

[16]Each of the articles in chapter 2 confronts various aspects of this issue.
[17]Harriett M. Bartlett, *The Common Base of Social Work Practice* (New York: National Association of Social Workers, 1970), p. 65.
[18]See Reid in chapter 3 and Setleis in Chapter 5 for a discussion of "the client as expert" idea.

a *need* perspective, with a definition of *what must be done.* This definition is best achieved through discussions between client and worker which culminate in an agreement on what can realistically be achieved; after which, the techniques and tasks required to satisfy those needs are selected. (This last step in the process has usually been the *first* step for the casework, group work, or community organization practitioners, who have tended to begin from a methodological perspective.)

The generalist must conduct his interventive acts either in conjunction with the client and/or with the client's consent or, in some cases, knowledge.[19] Given the variety of situations for which a generalist worker must have interventive skills, he or she must also have a means to integrate these skills with the requirements of a given situation into a meaningful structure of techniques. An "objectives framework" is such a means.

An objectives framework is built on the assumption that work has meaning only when it can be described and its end, or goal, is known. For example, a worker may sweep a floor (the action), for one or more reasons (the goal): "(1) to clean the floor; (2) to teach another person to sweep the floor; (3) to provide a housekeeper role model; or (4) to establish rapport, . . ."[20] Although sweeping the floor is a specific task, description of the worker's actions is not enough: one must also know the *reason(s)* for them. These two factors, what the worker does *and* what is accomplished, clarify the actions of social workers. The following twelve objectives illustrate the breadth of expectations for the generalist social worker. (These objectives are not listed in any order of priority nor are the skills necessary to achieve them elaborated upon here.) Client needs, as defined and clarified by the client and worker, will be the criteria for assignment of priorities.

1. Detection
The primary objective is to identify persons or groups who are experiencing difficulty (at crisis) or are in danger of doing so (at risk). A further objective is to detect and identify conditions in the environment that are contributing to the problems or are raising the level of risk.

2. Linkage
The primary objective is to steer persons toward the existing services that can benefit them. Its focus is on enabling or helping them to use the system and to negotiate its pathways. A further objective is to link elements of the service system with one another; this objective yields the essential benefit of direct

[19]See Gore and Schneiderman in chapter 2 and Riley, Taber, and Fantl in chapter 6 for varying but complementary views on this topic.
[20]McPheeters and Ryan, op. cit., p. 17.

contact between the person and the source of help and between elements of the service system.

3. Advocacy
The primary objective is to gain the rights and dignity of persons in need of help. The key assumption is that sometimes practices, regulations, and general conditions will prevent a person from receiving services, from thinking of fighting for services on his own behalf, and fighting for changes in laws, regulations, etc., on behalf of a whole class of persons or segment of society. Advocacy aims at removing the obstacles or barriers to the exercise of persons' rights or to the receipt of the benefits and use of the resources they need.

4. Evaluation
This involves gathering information, assessing personal or community problems, weighing alternatives and priorities, and making decisions for action.

5. Mobilization
The foremost objective is to assemble and energize existing groups, resources, organizations, and structures, or to create new groups, organizations, or resources, and bring them to bear on current or incipient problems. Its principal focus is on available or existing institutions, organizations, and resources within the community.

6. Instruction
Instruction is here an objective rather than a method. The primary objectives are to convey information and knowledge and to develop various kinds of skills. (A great deal of what has been called case work or therapy is, in careful analysis, simple instruction.) This is also needed for prevention of dysfunction and enhancement of social functioning.

7. Behavior change
This is a broad one. Its primary objective is to bring about change in the behavior patterns, habits, and perceptions of individuals or groups. The key assumption is that problems may be alleviated or crises prevented by modifying, adding, or extinguishing discrete bits of behavior, by increasing insights, or by changing the values and perceptions of individuals, groups, and organizations.

8. Consultation
The objective is to help other workers or agencies increase their skills and to help them to assist their clients in solving their social welfare problems.

9. Community planning
The objective is to assure that the human service needs of the community are represented and met as well as possible by groups and agencies at all levels—neighborhood, community, etc. This involves participating in and assisting neighborhood planning groups, agencies, community agents, or governments in the development of their programs.

10. Information processing
This objective (often ignored within social welfare) is to collect, classify, and analyze data generated within the social welfare environment. Included would be data about the individual case, the community, and the institution.

11. Administration
As with instruction, administration is here an objective rather than a method. The principal focus here is the management of a facility, an organization, a program, or a service unit.

12. Continuing care

The primary objective is to provide for persons who need ongoing support or care on an extended and continuing basis. The key assumption is that some persons will require constant surveillance or monitoring, or continuing support and services (for example, financial assistance, 24-hour care), perhaps in an institutional setting or on a community basis.[21]

An Individual Emphasis

The Basic Framework is intended to emphasize individual functioning: the generalist works with and for clients (defined as that system—individual, family, group, organization—for and with whom the generalist is pursuing some action). As we have said, the generalist is a direct service delivery agent, which means he can be the first line of contact for individuals who come to social welfare agencies in search of assistance, or he can also initiate contact by reaching out to a dysfunctional situation—such as a child abuse problem.[22]

Who the generalist works with, however, is a very different question from the object of his work, the *target,* which is defined as any system (individual, small group, organization) upon which the worker and/or client is acting. That a generalist works only with individuals does not mean that he works only with *single unit clients,* or individuals, who are also the only targets of his work. Client is that system (individual, small group, organization) for and with whom the worker is pursuing some action. Nor for that matter does this limitation imply that the generalist is concerned only with the functioning of individuals. Rather, the generalist works with individuals, who can be simultaneously client and target, to effect changes in their behaviors. We have defined the object of the worker's actions as his *target.* The *client* can be the target when, for example, a person comes to an agency to seek help for an emotional problem. The individual therapy that follows, with worker and client in a one-to-one relationship, makes the person both the client (that unit for whom the worker is doing something) and the target (the object of the worker's actions). He also has the requisite knowledge and skill to work with groups when this is a more effective client and/or target system, to achieve certain kinds of change. On the other hand, the generalist is acutely aware of the interrelationships of organizational conditions, community situations, and individual functioning. He has the requisite knowledge and skill to work with lower echelon decision-makers as clients and/or targets, on an individual basis, to seek changes and exceptions to regulations that are impinging upon the ability of his clients to function.

[21]Ibid., pp. 18–20.
[22]See Schneiderman in chapter 6 for a discussion of the social change–social control issue.

A Case Illustration

To clarify these ideas, we can use an example, necessarily somewhat oversimplified. (The chief purpose of the illustration is to delineate the actions and objectives of a generalist social worker and his relationship to a specialist, and to delineate the relationship between objectives and techniques.) A ten year old boy, the only child of working parents, is referred to school social services by his classroom teacher because of acting-out behavior. In her description of Homer's unacceptable behavior, the teacher had included that he usually sharpened his pencil as soon as the lead broke instead of having more than one pencil to minimize his trips to the pencil sharpener. Every day he asked to go to the restroom during class recitation instead of at recess. He seldom brought paper to school, preferring to borrow from other students. There was a variety of other similar behaviors that the teacher viewed as deliberate attempts by Homer to challenge her "authority" and/or to gain special attention from her. The teacher tried several unsuccessful disciplinary measures and was now seeking outside assistance—that is, outside the school resources.

Talking with Homer, the worker learns that there are no children for him to play with after school. He must go directly home from school on the bus, and is usually home alone for three hours before his parents return from work. Furthermore, because his parents work six days a week Homer is alone all day on Saturday, and the family seldom goes anywhere on Sunday.

The worker got in touch with Homer's parents. He learned they were in their present living arrangement because it was close to their work and enabled Homer to attend a "good" school. Homer's parents were aware of certain shortcomings in their present arrangement but had decided it was better for them than any of the alternatives they could afford. After interviews with the referring teacher and Homer's parents, the worker concluded that a good deal of Homer's unacceptable classroom behavior showed his need for relationships with his peers.

This same information can be related to Figure 1 (again, oversimplified). From the available information, the domains of living that are assumed to be in a state other than well-being include mental health (that is, Homer's acting-out behavior), financial resources (that is, both parents are working), education (that is, Homer's behavior defined as unacceptable by his teacher), housing (that is, the present living situation), leisure (that is, lack of playmates), and perhaps community integrity (that is, lack of opportunity for other, more satisfactory living conditions for this family).

Domains of living that are assumed to be in a state of well-being include physical health and employment (that is, both parents are working six days a week) and family integrity (that is, the quality of the relationships among members of the immediate family). Although these domains are assumed to be in a state of well-being because Homer's problem was manifested at school, this is but one of many legitimate interpretations that could be placed on this example.

It is as important to identify those domains of living that are in a state of well-being as it is to identify those that are dysfunctioning, for the domains in a state of well-being provide a resource for working on areas of dysfunctioning. For example, any effort to work with Homer's school-related problem will probably be somewhat easier since the family's integrity appears sound. The major obstacle to Homer's functioning is an environmental deficiency: he needs opportunities to be with his peers in other than the school environment, which in turn is related to the need for both parents to work—an integral cause of the family's current living situation.

Figure 2 schematically illustrates our description of the problem. Do not infer a linear cause-effect relationship between the affected domains of living identified and the attendant obstacles to functioning. Rather, the diagram indicates a reciprocation—that personal parental deficiencies are impinging upon the more clearly dominating *environmental* deficiencies which serve as the obstacle to Homer's unmet need —peer group relationships. This lack of peer relationships has affected several domains of living—his leisure, mental health, education, and the family's integrity. In turn, that Homer's need is unmet derives from impingement by several other domains of living—the parents' employment and financial resources, and the current housing situation. Finally, the integrity of the community in respect to adequate recreational opportunities has also been brought into question. In short, this diagram should be viewed as a picture of those domains of living that are related to Homer's need for peer group relationships, a need which was identified initially as a behavioral problem.

Figure 2, then, began with an identified need for peer group relation-

Figure 2. Domains of Living That Are Related to a Need for Peer Group Relationships

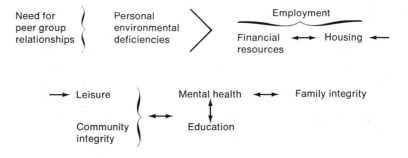

ships. This need has not been met because of certain deficiencies in Homer's environment. While the original problem was defined as one in which the mental health and education domains of living had been affected, these are now seen as only two of a number of domains that are an integral part of this unmet need, including the integrity of the family unit.

The nonlinear description is intended to emphasize two points:

1. Homer's identified problem, acting-out behavior, was initially associated with the educational domain of living. That his unmet need was initially defined as a behavioral problem suggests that the mental health domain was also in a state of less than well-being. Homer's unmet need is thus shown to come from the fact that a number of domains of living are in a state of less than well-being for Homer.

2. The lack of clearcut relationships among these domains of living and individual human needs suggests that any given need may be involved with a number of domains of living. This lack of definitive cause-effect relationships suggests that a worker must focus on needs rather than problems: for a worker to focus attention on need will help to minimize the notion of cause-effect relationships in favor of a multiple causation or holistic perception. To resolve any unmet need a worker must deal with a variety of factors that are related to it. Client needs, not necessarily an "identified problem" or a supposed "cause," are the primary objects of the worker's attention. Need becomes the basis for defining client goals and the attendant objectives, which are discussed later in the chapter.

The worker's contact with Homer's parents illustrates the *detection* objective: that is, an organizational decision (by the worker) was made to intervene in a situation (Homer's family) outside of the organizational environment (the school). Suppose that the worker has several more sessions with the entire family. It is decided to try to get Homer into a Boys Club near his school. The worker arranges to have a decision-making member of the Boys Club staff discuss this program with the family one Sunday. This action illustrates the *mobilization* and *linkage* objectives: the agency's normal procedures are changed and a need has been connected with a resource. At the same time, the family sessions have been used to help Homer and parents understand what Homer is doing and why. To satisfy the *behavior change* objective, we will further assume that these sessions are satisfying a part of Homer's need for attention, the need that is affecting his school behavior.

After learning about this program and understanding Homer's need, his parents decide to permit him to join the club. The father will pick Homer up at the club enroute home from work, another illustration of the *behavior change* objective. Suppose, however, that school policy requires children to go directly home from school. However little schools are able to enforce this regulation, nevertheless, if the above arrangements are implemented, the school, principal, social worker, teacher, etc., will knowingly violate a regulation. So the worker must seek an exception to this rule from one of that school's decision-makers —the *advocacy* objective. Here are two examples of a worker seeking exceptions to normal organizational procedures. In both instances, the worker's action was with specific individuals, decision-makers, in formal organizations.

But what if there are many "Homers" in the same school? What if the need for supervised after-school activities is common? The worker may decide that a major problem is in the domains of "community integrity" and "leisure," because many students have the same unmet need as Homer's. The focus has shifted to a much broader environmental deficiency; the domain affected is "community integrity."

The worker's objectives now move into the area of community planning to bring about a major organizational change; but changes of such scope are usually beyond the competence of a generalist. Although he had identified a need that requires action, the appropriate action now is to seek assistance from a more highly skilled practitioner, for example, a social planner, which illustrates the *consultation* objective. In the school setting this specialist may be the Chief School Social Worker, who has gained skill in these areas through work experience and continued education.

The generalist and specialist work together to develop a plan of action. The generalist remains a part of this new plan, documenting the specific needs of this school, such as determining the number of its students who would participate in an after-school recreation program —an illustration of the *information processing* objective. The generalist may contact parents in the district to enlist their support. A meeting of parents may be called to develop a vested interest group that would appear before the school board; such a strategy would embody the *community planning* objective. The planner would devise strategies and specify the kinds of documentation that are needed, but the generalist would assume primary responsibility for implementing these actions in his school district.

For community planning objectives, a knowledge of group dynamics and the skill to work with a task-centered group are most suitable. And the most appropriate method would be *community development,* which is "a process designed to create conditions of economic and social progress for the whole community with its active participation and the fullest possible reliance on the community's initiative."[23]

A generalist worker whose goal is organizational or community change might use community development. Of course, the emphasis

[23] *Social Progress Through Community Development* (New York: United Nations, 1955), p. 6.

is limited to locality development; when the goal is to change a local organization (such as the school above), and the most effective mechanism for achieving that goal is determined to be consumer pressure,[24] the community development method has particular relevance. But when the target is a larger system, such as a metropolitan or county school system, a very different method is required, one which may be beyond the generalist's competency.

A generalist can use community development skills in conjunction with the greater expertise of a social planner to bring about organizational changes; their working arrangement is a cooperative venture toward a specified goal. Crucial to the skill of the generalist is his ability to move from the specific to the general, to identify problems that can be better handled through policy changes and program development.

That is, although Homer remained a client and a target, a new client —children with unmet recreational needs—and a new target—the total school system—were added, which expanded the network of interventive acts by this worker. The generalist recognized that Homer's problem indicated a larger problem. The fact that Homer's need was shared by a number of students in the school suggested an organizational change was more an appropriate action than an exception to a rule. Recognizing the limits to his own level of competence, the generalist called upon a specialist in organizational change. The generalist did not refer the problem but remained as an active participant in the total effort to change this community.

The specialist worked at the top echelons of the entire school system while the generalist developed an action effort at the local school level. The generalist's focus was his particular school; the specialist's focus was the entire school system. Moreover, the specialist may have been working with a generalist in each school to undertake the same actions that the initiating generalist was taking at Homer's school. What could then appear before the school board is a vested interest group that included parents from the entire school system rather than one school —a most imposing group for a school board to face.

But suppose an inadequate budget made the school board unwilling to implement this plan. The planner may follow any one of many alternatives. *Mobilization* may become the major objective as the planner attempts to arouse community sentiment in favor of this proposal. He may, for example, decide to use the mass media to arouse public interest in a bond issue; such a strategy would incorporate *information processing* and *community planning* objectives. The planner's goal is to obtain a reallocation or increase in available funds so that the after-

[24]See Moore in chapter 5 for a discussion of the provider-consumer issue in organizing for social action.

school recreation program can be implemented. It should be clear that the worker must have other strategies in mind in case the first strategy fails.

Several variables are critical to generalist social work practice. A variable with special import to the social work process is the difference between a worker's client and his target. The *client* is that system (individual, small group, organization) for and with whom the worker is pursuing some action. The *target* is that system (individual, small group, organization) upon which the worker is acting. The client and target may be the same or they may be different. And with any client, the worker may have more than one target.

A second variable is related to the notion of risk: How great are the consequences for a client if a job is poorly done by an unskilled worker? Clearly, some situations require more knowledge and skill than do others. A person threatening suicide, for example, presents a greater risk than a parent anxious because parental authority is being questioned. The suicide threat involves an immediate crisis, the client's physical survival, and the worker who handles the client poorly may end up with a dead client. The risk for that client is extremely high, much higher than that for the anxious parent. For the parent, the problem would probably be long-term, and a poorly handled incident could be corrected.

In the school example there is also risk; the program in the offing would affect not only Homer's school but the entire school system. Although clearly not a life or death matter, this program nevertheless might be decisive in keeping a number of juveniles from becoming delinquent, for example. As such, it is a preventive effort; the element of risk is that there are many more people to be affected by the quality of the planner's work than are in any one school.

The element of risk makes it imperative that a social worker be able to determine whether he is competent to work with a given situation. He must know the limits of his competence and of his understanding of the situation with which he will be working, and the consequences to the client if he does a poor job. In short, the concept of risk can guide the generalist in defining the boundaries for his work.

A Model for Practice

The Social Work Process

Since social work practice is a dynamic interplay of a number of distinct phases of planned change, this process can be described as a series of steps roughly akin to those of the scientific method[25]—that is, characterized by the recognition and formulation of a problem, observation to collect data, the formulation of hypotheses, and the testing and confirmation of these hypotheses. As we said early in this chapter, the reader must remember that this is not a step by step process, as it is presented in the following pages, but a dynamic interplay of these phases.

Figure 3, a graphic illustration of the major phases of the social work process, combines certain ideas from general systems theory with the notion of process to indicate schematically the diversity of variables in this process. Each phase is transactional (◄——►); both worker and client recognize that each brings something to the process. And both are in a constant state of change with respect to these phases.

Because a worker would not be engaged if a client were able to cope with his own problem, the worker is seen by the client as having something to offer that he needs. The stress situation that brought a client to the worker must be dealt with at the outset. For example, the school social worker who saw Homer recognized a need to do something about Homer's behavior. Initially, the school had been the client and Homer was the target, when the worker was learning about Homer's home situation and attempting to ascertain the causes of Homer's unacceptable behavior—the initial stress. But by a subsequent redefinition of the problem Homer became the client and the school became a target, once the worker began to deal with the school policy that children go directly home from school.

We see here one of the facts of life in social work practice—the importance of the setting in which a worker is employed, for to a great

Figure 3. The Social Work Process

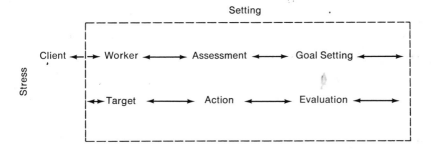

[25]Genevieve W. Carter, "Social Work Community Organization Methods and Processes," in *Concepts and Methods of Social Work,* ed. Walter A. Friedlander (Englewood Cliffs, N.J.: Prentice-Hall, Inc., 1958), pp. 220–22.

extent it will set boundaries on the kinds of client problems he will face. Social workers are usually employed by formal organizations, whose natures are such that they predefine much of what a practitioner is permitted to do. (For example, the school social worker does not take applications for public assistance; the adoptions worker in a child welfare unit does not work with juvenile delinquents on parole.)

Although few agencies have established formal policies that *prohibit* a worker from acting legitimately in any way he chooses to benefit a client, how a worker is introduced to an agency can leave him with the opposite impression. How agency policies and regulations are interpreted by administrators and supervisors can also affect the worker's notions of his autonomy.

Individual commitment also influences how a practitioner interprets agency policies. To a great extent, interpretation of policies is a matter of values: a professional who takes his professionalism seriously will place a primary emphasis on *what needs to be done.* (However, the size and complexity of his caseload may also curtail his ability to work thoroughly with each client.)

The worker's setting determines the kind of client a worker will see, as well as his activities directed to meeting the client's needs; and professionalism—the worker's commitment to the standards of the Code of Ethics—adds still more constraints. Acting in concert, these factors influence the boundaries for what a social work generalist will be able to do with a client.

Initiating the Process

The social work process begins when a condition of *stress* is identified. Stress, which is a situation involving threat, has three elements:

1. the stress factor, which threatens;
2. the value threatened;
3. the reactions, individual or collective, to the threat.[26]

The stress factor may arise inside or outside the system. The value threatened may be anything—a person's physical life; the social order; or opportunities for individual self-actualization, that is, an unmet need.[27] The reaction is what has been done by the threatened system to overcome the threat to the value.

In our earlier case illustration, Homer threatened the "order" value

[26]Jessie Bernard, *Social Problems at Midcentury* (New York: The Dryden Press, 1957), p. 70.
[27]Chris Argyris, *Personality and Organization, The Conflict Between System and the Individual* (New York: Harper and Brothers, 1957), pp. 49–53.

of the classroom. When none of the teacher's corrective reactions succeeded, Homer was referred to a school social services worker—an alternative resource, outside the classroom system but inside the school system.

Such a sequence is much the same with persons: when a person has failed, say, to remedy a stomach ache, he goes to a physician for assistance. The stress factor is the pain; the threatened value is life without pain. So, too, when a person comes to a social agency: he is in "pain"; a value is threatened; something has happened that the individual can no longer cope with on his own; and he seeks the assistance of an external resource.

Stress can occur at any level of a system. For example, an organization may identify a source of stress, such as an instance of child abuse, and initiate action. Potential sources of stress may be identified and preventive actions initiated, such as a family life education program in a community mental health center. It is even theoretically possible that a worker would penetrate the boundaries of his organization to intervene in an external system: the worker is then engaged in prevention, such as the family life education program mentioned above. The worker's objectives may be detection, linkage, or mobilization. Persons such as Homer's teacher seeking assistance from an outside resource are penetrating the boundary of an organization or external system to obtain outside help. The worker's objectives here may include evaluation, information processing, and behavior change.

A system can be defined by boundaries established by its observer.[28] But to be defined as a system it must have an organized set of interrelated subsystems or components that coact with each other within a specified physical region. The boundaries established by an observer relate to that physical region.[29] For example, the worker who considers prevention to be a legitimate part of his work may define the system within which he works to include all of the potential as well as current consumers of his particular agency's service. The worker who does not consider prevention a legitimate function of his work would define his boundaries as the formal organization within which he works. For the sake of clarity only, the boundary in Figure 3 may be considered that of the formal organization.

A worker within this system may be viewed as a subsystem: that is, a part of the system necessary to its functioning.[30] Social welfare organizations exist to provide a service to someone or something. The client, or consumer, is the recipient of this service. Clients and workers are

[28]James G. Miller, "Living Systems: Structure and Process," *Behavioral Science,* X (October 1965): 342.
[29]James G. Miller, "Living Systems: Basic Concepts," *Behavioral Science,* X (July 1965): 202.
[30]Miller, "Living Systems: Structure and Process," op. cit., p. 338.

essential elements of social welfare organizations—that is, they are sub-systems of a defined system.

At its simplest level, the social welfare system is an organization that employs social workers to provide specific kinds of services to specific kinds of clients. How a system defines its boundaries will significantly affect how a client is defined. Rehabilitation-oriented systems and workers will define a client along past and present recipients of service lines. Prevention-oriented systems and workers will expand this notion to include potential recipients of existing services, and will also tend to differentiate between the concepts of rehabilitation and habilitation —that is, will differentiate between the assumption that a person·had been functioning adequately and became disabled versus the notion that the disabled person had never functioned adequately.

At its most complex level, this system includes all of the service-providing agencies, public and private, and all of their recipients, past, present, and future. Such a system would also include the providers of resources, including those that provide agencies their manpower. This discussion will emphasize the least complex system possible, on the assumption that as the reader grows in knowledge, skill, and experi-ence, he will be able to generalize these basic concepts to larger, more complex systems.

In summary, then, the social work process is put into operation when a stress condition is identified by some unit, and initial counteractions to the stress do not return that unit to a stable condition; alternatives are employed, which may include the use of different resources, such as a social worker. The decision to initiate action against an identified stress is the first phase of the social work process—the client-worker transaction (⟵⟶)—in which the boundary of the setting is penetrated. The client is outside the system, since he is not defined as a part of the system, the setting in Figure 3, until the aforementioned client-worker transaction begins. Furthermore, he will remain a part of the setting only for as long as is necessary to work out a resolution of his stress situation. This may be for life, as with a recipient of Old Age Assistance, or for a few days or weeks, as with a potential suicide.

Assessment

Assessment is the second step in the process, initiated when a client comes to an agency. (When a worker decides to initiate a contact, to reach out, he has already made some assessment.) Even so, whenever the client-worker contact is made, an assessment is undertaken which involves both of these subsystems, client and worker, in a transaction.

Two major values underlie this premise. The client is assumed to know better than anyone else what his problem is and how he is being affected by that stress condition. The worker is assumed to bring certain kinds of knowledge and skill, and objectivity, to this phase. These may add a different dimension to the client-identified problem, for while "the customer is always right" tends to dominate this phase, the worker's expertise has something to offer: in a transactional situation each of the participants brings something to the assessment phase that will be of value to the final purpose of this relationship: resolution of the stress situation. It makes no difference who initiated this contact, the value premise of a transactional relationship holds.

Assessment begins with a statement of the identified stress situation. (The domains of living in Figure 1 are one view of the concept of need.) Client-identified needs are explored, causes and solutions for the problems are hypothesized. Need and problem are different concepts here: a *need* may be income, for example, with attendant *problems* such as malnutrition, inadequate clothing, and poor housing.

A term from general systems theory can be used to emphasize a critical feature of the assessment phase—*feedback.* By this concept two channels for communication exist; a part of any message that goes out on one channel will return to the sender, and the return message will reflect the receiver's understanding of the original message. If the return message accurately reflects the message originally sent, that communication incident is finished. If the message is incorrect, the sender must emit a new message (or messages) until the correct message is reproduced by the receiver.[31]

To achieve intended results, the assessment phase in social work practice must follow this process. Assessment is an ongoing process that must be a part of every other phase of the social work process. An ongoing assessment increases the probability that the work being done is appropriate to the goals that have been set and that the goals are appropriate to the client's needs and problems.

Goal Setting

Once the various aspects of a problem have been explored, the causes hypothesized, and solutions proposed, then the goal setting phase begins. The *goal*—the anticipated outcome of action or work undertaken by the worker and client—has two essential characteristics: (1) it is directly related to an hypothesized problem or need, and (2) it is stated in such a way that one can ascertain whether or not that goal has been achieved.[32]

[31]Miller, "Living Systems: Basic Concepts," op. cit., pp. 227, 228.
[32]*Key Factor Analysis Workbook* (Raleigh, North Carolina: Jarett, Rader and Longhurst, 1971), p. 6/08.

Because goals are anticipated outcomes, they should represent conditions that are acceptable to both the client and the worker, and therefore must be mutually agreed upon. At the same time, they should be realistic—that is, achievable. A worker may talk of achieving a series of goals, one related to another, and although some goals may not be immediately realistic, they might be achieved once certain preconditions, more short-term goals, are achieved.

The goal setting phase in social work practice can also be seen as a *contract,* by which two or more individuals, for us the client and worker, agree upon some outcome or end state. An agreed-upon end state or anticipated outcome is expressed as goals to be achieved. Since a quality of contracts is their liability to change, as agreed upon by the affected parties, this quality is of vital importance to the social work process. A contract, like a goal, can be changed as the client and the worker move through the social work process, as long as both worker and client agree to the proposed change.[33]

Targets

Once goals have been established and a contract has been made, the worker and client can then identify the targets. How many there will be at any one time will depend, among other things, on the needs and problems that are being addressed, the mutual understanding of the client's present situation, and the worker's skill. For example, a person may be both the client and the one and only target. Or a situation may be so complex or dynamic that a number of targets can be identified, as was true in our earlier illustration of Homer and the school system: as the worker moved into this case he redefined Homer from a target to a client, the parents became targets and then clients along with Homer; other targets became Homer's school, the Boys Club, Homer's peers, and finally the larger school system; and Homer and his parents remained targets throughout the process as well.

These targets are various-sized systems in which the worker may intervene. Remember: such interventions do not require of the generalist worker a high level of skill and knowledge with respect to each system; on the contrary, each of these interventions was seen to occur with representative individuals of that system. The only knowledge and skill required are *basic understandings* of these systems and the requisite skill to work with *appropriate* individuals at each level to achieve the desired goals. For example, intervention in the school and recreation organizations would require knowledge about the general structure

[33]Margaret Schubert, *Interviewing In Social Work Practice: An Introduction* (New York: Council on Social Work Education, 1971), p. 7.

and operations of formal organizations. The worker should know how those specific organizations function and how they resemble and differ from a more generalized structure. He should know where different levels of decisions are made and the person to contact in a given organization in order to achieve the particular goal that the client and worker have agreed upon.

The same requirements of knowledge and skill apply to work with families and other small groups: a worker has *basic knowledge* about the characteristics of various groups, and should have the skills to work with task-centered groups. Again, a generalist is not a highly skilled group worker who participates in group treatment, but, rather, one who employs group techniques where these are best to achieve an agreed-upon goal.

Action

The action phase of the social work process encompasses those specific tasks undertaken by a worker and client to achieve the agreed-upon outcomes. Each action may be considered from at least four perspectives: (1) the knowledge base required for that task; (2) the skill required; (3) the value premise upon which that action is based; and (4) the objectives of the work. Each of these factors *must* be related to a goal that has been agreed to with the client.

The reader should carefully differentiate between a goal and an objective: while a *goal* is client-oriented and is the anticipated outcome agreed upon by the client and worker, an *objective* is worker-oriented and directs what a worker does. Again, Homer's case can illustrate this difference. A need for Homer to have opportunities for after-school associations with his peers had led to the establishment of a goal—that he join a Boys Club. To achieve this goal, the worker found it necessary to mobilize a number of existing resources: mobilization was an *objective,* which called for gathering and energizing existing or new resources and bringing them to bear on existing problems. In other words, a goal influences the objectives that a worker will pursue, which in turn define the techniques a worker needs to achieve the agreed-upon goals.

Evaluation

The last stage in Figure 2 is *evaluation*—an on-going process that begins with the initial contact and ends only after the client-worker relationship is terminated. (Evaluation differs from assessment (described earlier) in that while assessment is directed to ascertaining the causes of stress, evaluation is directed to determining whether the hypothesized causes and attempted solutions were valid.) Evaluation is essentially a research process, a process of hypotheses, that begins when a worker plans an action and anticipates what will happen as a result of that action. The worker engages in that action and, we hope, tests his hypothesis by determining whether he has achieved the desired result. If so, he thinks he knows why and proceeds to the next action. If not, we hope he attempts to identify those factors (variables) that thwarted the anticipated consequences, and again attempts the action, now modified by his findings. This is research.

Research is appropriate for this phase of the social work process, since the scientific method is a problem-solving process. Because the scientific method imposes on a researcher an organized set of behaviors, an added impetus is placed on the client and worker to arrive at a clearly stated set of goals. And because a worker who must follow an organized set of behaviors to ascertain his level of effectiveness will carry this concern with evaluation throughout the social work process, his adeptness with both—evaluation and scientific method—in his practice are essential to a professional practitioner.[34]

Conclusion

The theoretical model for social work practice described in this chapter is based on the premise that often the recipients of social welfare services can be helped by a practitioner who can relate to a variety of needs, rather than by a specialist. This premise is based on the rapidly changing conditions in American society along with developments in our understanding of the individual, and the adoption of general and social systems theories by the social sciences. The generalist social worker measures the client's needs.according to the level of functioning in each domain of living; his goal is to raise inadequate levels of functioning to the status of well-being.

Both the generalist and specialist are needed in social work practice. Each complements rather than conflicts with the other, for their essential difference is where each practitioner begins: the generalist begins with client-defined needs and selects techniques appropriate to work on them; the specialist begins by judging the client's needs by their suitability to his particular method, and will refer the client to a different kind of specialist if his interventive repertoire and the client's needs are not congruent. The generalist will refer a client to a specialist if the client's need is beyond the generalist's skill, but the generalist will continue his relationship with the client for other unmet needs that do not require a specialist.

[34]Harris K. Goldstein, *Research Standards and Methods for Social Workers* (Chicago: Whitehall Company, 1968), pp. 11–14.

The work of the generalist practitioner is bounded by two assumptions: (1) he is the primary service delivery agent, with the basic knowledge and skill to work with the more common problems that clients bring to social welfare agencies; (2) his techniques are drawn from the major social work methodologies—that is, casework, group work, and community organization and social action, the basic knowledge and skills of which are the generalist's repertoire. Using a holistic frame of reference, the generalist draws upon the technique that is most appropriate for dealing with a specific client need.

The process for social work practice described in this chapter is essentially no different from other descriptions of the social work process, for all social work practice is fundamentally a problem-solving process, which is an adaptation of the scientific method: whether he is a specialist or a generalist the social work practitioner follows a prescribed set of behaviors with the primary purpose of solving a problem.

The concept of target presented in this chapter is the organizing premise for the body of this book. At the beginning of each chapter a commentary relates its content to the model presented here. Chapter 2 is concerned with a philosophical view of man and a value orientation to social work practice. The articles in chapters 3, 4 and 5 describe those elements of practice that a social work generalist must know as he intervenes with targets, whether they are individuals, groups, or organizations. Chapter 6 is composed of articles that illustrate social worker interventions from a generalist perspective, demonstrating interventions with targets ranging successively from the individual to the total system.

Health

Functions	Obstacles
Prevention	Lack of Access (Inaccessibility) Location

Detection
  Mental Illness
  Infectious Diseases
  Degenerative Illnesses
  Chronic Illness
  Acute Illness
	Transportation
	
	Lack of Availability
	  Quality
	    Facilities
	    Personnel
	  Quality

Maintenance of Good Health	Range-Diversity-Variety
Treatment	Lack of Ability to Pay or Purchase
Rehabilitation (Restorative Functions)	Lack of Knowledge and Information about Illness and about resources
Care	Lack of Motivation

	Opposition to Values and Beliefs
	  Stigma
	  Cultural Bias
	  Religious Scruples

	Restrictive Laws and Regulations
	Restrictive Policies and Practices

	Environmental Deficiencies
	  Garbage, Sewage
	  Rats, Pests, Vermin

Education

Functions	Obstacles

Basic Literacy (Reading, Writing)	Lack of Access (Inaccessibility)
	  Location
	  Transportation
	  Personal (Situational) Obstacles, i.e., child
	    must stay home and babysit

Preparation for Higher Education (Content)	Lack of Availability
	  Quantity
	    Facilities

Family and Social Living
  Skills
	Programs-Curricula
	    Personnel

"Hidden" Curriculum
  (Behavioral Maturity, Adaptive Skills)
	Quality
	  Irrelevant Curricula
	  Personnel
	    Improper Training

Extended, Continuing Education Avocational	Insensitivity

Leisure Time
  Hobbies
  Retirement
	Lack of Adaptive Skills
	  Work Habits
	  Conformity-Discipline
	  Grooming, Cosmetics

*Robert J. Teare and Harold L. McPheeters, *Manpower Utilization In Social Welfare* (Atlanta: Southern Regional Education Board, 1970), pp. 66–70.

                             General Introduction

Education

Functions	Obstacles
	Lack of Physical Necessities Diet, Nutrition Sleep Clothing
	Incongruent or Competing Values
	Destruction of Motivation
	Costs
	Restrictive Laws and Regulations
	Restrictive Policies and Practices

Employment

Functions	Obstacles
Securing Employment	**Lack of Access (Inaccessibility)**
Retaining Employment	Location Transportation

Conditions and Characteristics of Work
Working Environment (Light, Heat, Smell, Dirt, Risk)
Job Characteristics
  Security
  Status
  Meaningfulness
  Compensation
  Full Employment
  Advancement
	Personal Obstacle, i.e., need for child care during working hours
	
	Lack of Availability
	Quantity
	Diversity
	
	Lack of Information (about Job Opportunities)
	
	Negative Characteristics Inherent in Jobs
	
	Lack of Basic Educational Skills
	
	Lack of Specific Job Skills
	
	Lack of Adaptive Skills
	Grooming
	Discipline-Conformity
	Personal Habits
	  (Punctuality)
	
	Lack of Health and Stamina
	
	Personal Problems
	Transitory
	Chronic
	
	Restrictive Policies and Practices
	Race, Creed, Color
	Disability
	High Risks

Integrity of the Family

Functions	Obstacles
Husband-Wife Relationships	Composition of Family Ratio of Parents–children
Parent-Child (Child-Parent) Relationships	Age span (elderly–young) Sex
Sibling Relationships	Number of Members

Total Intrafamily Relationships	Role Conflicts
	  Authority Sources
	  Breadwinners

Extended Family Relationships
  (Aunts, Uncles, Grandparents, etc.)
	Psychological and Cultural "Drift"
	  Cultural Barriers

Autonomy and Individuality of Family Members	Achievement Changes Education Shifts

	Disability or Incapacity of Member(s)
	  Parent(s)
	  Breadwinner
	  Child (Children)
	  Elderly Member

	Prolonged Separation (of unit) Prolonged Absence
	  (of member(s))
	
	  Employment
	  Incarceration
	  Desertion
	  Military Service

	Termination of Family Unit
	  Orphans
	  Children grown
	  Widows, Widowers

	Lack of Adequate Resources and Necessities
	  Money
	  Food
	  Shelter
	  Clothing

	Disruptive Behavior on Part of Family Member
	  Acting-out
	  Alcoholism
	  Emotional Instability

Money

Functions	Obstacles
Provision or Securing of Income	Lack of Access (Inaccessibility) Inability to get credit
Retaining or Maintaining Income	Inability to get loans, financing
Management of Finances	Lack of Employment

	Lack of Availability
	  Poor money market
	  Lack of funds in general welfare and financial
	    assistance programs

	Lack of Information
	  Credit
	  Investments, Savings
	  Budgeting
	  Shrewd Purchasing (bulk purchasing, com-
	    parative shopping)
	  Sources of money

Money

Functions	Obstacles

	Loss of Buying Power
	  Fixed income (pensions, Social Security)
	  Inflation
	  Tax, Fee Inequities

	Vulnerability to Fraudulent Schemes
	  Home improvement
	  Used cars

	Lack of Motivation Vis-à-vis Saving, Investments
	Incongruent Values, Beliefs
	Laws, Regulations
	Policies, Practices Garnishment

Integrity of the Community/Neighborhood

Functions	Obstacles
Mobility (accessibility, transportation)	Lack of Access Transportation

Protection and Safety (physical, i.e., fire-police, legal, public health, psychological, social)	Location
	  Barriers or obstacles
	    Inability to negotiate

Shelter (public—low cost, institutions, detention)	Linkage of institutions, government, etc.

Growth and Development (individual and community)
  Cultural
  Educational
  Psychological
  Economic
	Lack of Availability
	  Quantity
	    Facilities
	    Manpower
	  Quality
	    Administration deficiencies
	      Planning

Enjoyment
  Recreation (organized or individual)
	Coordination
	      Enforcement
	      Delivery

Esthetic Experience
  Parks
  Architecture
	Evaluation of impact
	      Diversity

Permanence and Stability	Cost
	  Inability to raise funds
	  Inability to use available funds

Maintenance Public Works	

2

Foundations for Social
Work Practice

Both among professionals themselves and among the scholars who study professions there has not yet been agreement on the purpose of values or a philosophy for any given profession. One reason for this is the nature of values, which are statements of some idealized state, "the way things should be." In consequence the stated values of various professions are comprehensive enough to overlap to a great degree with those of other professions. For example, Schneiderman, in the first reading below, states that "All social work activity is directed to some change in the human condition." While this is a worthwhile ideal for social work practice, it does not tell us anything about social work that would distinguish this particular profession from others.

The essential issue to be dealt with in this chapter is whether or not values should be used as a means to define the boundaries of a profession. If values are indeed statements about idealized states, then we must say that while values should guide the practice of a profession they may not clarify the boundaries of that profession. That is, values serve as only one set of criteria by which to define the purpose of a profession. By their very nature they cannot be the sole major criterion. Values can carry no more than equal weight with several other factors in the prescription of social work practice.

The importance of values to social work is directly related to the issue of whether social work is a profession. Since not all occupations are professions, it must be established what conditions exist for members of the professional occupational group that are somehow different from those for members of other occupational groups. To begin with, the word "profession" implies that members of that group *profess* something. To profess means to *stand for* something, to *have a belief* that is openly acknowledged.

What an occupational group believes in is expressed in that profession's *Code of Ethics.* For social work, the beliefs are embodied in the National Association of Social Workers Code of Ethics. The first line of this Code indicates what the social work profession believes:

I regard as my primary obligation the welfare of the individual or group served, which includes action for improving social conditions.[1]

A second way to define the boundaries of the social work profession is a statement of purpose, about which there seems to be universal agreement: it may be summarized as the "enhancement of social functioning wherever the need for such enhancement is either socially or individually perceived."[2] This statement separates social work from the other helping professions by ruling out physical functioning (the purview for example of medicine) or legal functioning (the purview of the law), as its primary focus. While social functioning can, and often does, include the physiological and legal aspects of functioning, these aspects are not seen as the primary concerns of social work, but relevant only as they affect social functioning.

The specific concern of social work is with the individual's ability to realize his potentials within his society. There are no clearcut boundaries between social work and the other helping professions. On the contrary, concern with individual social functioning requires the professional social worker to engage a variety of other professional disciplines to help the individual realize his maximum potential. If any one factor can differentiate the social worker from other helping professionals, it is perhaps this one element: the social worker's knowledge and skill permit him to engage a variety of disciplines and systems of various sizes to help a client.

The Code of Ethics and the stated purpose of social work are acted upon to varying degrees by members of the profession according to how each member interprets these statements. This chapter presents

[1] *Code of Ethics,* National Association of Social Workers.
[2] Werner Boehm, *Objectives of the Social Work Curriculum of the Future,* Vol. I, Council on Social Work Education Curriculum Study, 1969 (New York: Council on Social Work Education, 1969).

a number of views on these issues, both for the social work profession as a whole and for the social work generalist in particular.

Three major themes can be found in all of the articles in this chapter: (1) the generally accepted purpose of social work is the enhancement of individual social functioning; (2) a major variable impinging upon individual opportunities for enhanced social functioning can be found in the political arena; and (3) "what needs to be done" must be defined *by the client,* rather than by some preconceived notion of what a worker can do that tries to fit a client's unique needs to these preconceptions. That is, the professional must be prepared to intervene in social institutions and systems at a variety of levels to help the client obtain whatever he needs to realize his aspirations and potentials. This requirement that a practitioner intervene in systems of different sizes suggests a need for a professional who has the requisite knowledge and skills to engage in a diverse set of behaviors related to client need. This kind of a professional was defined in the General Introduction as a *generalist.*

Schneiderman takes the position that social workers must arrive at some notion of the way things "ought to be" and attempt to achieve that state. His premise is that man is a growing, developing entity with the potential for creating something from nothing—that is, one cannot fully explain current choices by what has occurred in the past. Much the same notion is found in the two articles in chapter 3 by Atherton et al., in which it is proposed that the individual's selection of a desirable state of affairs should serve as the primary criterion of the way things "ought to be," and consequently that democratic political theory should be the foundation for the development of a social work value system.

Tillich lends support to this ideology by maintaining that every individual represents a unique situation for society's legal formal organizations, and such organizations deal best with common denominators. Recognizing that service to the individual is the ultimate purpose of all social work practice, Tillich sets a goal for social work that would develop a universal community of man wherein the aims of every individual become the universal aims of all individuals. With Schneiderman, Tillich calls for the social work profession to become more concerned with individual need. Need, then, serves as the criterion for selecting methods and techniques, rather than the opposite sequence, which held in the past, whereby needs were fitted to the available methods and techniques.

Gore adds another dimension to the purpose of social work in recognizing that human rights in general transcend those of any individual. Democratic political theory validates this position by identifying social justice and social equity as specific elements of the human rights question to which social workers must address themselves. Social workers must assume a responsibility for helping the deprived members of society to overcome any obstacles to their basic legal rights.

Lewis reiterates these points by delineating the effect political decisions have on the social worker's ability to work with clients. That is, the decisions of policy makers will influence the resources that are available for the use of the individual who strives for change in his status of functioning. Concern for individual enhancement must take the social work practitioner beyond the individual client to the policy making bodies.

Schwartz cautions against efforts to polarize the purpose of social work with an either/or issue. The private troubles of individual clients reflect, to varying degrees, larger public issues. The effective social worker is equipped to deal with both *private troubles* and *public issues* in a multidimensional, systemic frame of reference.

In summary, the values articulated in these readings identify a set of interrelationships among a client, his needs and rights, the situation in which he is functioning, the social worker who is involved with that client, and the agency that worker represents. The effective worker is cognizant of these interrelationships and can intervene at the *sources* of dysfunctioning or inappropriate interactions.

Values provide one boundary for the definition of the purpose of a profession and may be used to guide the behaviors of its members. Schneiderman takes the position that for social work practice this purpose can be premised upon democratic political theory, an ideological position that man is a rational, growing entity.

The Value Commitment of Social Work: Some Underlying Assumptions

Leonard Schneiderman

Reporting on the work of the National Association of Social Workers Commission on Social Work Practice, William Gordon notes agreement by the Commission that the ultimate value commitment of social work rests upon a conviction that, "it is good and desirable for man to fulfill his potential, to realize himself and to balance this with equal effort to help others do the same."[1]

Reprinted with permission of the author. Mimeographed, 1973.
[1]William Gordon, "A Critique of the Working Definition of Social Work Practice," *Journal of Social Work* (October 1962).

This statement implies that a difference is presumed to exist between what man may actually be at some given point in time and what he could ideally be, if allowed to "realize himself" and "to fulfill his potential." The statement further implies certain assumptions about man and his relationship and responsibility to other men. These assumptions need careful examination and development for they may be as important, if not more important, than the value statement itself.

What actually is man? What could man ideally be? How do we account for the difference?

Such questions would seem to be pivotal if we are committed professionally to contribute to man's fulfillment and self-realization, to his development from his actual to some preferred ideal state of being.

Is man inherently good or evil? Is man inherently social, asocial, or antisocial? Is man a creator or simply a creature? Is man's behavior conditioned or determined? Is man simply part of nature or beyond nature? Does all of this make any difference to social workers?

Why Are These Questions Important to Social Work?

All social work activity is directed to some change in the human condition. It would seem to be impossible to influence that condition, to influence man and his social reality, without some guiding notions not only about what man is but what man could be and under what conditions. It would seem impossible to set goals or policies for the future, to formulate social policy or therapy programs designed to "enhance social functioning" without some view of man and what it takes to influence him and toward what preferred ends. From a societal vantage point one of social work's functions is to help deviant persons to conform so that society will be less threatened and the individual will experience less conflict. All clinical treatment represents one of society's alternative ways of exercising social control over persons who manifest deviant behavior. A treatment service, the purpose of which is to "enhance" an individual's social functioning, necessarily contains distinct elements of control. If we are social control agents of society, how do we discover the right and the wrong, the good and the bad, the kinds of standards to enforce? What kind of a man is it who can subscribe to the standards we advocate?

There is an insistence in professional practice for a knowledge base both descriptive and prescriptive. Professions, unlike the sciences, are not primarily concerned with describing and analyzing the world but with attempting to influence it through some form of purposeful intervention. To do this we need to know how the world is, we need to know about the actualities of life. But, we need also to attach a value system to such understanding which aids us in defining the "ought to be" as a basis for setting goals and developing action programs to achieve these goals.

Facts do not speak for themselves and they are not in and of themselves problematic. Facts describe conditions. Conditions become problematic only when they are infused with value. Unless we have some picture of what man is, of what he could be, and under what circumstances, we lack a basis for evaluating the human condition and for setting the directions for purposeful change. Every public policy issue in the social welfare system today contains at its heart competing views of man. Does the value commitment of social work suggest an underlying consensus about what man is, about what he could be, or, are we neutral on such a question?

Some Different Views of Man

1. Natural vs. Transcendental Views of Man

Throughout the historical dialogue about man there has been a constant question of whether man is simply a creature of nature or God-like and a creator. Is man simply part of nature or can he transcend nature? Is man, in the words of Job, "but an insignificant creature of nature, here for a moment and wiped away as a shadow" or is man as described in the 8th Psalm, "a little lower than the angels."

What are some possible implications of these competing views for social work practice? Does social work's commitment to the concept of "self-determination" fit equally well into each of the contending views?

In the naturalistic view, man is seen as part of nature and can be studied and understood scientifically as we do the rest of nature. The world is viewed as continuous. Every event has its antecedent causative events. If we knew all that science will ultimately teach us, we could, according to this view, fully account for man and his behavior. The "ignorance theory" dominates the naturalistic view. It assumes that our inability to account for man is attributed, not to the intrinsic qualities of man himself, but to present limitations of knowledge.

The naturalistic view is not a simplistic view, for within it man is viewed as highly complex. Achieving understanding requires that we understand multiple and complex variables of a social, organic, psychological, cultural type and their interaction. The assumption is, however, that if we could understand enough, if knowledge was complete, as it perhaps some day will be, then we could fully account for man.

The transcendental view holds that science, that knowledge, in itself can never fully explain man and that this inability to explain man, to fully describe and to predict all that man does, is importantly, but incompletely accounted for by our ignorance. It is vitally important to reduce that ignorance. Our inability to explain man is, however, in part also accounted for by the fact that man has a potential to transcend the natural order of things. He has the capacity to choose, to create, to be rational. If man is simply part of a continuous world, as in the naturalistic view, and every event has its antecedent events, then man himself is best seen as a passive vehicle through which the antecedent events in his life operate. Concepts of self-determination, self-direction and choice would not seem reasonable in such a view.

Can science fully account for man? Can we ever know enough to conclude that human circumstances are beyond change, or, do we address ourselves to something divine in man, something creative, innovative and without historical precedent? Is our hope based essentially on the premise of ignorance, on hope born of the operation of as yet unknown natural factors, or, is it a hope born of belief in man's transcendental qualities; of his ability to make something out of nothing, in the sense that he has a potential for action in a way for which there exists no historical precedent in his life? Can anyone "know" what is best for other men, or, is man himself ultimately the best and only judge of his own interests? Can decisions be made for anyone which do not involve the effective participation of those affected?

2. Man as Social, Asocial, or Antisocial?

What is the basic human reality? Is society made up of discreet individuals who come together to form groups for their mutual protection and safety, so that the basic unit of society is the individual and the artifact, created for survival, the group?

Or, is the group the basic social reality with the individual, his identity, personality, and aspirations, all extensions of his group life? Is man inherently self-seeking and egotistical, out for personal gain at the expense of others, with selfishness curbed only by fear? Is every man basically at war with all other men? Is this the nature of social life? Is this the highest social ideal to which man's nature will allow him to aspire? Or, do men naturally aspire to live on good terms with others, to be part of and to contribute to group life, subordinating personal to group goals? Does fear socialize man, or, does fear dehumanize man?

These questions are of current and urgent importance for social policy issues facing this country today. Guaranteed annual income, the elimination of capital punishment, the availability of easy divorce and ready access to abortion all are fundamentally related to this basic question. Will guaranteed annual income and security bring out the best or the worst in man? Does fear motivate man to productivity? Is it "natural" for man to want to produce things of value for others? Do capital punishment and the fear of death motivate man to live on good terms with others? Will easy divorce lead to irresponsibility? Must men fear the punishment of a life-time of marital misery in order to be forced to act responsibly in the selection of a mate? Will ready access to abortion lead to growing promiscuity and irresponsible sexual behavior? Must man be frightened by the prospect of an unwanted pregnancy and a lifetime committed to an unwanted life in order to be deterred from irresponsible sexual behavior? Are men basically irresponsible and socialized through fear? Is it security, hope and a sense of self-competence born of success which ultimately socializes and humanizes man?

Such considerations are vitally important to us in our direct work with individuals and groups, in our understanding of limits and of controls.

The British intellectual, W. MacNeile Dixon, has said, "all forms of life, all organisms in which it is manifested, are engaged in an increasing struggle to maintain themselves against the disintegrating forces of nature. All are in conflict with each other for the same means of life, clan against clan, individual against individual. Each exists at the expense of others, and keeps his foothold only by success over the rest. How deep it goes, this warfare, you may conjecture if you remind yourself that the very trees of the forest are battling with each other for the light of the sun, and that the plants have their defensive armour, the rose and thistle their thorns, the nettle its sting. Make your heart iron within you, remember that to live you must kill either plants or animals."[2]

If as Dixon tells us, man is part of and at one with nature and if life is a war, a competition, with every man for himself, then indeed some must lose. Winning and losing are the inevitable concomitants of competition. We find losers all about us; the poor, the impoverished, the deprived and disadvantaged. Those who view life as massively competitive, view the losers as an inevitable consequence of living. It is "natural." It makes no more sense to be concerned about the plight of the losers, in such a conceptualization of man and society, than it does for the successful businessman to send his profits to aid and rescue a business competitor.

"Make your heart iron within you." In every competition there must be losers, no one ought to be shocked that one-third of the nation lives

[2]Edward Lindeman, *Science and Philosophy: Sources of Humanitarian Faith.* Paper delivered April 22, 1948, Symposium recognizing 50th anniversary of the New York School of Social Work and 100th anniversary of Community Service Society of New York.

Foundations for Social Work Practice

in deprivation. They are the losers; "natural" parts of any human system.

"Make your heart iron within you." Share nothing in taxes or in voluntary contributions to aid the losers. This makes no sense in a competitively organized society.

"Make your heart iron within you." The collective good is the sum total of every man for himself. Helping losers threatens to subvert our system. Regard those who express a stake, a concern in every man's well-being and welfare as an extension of their own, as subversives or as "do-gooders."

Questions concerning the nature of human nature are of basic importance to social work. Our methodology is predicated upon expressive rather than repressive approaches to human nature. We are oriented to man's nature as something to be lived out, to be ventilated, to be channeled, the source of his energy, his vitality, his growth and creativity. It is a view which assumes that human nature is not intrinsically evil; that it is, at least, perfectable and perhaps essentially good. It is a view which assumes that growth and maturity are the products of a satisfied human nature and not a repressed and denied human nature. The theories of personality development which form our basic knowledge foundation, whether they be those of Freud or Erikson or Maslow or others see growth toward maturity as a consequence of success, of achievement, of security, rather than of fear and denial.

3. Political Systems and Views of Man

What kind of a political system does it take to accomodate a man so conceived? If men have transcendental possibilities, and if only the individual can fully know his own interests, then any political system which falls short of the full participation in decision-making by all those who must order their lives by the decisions made is fundamentally deficient. It is for this reason that social work's view of man draws it naturally to an interest in democratic political theory. Democratic theory rests upon the supposition that man is capable of reason, of rational analysis and choice. That social, biological, cultural and psychological influences are very powerful and very important in influencing behavior, but that man can transcend these influences and exercise choice. Man has the potential to create something out of nothing in the sense that choice is not fully explained by what has gone before. One significant charge to a viable social welfare enterprise in a democracy is to work for the definition and the enhancement of those conditions under which man can make rational and responsible choices. Indeed social work's very commitment to the notion that "it is good and desirable for man to fulfill his potential to realize himself and to balance this with equal effort to help others do the same" requires it to delineate the political form of governance most compatible with this basic view of man.

To choose and to create are God-like functions. Is there a bit of the divine in man which makes him "but a little lower than the angels?"

The Scriptures tell us of man's profound difficulty when he presumed to be God-like, to think for himself, to transcend the natural order of things. Man's contemporary problem is clearly immortalized in the story of Adam and Eve. Man ate of the fruit and gained knowledge of good and evil. Gaining such knowledge, he gained also the burden of choice. He lost his innocence. He lost the safety of being at one with nature, of leaving his well-being to natural forces. He aspired, instead, to transcend the natural order of things by thinking and knowing and acting for himself.

Before that ruinous apple, man was as one with a safe, automatically operating universe, a kind of balanced aquarium, a kind of uterine life where all needs were completely and automatically met.

His fall from a state of nature necessitated that he seek a basis for decision making where previously no decisions were necessary. Man was required to act rationally and yet could not escape irrational forces.

The contest is, of course, still on. The question of man's capacity to provide for and to insure his own welfare through rational planning is yet to be demonstrated. It is not at all totally clear as yet whether man's creativity will be placed at the service of his survival or his self-destruction.

In social work we know that men do act irrationally. We believe, however, that ideally man can act rationally, that man can put knowledge to work to promote human welfare. Social work is itself a product of that belief. One vital charge to a viable social welfare institution in a democracy is to aid in creating the conditions under which man's rationality can be maximized and his irrationality minimized.

While we learn from Freud and Marx and others about the influences of unconscious and of social class conflict, for example, we regard these views as essentially incomplete in accounting for man. The views are seen as essentially undemocratic to the extent that they deny man's capacity to transcend unconscious and social class influences.

Edward Lindeman in addressing himself to an analysis of contemporary society, its stresses and strains, the increase in incidence of mental disorders, has adopted, it seems to me, a modernized version of the Adam and Eve story. Lindeman has ascribed heightened tensions, anxieties, neuroses and mental illness, etc. to the technological disruption of natural balances, a description which now requires that men make decisions to restore balances in nature which previously occurred naturally. The population explosion, for example, is as much a function of man's technology as of his biology.[3] Evidence of man's disruption of his natural environment is fully documented. It demands conscious analysis and planning to re-harmonize man's life with his natural environment.

Discovering the Moral Order

If choice is real; if man can choose, initiate, set in motion, create, rather than merely respond to antecedent influences, then we must account for ideas of right and wrong, for judgments concerning the desirable and the undesirable, the good and the bad. We must account for our moral experience.

A profession is committed to action and to doing. Decision making and action are impossible without some concept of the good life to which we aspire, without some moral and ethical commitment about the good and the bad, the right and the wrong. We must believe in something to have a basis for action. How do we discover what to believe in?

Action follows from commitment. Uncertainty tends to lead to passivity and submissiveness in action and to lack of assertiveness in approaching the social and the political order. Making decisions is a very painful business. For many it is something to be avoided. There is an inclination to "escape from freedom of choice" as Fromm has suggested, to submissiveness to an authoritarian rule.[4] There is also a tendency to deny the existence of choice by reference to a life dominated by immemorial custom and tradition which offers "the" right way to pattern one's life. Neither of these, it seems to me, can successfully support a professional enterprise oriented as it is to differential achievement of valued goals. What is the basis of the normative ideas which guide our professional practice?

1. Subjectivist's Views of the Moral Order

In this view moral experience is purely subjective. There is no objective right and wrong; all values are seen as relative. Since there is no objective reality, the moral realm is differently experienced by each person on a subjective basis. Ultimately the right and the powerful are indistinguishable. In this view, men are atoms socially, each with different, subjectively based concepts of right and wrong, all held together by force and a desire for safety from each other. Protection of life and property are the only moral realities.

---

[3]Unpublished notes given to the author when he was a student of Professor Lindeman's.
[4]Eric Fromm, *Escape From Freedom* (New York: Farrar and Rinehart, 1941).

2. Utilitarian Views of Morality

What is right and wrong ultimately depends upon its consequences, upon the calculus of pleasure and pain. What is right is what will maximize pleasure and minimize pain. The utilitarian view of right and wrong poses the question, "Does it work?" "Is it practical?" "Will it be 'successful'?"

3. Objectivist Views of Morality

These views hold that there is an objective world of value which exists independent of our image or of our knowledge of it as there is an objective physical reality. For example, the Ptolemaic view of the universe was objectively incorrect before the Copernican alternative. As man discovers the physical order so must man discover the objective moral order. Several approaches to the discovery of the objective moral order are possible:

a. *The Intuitionist View*—which holds that we can discover the objective moral order through intuition or revelation, for example, as revealed to us in the Scriptures or other sacred writings.

b. *The Classical View*—which holds that the objective moral order can be discovered through reason and through debate, through matching man's logical capabilities with the logic of the universe.

c. *The Democratic View*—which holds that one can discover the objective moral order through the function of a "general will" of all of the people, through the alchemy of group process in which people share and participate and discover the rules by which to order their existence.

Under what conditions can the general will function? The process requires at its very least:

1. full freedom of expression for everyone;

2. full access to public information, including a free flow of technical information from experts in a form in which it can be understood by the laymen;

3. a leadership which understands the nature of democracy, which proposes and suggests alternatives and does not dispose and threaten; which appeals to rational and not irrational; and which sees the ends of all men as equal and does not exclude anyone for racial, religious, economic or other reasons;

4. a level of social and economic and physical adequacy for all, sufficient to support a *common group life, a consciousness of kind, and the full, active participation of all members.*

For democracy to work there must be a minimum economic adequacy for all. The general will can function only through time and within a process of interaction and deliberation. There must be sufficient release from the immediate requirements of survival for the general will to function. Men cannot transcend the natural order of things unless they master the immediate requirements of nature. "Without bread the spirit dieth." The discovery of the moral order through the general will of the people requires a consciousness of kind, a substantial common life among people. For this to be possible, income levels must be sufficiently equal to support a substantial common life. If there are great income disparities, it becomes impossible to maintain group feelings and meaningful communication across lines of grossly different life styles, social classes isolated and ghettoized communities. Cultural and personality development are related to life experiences. In money currencies, life experience is a function of access to money, of what one can afford to experience, of one's access to resources, opportunities and power. Different life styles emerge for groups enjoying grossly different access to opportunities, resources and power. A substantial common life cannot develop across grossly different qualities of experience. Without it the general will cannot function.

The achievement of democracy depends upon the existence of a viable social welfare enterprise to create and to support those conditions which are prerequisite to the functioning and existence of a democracy.

As social workers, we must not only be concerned about enforcing the community's normative judgments, we must also examine the origin of those judgments and laws and measure the level of their legitimacy against the conditions necessary to achieve adequate definition of the general will of the community. Specifically, if all are to live by a community-defined morality then it must be a morality to which all have contributed definition. It must be a morality supported by full membership and participation in community life and by the achievement of minimum levels of decency and adequacy in standards of living.

Overview of Democratic
Ideas Relevant to Social
Work

1. Only persons shall be regarded as ends. No person shall be regarded simply as a means. There is a need to avoid a tendency in complex social organizations to reduce men to instruments for the achievement of purposes they have not helped to define. We talk frequently of economic man, man as a producer, as a consumer; man whose personal value is derived from his economic value. Such notions are basically offensive in a democracy for they cast man in the role simply as a means and not as the exclusive, legitimate end of societal organization.

2. Democracy assumes the possibility of rationality in humans. It is vitally concerned for success upon the definition of conditions most likely to support rational group functioning and decision-making.

3. Democracy distrusts experts. Trial and error in which there is general involvement is superior to expert judgment. If there are generally superior human beings, they are not thereby entitled to govern. Means and ends are inseparable. Involvement, personal growth are as important as the end to be achieved. Alienation from political, economic, and social processes cannot yield good results. In the final analysis each man is the best judge of his own interests and must therefore participate in all matters relevant to his self-defined interest. It is the aspiration for affiliation with others, for self-realization in a social context, that makes social stability possible through a full sense of membership and participation.

4. Human beings are morally equal. Each man occupies a position of equal importance to the society. No irrational means of discriminating against them is acceptable. Men have a right to get ahead and to advance economically as well as a right not to advance economically without sacrificing decency, self-respect and a right to life.

In sum, then, "it is good and desirable for man to fulfill his potential, to realize himself and to balance this with equal effort to help others do the same." Means and the ends are inseparable. The goals to be achieved are based upon conceptions not only of what man is but also of what man could ideally be. Methodological sophistication and treatment techniques can never replace or preceed in importance ideological clarity, clarity about who we are professionally and what we are about, clarity about basic value commitments and their underlying assumptions, clarity about the political forms most compatible with man's development and clarity about the role of social welfare systems in the nature and development of those political forms.

The values of a profession are one guide to the behaviors of its members. Tillich argues that a concern with individual need should be the overriding value for deciding the worker's actions. Techniques and methods are viewed as only means to be employed by the practitioner in satisfying those unmet needs that have been identified by their clients.

The Philosophy of Social Work

Paul Tillich

I have been asked to speak on the subject "The Philosophy of Social Work." No one can claim to give the philosophy of social work, and

Reprinted from *The Social Service Review,* Vol. 36, No. 1 (March, 1962), pp. 13–16, by permission of The University of Chicago Press.

Foundations for Social Work Practice

even a philosophy of social work is an enterprise which by far surpasses the limits of my ability and the time given me here.

What I shall attempt is to try to develop some ethical principles of social work which may be useful to reflect on and consider for those who do the work as well as for those of us who are only friends of such work but who may find their problems a mirror of the problems of human life generally.

Looking back in memory and with a little bit of pride at the twenty-five years of Selfhelp, its small beginning, its continuous growth, its power to last, I see a healthy tree which never tried to grow beyond the natural strength of its roots, but under whose branches many birds from many countries, and often of surprising varieties, found a transitory refuge. It might well be that this help is partly dependent on a sound philosophy of social work, a philosophy which lives not only in the minds but in the hearts of those who work as part of Selfhelp.

Therefore, when I agreed to speak today about the "philosophy of social work," I was helped by the idea that I did not have to develop concepts out of the air but had only to give a philosophical interpretation of the actual work of Selfhelp and the basic convictions underlying this work—convictions which we have developed, discussed, and transformed during the twenty-five years of our existence.

The basis of all social work is the deficiency of every legal organization of society. A perfectly functioning organization of the whole society, a social mechanism embracing all mankind would not leave room for social work, but such a mechanism is unimaginable. It is prevented by two factors, one which is rooted in what we call today in philosophical jargon "man's existential predicament," his insufficiency. The second factor is rooted in man's existential nature, the uniqueness of every individual and every situation. No total regulation, even if given in the best interest of everybody, ever has adequately functioned either in war or in peace. The disorder produced by totalitarian regulations in Nazi Germany during the Second World War is equaled by the disorder in food distribution in Soviet Russia during the present cold war. Neither intellect nor character of men is adequate to such a task. And even if they were in one part of the world, interferences from other parts would spoil the functioning of a perfect social organization. The fact on which Selfhelp is based, the European immigration, was for a long time beyond the reach of any existing legal organization of social needs. Spontaneous social work was the only way to solve the immediate problem.

But this is a minor part of our question. More important is the fact that even in the best legal organization of social needs, every individual represents a unique problem. Only in a society which suppresses individual claims for help can this problem be put aside, and not only individual persons but also individual situations between persons, or persons and groups, transcend the reach of any legal organization. It is the greatness of man that his freedom implies a uniqueness which prohibits his being absorbed into a social machine so long as he remains man. For this reason social work is more than emergency work, unless one defines emergency as a perpetual concomitant of the human situation—and that probably is true.

Certainly all social work tries to make itself superfluous and many forms of it have done so. And in all our discussions we often have asked ourselves whether we have already reached that stage, but each time we found a large number of emergency situations which required the continuation of our way of social work.

We tried to listen to the situation as we did in the years of our foundation, and in doing so we tried one of the great laws of life, the law of "listening love." It is one of the decisive characteristics of love that it listens sensitively and reacts spontaneously. As one of our early friends, Max Wertheimer, has indicated, situations have a voiceless voice. "Things cry," he used to say, but also what cries most intensively are situations. It was the cry of a particular situation which we hardly could have ignored and which drove us to found Selfhelp. And it was not only the beginning of our history in which this happened. Again and again we had to listen sensitively and to react spontaneously. It is certain that in some situations we were not sensitive enough and reacted not spontaneously enough, but it was a fundamental principle of our philosophy of social work.

Social work is centered in individuals. The most concrete, and therefore most important representative of social work is the caseworker, and for him is valid what is valid for the whole organization in its relation to the individual. He also must listen sensitively and respond spontaneously. He meets the individual and he is in the understandable temptation of transforming care into control. He is in danger of imposing instead of listening, and acting mechanically instead of reacting spontaneously. Every social worker knows this danger, but not always does he notice that he himself may have already fallen to this temptation. He should not make a harsh judgment about it, but from time to time he should restate the principle of "listening love" in order to dissolve any hardening mechanism in those who do social work.

The danger of which I am speaking is a tendency in every dealing with other persons to treat them as objects, as things to be directed and managed. It was always a symbol for me that the patients of the social worker were called cases. I do not know whether a better word can be found, but the word "case" automatically makes of the individual an example for something general. Who, I ask all of you, wants to be a case, but we all are cases for the doctor, the counselor, the lawyer, and certainly the social worker. He is not to blame for this inescapable situation, but he would be to blame if in his dealing with the patient, with this case, he makes him into an object for whom everything is determined and in whom spontaneity is suppressed. The question is whether the caseworker is able to see in his patient not only what is comparable with other cases or identical with what he has experienced in other patients, but that he sees also the incomparable, the unique, rooted in the freedom of the patient. It is the amount of love between the social worker and the patient which here is decisive—the listening, responding, transforming love.

Here, when I use the term love, as before, I certainly do not mean the love which is emotion; nor do I think of *philia*—of friendship which only really develops between the social worker and his patient, nor do I think of the love which is *Eros,* which creates an emotional desire towards the patient that in many cases is more destructive than creative; rather, it is the love whose name in Greek is *agape* and in Latin *caritas* —the love which descends to misery and ugliness and guilt in order to elevate. This love is critical as well as accepting, and it is able to transform what it loves. It is called *caritas* in Latin, but it should not be confused with what the English form of the same word indicates today —namely, charity, a word which belongs to the many words which have a disintegrated, distorted meaning. Charity is often identical with social work, but the word "charity" has the connotation of giving for good causes in order to escape the demand of love. Charity as escape from love is the caricature and distortion of social work.

Critical love, which at the same time accepts and transforms, needs knowledge of him who is the object of love. The social worker must know his patient. But there are two different ways of knowing. We may distinguish them as our knowledge of the other one as a thing, and our knowledge of the other one as a person. The first is the cognition of external facts about somebody. The second is the participation in his inner self—as far as any human being is able to participate in another one. The first is done in detachment, through an empirical approach; the second is done through participation in the inner self of the other one. The first is unavoidable, but never enough in human relations. The second gives the real knowledge, but it is a gift given alone to the intuition of love. Here the social worker is in the situation of all of us in our daily encounters with each other. No amount of factual knowledge about each other can replace the intuition of love, which remains love even if it judges.

A refinement of the empirical way of knowing man has been given to us by the psychology of depth, the very name of which indicates that it will be more than knowledge of an object, that it will know the person as a person, but with the means of analysis of the dynamics of his being. It is a way, one could say, between the two other ones. It is understandable that it was attacked from both sides, and still is, but also that it was eagerly taken over as a tremendous help for social work, as well as for other fields. In earlier years, it often made the social worker into a dilettante psychoanalyst, just as the minister in the alliance of religion and psychological counseling is in danger of establishing himself as a minor psychoanalyst—an attitude against which I have warned my students of theology for thirty years now.

But there are two dangers in this—schematism and dogmatism. It judges the object of analysis according to schemes with a relative validity but never fully applicable, and it is dependent on the doctrines of the different psychotherapeutic schools, usually judging on the basis of one of them. As the best analyst knows, personal participation in terms of mutuality, and this means the intuitive love, is never dispersible. No matter how refined the psychoanalytic matter may be, if you don't have a point of communion with the central person of the other one, all the methods do no good in the long run. Analysis is a tool, very refined, but not without the danger of missing the end by the way in which the tool is used.

This leads to the last and perhaps the most important question—the end, the aim, of social work. The aim has several degrees. The first degree is the conquest of the immediate need, and here the factor of speed is important. The necessity of accepting and being willing to bear the consequences of possible errors, even of helping somebody who doesn't deserve help, must be taken by the social worker. It is analogous with love which has the principle that it is better missing several guilty ones than condemning one innocent one. The second degree is the self-abrogation, the self-conquest of social help, as far as possible, by guiding the person into independence. This is attempted always in all social agencies, but we know it is not always possible. Then there is a third stage about which I want to say a few words. On the basis of the present situation as I have seen it in the young people in all the colleges and universities, and in many other people, we mainly need to give the people of our time the feeling of being necessary.

Being necessary is, of course, never absolute. Nobody is indispensable. Nevertheless, somebody who does not feel necessary at all, who feels that he is a mere burden, is on the edge of total despair. In all groups I found this widespread feeling of not being necessary. There are many reasons for every effect, but one of the reasons for this is that in our secularized society one thing is lost, namely, that, whatever their external destiny may be, people no longer have an eternal orientation, an orientation which is independent of space and time. It is the feeling of having a necessary, incomparable, and unique place within the whole of being. Herein lies a danger for uprooted and migrating millions. It is a danger for mankind itself, namely, to feel that their existence as a whole is no longer necessary. The easy way in which politically we are playing now with collective suicide is analogous to the phenomenon of individuals who have lost the feeling of a necessary place, not only in their work and community, but also in the universe as a whole.

This leads to a final aim of social work. In helping every individual to find the place where he can consider himself as necessary, you help to fulfill the ultimate aim of man and his world, namely, the universal community of all beings in which any individual aim is taken into the universal aim of being itself. That is the highest principle of social work and, of course, transcends the limits of its techniques. It is certainly understandable that this aim is not always conscious to those who have the burden of the daily work. On the other hand, it may give them a spiritual lift in moments when they feel grateful to hear a response from one of thousands whom we may have helped. It may be of inspiration to us to think that we contribute to the ultimate aim of being itself in our small way—and every individual's way is small. To give such inspiration may be a function of an hour of memory such as the present one.

The social functioning of individuals has long been recognized as the overriding purpose of social work practice. Hitherto, human need has been the focal point of efforts to actualize this concept. Gore maintains that the long-ignored human rights aspects of social functioning must be given as much attention as human need if the social work practitioner is to be an effective influence in contemporary society.

Social Work and Its Human Rights Aspects

Madhov S. Gore

I have a very definite feeling that social work will gain in depth and richness if its linkage with human rights can be rediscovered and respecified.

The origins of social work can be traced to the early beginnings of human society, and the origins of the concept of human rights can be traced to those societies in which the rule of law rather than rule by the whims of an autocrat came to be established. But the substantive

Reprinted from *Social Welfare and Human Rights:* Proceedings of the XIV International Conference on Social Welfare, 1969, pp. 56–68, by permission of the International Conference on Social Welfare.

goals pursued by social work and the nature of its activities have differed from society to society and from one period in history to another; equally, the scope and content of the rights of the individual as recognized by society have also varied according to time and place. Even today there is considerable variation between countries in what goes by the name of social work; and certainly there is a great deal of difference in what the countries actually concede by way of human rights to their citizens. It is, therefore, imperative that before undertaking a discussion of the human rights aspects of social work, we should indicate the society and the period of history with which we are concerned.

In regard to human rights, the point of reference is clear and specific. We are referring to the rights listed in the thirty articles of the Universal Declaration of Human Rights proclaimed by the General Assembly of the United Nations. While not every one of the articles may be of equal import to social work, the Declaration as a whole, the fact of its existence, its tenor, and some of its articles have a great deal of significance for social work values, goals, functions, and practice.

The Declaration and
Social Work

The Declaration of Human Rights is a long and complex document. Its thirty articles are spelled out in fifty tersely worded paragraphs. The Declaration is an affirmation of values, a statement of the aspirations of world conscience on behalf of the common man, and an indication of the direction in which the United Nations would like the nations of the world to move. The Declaration covers a wide range. It covers what are usually referred to as political and civil rights under a representative form of government; it covers the right to nationality, freedom of movement, and the freedom to seek asylum; it affirms human dignity, equality, and the right to freedom from discrimination and exploitation; it covers the freedom of thought and conscience; it covers the right to work and to be paid; and it covers the right to social security, to an adequate standard of life, and to the opportunity for the free and full development of individual personality. Finally, in a very significant addition, it refers to the duties of the individual to his community, in which alone the free and full development of his personality can take place.

The relevance of the Declaration for social work lies mainly in the fact that it unequivocally recognizes the worth and dignity of the person and asserts that he has a right to "seek the free and full development of his personality." Social work proceeds from the same basic assumption that the human individual is worthy in himself, independent of his material or social condition, and that it is important to provide him with every facility for the full development of his potentialities. Without the acceptance of this value much of social work would lose its meaning and sense of purpose and would seem rather like a response based on the social worker's sympathy or pity. While such sympathy and fellow feeling have been strong urges for social work in all societies and while they have been legitimated by religion and social usage, there is increasing recognition of the fact that by themselves they provide only one, somewhat inadequate, orientation to social work activity. The acceptance of the dignity and worth of the individual and the value of promoting his development is the other—and more important—orientation in social work today. In this acceptance one finds a common emphasis in the Universal Declaration of Human Rights and the values basic to social work.

Even in this point of contact there is a difference of approach which may appear to be inconsequential but which I believe is fundamental. Article 22 of the Declaration states that everyone is entitled, as a right, "to the realization . . . of the economic, social and cultural rights indispensable for his dignity and the free development of his personality." Social workers accept the free development of personality of their client as a basic value, but they are not always, in every society, able to regard it as a *right* of the individual, nor do the societies in which social workers function always accept the obligation to provide the individual with the opportunities for such fulfillment. The right of the individual to social security, to a minimum standard of life, and to opportunities for free and full development—even within the means available to the state—has been recognized only recently and not in the same way by all states. Some recognize the right to work and pay and to the protection of minimal income in the form of social security, but they do not necessarily grant freedom in religious, educational, or civic matters. Some grant the latter but do not concede the right to social security and income maintenance. Social workers have had to work in all these situations. They have sought to render services when no "rights" were recognized and when no law provided for special amenities and services to individual citizens, and in the greater part of the world they continue to work in these conditions even today.

Typically, social workers operate with the concept of needs—basic human needs—rather than of rights. The concept of needs can often go beyond the rights that are recognized in a given society. In this sense social work has a very different stance and approach from those suggested by the word "rights." Rights give rise to questions of justice—or at least of equity—in particular social arrangements. If the urge of a worker is for greater justice, his stance tends to be more heroic and his action bolder. The social worker's urge is for healing, alleviation, and soothing, and he tends to take on the less heroic but no less useful role of a constructive worker. The specific challenge he faces and the particular tasks he is called upon to perform are likely to vary from one society to another. The equation between human rights and social work is also likely to change from society to society. It would be useful to explore this suggestion a little further by examining the relationship between human rights and social work in different types of societies.

Four Types of Social Contexts

All typologies are inadequate, and typologies of societies are particularly unsatisfactory because of the complexity of phenomena that they attempt to summarize. But typologies are useful since they throw certain aspects of phenomena into bold relief for purposes of discussion. In the discussion of the relationship between human rights and social work it might be useful to distinguish between societies on two questions: Does a society recognize the obligation to provide its members with the freedom, the opportunities, and the facilities to achieve the maximum development of which they are capable? Independent of its value commitments, does the society have the material resources to enable it to provide such opportunities?

These questions are too broad and too vague to be applicable to particular known societies. One may also say that it is never possible to make categorical distinctions of the type implied by the questions. It is difficult to characterize societies as having accepted or not accepted the whole set of human rights. They may recognize some without recognizing others. Particularly, a distinction may be made between the civil and political rights of the individual on the one hand and the right to social security on the other; societies which accept one do not always accept the other. Yet, the questions are helpful in distinguishing among four types of social situations in which social work may function.

Consideration of the stage of economic development of a society becomes particularly relevant in respect to the right to social security. We can first distinguish between societies which *in principle* recognize social security obligations toward their individual citizens and societies which do not. Each group can be further subdivided into those which have the means to accept the responsibility for providing these opportunities and those which do not; that is, societies which are economically "advanced" and those which are "backward." Thus we have societies which have accepted obligations toward their members *and* have the means to meet these obligations and those which have accepted the obligations but do not have the necessary means. Also, we have societies that do not accept the obligations *although* they have the means and those which *neither* accept the obligations *nor* have the means to meet them.

The main concern of social work is to help individuals and groups to survive, to grapple with problems posed by their physical and social environments, and to achieve the full development of their potentialities. The recognition or nonrecognition of human rights by the society in which they work provides social workers with a value context which may help or impede their efforts, and so will the availability or nonavailability of material resources. In this sense the four types of social situations are likely to pose different types of challenges and give rise to differences in the goals, the methods, and the dominant concerns characteristic of social work in each of them.

In a society which has accepted the obligation of the collectivity to provide security to the individual and to gurarantee a minimum standard of life, social work can become one of the major instrumentalities for giving reality to the promise held out by the recognition of his "rights." If this society is economically advanced, the social worker will tend to be preoccupied with mobilizing resources, diverting them to particular areas which he considers of primary significance, and seeking the most appropriate way to provide assistance to the needy. As he finds that the basic problem of physical survival is gradually overcome, he will identify problems of social and psychological adjustment, organize his knowledge, refine his methods, and move toward the establishment of a profession.

In a society where these rights are not recognized, social work will have to serve as a means of awakening the conscience of the society so that they will be recognized. In the period during which the rights are not yet recognized, social work will have to mobilize resources on the basis of humanitarian and religious appeals and attempt to provide for the minimum needs of at least the most indigent sections of the population. It is unlikely that a profession can crystallize at this stage where those engaged in social work can expect no adequate recompense for their efforts and will often be expected to utilize their own means and materials before approaching others for help.

In societies which are economically advanced and have therefore the means to provide security, but have not formally accepted the individual's right to security, it is probable, though not certain, that social workers will find less resistance to their efforts to bring about a value change and to gain acceptance for the principle of the individual's right to social security. Social workers are likely to find it easier to evoke a response to their appeal in a society which has the material resources, even if it has not formally accepted the obligation, to provide security to the individual. To the extent that such a society has not accepted the individual's right to social security, the social worker will operate in an atmosphere of paternalistic charity and philanthropy rather than in an atmosphere characterized by recognition of the dignity of the individual.

Social Work and Its Human Rights Aspects

The right to social security was recognized only recently, and in most countries its recognition was associated with their growing economic ability to accept the responsibility implied in recognizing such a right. However, although they have some of the most idealistic political constitutions in the world and are in principle responsive to the concept of the individual's right to social security, they are without the means to implement their promises. Social workers in these countries find that policy-makers concede the validity of their plea on behalf of the needy but also simultaneously express their inability to help. This gives rise to an unreal atmosphere of sympathy for noble sentiments accompanied by an almost cynical inaction. In such a situation, social workers are likely to be led to believe that a value change has already been accomplished and that they have only to await the availability of material resources in order to offer the services they consider necessary. But the value change may be only superficial since it has never been tested in action, and the nonavailability of resources may only be a specious excuse for inaction.

Finally, there are societies which have not accepted the obligations toward the individual, nor do they have the resources required to meet them. In these societies, social workers are called upon to work at two levels—that of persuading the community to recognize the needs of some of its members and that of proceeding to meet them with the limited resources at hand. The services provided are likely to be directed merely to meeting the physical needs of food, clothing, and shelter since these are the only ones that are likely to gain support in the community. Social work will tend to be done primarily under religious auspices and sometimes with the help of individual philanthropists. Questions of human rights are likely to seem somewhat remote to social workers and clients alike.

I have deliberately refrained from identifying particular countries or parts of the world as belonging to one type or the other, not so much as a matter of strategy, but because I am conscious of the essential crudity of the suggested typology. One cannot easily group countries as having accepted or not having accepted the whole list of human rights. A country may accept some and not accept others. Also, even in the same country, particular rights may be accepted with reference to one section of the population on ethnic or religious grounds and not accepted with reference to others. This is likely to happen particularly in respect to civil and political rights. This may seem to violate the very concept of human rights since these rights, if they have any meaning at all, are in principle indivisible. Yet, no country has an altogether clear record in regard to human rights, and countries vary in the thoroughness with which they accept one set rather than another and also in the equability with which they make them available to different segments of the population. All societies thus live in the proverbial glass house and, mixing metaphors, one may say that none of them can allow its members to cast the first stone at another society.

This situation suggests that one should seek to apply the typology not so much to whole societies but to particular rights and to particular groups or subgroups in a society. It may even be that the availability or nonavailability of means also varies with reference to particular groups or particular "causes" within the same society. If one accepts the possibility that there could be variation within the same society, one would also have to accept the probability that within the same society social work would face a variety of challenges and be required to assume a multiplicity of roles.

The Social Worker's Role

It has often happened that in societies which have generally recognized the values affirmed by the Declaration and have also the means to meet the implied obligations, the efforts of social workers have naturally been devoted primarily to the operation and development of services. Not unusually, this has led to preoccupation with certain types of problems and services. In industrially advanced countries, social workers have tended to concern themselves with urban, industrial, working-class families. In fact, it may be true that professional social work arose largely in response to the problems of a rapidly industrializing and urbanizing society. The rural population did not receive the same measure of attention. This was a consequence of the assumption that the traditional institutions of the rural community would continue to meet the needs of the people and also of the assumption that somehow the problems due to change were more important than those arising from lack of change. The lack of organized resources and employment opportunities in the rural areas and the social workers' unwillingness to be consigned to the hinterlands may also have contributed to this situation. The consequence of all these factors has been that awareness of the existence of rural poverty and unmet needs has come with a shock to countries which have otherwise accepted the obligation to provide a minimum standard of life for their citizens and which have also the requisite material resources to meet this obligation.

Simultaneously, there has been another type of preoccupation and another type of neglect. In some countries, the acceptance and acclamation of the value implied in the political and civil rights listed in the Declaration has led to the social worker's concentration on his healing and remedial functions and to a neglect of his duty to serve as a watchdog for basic human values. Often, therefore, problems have arisen with a violence and an unexpectedness that have thrown the whole society into convulsions.

It may be asked whether activity in the movement for human rights generally, including political and civil rights, is within the scope of social work. The answer could be conditional, but in societies which have consciously and articulately accepted representative, democratic government and the equality of all their citizens, protecting the rights of minorities and insuring nondiscrimination through constructive action do form a part of social work. It is true that a measure of doubt, if not controversy, surrounds this area. It has been suggested that the stance of the social worker is likely to be gentler than the heroic stance of a rebel or a fighter, but it need not be less effective, and his role need not be less important to society.

Social Action and Social Work

Despite the suggestion that social action may be considered as a part of the three or four important types of activities engaged in by social workers, there has never been a clear understanding of exactly what its scope would be. Specifically, the question of whether the profession of social work should be involved in action which is likely to be unacceptable to some segments of a society and likely to affect the organized interests in that society remains unanswered—though such action is in full conformity with the basic values of that society. What, for instance, should be the role of the social work profession vis-à-vis the Negro problem in the United States, the Harijan problem in India, and the problem of colored immigrants in the United Kingdom? I think that in any examination of the human rights aspects of social work this question becomes crucial. What should be the role of the individual professional and of the profession as a whole in situations where the worth and dignity of certain individuals are denied although the society proclaims this value and generally accepts it in regard to other segments of so- . ciety?

One way of responding to this situation is to say that in their personal and professional lives social workers should not act in ways which would be in transgression of this value. This mode of response evades the issue by converting a question which is addressed to the profession into one addressed to the individual as a citizen. Obviously, even this response is valuable and shows the individual's commitment to a particular value. But it is not adequate.

Social Action and Political Action

Another response is to say that any organized social action is in the nature of political action and should be avoided because it is outside the sphere of social work and is likely to be divisive of the profession. This response merits serious consideration because it implies a certain definite concept of the nature of social work and of political action. I do not look upon social work as the only instrument for solving all human problems and I concede that the social worker in his professional role should avoid becoming entangled in the actions of political parties. Nevertheless, it is difficult to find any major program of social action which is bereft of all political significance. The important question is whether a particular problem is of such central interest to social workers in their professional capacity as to require them to act in the interests of their clients. I suggest that a social worker in one of the villages of India, in the working-class area of London, Manchester, or Birmingham, or in one of the racially torn neighborhoods of an American metropolis, cannot evade the responsibility of helping the deprived members of the population to overcome all obstacles to the exercise of their basic legal rights. In accepting this responsibility he need not adopt the methods of the political agitator. Every profession has its own means and methods. The question is not whether this sphere of activity belongs to social work, but rather how a social worker would respond in such a situation.

Characteristics of Professional Practice

There are certain inherent limitations to the practice of a profession, especially a profession like social work. A social worker has to have an agency to sponsor his action and a known client to whom his action is oriented. The prerequisite of an agency means that the action of the social worker has to have sufficient legitimacy so that it will be supported openly by at least a part of the community. Also, the professional has to act with reference to, or on behalf of, a client whether the client is an individual or a group. As an individual practitioner he cannot argue a "cause" in the abstract. Moreover, his methods must have the sanction of the profession. He cannot decide on the spur of the moment to pick up a poster and join a slogan-shouting group. Fortunately, this is not one of the methods of social work yet.

But where these conditions are fulfilled and where there are obstacles to the effective social functioning of his client, the social worker's responsibility to take interventive action is clear. This responsibility is not fulfilled by the response that as an individual he will not add to these obstacles and that he will not be prejudiced in his professional conduct. Minimally, he will be required to work effectively to enable his client to use fully all the services available in the community. In this pursuit he will use all his skills of persuasion and, if necessary, all the help that law can give to remove impediments to the legitimate exercise of his client's rights and to the normal fulfillment of his client's aspirations.

Not all obstacles to the exercise of human rights or to the functioning of an individual with dignity and freedom are tangible and such as can be legally removed. Also, there may be shortcomings in the law itself which need to be remedied. The individual social worker cannot, therefore, lean heavily on law to serve the interests of his clients. Legal battles leave scars, and if the worker is interested in furthering more harmonious relationships he cannot always brandish his legal stick.

The fact is that there are serious limitations to the change in community attitudes and values that an individual worker can achieve through his local action. On fundamental issues, such as the treatment given to minorities, attitudes in the local community are influenced and supported by attitudes in the larger society. At this level the individual social worker employed by a local agency cannot play an effective role. If social work is to serve as an effective instrument for giving reality to formally accepted values and rights, it will have to enter upon an action addressed to the whole society. This role has usually been assigned to a "social reformer." In so far as the social reformer questions and even rejects some of the widely held values and proposes the adoption of new ones, his role cannot be easily institutionalized and integrated into the activities of a profession.

The Profession and the Individual Professional

At this point the distinction between the scope of activities of the whole profession and that of the activities of an individual professional becomes significant. It is true that the effort to bring about a change in some of the values characteristic of a society, or a major segment of it, cannot easily be perceived as part of the activity of an individual professional, but I suggest that it can and should form a part of the activities of the profession as a whole. The professional organization at various levels and professional leaders in their individual as well as their representative capacity will have to undertake this task. This is an important role for the profession to play. It is a role that differs from that of a rebel and also from that of a repairman. It retains the constructive orientation of professional action. Yet it compels the profession to see beyond the fashions and prejudices of the present so as to identify and promote instrumental values and practices necessary for the realization of the goals of human dignity and equality which are at the core of the Declaration of Human Rights and which are fundamental in the practice of the social work profession.

The Human Rights
Perspective

Even from this perspective, social work will continue to be in the nature of an interventive action for the enhancement of the social functioning of individuals and groups. It will achieve this end through helping individuals and communities to grapple with problems of change at the social and psychological levels. But this perspective will lead social work beyond its confines. It will additionally identify and promote values and practices necessary for the realization of human rights through the use of means which are consistent with the rights of other individuals and groups. While this position is not unacceptable to social workers and will not appear new in its orientation, it has the advantage of clarifying what the moorings and long-term objectives of social work are. It will disturb the complacence of the individual social worker who may be tempted to acquiesce in the values of the local community even when they conflict with the broader sympathies of the profession. It will require and compel the organized profession to take clear positions on social issues. As distances are further reduced by even faster means of communication we shall be even more aware of the fact that the world is peopled by many races that speak many languages. In the midst of a plurality of cultures and values there will be need for the affirmation of one acceptable common denominator. The Universal Declaration of Human Rights provides this necessary standard and direction to all constructive action.

Within the limitations imposed by the need for constructive action this perspective will give social work a role to play in societies which are economically advanced as well as in those which are economically backward and in societies which have generally accepted the values articulated in the Declaration and those which have not.

I have suggested that the relationship between human rights and social work can be better understood if we appreciate the extent of value commitment to human rights which is characteristic of a society and its ability to transcribe this commitment into action. This commitment and the ability to transcribe it into action may vary not only from society to society but even between groups in one society and with respect to different facets of the Declaration. This varying equation between commitment and ability provides one of the major determinants for the type of social work practice that will emerge or stabilize itself. And since this equation is a varying one, our concept of the nature of social work will have to be broad enough to provide for the variations in practice.

The social work practitioner is frequently seen by the client as a representative of a social agency rather than as one concerned with the client's unmet needs. Lewis presents two sets of principles for social work practice, trust and distributive justice, that he purports can so guide professional behavior as to overcome this potential conflict between the client's and the worker's views of the purpose of their relationship.

Morality and the Politics of Practice

Harold Lewis

Science first developed as a method, then as a body of knowledge, and, more recently, as a social institution. Scientists now overwhelmingly assume roles as professionals employed by large organizations, universities, and governmental agencies. The human service professions similarly have found themselves emphasizing their methods, their knowledge base, or their institutional self-interests at different points in their history. The concern for consequences which justify practice and the values that direct such concerns are frequently overlooked in the history of science but can hardly be ignored in the development of a profession. When such values are evident in the product of professional effort, they constitute its morality.

Our nation and the helping professions are currently experiencing a moral crisis. This crisis is manifest in every issue confronting the social work profession, challenging its very existence. Questions of manpower, professional and paraprofessional; of auspices, public and voluntary, profit and nonprofit, religious and nonsectarian; of advocacy and treatment; of generalist and specialist; and of policy and practice cannot be understood without confronting the moral crisis and cannot be resolved without some commitment to deal with the issues posed.

Although the sciences have helped orient us to issues affecting our means, and the applied humanities have oriented us in our choice of ends, our profession utilizes a blend of both, formulated as principles and guidelines for practice. These practice principles define the performance expected of the principled practitioner and his commitment to a moral practice. Morality produces a set of values and seeks to generate trust and justice in reciprocal human relationships.

Reprinted with permission of the author and The Family Service Association of America from *Social Casework,* Vol. 53, No. 7 (July 1972), pp. 404–417.

The reluctance of professional social work to engage in authoritative services—to doubt the possibility of a professional service in circumstances where the recipient is an unwilling participant—stems in part from assumptions concerning the minimal moral maturity essential for a truly helpful relationship.[1] The worker who assumes willing engagement and freedom of choice is reluctant to initiate a relationship of fearful dependency with an obedience and punishment orientation. He is equally reluctant to enter into a self-serving reciprocity where contact and exchange are characteristically egoistic and opportunistic. As a minimum, almost all of the psychological approaches which provide the conceptual underpinnings of practice imply at least some conforming to a stereotypical image of natural role behavior. The conforming may be only a concession to please with a "good-boy" intention. Where this minimal implication is absent, the recipient is likely to resist involvement in a service relationship that expects some degree of commitment on his part.

The recipient who is motivated to use the help to be given and who evidences a willingness to conform to rules is more commonly found. He behaves in an appropriate manner, as defined by the service source, even when rules and behavior may be viewed by him as burdensome additions to the conforming role—necessary and entered into only because failure to fulfill them can deny him access to the resources which he badly needs. Studies of helping relationships usually find such recipients among the more successful cases of short-term service—able to sustain their participation in the helping process long enough to transact the transfer of resource which prompted their seeking help and maintain their conforming role behavior.

This degree of commitment, nevertheless, is rarely seen as sufficient for achieving a more ambitious psychological influence in a counseling transaction. For long-term helping, conforming behavior would seem to require adherence to shared standards, rights, and obligations involving a contractual, legalistic orientation, based on a mutual willingness and expectation of positive consequences. This level of moral maturity usually cements the relationship with mutually satisfactory intentions, releasing energies for growth-yielding experiences, generally seen as a major goal of long-term service. It is but one step further in moral maturity for the recipient to pattern his behavior on the basis of conscious and universal logical principles founded on mutual respect and trust. The recipient who has achieved this level of moral maturity is

[1]The concept of moral maturity and the stages of maturity discussed are based on Lawrence Kohlberg's work on stages of moral maturity. See Lawrence Kohlberg, *Acquisition and Development of Values: Perspectives on Research* (Bethesda, Md.: U.S. Department of Health, Education, and Welfare, Public Health Service, National Institute of Health, The National Institute of Child Health and Human Development, 1968), pp. 16–22.

more likely to be psychologically free of handicapping attitudes and behavior. He can initiate and terminate engagement in the helping relationship with minimal need for structure-rules and procedures.

These levels of moral maturity depict different degrees of morality, evaluated from the perspective of the profession's view of a recipient's mature behavior in a helping relationship. Although these levels suggest a progression with reference to dependence-independence, they evidence no such progression with respect to commitment to behavioral norms appropriate to each level. For example, at the lowest level of morality, dependence on outside rules is greatest; at the highest level such dependence is practically nil. The degree of the recipient's involvement with the helper, however, will fluctuate at any level of the dependence-independence continuum. Professional authority is appropriately exercised in relation to the recipient since this authority is earned through furthering the moral maturity of the recipient in his service role. In sharp contrast, the exercise of professional authority to compel commitment and the involvement in service it would entail is more appropriately viewed as authoritarian and unprofessional. This difference is fundamental and poses the central issue that confronts the human service professions in our country today.

There is work to be done in achieving a level of self-trust that supports one's risking independent behavior when the professional worker helps contribute to the clarification of tasks, monitors behavior, identifies weaknesses, and expands on alternatives. The consequences of such effort is evident to the recipient in his own experience. The recipient, in effect, is able to know and claim his own growth. He can willingly yield some control to the helper, whose authority is knowingly based on the recipient's belief in the helper's capacity to provide the service needed. It is an authority based on means, not on ends.

Commitment, on the other hand, is a matter of trusting the other's intentions, not his competence. It depends on factors affecting, but extending far beyond, the relationship. Thus, in a society where social practice and policies evidence a lack of regard for distributive justice and privacy, trust is the earliest victim. Such practices and policies are increasingly evident at all levels of our own national life. A pervasive immorality is contributing to deterioration of the humane context of professional practice. If this destruction of trust is allowed to continue, it will, in time, no longer be possible to engage in an ethical social work practice. Instead, a dehumanized welfare service, void of a caring human interface, will take its place. Such dehumanized service will provide a computerized, plastic, and efficient tool for national pacification, programming people who will be known by the company that keeps them and by their code numbers in an omniscient surveillance memory bank.

Importance of Trust

Consider what characterizes a relationship without trust. A relationship without trust is burdened with fears. It entraps the parties involved in a labyrinth of unfathomables: guessing intentions, deciphering motives, or searching for meaning that arouses or placates doubts. Without trust, a relationship may breed contempt when it intends respect or create anxiety when it wishes to comfort. Lacking this element of reciprocity, it will also be deficient in friendship and love.

Social workers experience circumstances in their practice that foster distrust in their clients and in themselves. Common to such circumstances are requirements that foreclose on choices by limiting alternatives. In social work practice, choices are most often denied where resources are lacking. The poor and the powerless, those with the least and needing the most, are frequently the victims of such denials, promoting their distrust. Thus, in service encounters that ask for mutual engagement for good and humane reasons, the expectation of mutual trust may, for many, be most unreasonable. Certainly, in times such as we are now experiencing, where social workers and services are being separated from the poor by deliberate national and state policies, there is good and sufficient reason for distrust.

In a helping relationship, trust functions to support dependence without fear of self-effacement; to inculcate an expectation of joint, mutually beneficial effort—despite differences in kind, frequency, and intensity of involvement; to reinforce the belief that assigned obligations will be fulfilled and cooperative effort sustained, reassuring participants who might otherwise fear betrayal. Trust serves as an organizing device that facilitates the communication of a moral tone to a helping relationship. These functions, composed of elements that signal the basis for trust, may be evidenced in the circumstance, in the process, and in the participant's attitude and behavior in the relationship. It will be undermined where racial, class, cultural, and ethnic differences deny equal and fair access to available resources. A society—its institutions and its welfare programs—which fails to see all persons as ends in themselves (whether they be Vietnamese or Americans), which in its actions fails to give equal weight to the interests of each person affected by an action, or which departs from this equality in a way that grants unequal benefits without regard for the expectation of the least advantaged is necessarily unjust in its distribution of resources and is not to be trusted. It is crucial for the social work profession to develop and support practice principles that will instill trust in the helping relationships associated with its services. Such principles should generate rules that would commend agencies and workers in the offer of service and in the helping situation to act in a trustworthy manner.

Practice Principles

The first set of practice principles deals with fair and equal access to service. These principles assume that an absence of justice in the offer and initiation of service will seriously undermine that confidence on which trust relies.

1. The conditions that determine the availability of service should be uniformly applicable to all partaking of it. Deviations from these conditions are justified only when they can be shown to be to everyone's advantage.

This principle recognizes that trust develops with the expectation that each request for help will receive the same consideration, will be evaluated on the basis of appropriate and similar criteria, and will be judged by its intrinsic merit as a claim on service resources. No person will be privileged without good and apparent reason or without some provision for those thereby disadvantaged. An example of privileged consideration in keeping with this principle is the selection of a request for special care and treatment where potential for enhancing new knowledge exists. An example of privileged consideration that contradicts this principle is the bypassing of a waiting list in order to facilitate access to service resource for a recipient who makes claim based on friendship, kinship, or some other irrelevant criteria. This principle also recognizes the chronic limitation of available resources; it cautions against exhausting their supply without provision being made for those who will be unserved for reasons over which they have no control and which otherwise are not grounds for exclusion.

2. No more should be asked of the recipient in a service relationship than is necessary and sufficient to transact the intended service. Involuntary involvement of a recipient in service for his own protection or that of others should provide for the defense of the recipient's rights by persons and procedures not under the control of the service source or an agent pressing for such involvement.

This principle proposes an allocation of resources and provision of procedures to protect a recipient against unwarranted intrusion upon his privacy. Where privacy is denied an individual against his wishes, he is thereby deprived of an essential element of trust: the choice to share a part of himself that he can otherwise choose to keep from public view. In such intimate relationships as love and friendship, the granting of access to one's otherwise private self is frequently the most convincing expression of trust. Requesting information in a service relationship must clearly demonstrate its relevance to the use the recipient will make of the service and to his appropriate participation in it. Only under these circumstances can the recipient exercise choice in self-revelation and trust the intentions of the offer of service.

Compelling a person to enter into a relationship which inevitably must subject parts of his thoughts, attitudes, feelings, and behavior to the scrutiny of another is tantamount to victimizing him by robbing him of an area of personal authority and thereby arousing his distrust. External authority, when imposed and not contracted for, communicates to the person imposed upon intentions that are suspect, for they threaten his freedom of choice and self-determination. Without a reasonable and adequate appeal against imposed authority, it will convey an authoritarian tone to the relationship this imposition establishes. The intervention without request—whether motivated by an intention to protect others or to protect a person from his own self-destructive behavior— is most often justified on grounds that the person involved cannot be trusted to behave in a socially acceptable manner. This distrust breeds further distrust, which, although it can never be totally removed, can be mitigated by providing access to a higher authority empowered to subject the intrusion to a test of validity, under circumstances not entirely in control of the instigating authority.

An example of the application of this principle would be in a process whereby eligibility for public assistance is determined on the basis of the specific, immediate, and shared evidences of financial need. Another example of the application of this principle would be in a child neglect case in which a presentation to a court makes provision for an attorney to represent the client, overseeing the interests of the family charged with neglect. An example of the failure to comply with this principle is determining eligibility for a service through requirements concerning political, religious, ethnic, or other personal preferences having no direct bearing on the determination of need for the resource requested.

3. The restraints implicit in the conditions for offering or making claims for service should not be posed as a threat. The risks and obligations entailed in a service relationship should not unfairly burden any one participant.

Given the excess of demand over supply associated with the provision of services, preferences must be exercised. In arriving at such priority decisions, some recipients will be disadvantaged. Such disadvantage will frequently ask of the group affected that they risk the uncertainties of delay and incomplete provision and undertake greater obligation of justification of need than is otherwise required. Recognizing this fact, this principle requires that such differential treatment be based on legitimate and relevant criteria, be openly arrived at and uniformly applied, and be subject to ongoing review lest a just procedure in time perpetuate an unjust burden. Where the recipient perceives unequal treatment as unjustified, fairness is doubted and distrust promoted.

This principle cautions against surrounding otherwise fair and equal access to service with conditions that promote privileged treatment based on unequal talents and status. It is unreasonable to expect persons seeking help to have confidence in processes and procedures which evidently channel their requests into categories of service provision differing in quality and quantity when such assignment is based on social status and conditions over which they have no control or on natural differences not subject to alteration by their own conscious and reasoned effort. The application of criteria that are unrelated to the elements relevant to the request and that are not subject to the influence of the helping resource as a condition of access must inevitably deplete the recipient's image of himself as a source of power and influence over his own condition. This depletion threatens his sense of self-determination. Similarly, priority considerations determined by such criteria do not order preferences on the basis of need, motivation, or capacity, but on competitive evaluations. These evaluations are likely to penalize, for reasons over which they lack control, those persons who are most disadvantaged. Fair and equal access must anticipate natural and social restraints and not be conditioned by them.

An example of this principle is the fair manner in which provision is made for a waiting list and fee assignment in a child guidance clinic. An example of the failure to apply this principle is the practice of "first come, first served" allocation of resources, without consideration of unequal opportunity or capacity for initiating request. This lack of consideration is often evident in the allocation of concrete resources such as day care, homemaker, camping, or financial emergency relief funds.

4. The offer of essential concrete services should include alternatives for the intended beneficiary. Lacking alternatives, the offer should be made as a matter of right, as free of conditioning tests as possible.

This principle primarily concerns the provision of such basic human needs as food, clothing, shelter, and medical care. Where survival depends on access to these resources, it is unrealistic to expect persons needing such assistance to trust a relationship that intervenes between their request and access to the resource. To the applicant who understandably assumes his own continued survival to be a fundamental right, a requirement that limits this right represents a threat to his existence. He can hardly avoid the implication that his claim is in some way doubted and that he is not entirely to be trusted. Under these circumstances, reciprocal involvements intended to enhance social and psychological functioning may be viewed as barriers, not aids, to access.

Foundations for Social Work Practice

They would appear to hold little promise of effective consequences.

An example of the application of this principle is the provision of unemployment compensation as a right. Another example is the provision of emergency medical care after natural catastrophes. An example of the contradiction of this principle is in the uniform requirement that indigent recipients participate in a counseling service as a condition for emergency relief or medical care.

5. The recipient of service should have the opportunity to experience his role in its provision as a test of its fairness and not be expected to assume such fairness as a precondition for service.

This principle accepts as an unavoidable accompaniment of a trusting relationship the risk entailed in revealing oneself to another, relinquishing thereby some element of personal autonomy and self-determination. Deciding on what and how much to risk involves the recipient and helper in ambiguous situations whose scope and consequences cannot be entirely anticipated. Thus, each new encounter with a helping process requires of its participants a willingness to consider the intent of the other partly on the basis of past experiences, but always on the basis of performance in the here and now. Foreclosing an existential criterion by which participants can evaluate fairness limits the choice to risk based on what is new and different in this encounter. This limit denies to each participant the opportunity to be judged anew. Emerging changes and growth may in these circumstances be discounted for the sake of relative certainties projected from earlier evidences. In some ways, such projections may become self-fulfilling and in other ways may undervalue existing potential. In either case, a fair hearing of a current request may be denied.

An example of the application of this principle is the provision for an initial phase on service for mutual exploration of the resources requested, the resources available, and the conditions for their utilization. An example of the contradiction of this principle is the requirement of detailed, personal history data on application forms, without any explanation of their intended use nor any clear statement of their relevance to the decision affecting the applicant's access to service.

The second set of practice principles pertains to the need to provide opportunities in each service encounter to share risks, to engage in frank and responsible expression of feeling and thought, and to evidence dependable and consistent behavior in order to promote trust among participants in a helping relationship.

6. The worker should seek to enlarge on choices available to the recipient, including those proposed by the recipient and those newly developed in the course of rendering the service.

This principle regards choice as significant in moral behavior. Choice is as essential for trust as opportunity is for self-realization. Choice increases opportunities for error. Where there is no possibility of error, there is also no basis for trust. Willingness to act in uncertain situations is a necessary condition for determining one's commitment to the goals of a relationship which entails some risk to one's self.

Without choice, decisions are foreclosed. The recipient, denied the option of selecting among alternatives, is limited in the risks taken. Where the offer of service is tightly bound by requirements and where resources are limited, the recipient may be faced with a take-it-or-leave-it decision. In these circumstances, neither the worker nor the recipient has reason to experience together the exploration of alternatives so essential to a trusting relationship. Enlarging choices thus constitutes a significant source of evidence on which convictions about intentions and expectations can be developed. Where new choices evolve from the worker-recipient interaction itself, a natural bond can evolve that cements the relationship with the commitment of both parties. The binding nature of joint discovery reinforces in the explorers a sense of their mutual competence and importance. Finally, the attitude that conveys an intention to seek after options is likely to be one that is hopeful. An atmosphere of hope, associated with choice, communicates belief in potential and thereby encourages trust.

An example of the application of this principle is a community's providing a range of supervised housing services for the aged, with varying degrees of supervised care provided. Such provision makes possible relevant choices based on recipient need rather than making do with limited alternatives that may further undermine the full potential for self-care of the aged person involved. An example of the failure to adhere to this principle is a community child welfare program in which a lack of provision for halfway houses, specialized institutions for the emotionally disturbed, sufficient foster-home care, and care away from home perpetuates conditions of child neglect and dependency through the very structure of service intended to alleviate such conditions.

7. Potential recipients should be informed about programs for which they are eligible. Participating recipients should know when resources sought and promised are no longer on hand. Failure to utilize a service or sustained participation in a program of service ought not to be based on ignorance of the facts concerning the availability of resource.

It is not uncommon for channels of communication to handicap further those already handicapped. The lack of awareness of available services on the part of economically and socially deprived persons has been documented many times over. Failure to reach eligible populations in need with information of their rights and opportunities rein-

Foundations for Social Work Practice

forces in them a deep disbelief in the intention of those offering a service and a distrust of procedures used to determine eligibility for the service. Similarly, doubt as to program intentions is inevitable when recipients are initially involved in a relationship on the basis of a promised provision of resource and subsequently are sustained in this relationship despite knowledge on the part of the service source that the original resource requested has been exhausted or is no longer available.

An example of the application of this principle is the program of the Veterans Administration which utilizes a variety of channels to inform veterans of their rights and of available resources. A further example is the provision of ombudsmen services to protect the clients' rights to services that are promised by programs in which they are involved.

An example of the failure to apply the first element in this principle is the denial of public assistance in many instances to poverty-ridden persons primarily because they remain ignorant or misinformed of their rights. Failure to apply the second element in this principle is the commitment of persons to institutional care for purposes of treatment when, in fact, treatment resources are so scarce as to be practically unavailable to the recipients who are thus retained in a custodial setting with little expectation of a change in their condition.

Importance of
Distributive Justice

Clients of social service programs are among the most disadvantaged persons in our society. Social workers employed in these programs normally serve such disadvantaged clients directly or work with persons interested in promoting services for them. A principal moral justification for professional social work practice is therefore to be found in the dedication of the practitioner to the improvement of the circumstances and expectations of these clients. A helping profession not based in a morality inspiring a just order risks encouraging a practice that promotes an unjust one.

Distributive justice, while by no means the whole of a just order, is a particular concern of a helping profession serving the disadvantaged. If it penalizes the least advantaged, it defeats efforts intended to aid the disadvantaged.

An ethical imperative intended to guide the behavior of persons seeking distributive justice has been proposed by John Rawls. Professor Rawls utilizes social contract theory and a set of value expectations which rational persons may be presumed to want (that is, liberty and opportunity, income and wealth, health and educated intelligence, and self-respect) and proposes the following necessary conditions for distributive justice:

a. Each person is to have an equal right to the most extensive basic liberty compatible with a similar liberty for others.

b. Social and economic inequalities are to be arranged so that they are both:

(i) reasonably expected to be to everyone's advantage and
(ii) attached to positions and offices equally open to all.[2]

Professor Rawls assumes a framework of social institutions in which fair equality of opportunity obtains. His second condition suggests an ethical imperative: ". . . the higher expectations of those better situated in the basic structure are just if and only if they work as part of a scheme which improves the expectations of the least advantaged members of society."[3] He also assumes that the first condition must be satisfied before the second can be met.[4] Thus, the principle of equal rights to liberty becomes a preliminary condition to the establishment of justifiable inequalities. These conditions and the derived ethical imperative seem compatible with the goals of service voiced in the professional literature of social work and in statements expressing program intentions of social service.

Social institutions incorporate into their practices those established patterns of behavior which they are charged to maintain in the society that supports them. While they may differ in their functions in relation to the *status quo*—some primarily concerned with control or maintenance, others with the restoration or restructuring of social relationships among competing groups—all are directly involved in activities or events which inevitably favor some and may discriminate against others.[5]

With knowledge of the role of social institutions in any society and of the ethical imperative earlier enunciated for achieving distributive justice, it is possible to formulate principles intended to promote distributive justice that should enhance the work of social workers, whatever their practice concentration.

Practice Principles

1. The profession and its associated institutions must, in the work and attitudes of their constituents, combat unfair discriminatory practices or be judged as perpetrating the disadvantages they entail.

[2]John Rawls, Distributive Justice: Some Addenda, *Natural Law Forum,* 13:51 (1968).
[3]Ibid., p. 59.
[4]John Rawls, A Theory of Justice, mimeographed, January 1970, p. 65. (Draft of book distributed to Fellows, Center for Advanced Study in the Behavioral Sciences, Palo Alto, Calif., February 1970).
[5]Bruce Eckland and Donald P. Kent, Socialization and Social Structure, in *Perspectives On Human Deprivation: Biological, Psychological and Sociological* (Bethesda, Md.: U.S. Department of Health, Education, and Welfare, Public Health Service, National Institute of Health, The National Institute of Child Health and Human Development, 1968), pp. 187–215.

Foundations for Social Work Practice

This principle includes in its formulation a denial of the possibility of a neutral stance toward racism. This principle assumes that one cannot enter the stream of community life and remain dry; nor can one avoid some deflection of its flow. Either the worker imparts a principle in his practice or departs from it; his actions provide the evidence by which his adherence to principle can be judged.

2. In choosing program goals and purposes, it should be assumed that ability and motivation among the disadvantaged are more widespread than is opportunity.

3. Institutionalized restrictions which limit opportunities, as well as the personal shortcomings of the client which may curtail his options, are legitimate targets for change.

This principle carries with it the implicit expectation that the worker will be knowledgeable in actions intended to change institutional structures as well as actions intended to structure personal and interpersonal change. It does not assume that these need be separate or qualitatively distinctive actions. The principle further recognizes that institutional arrangements in troubled communities must not model professional and organizational goals but serve them. If the profession is to act in accordance with its commitment to distributive justice, it must be prepared to transform itself and other community institutional structures and agencies employing social workers.

This third principle visualizes a societal and personal component in every service encounter. In seeking to maximize the client's utilization of resources, the worker's causal interests direct him to focus on personal and social restraints, which determine the current opportunities available to the client. He would be so directed whatever the nature of the client's problems, whatever their etiologies. Utilization of service appears in practice as action and, in the context of the helping process, is an important form of social action. It is not likely to be enhanced without client involvement on his own behalf. Nor can it be enhanced where opportunities available for improved utilization are so limited as to deny choice.

4. Opportunities to participate in the development of programs, in the formulation of policies and procedures, as well as in the practice decisions directly affecting their lives, must be afforded the disadvantaged as a minimal expectation of organizations and practices intended to help them.

It makes little sense to see individuals and institutions as beneficiaries of service, while denying them a central role in its development. The fourth principle, therefore, requires organizations and professionals intent upon helping people to include those for whom their services are intended in all phases of the social processes whereby needs are identified and resources are organized and distributed to meet these needs.[6] The knowledge basis for the propositional element in this principle has received extensive documentation in the literature of social work, particularly as a result of the experiences of recently developed antipoverty, community mental health, and client self-help programs. This principle does not require that those who are intended to benefit directly from the program have control of it, but it does not exclude this possibility. There is increasing evidence that many client groups favor such control, and experience may prove that it is an essential ingredient for sound practice. Conceivably, client control may provide one of the more important opportunities which traditionally have been denied to the disadvantaged in our country.

Characteristics of the Practice Principles

All the principles cited may be generalized to cover a variety of immoral practices known to be prevalent in our society, including denial of fair opportunity to racial and religious minorities, to women, to handicapped persons, to the aged, and to the poor. The propositional elements are derived from known facts about social institutions and their functions in any society, about discrimination and its impact on all groups thereby disadvantaged, and about changes that are required if evident inequities in opportunity are to be eliminated. The ethical commendations are derived from the ethical imperative accepted as essential for the achievement of distributive justice and trust. Together, these propositional and value statements justify the principles proposed. The experiences of social workers also serve to justify them in a way that encourages their acceptance in practice.

The social worker, in his professional and nonprofessional experience, has the opportunity to observe and evaluate the unjust and untrustworthy practices of the community in which he lives and works. He stores in memory these perceptions of prevalent social inequalities and refers to them when he seeks to understand events and circumstances new to his experience. Certainly life experiences differ among social workers and such differences extend to the social context and circumstances of their encounters with various forms of discrimination. There are workers who have been the victims of unfair behavior and others who have practiced such behavior without a conscious aware-

6Roland L. Warren, Toward A Non-Utopian Normative Model of the Community, *American Sociological Review,* 35:219–28 (April 1970).

Foundations for Social Work Practice

ness of its implications. There are, undoubtedly, some who have rationalized the injustices they have observed, attributing evident inequities to the influences of fate, faith, or fundamental biological differences. Whereas some workers would find support for the suggested practice principles in their total life experience, others would view these principles as contradictory to what nonprofessional and even certain professional experience would suggest.

Workers who would accept these principles for professional practice but deny their applicability to their own behavior when not involved in professional work would have to manage serious inner-directed conflict. One may suppose that the mental compartmentalization of behavior norms that must accompany such contradictory directives is likely to be successfully maintained when reinforced by external influences. Social structures, community norms, and institutions appear to facilitate and reinforce mental compartmentalization of behavioral roles by supporting differential role expectations in different settings. Increased dependence on such external structures to sustain mental compartmentalizations would ultimately deprive the worker of considerable freedom to respond imaginatively to client need situations, reinforcing a more rigid, habituated role-dominated practice. This is a heavy price to pay, but probably unavoidable if inner-directed conflict is to be controlled.

Experience teaches us to accept as a matter of fact the ability of most persons to engage in inconsistent behavior; we accept it as normal provided that contradictory behaviors are not simultaneously evident in the same social context. A helping profession (and its associated institutions) which promotes such inconsistencies, however, cannot expect to compartmentalize them so readily. Policies and procedures are never entirely private in an institution; the tensions generated by contradictory policies are communicated to the practitioner and his clients and are not likely to be fully absorbed in intraorganizational stresses and strains. The profession can hardly afford to be inconsistent in its principled behavior lest it be judged dishonest to the degree that its rules subvert professed intentions. If, for the individual, inconsistent behavior in professional and personal activities can be depleting of energy and resource, for the profession it can be calamitous.

There is a process, not clearly understood, whereby the principled behavior is achieved. For the individual worker there is the need to determine for himself that the propositions and ethical commendations of the principles to be followed are true and right, and this determination normally requires that he experience in practice the positive consequences that follow upon their application. He may, in relation to the principles proposed, find personal and social reasons for supporting their directives, recognizing that they are intended to increase the choices open to recipients. As he works with recipients and discovers for himself how personal and social factors contribute to the conditions he seeks to change, he will compose for storage in memory the self-confirming proofs that develop and sustain convictions and will be more willing to act on them.

One cannot legislate an inner-directed adherence to an ethic or truth, but one can promote a context that encourages such adherence. A practice environment that is increasingly intolerant of workers who profess ideals but fail to evidence conviction about them in their work is likely to inspire principled behavior. This fact is sensed by workers seeking employment in such agencies who assume that they will be encouraged to do likewise.

The social work profession attaches considerable importance to its code of ethics and similarly seeks a community environment that is sympathetic and encourages the profession to act on the basis of its convictions. While the profession is aware of its limited capacities and deficiencies in skill, there is much evidence of community restraints and deprivations that harm programs employing social workers, severely limiting their opportunities to achieve at the level of their known capacities.

A measure of a practitioner's skill is his ability to take into himself both the recipient-situation and worker-situation and to develop a balanced perspective which frees him to act on the basis of practice principles. The processes which the practitioner experiences in developing and sustaining a conviction to act on the principles must include work and the opportunity to observe the consequence of his work. The assumption long held by social work educators that methods are mastered in their application rests in part on this necessity to do in order to know what acting on a principle really means.

Patterns of worker activity provide the vehicles through which guiding principles are actualized. "By their deeds ye shall know them" accurately describes the role of action in the appraisal of professional intentions.

The Politics of Practice

Practice principles impart a moral component to professional service when they influence the worker's use of self in action, guiding his political choices. Politics concern the processes whereby priority decisions affect the allocation of resources (including the worker's own professional competence) and in this sense no professional practice can be apolitical. Given the ethical imperative that we have chosen to inform the principles cited, it is possible to define a morally destructive practice as one in which rational, programmatic, or personal priorities evidence preferences which further benefit the advantaged without increasing the expectations of the least advantaged. Such priorities can only be enforced by coercion, compelling those they further disadvantage to accept them. It is such coercion we call authoritarianism and which we identify in professional practice as unprincipled.

The priority question, "What should be the order in which I (we) do what I (we) can for this recipient (program)," is necessarily complex. It seeks a list of possibilities among which a choice must be made, some measure of their interdependence, and the sequence in which those possibilities chosen will be acted on. Thus, three different questions are incorporated in the one: What can I (we) do? How does the choice of one influence the others? What order of actions is required? These three questions differ in the type of answers they seek. The first requests information; the second asks for a propositional statement establishing the relationship recovered in answer to the first; the third resembles what John M. O. Wheatley calls a deliberative question, wanting a decision. In answer to the first question, a "true or false" test may be applied. In response to the second, one can propose a procedure for proving whether, in fact, the relationships specified are what the proposition asserts. For the third, what is called for is a decision rather than an assertion:[7] an answer that is neither true nor false. The first and second questions seek knowledge—"know-that" statements, for example; the third draws on imperatives. Since decisions are dispositions to behave in a certain manner if certain conditions are realized, the value component entailed in an answer to the third question is clear. What the inquirer wants in answer to the decision question is not a prediction, but suggestion or advice.[8]

The social worker employed by a social agency is not free to exercise his preferences in determining his clientele, workload, or problem to be dealt with in practice. Priority decisions that have culminated in the program of services offered by the agency limit his opportunities. It is not difficult to identify the many prior decisions that have shaped an agency's program and the political and economic interests they reflect. These decisions are manifest in program budgets of financing bodies and in the attributes of persons serving on those bodies that pass on plans and policy. The agency's goals, purposes, policies, and procedures are themselves conditioned by prior decisions and in turn set limits within which the worker's choices are exercised.

The worker must deal with two situations which necessitate personal priority decisions, given the constraints flowing from agency program preferences. He must, at any one time, decide how to allocate his

[7]John M. O. Wheatley, Deliberative Questions, *Analysis,* 15:49–60 (January 1955), p. 55, footnote.
[8]Ibid., pp. 52, 56.

personal resources among all the clients requiring his services. He must also decide on the allocation of those resources designated for a particular client. These two decisions undoubtedly have their distinctive, as well as common, attributes. These personal priority decisions can be contrasted with the priority decision process occurring in social policy and planning activities.

It is customary in social work to think of priorities as an aspect of the planning and policy decision processes of groups, organizations, and communities, but rarely, if ever, as an integral part of the worker's practice wherein he decides how to budget and allocate his own personal resources. Actually, the worker's efforts to cope with value-preference issues in practice evidence all the issues identified in planning and policy choices situations if we accept the following list of such issues as indicative:

there are conflicting values at stake;

value questions must often be posed in an "as if" form;

it is difficult to clarify just what the prevalent values or preferences are;

values are not always transitive;

there is often dispute as to whose choices are relevant or most relevant to the decisions to be made;

it is difficult to translate technical issues into their value consequences in a completely objective fashion.[9]

The social worker may accept as a "given" the agency's allocation of its resources, recognizing the priority choices such allocations evidence in its program goals. He may also accept as a "given" the preferences expressed by his clientele regarding problems to be worked on, the nature of help desired, and acceptable outcomes. He, nevertheless, must then ask himself, whatever are the restraints of these "givens" circumscribing his choices: How shall I allocate my own resources? What investment of self ought I to make in a particular service transaction? In what order should my abilities be committed in meeting the demands evidenced in this one practice encounter?

The approaches to decision making suggested for those concerned with problems of valuations in social policy and planning hardly suffice for this inner-directed choice process.[10] The concern in the former is with processes and procedures for enabling others to achieve consensus on goals and purposes, often in conflict-laden interpersonal situations. Self-directed valuations, having as their intent the recovery of

---

[9]Alfred J. Kahn, *Theory and Practice of Social Planning* (New York: Russell Sage Foundation, 1969), p. 107.
[10]Ibid., p. 126.

guides for actions that realize the worker's allocation of his own resources, involve other matters.

For example, while compromise is often an acceptable ploy in social
planning, one does not compromise with one's self—one compromises
one's self. Consensus is important to social planners, but one does not
look for consensus or majority opinions in inner-choice decisions, nor
does one avoid the need to choose by delegating the choice to others.
Such delegation is itself the choice. Dividing the circumstances conditioning the need for the self-directed professional priority question may
be helpful; involving others in identifying the alternatives and their
consequences may clarify and focus the worker's perspective; but in
the end he, and he alone, will have to decide how to allocate his
resources in each practice encounter within the "givens" that limit his
options.

In seeking to recover guidelines for action, the worker's theory and
value preferences no doubt point him in certain directions and limit the
range of possibilities he will consider in arriving at "inner" priority
decisions. The external parameters that circumscribe his available possibilities, such as the agency and client conditions, certainly restrict his
range of choices and serve a justifying function as well as an orienting
one. The "realities" to be reckoned with are likely to be accounted for
in the theory and goal preferences of the worker. These realities would
tend to assure, whatever the worker's choices, that "what is" in practice will largely determine "what should be." Another element that will
influence the worker's choice of theory and values will be his own
response repertoire, which sets limits on what he can personally consider as possible choices.

The worker must also establish a tentative agenda which maps his
inner-directed inquiry. This agenda sets forth a set of problems to be
dealt with in order that the priority decision appropriately relates to the
practical intent of his efforts. Thus, the worker must determine (1)
whether the recipient has a legitimate claim on his resources, (2) what
the recipient would have to do in order to avail himself of these resources, (3) what the worker would have to do to render the agency's
services in this instance, (4) what other claims on worker resources are
conditioned on this particular allocation and the relative merit of each,
and (5) what resources are to be allocated in light of the answers
obtained to questions one to five.

The substantive materials which constitute the content that characterizes these agenda items are generated in the interaction of worker and
recipient. Whereas the worker may be aware of this inner agenda
relevant to each service request, he is only able to establish the order
and scope of his consideration of these agenda items through the ex-
changes with the recipient that occur in the "intake" process itself.

Morality and the Politics of Practice

Thus, the prevalent view that service begins with the process of determining eligibility and does not wait on priority decisions seems realistic. It is inevitable that a certain amount of worker resource be expended in determining his time and energy allocations, and this expenditure necessarily influences the future direction of relationships that will obtain with the recipient. This item apparently ranks first in whatever priority scheme he later evolves.

The worker's inner-directed agenda must not be confused with the program of work that the worker and recipient jointly agree upon to govern their contacts. Although the "inner" agenda is, as noted, dependent on the "outer" agenda in certain respects, it is neither temporally nor spatially bound by the latter. The worker's professional questions which he puts to himself, while similar to those entering into any priority decision process, nevertheless, have their own characteristics.

The worker's complex self-directed question assumes that there are possibilities—that a choice exists—and he would want all likely ones to be listed. It does not, as far as he is concerned, assume that there is an indeterminate number of such possibilities. The worker seeks answers that commit his existing capacities. Moreover, he has been oriented by agency and recipient conditions and by his own professional theories and values to remove from consideration all possibilities that do not meet certain special qualifications.[11]

The "special qualifications" that serve to limit alternatives for the worker do differ from those that may limit the range of possibilities considered in the social policy and planning situation. In the first (approximation of possibilities), the worker will be guided by "thou shalt nots" which prescribe prohibited cases and focus his attention on recoveries that can count. This internal censorship clearly cannot prevail in social processes wherein the various interests influencing the priority choices must first reach agreement on those "shall nots" in order to proceed with the listing of possibilities.

Establishing the interdependence of possibilities, in order to arrive at the number of truly independent choices available, and determining which choices necessitate others as prerequisite or consequence can only follow, not precede, the listing of possibilities. This sequence, of course, is not unlike that which is evident in the interplay of preferences in interpersonal and intergroup priority processes. In the self-directed query, however, both the possibilities and their associations are presumed to be likely and in the interest of the recipient. In the social policy and planning choice situation, this is hardly the case where heterogeneous interests are represented.

[11]Charles L. Hamblin, Questions, in *The Encyclopedia of Philosophy*, vol. 7, ed. Paul Edwards (New York: Macmillan Co., 1967), pp. 49–51.

In any case, the initial priority decision cannot precede some approximation of responses to questions noted at the outset of this discussion of priorities. This order of precedence does not mean that the worker is committed to an unbreakable chain of consequences in arriving at his initial decision. All possibilities and their interdependence probably will not be recovered or discovered in time for the initiation of action. The process is a continuous one, with feedback serving to open new options not previously stored in memory. Stored options are sometimes recognized as appropriate only after the worker-recipient interaction develops.

In the social planning situation, collective decisions are reached usually after considerable investment of effort on the part of those whose interests are represented in the process. These decisions are not easily altered and are not as susceptible to change through the corrective influence of feedback transmitted in the course of their implementation. Resources committed to one purpose often deny sustenance to others —terminating certain interests' representation in the bodies responsible for policy, planning, and decision making and denying them further claim to a voice in setting or altering priorities.

The decision taken in response to the self-directed questions may be more readily altered as a result of experience in its implementation. It is private in the commitment it entails and more open to self-correction, not having to contend with the fault-finding that publicly admitted error in political judgments normally provokes. It is true that the worker's resources are limited and allocations to one purpose will deplete resources to be used in another. To the degree that the decision is the product of a single judge, however, judgments will be contingent on self-selected criteria reflecting the worker's natural preference for flexibility in the investment of his self in a given practice engagement.

A unique aspect of the self-directed question is its monostylous nature. What the worker finds attractive will more than likely influence his preferences. Since the alternatives to be ordered are inseparable from the style in which they are formed, the elements of style-conflict or style-complementarity which are present in interpersonal decision processes are absent in the worker's inner choices. Stylistic bent affects inner-directed query in another fashion that is somewhat unique.[12] The worker anticipates that what he decides will be what he has to carry out in practice. Knowing this, he is likely to prefer those alternatives which he judges will prove, in application, most congenial to his own style. Thus, style influences the possible alternatives selected for consideration and affects their ranking. It is not surprising, therefore, to observe how often diverse situations requiring dissimilar activities on

[12]T. A. Sebeok, *Style In Language* (Cambridge: M.I.T. Press, 1960), pp. 289–92.

the part of the worker manifest his individual style in their realization.

The social and the personal priority determination processes have deliberately been contrasted in order to use their differences to clarify elements peculiar to the inner-directed query. The comparison was also intended to highlight similarities, which suggest the "political" attributes of professional thought processes. Though deserving more discussion than it has been given, this subject seemed important to identify. The worker's priority decisions inevitably influence his practice, yet rarely are recognized for what they are: *His own approximation of his view of just and trustworthy behavior.*

The reluctance to engage in authoritative services previously noted stems in part from assumptions concerning the minimal moral maturity essential for a truly helping relationship. Levels of moral maturity were used earlier to identify the recipient's behavior. The same analysis applies to the moral behavior of the worker, particularly as such morality is manifest in his inner-priority decisions—his practice politics. Finally, the context of practice—our society's morality or immorality as evidenced in its priorities—can support the reciprocal relationships of the human service professions but currently is undermining them by destroying trust, invading privacy without which trust is impossible, and perpetrating distributive injustice on a massive scale.

Drawing upon systems theory, Schwartz argues that social workers must become more knowledgeable of system theories. The either/or polarization of the "social" vs. the "psychological" is no longer a relevant issue when systems theory is applied. The focus of social work practice is on how the individual interacts with larger systems, his total environment.

Private Troubles and Public Issues: One Social Work Job or Two?

William Schwartz

There are certain human issues that are never laid to rest. They are "solved" by the best minds of every generation, yet they remain troublesome, suspended, permanent centers of uneasiness. These issues tend to persist in the same form in which they began—as polarized absolutes between which we are asked to choose. We are urged to

From National Conference on Social Welfare: *The Social Welfare Forum,* 1969, pp. 22–43. Reprinted with permission of Columbia University Press.

Foundations for Social Work Practice

decide whether we are for the individual or the state, for freedom or discipline, nature or nurture, means or ends, structure or process, the past or the future. The specific controversies change, but the demand is always the same: you must be for the one or the many; you are a process man or a goals man; permissive or restrictive; for stability or for change; and so on into dualism after dualism.

These "choices" never satisfy. We feel trapped in the array of absolutes, wanting some of each and feeling that the problems have somehow been misstated. Those who have only to speculate about life can abstract the problems from the people and be satisfied with the clean ring of deductive logic. But those who must put the issues to work must look for solutions that not only include both polarities—the how and the what; the means and the ends; and the rest—but integrate them so completely that they cannot be pulled apart into false alternatives and inoperable choices.

The dualisms make it necessary to create *religious* solutions rather than technical ones, those where faith is more important than fact and strong belief is its own justification. Having sworn allegiance to one of the alternatives, there is no need for evidence, for records, for research, or any other effort to translate objectives into ways of achieving them. There is a kind of magical quality about it, a form of prayer, where solutions are invoked by forming the proper words and saying them with a certain emphasis and conviction. Hutchins, for example, urges the "pursuit of knowledge for its own sake"[1] (the content *vs.* process dualism) in the following tones: "Education implies teaching. Teaching implies knowledge. Knowledge is truth. The truth is everywhere the same. Hence education should be everywhere the same."[2] He tells us further that "the aim of education is to connect man with man, to connect the present with the past, and to advance the thinking of the race. If this is the aim of education, it cannot be left to the sporadic, spontaneous interests of children or even of undergraduates."[3] His conclusion is irresistible, a haunting strain from the old days: "One objection may be that the students will not like it, which is, as we have seen, irrelevant."[4]

A frequent consequence of the polarization of complex problems is that the adversaries forget who their real enemies are and fall on those closest to them. What ensues is a kind of "family quarrel" which takes on a ferocity not ordinarily wasted on strangers. The following was written by social workers about other social workers in public welfare:

[1] Robert M. Hutchins, *The Higher Learning in America* (New Haven: Yale University Press, 1936), p. 36.
[2] *Ibid.*, p. 66.
[3] *Ibid.*, p. 71.
[4] *Ibid.*, p. 86.

. . . recipients who have now learned to organize and fight the welfare system may not submit any longer to the preachments of case workers. Indeed, the movement may soon demand that welfare workers stay out of the ghettos and barrios, thus putting a halt to routine invasions of recipients' homes which take place under the guise of establishing rapport and conducting rehabilitation (in probable violation of the Fourth Amendment).[5]

Each profession creates its own versions of these dilemmas, with their trumped-up "choices," the verbal magic, and the family quarrels. But since they are professions, the frustrations are particularly acute. Professionals are paid for doing, for operationalizing, and not simply for speculating on the nature of life. The need for technical rather than dogmatic solutions is inherent in their social role. Although they may sometimes be a little apologetic about it, the fact is that their stock in trade is technique, and society holds them responsible for their ability to perform their work with skills not available to the ordinary citizen. How-to-do-it is the bread and butter of the lawyer, the doctor, the engineer—and the social worker. Without it they fail to differentiate themselves from the knowledgeable public, the informed layman, and the rest of those in society who are alive to its issues and have opinions about them. The professional distinguishes himself not by his general wisdom, his philosophy, or his goals, but by his ability to perform an operation, teach a class, build a bridge, plead a case, or use the resources of a community to help a person in trouble. Those who have studied the sociology of the professions have made a special point of their relationship to action and to skill. Parsons notes that "the professional man is thus a 'technical expert' of some order by virtue of his mastery of the tradition and the skills of its use."[6] And Wilensky and Lebeaux state that "the profession represents a monopoly of skill, which is linked to standards of training and which justifies a monopoly of activity in an area."[7]

Thus, when these polarizations appear in the professional arena, they are disruptive of technical advancement. They may serve for a while to dramatize important issues,[8] but the banner-waving, the quarrels over abstractions, and the ritualistic emphasis on goals without means, all impede the work on the central professional tasks. The dualisms inhibit action, and the term "technique" itself becomes invidious rather than the symbol of highest achievement.[9] As long ago as 1920, it was Edward Lindeman, always sensitive to this problem, who complained:

[5]Richard A. Cloward and Frances Fox Piven, "Finessing the Poor," *The Nation,* October 7, 1968, p. 332.
[6]Talcott Parsons, "A Sociologist Looks at the Legal Profession," in *Essays in Sociological Theory* (rev. ed.; Glencoe, Ill.: Free Press, 1954), p. 372.
[7]Harold L. Wilensky and Charles N. Lebeaux, *Industrial Society and Social Welfare* (New York: Russell Sage Foundation, 1958), p. 284.
[8]This point was made to me in a conversation with Dr. Hyman Weiner.
[9]See, for example, Alvin L. Schorr, "The Retreat to the Technician," *Social Work,* IV, No. 1 (1959), 29–33.

But we have been surfeited with the sentimental appeals in all spheres of social work. And sentiment, unsupported by scientific fact and principle, saps the dynamic forces of community life, making of our attempts at social progress a series of trial-and-error, hope-and-delusion spasms. . . . What we ask of the specialist is technique which rings true and organization which is unselfish.[10]

It is not that sentiment is unimportant to professionals. On the contrary, their hopes and convictions are indispensable to them as they work. It is simply that these are preludes to action, not accomplishments in themselves or debaters' points that carry their own ring of finality. Such have been the issues of "child vs. curriculum" in education, "justice vs. mercy" in law, "innate vs. cultural" determinants in psychiatry.

Social work has created its share of these dilemmas. It has had its "diagnostic vs. functional"; it is currently enjoying its "generic vs. specific"; and there will be others. But the granddaddy of them all, the oldest and still most vigorous, is the issue of the "social" vs. the "psychological"—its responsibility for social reform on the one hand, and individual help to people in trouble on the other. The issue has all the elements of the classical dualism, with the polarized abstractions, the family quarrel, the self-realizing objectives, and the persistent, unsolved feeling despite the attention of the best professional minds of every generation since social work began. In today's unstable and uproarious American scene it has taken on new forms, a new language, and a fresh sense of urgency.

As always, the problem has been identified by each generation in its own terms. In 1913 Porter Lee was already engrossed in his search for the connections between the spirit of reform and the technical problems of service to people. He called it "the crystallizing of enthusiasm into programs,"[11] and he said:

To go from concept to program and from program to technique is to take the long dreary drop from ideals to routine, from the heroic to the humdrum, from enthusiasm to devotion. But technique is still the factor which rounds out our march towards social justice and every social program must in the end stand or fall upon the quality of its technique.
. . . seen in its true relation to the other aspects of social work [technique] is as vivid and as appealing as the ideas which ought to guide it.[12]

Then, in 1929, Lee summarized the issue as that of "cause vs. function" and tried to reconcile the two. Beginning with Bryce's notion that the struggle for democracy comes not out of positive ideas but from the

[10]E. C. Lindeman, "Organization and Technique for Rural Recreation," in *Proceedings of the National Conference of Social Work* (Chicago: University of Chicago Press, 1920), p. 324.
[11]Porter R. Lee, "Technical Training for Social Work," in Lee, *Social Work as Cause and Function and Other Papers* (New York: Columbia University Press, 1937), p. 29.
[12]*Ibid.*, pp. 30–31.

need to remove certain tangible grievances,[13] Lee pointed out that "a cause is usually a movement directed toward the elimination of an intrenched evil."[14] When the evil is disposed of, the interest lessens. He went on to say:

The momentum of the cause will never carry over adequately to the subsequent task of making its fruits permanent. The slow methodical organized effort needed to make enduring the achievement of the cause calls for different motives, different skill, different machinery.

. . . an outstanding problem of social work at the present time is that of developing its service as a function of well-organized community life without sacrificing its capacity to inspire in men enthusiasm for a cause.[15]

Much earlier, Mary Richmond had written of the "wholesale" and "retail" methods of social reform, avowing her strong belief that "the order of march for most minds is from the particular to the general,"[16] asking her followers to "stick to the individual case," and concluding that "the whole of social reform is in the retail method, when we follow faithfully wherever its careful working out may lead."[17] Even earlier, in 1896, she had warned against the diversionary effects of the settlement movement.[18]

Clarke Chambers, reviewing the "wholesale-retail" dimensions of social work, states that "over the past 40 or 50 years, it was inspired more by St. Sigmund than St. Karl,"[19] and continues:

And so the two overlapping phases of social work continue to exist, not always harmoniously, but certainly in interdependence—the one focused on the individual and his welfare, strongly influenced by the psychological disciplines, introspective, dealing in personalized, retail services; the other concerned with reform, with reconstruction, informed primarily by the social sciences, extroverted, dealing in group or community or wholesale services.[20]

Chambers's analysis of the tensions between the "prophets"—those who thunder and hold up absolute standards—and the "priests"—those who minister, listen, and judge not—illustrates what I have called the

[13]James Bryce, *The American Commonwealth* (London and New York: Macmillan, 1888).

[14]Porter R. Lee, "Social Work as Cause and Function," in Lee, *op. cit.,* Presidential Address, National Conference of Social Work, 1929, in *Social Work as Cause and Function and Other Papers* (New York: Columbia University Press, 1937), p. 3.

[15]*Ibid.,* pp. 4, 5.

[16]Mary Richmond, "The Retail Method of Reform," in Joanna C. Colcord, ed., *The Long View* (New York: Russell Sage Foundation, 1930), pp. 215–16.

[17]*Ibid.,* p. 221.

[18]Mary Richmond, "Criticism and Reform in Charity," in Colcord, *op. cit.,* pp. 50, 51.

[19]Clarke A. Chambers, "An Historical Perspective on Political Action *vs.* Individualized Treatment," in *Current Issues in Social Work Seen in Historical Perspective* (New York: Council on Social Work Education, 1962), p. 52.

[20]*Ibid.,* p. 53.

"family quarrel": "Between the 'movers and the shakers' on the one hand, and the 'seekers and the sojourners' on the other there has often been misunderstanding and bad blood."[21]

Kenneth Pray wrote of "workmanship" and "statesmanship."[22] Others have stressed the polarities of clinician and activist, technician and reformer, Freud and your favorite sociologist, the "service" and the "movement." A few years ago, I tried my hand at the service-movement theme:

When a profession is young, a considerable proportion of its thought and energy is devoted to the process of calling attention to the social need out of which it grew. From its special vantage point, the new group is intensely aware of this need, of the importance of doing something about it, and of the necessity for arousing a similar sense of urgency in the minds of the general public. This is another way of saying that a profession begins as a *movement;* its primary function at this stage is to agitate for a place on the social agenda, its workers are dedicated to the cause and its advocacy, and its major spokesmen are social philosophers, energetic social advocates, and commanding personalities who call attention to themselves and to the objects of their concern.

As this effort begins to achieve some success, and as the group and its cause begin to take on some stability and permanence within the social division of labor, the concerns of the profession undergo a gradual shift from the problems of social *advocacy* to those of social *effectiveness.* Having established the social need as a proper object of society's attention, it remains to be shown that the profession can do the job and do it well. Increasingly, then, a greater proportion of professional energy is diverted from what *should be* to what *is.* The concern with ends becomes a growing curiosity about the means for achieving them; the stress on intentions, motives, and enthusiasms gives way to a larger preoccupation with efficiency and productivity; and the working skills of practitioners take on a greater significance than their ability to formulate statements of philosophy and aspiration.

. . . That the emphasis on means can be used to evade social responsibility is, after all, no more surprising than the earlier discovery that the preoccupation with goals can be used in the same way. Both dangers simply point up the challenge to the modern profession: to draw upon a growing knowledge of social reality, to frame a sense of purpose consistent with that reality, to conceptualize its practice in forms that make it testable and teachable, and to retain in the process its initial vigor, its power of advocacy, and its driving vision of what society should be like.[23]

This would seem to have tucked the issue away rather nicely—except that in the six years since that was written, the world changed again, and the cause-function dilemma became sharper and more demanding than ever before.

[21]*Ibid.,* p. 54.
[22]Kenneth L. M. Pray, *Social Work in a Revolutionary Age and Other Papers* (Philadelphia: University of Pennsylvania Press, 1949), p. 231.
[23]William Schwartz, "Small Group Science and Group Work Practice," *Social Work,* VIII, No. 4 (1963), 40–41.

In today's world, the initiatives have changed, and the actionists within the profession are no longer in the minority. It is the "psychological" emphasis now that is on the defensive, and, at least in the literature and the open forums, the militants rule the roost. This does not resolve the historic dilemma, or even ease it; it simply drives it underground. The battle for supremacy continues, the impossible choices, and the family quarrel.

Thus Eveline Burns tells us that "the center of gravity has shifted away from an emphasis on what goes on inside the individual to an emphasis on improving the functioning of society"[24]—without explaining how such a shift takes place and how, specifically, one manages to choose between the two. The fact is that no such choices are made within the professional arena; the practitioners on whom troubled people depend could easily explain to us that their clients would take small comfort from knowing that the social workers are out somewhere "improving society."

As the rhetoric mounts, the polarities widen. Against Vinter's sideswipe at "group workers in search of a cause"[25] there is Frankel's accusation that the social worker "is tinkering with the broken products that are brought to the repair shop, but he is not asking himself why so many of these broken products have been brought in."[26] Roy Lubove urges us to eschew the "service role," become "hawks" instead of "doves," and "confront the hard questions of power and income redistribution."[27] Typically, he does not tell us which of the social services he would eliminate and what specific forms his "confrontation" might take.[28]

In effect, what began as a necessary and overdue attack on the idea that if the *people* are changed the system will take care of itself, has turned into its opposite: if the *system* is changed, the people will take care of themselves. The reaction against purely psychological explanations has been so fierce that it has produced purely sociological ones, spawning analyses that romanticize "action" as the previous ideas romanticized "insight" and glorify structural solutions as we previously glorified individual ones.

In the process, a new utopianism has emerged, with much talk about "destroying systems" and "power and income redistribution"—all

[24]Eveline M. Burns, "Tomorrow's Social Needs and Social Work Education," *Journal of Education for Social Work*, II, No. 1 (1966), 16.

[25]Robert D. Vinter, "Group Work: Perspectives and Prospects," in *Social Work with Groups, 1959* (New York: National Association of Social Workers, 1959), p. 147.

[26]Charles Frankel, "Obstacles to Action for Human Welfare," in *The Social Welfare Forum, 1961* (New York: Columbia University Press, 1961), p. 281.

[27]Roy Lubove, "Social Work and the Life of the Poor," *The Nation*, May 23, 1966, pp. 609–11.

[28]See William Schwartz, "Bucking the System," letter to the Editor, *The Nation*, June 27, 1966, pp. 762, 780.

naïvely set within the existing economic structure. Cloward and Piven actually propose to end poverty by forcing public welfare out of existence and creating a guaranteed annual income, which, whatever its merits, is not likely to escape the limits of least eligibility and soar too far above the present rates of public assistance.[29] Eisman's vision is dramatic: "Social work, a profession dedicated to planned social progress, has the ability to develop skills and insights needed to bring about a successful welfare-class revolution."[30] Others would dispense with the profession itself, the prime scapegoat for the plight of the poor. Here the attack is no longer directed to the bad practices of social workers, but to the social work institution itself: "It may even be unfair," concludes Lubove, "to ask a dove to become a hawk."[31]

The "Advocacy" Variation

The most recent effects of the cause-function dilemma are evident in the present preoccupation with the "advocacy" role now being pressed by a committee of the professional association[32] and discussed at some length in a recent issue of the professional journal devoted to the subject.[33] As explained by one of its major proponents:

. . . the role of advocate has been co-opted from the field of law. Often the institutions with which local residents must deal are not even neutral, much less positively motivated, toward handling the issues brought to them by community groups. In fact, they are frequently overtly negative and hostile, often concealing or distorting information about rules, procedures, and office hours. By their own partisanship on behalf of instrumental organizational goals, they create an atmosphere that demands advocacy on behalf of the poor man. . . .

In short, the worker's posture, both to the community residents and to the institutional representatives with whom he is engaged, is that of advocate for the client group's point of view. While employing these techniques, the worker is not enabler, broker, expert, consultant, guide, or social therapist. He is, in fact, a partisan in the social conflict, and his expertise is available *exclusively* to serve client interests.[34]

Beginning with a real social problem—the breakdown of service to people in need—the advocates, with the best will in the world, find no

---

[29]Richard A. Cloward and Frances Fox Piven, "A Strategy to End Poverty," *The Nation,* May 2, 1966, pp. 510–17.

[30]Martin Eisman, "Social Work's New Role in the Welfare-Class Revolution," *Social Work,* XIV, No. 2 (1969), 86.

[31]Lubove, *op. cit.,* p. 611.

[32]National Association of Social Workers (NASW) *Ad Hoc* Committee on Advocacy, "The Social Worker as Advocate: Champion of Social Victims," *Social Work,* XIV, No. 2 (1969), 16–22.

[33]See *Social Work,* Vol. XIV, No. 2 (1969).

[34]Charles F. Grosser, "Community Development Serving the Urban Poor," *Social Work,* X, No. 3 (1965), 18; italics added.

way but to create a permanent "social conflict" between an unchange-ably evil system and a hopelessly alienated client. The worker must then "choose" the client and devote himself "exclusively" to his interests. "To whom, then, is the worker's primary responsibility: the agency or the client? If the former, the issue is simply met. If the latter—as in the case of the advocate—the agency may well become a target for change."[35] If, indeed, the worker feels that it must be the one or the other, he can do no less than choose the client and be prepared to cast his lot with the enemies of those who pay his salary. But this, of course, is the ultimate dualism, the polarization of the people and their own institutions. The advocate must now, presumably, agree with the very establishment he despises that the agencies are the natural enemies of the people who need them. "Change the people" has become "change the system," since they can no longer hope to change each other through the skilled use of the client-agency encounter.

The results are predictable. Again, much of the talk is revolutionary, but it is essentially romantic rather than programmatic, because social workers do not lead revolutions. Within the professional context it turns into a kind of "let's-you-and-him-fight" position that confuses both clients and workers.

From the first false choice, others emerge. The NASW *Ad Hoc* Committee tells us not only that "the obligation to the client takes primacy over the obligation to the employer,"[36] but also that "NASW has an obligation to the worker that takes priority over its obligation to the agency."[37] Wineman and James extend the approach to the social work schools, setting them against their training agencies and demanding that the student be given an opportunity to see his school "put its action where its mouth is."[38] And so it goes: school against agency; agency against professional association; social work practitioner against social work administrator; "social worker" against "welfare worker";[39] some clients against other clients.[40] All is absolute, all is split into halves, and all is stereotyped.

Indeed, the split is so sharp that in the advocacy programs put forward by both the *Ad Hoc* Committee for the professional association and Wineman and James for the social work schools not one of the many steps proposed calls for an offer of assistance to the agency itself. It is as if any contact with the agency system would contaminate them, or throw their identification with the poor into serious question.

[35]George A. Brager, "Advocacy and Political Behavior," *Social Work,* XIII, No. 2 (1968), 7.
[36]NASW *Ad Hoc* Committee on Advocacy, p. 18.
[37]*Ibid.,* p. 21.
[38]David Wineman and Adrienne James, "The Advocacy Challenge to Schools of Social Work," *Social Work,* XIV, No. 2 (1969), 32.
[39]See Eisman, *op. cit.,* p. 82.
[40]See NASW *Ad Hoc* Committee on Advocacy, *op. cit.,* p. 19.

But, as always, the problem of method is the most serious. The disdain for means is evident in the definition of "process" as a straw man: ". . . the process orientation is distinct from the others in that process is valued for its own sake"[41]—an accusation frequently made but impossible to document. Brager points out that "although the concept [of the social worker as advocate] is both important and in current use, its methodological implications have not yet been seriously considered."[42] Nevertheless, some discussion of tactics must be held sooner or later, and here we find ourselves developing a literature of guile, with Machiavelli as the new culture hero. Brager cites studies to show that people in influencing roles, as well as bright college students, are in significant agreement with Machiavelli's ideas.[43] He points out that "in the context in which social workers function, advocacy requires political behavior, and political behavior includes manipulation."[44] In action, the method looks like this:

He [the social worker] must then walk the tightrope between conflicting demands. If client identification is uppermost to him, he will present the case to his agency in a way most likely to garner support for a client-oriented course of action. This may require that he minimize the risk to his agency while underscoring the importance of his client's interests. He may even argue the case with more passion than he feels, if he believes that his emotional tone will positively affect his gaining administrative support. He will, in short, engage in political behavior.[45]

It is important to note that guile is not reserved for the employer alone; it is elevated to a general methodological principle. It is recognized, however, that the approach has some dangers, and Brager's discussion of professional technique concludes:

The potential costs of political strategies must always be assessed against their potential gains, so that one's morality is supported by expedience. Social workers may use up their currency as, for example, when a person develops a reputation for guile. With his motives suspect, his hidden agendas revealed to view, and his word in doubt, he can hardly be an effective advocate. Since people resent being treated as means to an end rather than ends in themselves, those who appear to use them instrumentally are likely to be ineffective.[46]

Precisely so; and the advocates present clear evidence of how manipulativeness emerges from an unresolved means-ends problem. The fact is that manipulation, which C. Wright Mills defines as the

[41]Brager, *op. cit.*, p. 9.
[42]*Ibid.*, p. 6.
[43]*Ibid.*, pp. 9, 14.
[44]*Ibid.*, p. 9.
[45]*Ibid.*, p. 8.
[46]*Ibid.*, p. 14.

"secret exercise of power,"[47] diminishes both those who use it and those on whom it is used. To people in need, it makes little difference whether they are being pushed around by "good guys" or the "bad guys." The loss of freedom and dignity is the same.

The methodological issue is deeply troublesome for many within the advocacy camp itself. Specht states:

The question for the professional is whether his objective is to enable people to make choices or to assert *his* choice and cast his lot with those who have arrived at *the* solution. Social work operates in a framework of democratic decision-making, and if one decides that the framework is no longer viable, then there is no profession of social work to be practiced.[48]

Finally, the family quarrel is pushed to its furthest point when the *Ad Hoc* Committee recommends to NASW a program that would go beyond "mere urging" in holding members to the "obligation under the Code of Ethics to be an advocate," and states that "under certain circumstances . . . the obligation is enforceable under the Code of Ethics."[49] It is further noted that the NASW Commission on Ethics "reviewed these findings . . . and . . . interprets the Code of Ethics as giving full support to advocacy as a professional obligation."[50] Unfortunately, the Committee itself deplores the general lack of understanding of advocate behavior and admits that "most social workers seem wholly deficient in this area."[51] Thus the members of the professional association seem about to be punished for not doing something that has not yet been defined.

The motives of the advocates are not in question here; it is the analysis that is weak. They subvert their own real identification with the poor and the oppressed by their neglect of the dialectics of the client-agency relationship. An agency is not a static organism with no play of internal forces; and those who insist that it is must cut themselves off from the most progressive elements within it, and take their clients with them. It was Brager himself who said that the agency is "a coalition of diverse interests"[52] and that "the task is to foster that influence within the agency coalition, so that goals congenial to the value system of social work may be specified and attained."[53]

[47]C. Wright Mills, *The Power Elite* (New York: Oxford University Press, 1957), p. 316.
[48]Harry Specht, "Disruptive Tactics," *Social Work*, XIV, No. 2 (1969), 13–14. See also, for a discussion of the "troubles and issues" theme, Ronald A. Feldman and Harry Specht, "The World of Social Group Work," in *Social Work Practice, 1968* (New York: Columbia University Press, 1968), pp. 77–93.
[49]NASW *Ad Hoc* Committee on Advocacy, *op. cit.,* p. 21.
[50]*Ibid.,* p. 21 n.
[51]*Ibid.,* p. 20.
[52]George Brager, "Goal Formation: an Organizational Perspective," in *Social Work with Groups 1960* (New York: National Association of Social Workers, 1960), p. 35.
[53]*Ibid.,* p. 36.

One Job or Two?

The psychological-social dilemma has cut so deep as to suggest to some social work educators that society would be served best by a "two-track" system of social work education. Such an arrangement would create two broad specializations in the profession: the "technicians," who would devote themselves to the tasks of practice, treatment, and psychological theory; and the "planners," who would be taught the theories and strategies of social policy and action. Miller and Rein suggest, in one of their "models for change," the separation of casework from the other social work fields and discontinuance of the search for the "generic."[54] Kahn remarks on the variety of new social roles required of the profession, and issues a call for "some other kinds of people" who "would have to be appraised by new criteria and . . . perhaps even trained in new ways."[55] Burns draws her implications for professional education as follows:

In place of the "methods" ideology, it should be recognized that there are two types of professional workers who are differentiated by their *professional objectives.* The first, the social caseworker, is concerned with bringing about change in the individual and is essentially clinically and therapeutically oriented. The second, the social welfare specialist, is concerned with change in social institutions and is non-clinical. One could also differentiate them by saying that the professional activity of the first justifies—indeed, requires—certification or licensing (because an unqualified person can do so much harm to the individual client) whereas the second does not. Freed from the necessity to pattern itself on the clinical model, the curriculum of the social welfare practitioner could then be developed in accordance with the nature of its subject matter, the presenting of problems, and the professional orientation of its students, whether they are aiming toward community organization, leadership in a variety of roles, administration, or research.[56]

A half-licensed profession would indeed be a living symbol of the schizophrenia induced by the failure to understand the connections between private troubles and public issues. To create a "department" for each would in fact institutionalize the very evils they mean to solve. The "clinicians" would be shielded from any further pressure to bring the weight of their experience with people in trouble to bear on the formation of public policy; and the "social planners" would be set free from the realities of practice and left alone to fashion their expertise not from the struggles and sufferings of people but from their own clever and speculating minds. It would be as if the legal profession were to

[54]Miller and Rein, *op. cit.*
[55]Alfred J. Kahn, "The Function of Social Work in the Modern World," in Alfred J. Kahn, ed., *Issues in American Social Work* (New York: Columbia University Press, 1959), p. 38.
[56]Burns, *op. cit.,* p. 18.

decide to train its lawyers in one curriculum and its judges in another. Practice and statesmanship are functions of each other, and each is informed by the demands of the other. The planner who has not practiced will be as shallow in his policy-making as the practitioner who has not made his impact on policy will be in his work with people.

Thus, the question for the profession is whether it now gives itself over to the polarization of the individual and the social, building it into its very structure, or tries to see more deeply into the connections between the two so that it may create a single vision of the professional function. To remain split in this way is to remain uncertain of our identity, accusing each other of not being the "real" social workers, and providing the forces of reaction with the ammunition they need to keep watering down programs and diluting services to people in need. If, on the other hand, we can find a function that will integrate insight and action, service and policy, psychology and sociology, the individual and the group, the people and their institutions, we may develop a profession that spends much less energy on the family quarrel and more on building a unified conception of professional knowledge and skill. The problem is deeply felt in many corners of the profession. "It is not fitting," says Konopka, "for this profession to indulge in the destructive practice of arguing an 'either-or' position—either direct help to individuals or a change of society."[57] And a graduating social work student said to me, in a last-semester seminar: This school has taught me to be a good caseworker; and it has also taught me to be ashamed of it."

Toward a Single Focus

How can we merge the twin images of individual and social need into one? In a complex and disordered world, there are forces constantly working to pull them apart, and the search for unity is an old one. Back in the social ferment of the Progressive Era, James Mark Baldwin studied the relationship between psychology and sociology and commented, in 1911:

It is, to my mind, the most remarkable outcome of modern social theory—the recognition of the fact that the individual's normal growth lands him in essential solidarity with his fellows, while on the other hand the exercise of his social duties and privileges advances his highest and purest individuality.[58]

[57]Gisela Konopka, "Social Values and Social Action: the Place of History in the Social Work Curriculum," Annual Program, Council on Social Work Education, 1967.
[58]James Mark Baldwin, *The Individual and Society; or, Psychology and Sociology* (Boston: Richard G. Badger, the Gorham Press, 1911), p. 16.

Mary Follett searched for "a method by which the full integrity of the individual shall be one with social progress."[59] She preferred to think of "individual" and "social" rather as the "short view" and the "long view."[60] And she said: "The problem of democracy is how to develop power from experience, from the interplay of our daily, concrete activities."[61] Eduard Lindeman saw "adjustment" as a "dual process," noting that "the forms of social organization need to be adjusted in such a manner as to produce cohesion among the constituent units, and the individuals need to be adjusted to the social forms without sacrificing their essential freedom."[62] The literature is huge, and we have established again and again the general thesis that "it is only through social survival that the individual survives, but it is only through the survival of the individual and of some measure of his self-centered concerns and ambitions that society survives."[63]

In our own time, C. Wright Mills has seen most clearly into the individual-social connections and their implications for professionals identified with social struggle. He points up the distinction between what he calls the "personal troubles of milieu" and the "public issues of social structure,"[64] and notes that *trouble* is a private matter, while *issue* is a public one. Most important, he stresses that each must be stated in terms of the other, and of the interaction between the two. Taken in time, this way of posing the problems of an era brings us closest to its central characteristics. The task of the social scientist, he continues, is to clarify both the private troubles and the public issues of his time; it is here that the sociological imagination is most needed.

Earlier, Mills had said: "It is the task of the liberal institution, as of the liberally educated man, continually to translate troubles into issues and issues into the terms of their human meaning for the individual."[65] In this light, the polarization of private troubles and public issues cuts off each from the reinforcing power of the other. There can be no "choice"—or even a division of labor—between serving individual needs and dealing with social problems, if we understand that a private trouble is simply a specific example of a public issue, and that a public issue is made up of many private troubles. To speak of confrontation as an alternative to service is to betray one's misunderstanding of both.

Every agency is an arena for the conversion of private troubles into public issues. The agency begins, in fact, as an effort to provide a service

[59]Mary P. Follett, *Creative Experience* (New York: Longmans, Green, 1930), p. xiv.
[60]*Ibid.*, pp. 37, 38.
[61]*Ibid.*, p. 197.
[62]Eduard C. Lindeman, "From Social Work to Social Science," *New Republic,* June 2, 1926, p. 48.
[63]Arthur T. Jersild, *Child Psychology* (3d ed.; New York: Prentice Hall, Inc., 1947), p. 158.
[64]C. Wright Mills, *The Sociological Imagination* (New York: Oxford University Press, 1959), p. 8.
[65]C. Wright Mills, *The Power Elite* (New York: Oxford University Press, 1957), p. 319.

that is of specific consequence both to society and to its individuals; each system is a special case of the individual-social encounter. That there are quarrels over ownership and the terms of the contract is not surprising in a class society. And that, in a badly organized collective where the few rule the many, there will often be a nasty feeling between the service and its people is to be expected. But the fact remains that the basic relationship between an institution and its people is symbiotic; each needs the other for his own survival. Each individual needs to negotiate the systems with which he must come to terms—school, welfare, occupation, neighborhood, and others. Each agency, on its part, needs to justify its existence by serving the people for whom it was designed. It is a form of social contract; and when the arrangement goes wrong, as it frequently does, those who claim that the contract is broken do no service to the people or to the agency. The arena of need remains the same, and the symbiosis remains intact—merely obscure to the unpracticed eye.

In the individual's struggle to negotiate the various systems of demand and opportunity that his society offers him, he will, wherever it is made possible, enlist the aid of people who have similar tasks and similar systems to manage. The peer group or mutual aid system then becomes a way of helping him negotiate the larger system and getting what it was designed to offer him. It cannot, however, substitute for the institutional structure and provide the volume of resources available to the larger society. What it can do is strengthen its members and heighten their sense of poise and security in the processes through which they reach out to fulfill the terms of the symbiotic relationship. The institutions are theirs; they do not belong to anyone else, for there is no one else. And the move is toward the agency, not against it—to make the system-representatives listen if they are not listening, to take responsibility for their part in the process, and to institutionalize their own roles in the service encounter. The client and the clients together need their institutions; they have no stake in destroying them.

The agencies, as do the clients, reach out with all the strength at their command at a given moment, and all the ambivalence. They have devices dedicated to both stability and change, and their managers are torn between the need to make people fit into preconceived structures and the desire to create and to innovate. They are not devils, they simply represent both the worst and the best motives of the communities that pay them. In Bertha Reynolds's words:

Our agencies are social institutions, molded by the same contending interests in our communities that produce both the relationships which bring people together and those that drive them apart. Whatever we find in our communities, we find also in social agencies.

Foundations for Social Work Practice

Social work and social living, then, instead of being in contrast, or being artificially brought together, are inextricably mixed, and inseparable.[66]

On the ambivalence of systems, Lippitt, Watson, and Westley offer the following in their analysis of systems, individual and social:

We need always to remember that when examined closely all dynamic systems reveal a continuous process of change—adaptation, adjustment, reorganization. That is what we mean by dynamic, by being alive. . . . But it is equally true, as we can learn both from experience and from the results of scientific studies, that all these systems exhibit a high degree of stability, constancy, or rigidity, in many aspects of their operation and organization.[67]

Thus the problem, throughout modern society, is one of complex, ambivalent systems that are hard to negotiate by all but the most skillful and best organized. How can such systems be kept functional? What they need, and what each tries feebly to provide in some form or other, is a force within the system itself that will act as a hedge against the system's own complexity. Its charge is to see that people do not get lost, that the system does not overpower its consumers, and that the processes through which client and system reach out to each other remain viable. Although this is a system role, necessary to its proper functioning, it places the role-occupant in a unique position in which he is not exclusively identified with either the client or the agency, but with the processes through which they reach out to each other. The practitioner is required neither to "change the people" nor to "change the system," but to change the ways in which they deal with each other.

I believe that it is this "mediating" or "third-force" function for which social work was invented and that historically it is the function in which it has done its best work.[68]

A Professional Function

Rein and Riessman discuss a "third-force" role for the community action programs (CAPs), in these terms:

These new programs constitute a form of third party intervention between the poor who represent the demand side of the social service market system and the established community institutions who represent the suppliers of service.

[66]Bertha Capen Reynolds, *Social Work and Social Living* (New York: Citadel Press, 1951), p. viii.

[67]Ronald Lippitt, Jeanne Watson, and Bruce Westley, *The Dynamics of Planned Change* (New York: Harcourt, Brace & World, 1958), p. 10.

[68]For a fuller development of the mediating construct, see William Schwartz, "The Social Worker in the Group," in *The Social Welfare Forum, 1961* (New York: Columbia University Press, 1961), pp. 146–71.

As a third party they fully represent neither, but rather they are an attempt to produce a better juncture between both. They can be seen as a strategy for bringing together the citizen and the bureaucracy; its techniques of "linkage" are an attempt to provide greater coherence into a highly fragmented system.[69]

What I have called the "hedging" role in complex social systems has been institutionalized in many forms throughout the world. Rein and Riessman discuss a number of these phenomena in this country and Europe, citing the political clubs, the various information and referral services, the trade union counselors, the veterans' representatives, the British Citizens' Advice Bureaux, the Swedish Ombudsman,[70] and others.[71] These, however, and the third-party role that Rein and Riessman describe for the CAPs, are positions taken up outside the system to be negotiated; many, like the Ombudsman, direct themselves largely to abuses of government authority.

Where, on the other hand, such a function originates within the agency itself, the image is that of a built-in monitor of the agency's effectiveness and a protection against its own rigidities. From such a position, the social worker moves to strengthen and reinforce both parties in the client-agency relationship. With the client, and with mutual aid systems of clients, the worker offers the agency service in ways designed to help him reach out to the system in stronger and more assertive ways, generalizing from his private experiences to agency policy wherever possible and avoiding the traps of conformity and inertia. In many instances, the activity thus produced is similar to that desired by the advocates except that the movement is toward the service and the workers are interested in the process rather than having lost faith in it.

With the system—colleagues, superiors, and other disciplines—the worker feeds in his direct experience with the struggles of his clients, searches out the staff stake in reaching and innovating, and brings administration wherever possible into direct contact with clients who are seeking new ways of being served. The role is difficult, but it is not new. It is what we have meant all along by the "social" in social work and have implied by our interest in "social functioning," "social relationships," the terms "psychosocial" and "social problems." We have long been agreed that the social worker is somehow related both to the

[69]Martin Rein and Frank Riessman, "A Strategy for Antipoverty Community Action Programs," *Social Work,* XI, No. 2 (1966), 3.

[70]For a discussion of the Ombudsman role in various countries see Donald C. Rowat, ed., *The Ombudsman: Citizen's Defender* (London: George Allen & Unwin, Ltd., 1965). See also Richard A. Cloward and Richard M. Elman, "Poverty, Injustice and the Welfare State. Part I: An Ombudsman for the Poor?" *The Nation,* February 28, 1966, pp. 230–35.

[71]Rein and Riessman, *op. cit.,* pp. 4–8.

individual and to the society in which he lives. Some have even understood that it is the individual *in* society. But the term "social functioning" has not explained enough, because *all* human functioning is social functioning.

When we begin to ask, as Gordon does, "What does the social worker intervene *in?*"[72] we go beyond the social worker's "interest" in the individual *and* society to the kinds of *processes* to which he is related. Bertha Reynolds's "We are ever and always a *go-between* profession"[73] is closer because it moves to *action.* But a new element is needed, and that is the energy that flows between the individual and his systems. That is what the social worker intervenes *in,* and it is for that function that he needs all his specialized knowledge and skill.

The skills, it should be emphasized, are directed not only to clients, but to system-representatives as well; both require the same sensitivities, the same listening, the same partializing, generalizing, reaching for negatives, decoding messages, and the rest. We are collecting records of such "systems work," and Weiner has made valuable contributions from his work in hospital settings and the trade unions.[74]

The mediating function is a skillful one, but it does not "retreat into technique"; on the contrary, the engagements of people with their systems aim at real confrontations on real issues. This is not a call for peace, for there is no peace. The struggle is of a different order, designed to mobilize agencies rather than destroy them. There are other forms of social action—disruptive, revolutionary—and we have a right to join them. But we have no right to confuse this with the professional function, for we must then find ourselves exploiting people in need in order to satisfy our own need for social protest. As long as our living is made in the professional arena, our responsibility is to make *those* processes as dramatic and as vital as we can. If we can help to revolutionize the nature of service and the relationship of people to their agencies, we will have performed an important, and difficult, social function. The *cri de coeur* is from our young advocate:

If we believe it is possible to move the community, we can continue to work for change through its institutions. If it is not possible, then God help us all, for then we must either continue to act in a drama that has lost its purpose or join in the destruction of society.[75]

[72]William E. Gordon, "A Critique of the Working Definition," *Social Work,* VII, No. 4 (1962), 12.
[73]Bertha C. Reynolds, "The Social Casework of an Uncharted Journey," *Social Work,* IX, No. 4 (1964), 17.
[74]See Hyman J. Weiner, "Toward Techniques for Social Change," *Social Work,* VI, No. 2 (1961), 26–35. See also Hyman J. Weiner, "A Group Approach to Link Community Mental Health with Labor," in *Social Work Practice, 1967* (New York: Columbia University Press, 1967), pp. 178–88.
[75]Specht, *op. cit.,* p. 15.

Selected Bibliography

Bartlett, Harriett M., "Toward Clarification and Improvement of Social Work Practice," *Social Work*, 3(2), April 1958, pp. 3–9. A view of the full scope of social work practice is attempted with the focus on trends and issues, priorities, and need for long-range study. Included is the Working Definition of Social Work Practice as a useful frame of reference.

Day, Peter R., "Communication and Social Work Roles," *Case Conference*, 15(6), 1968, pp. 239–42. The dilemmas faced by social workers and the roles necessary for them in this time of rapid social, political, and economic change are presented. The challenge remains for social workers to find ways to influence change that will develop individuals who can function rationally and autonomously in a variety of spheres of living.

Glazer, Nathan, "Interethnic Conflict," *Social Work*, 17(3), May 1972, pp. 3–9. Interethnic and interracial conflict are discussed as continuous, closely linked phenomena. The federal government's role in promoting equality among conflicting groups is examined.

Laroque, Pierre, "Human Rights, Social Work and Social Policy," *International Social Work*, 12(3), 1969, pp. 3–13. The need to reconcile civil rights and social rights of people so as to promote dignity and solidarity is discussed in terms of defining and formulating social policy.

Levy, Charles S., "The Value Base of Social Work," *Journal of Education for Social Work*, 9(1), Winter 1973, pp. 34–42. Values are organized along three dimensions which can be related to all professional practice. Values can be used as guides that would help to clarify social work practice for the client, practitioner, and larger society.

Levy, Charles S., "The Context of Social Work Ethics," *Social Work*, 17(2), March 1972, pp. 95–101. Practice reality requires social workers to deal with conflicts of interest and make difficult choices. The social work service situation must be examined to consider the ethical issues involved.

Rein, Martin, "Social Work in Search of a Radical Profession," *Social Work*, 15(2), April 1970, pp. 13–28. Radicalization of the social work profession is examined for the role of the professional association and the social worker's changing activity. A radical casework approach is recommended as the enduring strategy to follow.

Turner, John B., "In Response to Change: Social Work at the Crossroad," *Social Work*, 13(3), July 1968, pp. 7–15. The ability of social work to remain relevant to the ever-changing problems of society is questioned. Proposals enabling social work practitioners and organizations to become more responsive to changing needs and demands are presented. The alternative is a decreasing responsibility for social work in relation to the human condition.

Younghusband, Eileen, "Intercultural Aspects of Social Work," *Social Work*, 3(1), Spring 1966, pp. 59–65. An examination of social work values, relationship with the social sciences, course of professional development, and uses and limitations of practice modalities is presented from an intercultural perspective. Broad implications for the social work profession are proposed for consideration.

3

The Individual as Target

The enhanced social functioning of individuals has been set forth as the primary purpose of social work practice—and this means *all* social work practice, including both direct and indirect service to individuals. That is, the agency administrator responsible for implementing higher level policy decisions should be as concerned with the effect those policies have on how and what services are delivered as is the practitioner directly engaged in their delivery to clients.

We take the position, with Schwartz ("Private Troubles or Public Issues," chapter 2) that when the individual is specified as a target, we are dealing with a set of interacting variables. The three most obvious variables are: (1) the client, what he wants and needs; (2) the worker, what he is able to do for the client's wants and needs; and (3) the policies of the social welfare system, what can be done within the constraints of the given society. To effectively intervene in a situation with these interacting variables, a worker must have the requisite knowledge and skills to work with individuals on a one-to-one basis, in groups, and as decision-makers in formal organizations. Such a worker is the generalist.

In this chapter we focus on those situations in which an individual has experienced stress that he has been unable to alleviate with his own resources, and a social welfare agency has become an alternative re-source. This creates a new situation for the client wherein the resources of another system are brought to bear on his problem(s). The initial phase of the social work process begins when a problem is isolated that the client and worker agree will be the object of their attention. These endeavors focus upon the client and that segment of the environment that is impinging upon his opportunities to resolve the stress situation —unmet need or unfulfilled right—that brought him to the agency.

One method the generalist may employ when intervening in these problems is social treatment, and the articles in this chapter present various aspects of this particular modality. Social treatment makes no prior assumptions about what causes clients to come to social welfare agencies, but instead emphasizes functioning and those obstacles in the individual's environment and himself that impinge upon his abilities to function. The first article, Gelfand's, reviews seven treatment trends that mark a direction social work practice should follow if it is to become more responsive to individual client needs.

Siporin reviews current conceptions of social treatment as a practice modality and identifies their similarities to the views held by practition-ers prior to the impact of psychological theory on social work. Current social treatment theory is presented as a blend of the two valuable theoretical formulations, psychological and social theory. For although personality growth and behavioral change continue to be the central objectives of social treatment, it is recognized that they interact with environmental conditions and structures.

Social treatment has a systemic quality that requires that a worker have a comprehensive approach—that he deal with a dysfunctioning social system as well as with the individual personality. Social treatment requires one to recognize that each individual is a member of a group and therefore subject to group pressures. At the same time, an in-dividual has unique needs. Social treatment recognizes and deals with these interacting (and sometimes conflicting) demands. Tasks that will affect all the parts (the individual, the problem, the situation) and the total system become the whole of a case gestalt. The worker's role is active: he directs, is assertive, and influences decisions so that he is able to intervene and institute processes for change.

Social treatment concentrates on individual social situations. A social situation consists of the behavior of individuals within an immediate environment in a larger social system. The larger social system includes a number of overlapping "immediate environments" or subsystems in which individuals and groups function. "Immediate environments" contain cultural variations and formal organizations that influence in-dividual and group behaviors. Interacting subsystems within a larger system require the practitioner to intervene and change systems and people.

Atherton et al. propose an alternative to the disease model for providing services to people. Their model of intervention, based on role and systems theories, begins with a value premise that "the most desirable state of affairs for people is one that allows maximum freedom of the individual in his personal affairs as long as he harms neither himself nor others." (Again this is a position based on the fundamentals of democratic political theory.)

Siporin identifies role theory as the primary criterion for identifying those areas of dysfunctioning that will be targets for social work intervention. The assumption underlying interventions is not pathology, but rather an incongruence between role expectations and actual role behaviors. As in Siporin, in Atherton et al. the social worker will entertain no preconceived notion of where the incongruities occur. The problem may lie within the individual, a larger system, or the situation. The worker's task is to identify the source of this problem and to work with all of the systems that are influencing these incongruities.

That all affected systems must become involved in any interventive act is an acknowledgment that interactions occur among those systems and that no one system is the exclusive source of a given stress situation. Role theory considers both actual behaviors and expected behaviors. Both behaviors must be changed if any dysfunctional situation is to be resolved. Siporin and Atherton present schemes for identifying appropriate points of intervention and related worker behaviors. The assumptions and modes of intervention offered by social treatment begin from a premise similar to that of the social work generalist.

Reid assumes the professional practitioner has the requisite knowledge and skills to intervene in systems of various size. Although one of these systems is the individual, there is no preconceived notion, in this generalist approach, that the problem identified by the individual is inherent to that person. The client identifies a dysfunctional situation; client and worker hypothesize its sources, then act to alter those conditions. Their actions may, and frequently do, include work with individuals who become targets of the worker's efforts. Their actions may also, and usually should, include other systems that are interacting with that individual. Herein is the essence of the generalist approach to social work practice. The professional recognizes the existence of interacting systems and is prepared to intervene in those systems. The individual is one of these systems that can be a target of the worker's interventive efforts.

Interventive acts meant to influence the behaviors of individuals occupy a significant amount of a generalist's
time. Gelfand identifies seven trends in social treatment
theory that are having a significant impact on social work
practice theory. Social treatment suggests a variety of
intervention strategies that may be pursued with respect
to systems of different sizes.

Emerging Trends in
Social Treatment

Bernard Gelfand

More than half a decade has elapsed since the critics of social treatment
began their condemnations of its established practices. During this
period, the methods of social treatment, most particularly those of
casework, have been assailed on all sides; irrelevant, unresponsive, and
ineffective were some of the charges leveled against the methodologies
of social practice.[1]

The time is now appropriate to assay whether changes have occurred
within the compass of this field. Has social treatment, in relation to both
theory and practice, responded to the critical commentaries and pressures placed upon it? In addition, has the stress of a rapid expansion
of scientific knowledge effected changes?

The purpose of this article is to identify the significant modifications
in social treatment during the past five-year period, to catalog these
alterations, and to explicate them with valid documentation.[2] An attempt will also be made to assess the possible effect of each of these
changes on social treatment in the future. The list of social practice
modifications that follows should by no means be considered exhaustive; it is, rather, merely indicative of some of the major changes that
have recently materialized. Those trends that appear most significant
for social treatment methods are (1) an increasingly eclectic theoretic
orientation to practice, (2) an expansion of the role functioning of the
social practitioner, (3) an integration of the peer-helping concept into
treatment practice, (4) an increasing understanding and consideration
of the complexities of the environment, (5) an emphasis upon behavior-

Reprinted with permission of the author and the Family Service Association of America from *Social
Casework,* Vol. 53, No. 3, 1972, pp. 156–162.
[1]See, for example, Richard A. Cloward and Irwin Epstein, Private Social Welfare's Disengagement
From the Poor: The Case of Family Adjustment Agencies, in *Social Welfare Institutions: A Sociological
Reader,* ed. Meyer N. Zald (New York: John Wiley & Sons, 1965), pp. 623–44; and Scott Briar, The
Casework Predicament, *Social Work,* 13:5–11 (January 1968).
[2]The writer is indebted to Steven Hagerty, doctoral student, School of Social Work, University
of Ontario, for his help in clarifying parts of this article.

ally oriented technologies, (6) an elaboration of the system concept in diagnostic consideration, and (7) an increasing "ephemeralization,"[3] that is, the ability to accomplish more with less utilization of time, energy, and personnel.

Eclecticism

It is apparent that social treatment has significantly expanded its practice theory base. The psychoanalytic model of practice has been deemphasized in many schools of social work, and, along with this trend, a variety of practice approaches that readily lend themselves to the practice field has been introduced. Role theory, for example, has been helpful to those who work with marital dysfunctioning; William Glasser's reality model also has been of assistance to those practitioners in the fields of corrections and child protection.[4] Although the practice field has not, as yet, produced many reports about the introduction of behavioral techniques, it must be considered that this group of relatively well-validated techniques eventually will affect the practice of social treatment.[5]

No longer do practitioners subscribe to one theoretical position for practice. A generalization now frequently made is that as client problems differ, so too must practice theories in order to apply theory to problem. Only unsophisticated and dogmatic practitioners continue to force all client problems into psychodynamic categories.

As casework has made strides by adding other perspectives to its practice base, group work has advanced by delineating various models for practice.[6] These models can be applied differentially depending upon the social context and client population served. James Whittaker's article relating stages of group development and the roles applicable for workers in each of three basic group work models is evidence of the ability of practice theorists to specify the techniques utilized in various methods.[7]

Because of an increasingly expanding body of knowledge and the awareness by clients of this knowledge expansion, the necessity for an eclectic position will grow. Practitioners, as a matter of course, will have to master a number of theoretical models and the principles and techniques derived therefrom.

[3]Concerning the term *ephemeralization* as used in this article, see Richard Buckminster Fuller, *Utopia or Oblivion: Prospects for Humanity* (Toronto: Bantam Books, 1969), pp. 3–10.

[4]William Glasser, *Reality Therapy* (New York: Harper & Row, 1965).

[5]Edwin J. Thomas, ed., *The Socio-Behavioral Approach and Applications to Social Work* (New York: Council On Social Work Education, 1967).

[6]Catherine P. Papell and Beulah Rothman, Social Group Work Models: Possession and Heritage, *Journal of Education for Social Work*, 2:66–77 (Fall 1966).

[7]James K. Whittaker, Models of Group Development: Implications for Social Group Work Practice, *Social Service Review*, 44:308–22 (September 1970).

Role Expansion

Practitioner roles have been radically modified as a result of the devastating criticisms of the role constriction of social practitioners in the past.[8] Practitioners, both in the public and voluntary fields, now use more diversified and flexible treatment methods. Client needs, no longer perceived as stemming only from intrapsychic sources, can now best be met by a worker actively engaged with the network of social agencies.

Many social practitioners trained in the clinical model have experienced difficulty in assuming such active roles as broker and advocate. Many of these workers argue that such roles are most appropriate for serving low-income clients, without recognizing that their middle-class clients can, in the social confusion that characterizes the urban milieu, be as voiceless and as powerless as the poor in finding and obtaining important social services.

It is imperative that the practitioner incorporate active, assertive roles into his professional repertoire. Furthermore, as new roles are developed for practitioners, there will be an expansion of functional roles. A possible future role for the social practitioner may be the identification of groups of persons in the process of "becoming," that is, making transition from one role or status to another.

By linking these groups to peer helpers who are aware and sensitive to the difficulties inherent in the transitional situation, the social worker will provide a service that should help cushion the shock of change. For example, people moving from rural to urban settings frequently experience a variety of disorganizing events based upon environmental differences inherent in the change from one milieu to another. Providing such a transitional group with helpers who have coped with this type of adjustment problem may be offering the most relevant kind of assistance.

Peer Helping

Only reluctantly did social practitioners begin to understand and to employ the tool of peer helping. William Schwartz has been one of the few social practice theorists who has insistently emphasized peer helping through his concept of the group as a mutual aid system.[9]

The major impetus for the extended use of the concept into social practice has come from nonprofessional sources; a host of self-help groups, such as Synanon, Alcoholics Anonymous, Weight Watchers, and ex-patient therapeutic clubs, have effectively utilized this device

[8]Briar, Casework Predicament, pp. 7–8.
[9]William Schwartz, The Social Worker in the Group, in *The Social Welfare Forum, 1961* (New York: Columbia University Press, 1961), pp. 146–71.

for therapeutic intervention. Perhaps the main resistance to this idea has come from the professional practitioner's past insistence that he was the most significant source of social assistance. The great proliferation of self-help groups that emphasize peer-helping methods is itself a reaction to professionalism and the rigid helping roles to which it adhered in the past.[10]

It is recognized that peer helping, beyond the assistance it provides to others, has benefits for the helper.[11] Peer helping works most effectively when the peer helper is perceived by the person receiving help as both peer and not peer. The receiver of help identifies with the peer helper on the basis of problem similarity and attempts to model himself upon the aspect of the peer helper that is different.

Group workers have gained increasing awareness of the importance of stimulating peer-helping processes in their groups. Those social practitioners who work with families are recognizing that a strong family system is characterized by a process similar to that of peer helping. In a rapidly changing urban society typified by high levels of locational mobility, the family, by acting as a mutual aid system, can counteract and neutralize the shock of social displacement.

The Environment

The profession has long identified "manipulating the environment" as one of the major tasks of the social practitioner. Unfortunately for those practicing social treatment, the information and knowledge required to understand and modify the environment in positive ways have been lacking until relatively recently.

Although social workers were the first urban reformers, their concern for environmental modification seldom took the form of systematic research into its consequences for client behavior. Several factors converging in the 1950s and early 1960s reawakened in social work, as well as in all society, a keen interest in environmental reform. One factor was the publication of the influential *The Affluent Society* in which John Kenneth Galbraith articulated his theory of social balance.[12] A second factor was the rediscovery of a segment of society that was not part of this affluence—the invisible poor. As a result, sociocultural concepts were reincorporated in the social work knowledge base.[13]

---

[10]O. Hobart Mowrer, *The New Group Therapy* (Princeton, N.J.: D. Van Nostrand Company, 1964), p. iii.

[11]Frank Riessman, The Helper Therapy Principle, *Social Work*, 10:27–32 (April 1965).

[12]John Kenneth Galbraith, *The Affluent Society* (New York: New American Library, 1958), pp. 198–211.

[13]See, for example, Herman D. Stein and Richard A. Cloward, eds., *Social Perspectives on Behavior* (Glencoe, Ill.: Free Press, 1958); and Herman D. Stein, The Concept of the Social Environment in Social Work Practice, in *Ego-Oriented Casework: Problems and Perspectives,* ed. Howard J. Parad and Roger R. Miller (New York: Family Service Association of America, 1963), pp. 65–88.

In rapid succession there has been a plethora of environmental studies from a variety of disciplines, with each study adding richness and complexity to the once transparent concept of environment. Studies of sensory deprivation, information overload, life-change patterns resulting from social stress, cultural patterns evolving from communication, and life events associated with psychiatric impairment have demonstrated how environment can be as potent a determinant of physical and psychopathological consequences for clients as can unresolved intrapsychic conflict.[14]

The evidence from environmental studies strongly suggests a multicausal theory of psychic and social dysfunctioning wherein the stress generated from a rapidly changing and turbulent environment acts as the necessary but not sufficient condition for breakdown. Such stress, combining and interacting with individual vulnerabilities either contracted from early learning experiences or constitutional factors, is the element that leads to most psychosocial failures in functioning.

Such a theoretical explanation of social breakdown is hardly an original one; it is the *factual data* upon which this exposition is based that is new. There appears to be scant doubt that appropriate environmental modifications can effectively prevent individual dysfunctioning.[15] The major task of the environmental and social sciences is now to specify clearly the populations that are highly vulnerable to environmental stresses. It will be essential to continue to introduce this knowledge of environment into social work curricula in order that social practitioners may be equipped to identify and modify its potent effects.

Behavioral Emphasis

There is presently a trend in practice toward specifying changes in client problem behaviors; this trend runs counter to the long-standing preoccupation of social practices with changing inner states and mental attitudes. Since the introduction of learning concepts into social practice by Edwin J. Thomas, practitioners have become more demanding of themselves in defining response change goals.[16] There now appears to

[14]Eric E. K. Gunderson, Emotional Symptoms In Extremely Isolated Groups, *Archives of General Psychiatry,* 9:362–68 (October 1963); James G. Miller, Input Overload and Psychopathology, *American Journal of Psychiatry,* 116:695–704 (August 1960); Richard H. Rahe et al., Social Stress and Illness Onset, *Journal of Psychosomatic Research,* 8:35–44 (March 1964); Richard H. Rahe, Joseph D. McKean, and Arthur J. Ransom, A Longitudinal Study of Life-Change and Illness Patterns, *Journal of Psychosomatic Research,* 10:355–66 (May 1967); Edward T. Hall, *The Hidden Dimension* (Garden City, N.Y.: Doubleday & Co., 1966); Jerome K. Myers, Jacob Lindenthal, and Max P. Pepper, Life Events and Psychiatric Impairment, *The Journal of Nervous and Mental Disease,* 152:149–57 (March 1971).

[15]See, for example, Alvin Toffler, *Future Shock* (New York: Random House, 1970), pp. 334–46; and Gerald Caplan, *An Approach to Community Mental Health* (New York: Grune and Stratton, 1961), pp. 3–10.

[16]Edwin J. Thomas, Selected Sociobehavioral Techniques and Principles: An Approach to Interpersonal Helping, *Social Work,* 13:12–26 (January 1968).

be a *response-centered* orientation in the practice field as opposed to the older *organism-centered* approach.

Some of the concerns that social practitioners had voiced about behavior modification methodologies have been relinquished; criticisms about client manipulation, for example, have been dispelled when it was recognized that behavioral methods required as much or more client participation as the more traditional practice approaches. In addition, less professional mystification is involved; the client knows in behavior modification that the practitioner is attempting to change bothersome behavior.

To a great extent the difficulty that many social workers have in accepting these methods still remains. Specifying the reason for this resistance to its acceptance may assist in dispelling it. Behavioral methods demand from the worker greater discipline and precision than do more traditional practice methods. They require him to plan treatment steps concretely; to understand clearly the client's sociobehavioral situation that is supporting his behavioral difficulty; and to measure clearly and quantitatively, both before and after treatment, the frequency of the client's problematic behavior. This last operation may be at the heart of the stubborn refusal of many workers to utilize these methods, for to measure quantitatively one's own practice efforts is to measure palpably one's own effectiveness.

Warren Bennis has noted that the time lag between a technical discovery and its reliable application has steadily decreased from thirty years prior to World War I to only nine years following World War II.[17] Using these figures for prediction, we may estimate that by 1975 social practitioners coming from master's degree and bachelor's degree programs will be prepared to use these behavioral methods with regularity. These methods by that time will be accepted as standard tools of social practice.

System Concept

Social practitioners have been utilizing the system concept upon an intuitive basis perhaps since the beginning of the casework method. For Mary Richmond, casework was family casework and she seemed to understand that change in one part of the system agitates the whole.[18] Many family caseworkers and therapists routinely record these systemic changes. Family therapists who have theorized about their observational data have added to the understanding of the system concept

[17]Warren G. Bennis, Beyond Bureaucracy, in *The Temporary Society,* ed. Warren G. Bennis and Philip E. Slater (New York: Harper & Row, 1968), p. 56.
[18]Mary E. Richmond, *Social Diagnosis* (New York: Russell Sage Foundation, 1971), pp. 137–44.

through their analysis of the family as a communication system with definite purposes for the rearing of children.[19]

Perhaps the most important principle derived from the field of operant learning is that all behavior change is contingent upon the client's systemic relations; the client's future behavior is dependent upon the effects of his environment on him.[20] The individual's environment—the system in which he is a functional part—controls to a great degree the type of individual he will become. This principle reflects the convergence of three concepts that are helpful in understanding personal development: individual behavior, system, and environment. Howard Becker, from a sociological framework, has analyzed the constraints placed upon the individual's behavior as he is imbedded in specifiable socioenvironmental systems.[21]

One important consequence of the system concept for practice workers is the influence it has regenerated in environmental concerns because the major question that requires an answer is To what part of the client's system should the practitioner address himself? System as so perceived is a conceptual diagnostic tool that demands of the worker a more critical sensitivity to that rapidly changing admixture of things and mediums we call environment.[22] If only for its powers to sensitize the milieu, the teaching of the system concept will continue to be given a prominent role in the diagnostic education of the social practitioner.

Increasing Ephemeralization

A technological revolution has occurred in the electronics field in which the miniaturization of parts has allowed the designers of electrical systems to do more with less. As Buckminister Fuller has surmised, ephemeralization is a trend in nearly all of today's scientific-technologic endeavors.[23]

Social treatment has made rapid strides in its ability to ephemeralize, that is, to provide more and better service to clients through the expenditure of less time, energy, and personnel. Since the development and application of the crisis concept, a host of situations have now been identified that require brief, skillful interventions and that deliver to

[19]Theodore Lidz, Alice Cornelison, and Stephen Fleck, *Schizophrenia and the Family* (New York: International Universities Press, 1965); Gregory Bateson, Donald D. Jackson, and John Weakland, Toward a Theory of Schizophrenia, *Behavioral Science*, 1:251–64 (October 1956); and David Hallowitz, The Problem-Solving Component in Family Therapy, SOCIAL CASEWORK, 51:67–75 (February 1970).

[20]Charles B. Ferster, Reinforcement and Punishment in the Control of Human Behavior by Social Agencies, *Psychiatric Research Reports*, 10:101–18 (1958).

[21]Howard S. Becker, Personal Change in Adult Life, in *The Planning of Change*, ed. Warren G. Bennis, Kenneth D. Benne, and Robert Chin (New York: Holt, Rinehart & Winston, 1969), pp. 255–67.

[22]Roger Barker, *Ecological Psychology* (Stanford: Stanford University Press, 1968), pp. 159–67.

[23]Fuller, *Utopia Or Oblivion*, pp. 3–10.

clients relief from stress and the possibility for growth.[24] The recent work of William Reid and Ann Shyne, investigating and comparing the effects of brief and extended treatment services to couples experiencing marital and parent-child difficulties, has led to additional exploration of learning ways of accomplishing more in social treatment with less disbursement of the social worker's time and energy.[25]

As professional social workers are called away from treatment practice to the fields of administration, planning, and teaching, the practice of social treatment increasingly will become the responsibility of less trained workers, recruited from undergraduate social welfare programs and community colleges.[26] These changes in the personnel practicing social treatment will force social work educators in these institutions to train these future practitioners as rigorously as do those educators presently in the professional schools. Approaches are now being developed that quicken the pace of transmitting core concepts of social treatment.[27] There is an extensive body of research literature validating the effectiveness of lay counselors in a variety of situations in the helping professions.[28]

Additional evidence of ephemeralization in the social practice field is shown by the increasing attention that casework practitioners have paid to the group as a treatment vehicle, which suggests that in the future less importance will be attached to one-to-one contacts by all practice personnel. One might predict that the preferred mode of future social treatment will be delivered in large groups which have relatively few contacts and in which the principle of peer helping is emphasized.

The trend toward ephemeralization in order to deliver more and better services to a greater number of persons will place great pressure upon the educational and practice fields to devise new technologies. If we can begin to redirect our thinking away from the notion that more service, in relation to time and energy expended, automatically means more effective service, perhaps we may begin to think more creatively about our service delivery problems.

Conclusion

The writer has attempted in this article to identify and discuss seven significant trends in the field of social treatment. The discussion of

[24]Howard Parad, ed., *Crisis Intervention: Selected Readings* (New York: Family Service Association of America, 1965).

[25]William J. Reid and Ann W. Shyne, *Brief and Extended Casework* (New York: Columbia University Press, 1969).

[26]Arnulf Pins, Changes in Social Work Education and Their Implications for Practice, *Social Work,* 16:6–9 (April 1971).

[27]Charles B. Truax and Robert R. Carkhuff, *Toward Effective Counseling and Psychotherapy: Training and Practice* (Chicago: Aldine Publishing Co., 1967).

[28]Robert R. Carkhuff, Differential Functioning of Lay and Professional Helpers, *Journal of Counseling Psychology,* 15:117–26 (March 1968).

several of these emerging features of practice showed that some of these trends are interrelated. For example, it is not possible to discuss behavioral methodologies without consideration of the concepts of milieu and system. Another example of interconnection between trends is that ephemeralization occurs through the use of the peer-helping concept to promote the aim of doing more with less.

How can the changes that have occurred in social treatment be evaluated? If one agrees that the trends identified are in the process of becoming established, then one must also agree that practice has responded vitally to the stresses that have been placed upon it. In perhaps half a decade, social treatment theory, concepts, and methods that have helped renew the practice field have been introduced and developed.

A word of stricture must be invoked. Many of the concepts adumbrated in this article require use and embellishment. Concepts grow old and some even die; however, old and dying concepts are not necessarily poor for practice use. Their death can in many instances be attributed to a lack of creative response in the users.[29] Social practice in the future will be required to introduce creative new concepts and to elaborate constructively those that are old and that have stood the test of effectiveness.

[29]The role constriction of caseworkers through time is a prime example of the withering and near death of such important worker-role conceptions as broker and advocate.

There is some debate in the social work literature as to whether social treatment is a new approach to intervention with individuals or a return to a practice model of an earlier period. Siporin notes how current generalist orientations to practice resemble earlier views, but then differentiates contemporary society from earlier times and indicates how the demands and knowledge requirements imposed upon the contemporary practitioner likewise differ.

Social Treatment: A New-Old Helping Method

Max Siporin

Major changes in social work method have taken place in recent years as part of the social work profession's response to the crises and

Reprinted with permission of the National Association of Social Workers and the author from *Social Work,* Vol. 15, No. 3, 1970, pp. 13–25.

upheavals of our time. These changes have resulted in the emergence of professional modes of helping services that have important points of similarity with those of an earlier era of social reform.

From 1892 to 1917, and especially at the beginning of this century, the new profession of social work emphasized social legislative action, social institutional reform, and broad preventive programs as its preferred methods of practice. However, there was also a climate of opinion within certain social work circles that depreciated direct services to individuals and family groups. As Richmond later recalled, she was one of the caseworkers who were "often waved aside as having outlived [their] usefulness" because "legislation and propaganda, between them, would render social work with and for individuals unnecessary."[1]

At this same time, though, there was a remarkable and common development, within both the Charity Organization Societies and the social settlements, of a social work helping method for use with individuals and families. It was variously called charity work, scientific philanthropy, friendly visiting, social casework, or social treatment. Of course the method that came to be known mostly as social casework had a long history. But it was during this social reform period that it gained a distinctive identity. It became a way of providing a wide range of individualized services in what today might be called a multifunctional set of procedures. The method evolved at a time when social workers were less fragmented and more unified in their helping approaches. They had a broad, idealistic yet realistic vision of serving the individual and society. They sought to aid the individual as a social being and the family as a social unit and thus help create a new social order in which poverty and ill health could be prevented. The method they fashioned was highly conceptual and creative. It continued to have a great vitality in practice and in the development of practice theory during the 1920s and thereafter.

This methodological orientation suffered a decline in usefulness and popularity after 1917, when many social workers committed themselves to individual moral reform and psychoanalytic forms of therapy. It is indeed fortunate that in recent years the older, more traditional, larger conception of the social work helping method has been rediscovered and found relevant for current needs. There has been a rapid and exciting renewal of its development in social work practice and education. It is being referred to again as social treatment and also as comprehensive casework or clinical social work.

In this paper the concept and characteristics of social treatment will be examined both from a historical point of view and as they seem to be unfolding today. This discussion is based in large part on an analysis

---

[1]Mary E. Richmond, *The Long View* (New York: Russell Sage Foundation, 1930), p. 586.

of current and emerging social work practice with individuals and families carried out by the author and his students. In examining practice and the relevant literature, there was a particular concern to determine how a problem-task focus is changing the patterns of helping procedures used by social workers in clinical practice, for example, in regard to the problems of alienated poverty, juvenile delinquency, child abuse and neglect, vocational maladjustment, psychosis, and marital conflict. What follows, then, is both a charting of current changes and a foreshadowing of new and needed developments in direct social work services to individuals and family groups.

The Concept

The term "social treatment" was used by many social workers prior to World War I and during the 1920s to mean social case treatment and social casework as well as to refer to its action-change aspect. Witmer observed that during the "social reform era of social work," social treatment was conceived largely in terms of the organization and coordination of community resources, so that social casework had a "community organization aspect."[2] It included family rehabilitation efforts as well as aid to individuals. This was the period when the procedures of what came to be called group work and community organization had not yet been separated out as specialized methods, but were part of a natural way by which one helped individuals and families. The social casework method as practiced before 1917 is described as having been family centered and as "group work with families."[3]

For Richmond, social treatment complemented social diagnosis as one of the two basic components of "social casework," a term she had resisted and did not care for.[4] She regarded social treatment as a "combination of services" through which "readjustments" were made within the individual and the social environment through "reeducation of habits," "the influence of mind upon mind," and changes in the network of social relationships among family members, friends, neighbors, religious congregations, schools, and so forth. Lee held that social treatment should incorporate financial relief programs; he later explicated this method as helping individuals and families through "executive"

[2]Helen L. Witmer, *Social Work* (New York: Farrar & Rinehart, 1942), pp. 161–180.
[3]Bertha C. Reynolds, "Rethinking Social Casework," *Social Work Today,* Vol. 5, No. 4 (April 1938), pp. 5–8; No. 5 (May 1938), pp. 5–7; No. 6 (June 1938), pp. 5–8.
[4]Mary E. Richmond, *What is Social Case Work?* (New York: Russell Sage Foundation, 1922), pp. 90, 108–112, and 122. On her preference for the term "friendly visiting" over that of "social casework," *see The Long View,* p. 97.

procedures (managing a service program) and "leadership" (relationship-motivational) procedures.[5]

This enlarged and wide-ranging conception of method was underlined by a number of social work leaders. Abbott, for example, spoke of social treatment (meaning social casework) as a "broad field [containing] the whole science of human relations," rather than limiting it to the specialized procedures of psychiatric social work.[6] In the Milford Conference report in 1929 social treatment was viewed as blending in a generic way the content of the social casework "specializations" that had arisen by that time.[7]

Despite the increasing dominance of the psychoanalytic point of view, there was a continued development of ideas about social treatment that amplified Richmond's conceptualization. Sheffield urged a "situational approach" in social casework in which "group adjustive" and "social learning" processes, involving changes in social perceptions and social relationships, could aid personal maturation and "family reeducation."[8] Reynolds emphasized the sociopsychological bonds between client and community and the need for environmental change to meet clients' needs.[9]

Young presented social treatment as "a method of social therapy" for the juvenile delinquent that would achieve

not only changes in his habits and reactions but changes in the social relations which he maintains with his family, school and other groups, changes in the community and its institutions.[10]

She also considered treatment primarily a "reconditioning" and "reeducation process," and, like Sheffield, gave prominence to "redefinition of the situation." This method included the "services of many professionals and resources," as well as the treatment of the family group and family life education about housekeeping and "child-training" practices.

In this perspective there was a remarkable interest in social processes and group dynamics, in emergent social values and purposes. Thus

[5]Porter R. Lee, *Social Work as Cause and Function* (New York: Columbia University Press, 1937), pp. 39 and 191–199.
[6]Edith Abbott, *Social Welfare and Professional Education* (2d ed.; Chicago: University of Chicago Press, 1942), pp. 48–49.
[7]*Social Case Work: Generic and Specific* (New York: American Association of Social Workers, 1929).
[8]Ada E. Sheffield, *Social Insight in Case Situations* (New York: Appleton-Century Co., 1937).
[9]*See* Reynolds, op. cit.; and Reynolds, "Between Client and Community," *Smith College Studies in Social Work,* Vol. 5, No. 1 (September 1934), pp. 5–138.
[10]Pauline V. Young, *Social Treatment Probation and Delinquency* (New York: McGraw-Hill Book Co., 1937), p. 290.

Richmond became enthusiastic about the new "small group psychology" that would provide a "stronger technique" for social treatment.[11] Reynolds sought to revive the direct social reformist intentions of the earlier period of practice. Lindeman conceived of "social therapeutics" as a form of social work practice in which "the forms of social organization" are adjusted "to produce cohesion among the constituent units, and the individuals . . . adjusted to the social forms without sacrificing their essential freedom."[12] This kind of procedural orientation was well expressed by Young, who sharply differentiated social treatment from psychotherapeutic casework:

Social therapy means linking the person to the structure and function of the social group which influences him, sustains him, and at the same time requires his support, cooperation, and the sharing of responsibilities for the common wealth. . . . It promotes the inherent social impulses of human beings and releases their energies for activity and service. Integration and participation in group life on a democratic basis creates that "wider social self" which tends to make life meaningful and useful. The socialized person tends to accept responsibility not only for himself but for others . . . he tends to develop a social philosophy of life. . . . In short, mobilization of the latent powers of the family and group cooperating in full strength is one of the basic social techniques in aiding the person and the family to aid themselves and others.[13]

The social therapists were, however, out of tune with the prevailing Freudian ethic and the preoccupation with effecting personality change through psychological procedures. Virginia Robinson, Charlotte Towle, Gordon Hamilton, and others helped to redirect social caseworkers toward a psychotherapeutic ideology. The term social treatment fell into disuse and was replaced by references to the limited procedures of "environmental manipulation."[14]

Today the revived term social treatment is again an attempt to distinguish a pattern of direct service quite different from psychotherapeutic casework. There are certain negative connotations about alternative rubrics, such as comprehensive casework and clinical social work, that are avoided by the older term. In the social treatment approach the therapeutic objectives of personality growth and change remain of central importance, but they are regarded as inextricably bound up with and conditioned by social environmental structures and changes, par-

[11]Richmond, *The Long View,* pp. 484–491.

[12]Eduard C. Lindeman, "From Social Work to Social Science," in Robert Gessner, ed., *The Democratic Man* (Boston: Beacon Press, 1956), p. 208.

[13]Pauline V. Young, *Social Case Work in National Defense* (New York: Prentice-Hall, 1941), p. 215.

[14]Gordon Hamilton, *Theory and Practice of Social Casework* (2d ed.; New York: Columbia University Press, 1951), pp. 246–249.

ticularly in family and community situations. The return to the concept of social treatment marks a major shift back to traditional perspectives, to a concern with person and situation, family and community values, and socially progressive purposes and processes.

The Method

Social treatment may be defined as a general method for helping individuals and family groups cope with their social problems and improve their social functioning. The scope and boundary of this method are determined by the focus of attention and effort on direct assistance to individuals and family groups, with their individualized problems and functioning.[15] This is in contrast to interventive programs aimed at helping to change neighborhood groups, social organizations, communities, or social welfare institutions to improve their corporate functioning. It has been fallacious to consider the casework method as being limited to one-to-one relationships between the social worker and client. This limitation forced therapeutic purposes to become narrow, fragmentary, and therefore inadequate for the attainment of needed objectives.

To help people with their social problems the systematic, skilled implementation of an extensive repertoire of specific, concrete procedures and resources, of powerful ways and means, is required. Traditionally these procedures consist of assessment, planning, implementation, evaluative feedback, corrective, and continued action activities. The intention is to assert influence through such procedures and processes so as to effect desired change in individuals, social environments, or, usually, in both systems and in the relationships between them.[16] The social treatment method thus consists of interventive procedures in which the social worker uses relationships with individuals, families, small groups, organizations, milieus, and communities and intervenes purposefully, adequately, and effectively in these systems to help individuals and families resolve their problems. Psychotherapy is but one set of procedures within the method of social treatment.

It is now recognized that many social workers in direct service use

---

[15]Method as used here refers to purposeful, instrumental activity—an orderly use of means and procedures—including the application of knowledge, attitudes, and skills to accomplish tasks and achieve goals. As Buchler explains, it is "a power of purposive manipulation in a specific recognizable form and order of activity . . . a reproducible order of utterance . . . a tangled cluster of doings, makings and assertings." Justus Buchler, *The Concept of Method* (New York: Columbia University Press, 1961), pp. 135–144.

[16]*See* Richmond, *The Long View,* p. 576; Hamilton, *op. cit.,* p. 239; and "Working Definition of Social Work Practice," in Harriett M. Bartlett, "Toward Clarification and Improvement of Social Work Practice," *Social Work,* Vol. 3, No. 2 (April 1958), pp. 3–9.

interventions that have been thought of as casework, group work, or community organization procedures.[17] But as Meyer has well asserted: "The traditional separation of casework, group work and community organization is no longer tenable."[18] Such an approach implies a rejection of ritualistic, methodical activism and a deemphasis on method in the sense of a "methodolatry" that lacks regard for aims and results.[19] Social treatment calls for a focus on the problems, goals, and tasks to which method is addressed.

Problem-Person-
Situation Model

Social treatment also represents a return to the problem-person-situation model that has been the basic, traditional model for casework.[20] It was Richmond who articulated this theoretical structure when she defined social diagnosis as the identification of the "social difficulty" (or "social need") of the human being and of his social situation.[21] What has also been referred to as the person-in-situation perspective was further developed by Cannon and Klein, Sheffield, Reynolds, Young, and Hamilton and was recently restated by Hollis.[22] It is a definite theoretical framework that was in large part abandoned when social work became preoccupied with psychodynamics and psychopathology.

This traditional model offers a more suitable alternative to the medical symptom-illness view of social problems. Furthermore, it clarifies and emphasizes the concepts of problem and situation (as distinguished from the concept of personality) more than does psychotherapeutic casework. The psychosocial problems of clients are now better understood as difficulties in social functioning and social relationships, as social disability and deviant behavior. They are therefore reactions to and outcomes of maladjustive transactional processes between person and situation, not properties of a person or situation.[23]

The traditional framework can now be understood as representing

---

[17]Harriett M. Bartlett, "Characteristics of Social Work," *Building Social Work Knowledge* (New York: National Association of Social Workers, 1964), pp. 1–15.

[18]Carol H. Meyer, "The Changing Concept of Individualized Services," *Social Casework,* Vol. 47, No. 5 (May 1966), pp. 279–285.

[19]Buchler, op. cit., pp. 105–106.

[20]*See* Bernece K. Simon, "Borrowed Concepts: Problems and Issues for Curriculum Planning," *Health and Disability Concepts in Social Work Education* (Minneapolis: School of Social Work, University of Minnesota, 1964), pp. 31–41.

[21]Mary E. Richmond, *Social Diagnosis* (New York: Russell Sage Foundation, 1917), p. 62.

[22]M. Antoinette Cannon and Philip Klein, eds., *Social Casework: An Outline for Teaching* (New York: Columbia University Press, 1933); and Florence Hollis, *Casework: Psychosocial Therapy* (New York: Random House, 1964).

[23]A situation is a segment of the social environment that has meaning for the individual and refers to some social group in focused action at a certain time and place. Person-situation relationships become a focus for interventive effort, particularly for personality and identity change.

a systems model based on three interdependent, interacting elements: problem, person, and situation. Such a gestalt exhibits systemic, structural, functional, and change characteristics. Causality becomes a matter of a system's structure and part relationships, rather than of individual responsibility and blame. Behavior becomes problematic and deviant when defined as dysfunctional for the system's needs. Social workers are pulled away from a predilection for intrapsychic conflict issues, and resources become important elements for input-outcome relations.

From such a wide and holistic viewpoint, it is easier to see that interventive change in one variable of the system affects its other parts and thus affects the equilibrium and functioning of the whole. This means that strategic intervention has wide, amplifying consequences, as was noted by the pioneer social workers.[24] The systemic character of social treatment thus calls for a comprehensiveness in the helping approach and a concern with both dysfunctional personality and social system, with interactive personal and group objectives and tasks that will affect the parts and the whole of the case gestalt. Especially important is the need for feedback information loops and a self-monitoring kind of self-awareness to enable self-corrective, goal-directed interventive behavior.

The problem-person-situation model, because of its complex and multifactorial character, compels social workers to seek out and make use of a variety of theories and the interventive approaches, strategies, and programs derived from them. Thus we find ourselves applying relevant aspects of theories about social problems and deviant behavior; adapting personality change approaches based on psychoanalytic, behavioral learning, and humanistic-existentialist theories; and implementing social-situational change approaches based on theories about social situations and groups and marital, family, milieu, organizational, community, and welfare systems. Each of these theories offers some mode of response to different aspects of therapeutic tasks. Practice "theory" needs to be eclectic and must evolve integrative links for the operational use of personality and social system theories, such as propositions about deviant behavior, role, identity, social situation, crisis, and conflict resolution. It would appear that during the past quarter of a century social workers have unknowingly evolved an integrative framework of personality and situational change procedures under the guise of "crisis therapy," whose principles seem to be applicable in both

[24]*See,* for example, Richmond, *What is Social Casework?* pp. 136–139. For a helpful discussion of systems theory, *see* Walter Buckley, *Sociology and Modern Systems Theory* (Englewood Cliffs, N.J.: Prentice-Hall, 1967), pp. 55–70; and Gordon Hearn, ed., *The General Systems Approach* (New York: Council on Social Work Education, 1969).

short-term and long-term interventive programs with individuals and family groups.

Within the context of social treatment the concepts of diagnosis and treatment take on different connotations and operational procedures. There is a greater tendency to apply phenomenological perspectives in understanding the social situation and the subjective world of the client as he experiences them. There is an explicit *assessment of the social situation,* including an appraisal of the structural adequacy and functional efficiency of the family and other groups, organizations, and communities in which the client is an active member. Social workers find that they are again more directly concerned with the assessment of work-employment situations and the vocational functioning of clients and that they actually do much vocational counseling without recognizing that it has remained a basic function for social workers in many settings.

Social workers are more interested now in *personality assessment* that emphasizes the sociopsychological, interactional aspects of personality. This requires them to evaluate and help individuals with their self-concepts and self-esteem, which are related to social, personal, and self-identities; social skills and interpersonal competence; and social learning and social reinforcement processes. There is a growing conviction about the validity of social work's characteristic way of helping clients with difficulties in social functioning and relationships so as to help resolve identity crises and social conflicts and to enable individuals and groups to achieve self-realization and development. Perlman has helped revitalize this orientation in her discussions of persona and identity.[25]

The therapeutic or *action-change process* is also understood in different terms. Such elements as skills, resources, and relationship are applied in a plan or program of action in which services and procedures are combined to realize specific tasks and goals. A basic element of treatment is a shared diagnostic experience between worker and client in which redefinitions of the client's situation and problems take place and mutual problem-solving plans are formulated. The task program is then carried out through the use of one or more strategies involving roles to be performed by the worker, client, and others, as well as specific resources and tactics to be used in some sequential order of process. The social worker's helping interventions are more than "techniques"; they are change-inducing units of behavior and are essentially interactional role performances responsive to heuristic task requirements.

[25]Helen Harris Perlman, *Persona* (Chicago: University of Chicago Press, 1968).

The Individual as Target

Situational interventions are concerned with changing relationship and functioning patterns in a group and with altering the group's focus of attention and effort, its definition of experience, and its time-space characteristics. The family and extended family thus become a client, and intake is understood to involve inducting the family unit into the role of client. Change programs are geared to influence organizational and community networks. Marital, family, and milieu therapies as well as family life education programs are again reestablished as basic social work services. The provision of a situational support and reinforcement system for new behavior and interpersonal relationship patterns is of critical importance in the rehabilitation and resocialization programs of social treatment. For example, in order for a woman to become a more effective mother, she may have to be helped to gain a new understanding of herself and resolve a negative self-image and transference reaction that confirm her to be rejecting and inadequate. In addition her home situation may be transformed into a learning experience. The mother, father, and child, individually and as a family unit, may be guided in learning new attitudes, self-expectations, and role performance skills. Also, family and neighborhood situations may be changed to create a positive environment that is socially reinforcing of more adaptive behavior and relationships.

Problem-Task Focus

Another aspect of the method of social treatment is its *problem-task focus.* The problems of social work clients can be understood as difficulties in completing crucial life tasks, especially the developmental tasks of identity formation and change and transition to new social roles and relationships that occur during the crises of life cycles and careers. Studt describes "task focus" as situational diagnosis and planning, an emphasis on interventive strategies, and a process of establishing and guiding task-oriented working relationships that center around the therapeutic organizational role of the client.[26] The social worker thus becomes a "strategy guide," implementing various kinds of resocializing strategies, with method being adapted creatively to task needs.

A problem-task focus operationally involves identifying and translating a problem into a task or set of tasks to be completed that will overcome obstacles, relieve stress, and achieve desired and specific goals. The accomplishment of such tasks calls for certain essential elements—problem-solving attitudes, motivation, knowledge and skills, resources, consensual goals and strategies, and focused energy (elbow

---

[26]Elliot Studt, "Social Work Theory and Implications for the Practice of Methods," *Social Work Education Reporter,* Vol. 16, No. 2 (June 1968), pp. 22–24 and 42–46.

grease)—to be contributed by the client, social worker, social welfare aides, relatives, and other persons who may be available. Thus a depressive reaction on the part of a wife may be redefined as secondary to a marital conflict. Helping efforts would aim to resolve the conflicted role expectations and role performance difficulties between husband and wife, children, and in-laws, and would aim to help the couple learn the competencies needed for a satisfying marriage.

The problem-task orientation places responsibility on the client for conscious participation in decisions regarding goals, risks, costs, and resources to be used in achieving results. Rather than assuming the role of a dependent patient, the client becomes responsible for himself and the social worker acts as a task collaborator. This is a more democratic and efficient division of labor. The organizational role and treatment career of the client offer arrangements through which he can change deviant and discredited identities and learn new values and skills.[27]

The multiple, complicated, severe, and chronic problems often presented by clients also require many different kinds of helping persons —what Studt calls a "work group."[28] Such a helping system may consist of the social worker and client, his relatives and work colleagues, other social workers and helping professionals, as well as social work aides. The social worker often serves as a central member and "clinical team leader." Tasks, rather than cases, may be referred when necessary to obtain external resources or expertise. There is much less dependence on psychiatric consultation or supervision. A premium is placed on role variety, the phasing and coordination of task effort, and team cohesion and morale.

Task structure becomes an important determinant of change strategies and roles as well as of group leadership. The structural elements may be identified, according to Fiedler, in terms of "decision verifiability," "goal clarity," "goal path multiplicity," and "solution specificity," so that tasks can be programmed in step-by-step fashion.[29] Fiedler also suggests certain characteristics of a task: the degree of the task's structure and stress, the interlocking of effort by group members, and the degree of chance or skill perceived as being involved in its completion. The effectiveness of group leadership in utilizing task-oriented or relationship-oriented styles and the productivity of the group are therefore determined by the task structure, the type of group involved, the nature of leader-member relationships, and the position and power of the leader.

[27]Max Siporin, "Deviant Behavior Theory in Social Work: Diagnosis and Treatment," *Social Work* Vol. 10, No. 3 (July 1965), pp. 59–67.

[28]Studt, op. cit.; and Studt, "Fields of Social Work Practice," *Social Work,* Vol. 10, No. 4 (October 1965), pp. 156–165.

[29]Fred E. Fiedler, *A Theory of Leadership Effectiveness* (New York: McGraw-Hill Book Co., 1967), pp. 22–35 and 142–147.

One implication of these ideas about task focus and group leadership is that the group leadership role may alternate among worker, client, and others, depending on task needs. Also, it becomes a basic therapeutic objective to improve the leadership competence of the family and group members and the group's problem-solving skills. In addition the natural, unofficial helping system of mutual aid available to an individual and family needs to be strengthened to help them meet recurrent crises of the life cycle. Then the social worker can phase himself out of the client group and terminate treatment.

Role Intervention

Today the social worker is more helpful in group leadership and membership roles rather than limiting himself to being a confidante or "guru" in intimate encounters with individual clients. He needs to know and be skilled in both individual and group helping procedures and know how to be a group discussion leader. The helping stance is an activist one; he must be direct, self-assertive, and influential so that he can intervene and set in motion change processes that can alter severely pathological interaction patterns, particularly in family crisis situations. The activist, interventive posture has been well described in the case of the worker as family group therapist, but it needs to be extended to other helping situations.[30] Such an orientation encourages a more positive, autonomous kind of self-image for the worker, is self-confirming, and encourages him to be more responsible and accountable for his practice.

The social worker also needs to learn to make a more conscious, direct, and therapeutic use of his authority so that he can alter power structures and communication patterns in a disorganized family, terminate vicious self-reinforcing habitual cycles of sadomasochistic relationships, or obtain scarce community resources. Not only in protective cases involving abused or neglected children, but in many other kinds of situations as well, therapeutic tasks demand a firm, limited, and directive influence based on important professional and personal forms of authority as well as on agency-delegated bureaucratic authority. The client views a therapeutic use of authority as a real, powerful influence on his behalf. Such exercise of authority needs to be consistent with democratic ethics and forms—allowing freedom and choice for the client—within the collaborative contract and relationship between client and worker.

As a representative of the social work profession, the social worker

---

[30]Arthur L. Leader, "The Role of Intervention in Family Group Treatment," *Social Casework,* Vol. 45, No. 6 (June 1964), pp. 327–332; and Virginia Satir, *Conjoint Family Therapy* (Palo Alto, Calif.: Science and Behavior Books, 1967).

takes on a multifunctional orientation as he seeks to help realize the profession's institutional and societal tasks. He does this by using helping processes that are problem solving, educational, therapeutic, and socially integrative. These processes articulate with the functional prerequisites of personality and social systems identified by Parsons as system "pattern variables" of pattern maintenance, integration, adaptation, and goal attainment.[31] The helping processes are also linked to outcomes of identity confirmation, social inclusion and adjustment, growth and competence, and productivity and self-realization for individuals and collectivities. In turn the helping processes are fulfilled through a wide repertoire of helping roles. These multidimensional relationships are listed in Table 1.

In social treatment the social worker serves as a system change agent for both personality and social systems. He seeks to be active and effective at several levels of intervention, choosing targets and entry points in individual, family, group, organizational, community, and institutional structures and domains of functioning. Geismar, Spergel, and

TABLE 1. Role Intervention Model for Social Work Practice with Personality and Social Systems

System Task-Functions	Outcomes	Helping Processes	Helping Roles
1. Adaptation	Viability Growth Competence	Education Socialization	Social parent, socializer, teacher, guide, model, reinforcer, norm-sender, norm-bender, social reformer, social planner, researcher.
2. Integration	Integrity Solidarity Interdependence	Relational Friendship Communion Inclusion Mutual Aid	Social parent, friend, big-brother, supporter, protector, integrator, liaison, mediator, advocate, community organizer, social conscience.
3. Pattern Maintenance	Autonomy Stability Identity-Repair	Rehabilitation Therapy Correction	Rehabilitator, therapist, healer, restorer, care-giver, mender, consoler, confessor, guru, social controller, regulator, limit-setter, rule-enforcer.
4. Goal Attainment	Productivity Creativity Self-realization	Problem-solving Crisis and conflict-resolution Task-performance	Counselor, adviser, enabler, expert problem-solver, trouble-shooter, broker, referrer, expediter, arbitrator, discussion-leader, gate-keeper, resource-person, coordinator, administrator, work-manager consultant, certifier.

[31]Talcott Parsons, "Pattern Variables Revisited," *American Sociological Review,* Vol. 25, No. 4 (August 1960), pp. 467–483. For an effort to relate these Parsonian pattern variables to helping roles in residential treatment, *see* Howard W. Polsky and Daniel S. Claster, "The Structure and Functions of Adult-Youth Systems," in Muzafer Sherif and Carolyn Sherif, eds., *Problems of Youth* (Chicago: Aldine Publishing Co., 1965), pp. 189–211.

others have illustrated this multilevel approach in the provision of individualized services.[32] There is, however, a growing awareness that it is through his role performances in situational interventions that the social worker gains entry and effects change for personality and social systems, including the social welfare system.

Role performances are extremely important in carrying out helping interventions. A social system consists of patterns of role relationships actualized by people in social situations. Meaningful action is role-patterned behavior oriented toward symbolic or overt situational interaction with others. One has to be a role-actor to participate socially and function as a human being. Role performances thus are ways of getting jobs done and of meeting reciprocal needs for identity and reality confirmation. They also dramatize and idealize a social situation so as to maximize one's influence on the behavior of others.[33] Therefore, it is through his role performances that the social worker acts in reciprocal and collaborative relationships with clients and carries out the jobs of giving information, changing attitudes and behavior, motivating, limiting, modeling, and so forth.

In order to have maximum therapeutic influence, the social worker needs to provide effective role performances in which he is genuine and committed. The roles may be culturally defined and should be geared to the client's expectations. But they will be interpreted personally by each worker and enacted in highly individualistic styles. Even when they are part of the social rituals of degradation or conversion ceremonies, the social worker may have to improvise the helping roles in response to the often unpredictable contingencies of situational events and the often unpredictable behavior of clients and others.

In social treatment processes, the social worker is active either within or outside a social agency office and intervenes directly or indirectly in the client's life situations. He accomplishes his therapeutic tasks through an extensive repertoire of general and specific situational roles.[34] The most highly valued role—therapist—is now often overshadowed by other diverse roles such as integrator and friend, problem-solving expert and innovator, mediator and negotiator, liaison person and coordinator of resources (broker), spokesman (advocate), and especially teacher.

The therapeutic work of consoling, nurturing, and confirming the

[32]Ludwig L. Geismar, "Three Levels of Treatment for the Multiproblem Family," *Social Casework,* Vol. 42, No. 3 (March 1961), pp. 124–127; and Irving Spergel, "A Multi-Dimensional Model for Social Work Practice," *Social Service Review,* Vol. 36, No. 1 (March 1962), pp. 62–71.
[33]Erving Goffman, *The Presentation of Self in Everyday Life* (New York: Doubleday Anchor Books, 1969), pp. 17–76.
[34]For a definition and discussion of situational roles, *see* Max Siporin, "Private Practice of Social Work: Functional Roles and Social Control," *Social Work,* Vol. 6, No. 2 (April 1961), pp. 52–60.

self-worth and identity of a client needs to be done in conjunction with helping actions of the friend and social parent. The resolution of intra-psychic and interpersonal conflicts and the integration of new identities and social roles as well as the integration of individuals within collectivities are now seen as reciprocal aspects of a social inclusion process carried out with peers and parental surrogates.

The social worker is, as always, expected to be an expert trouble-shooter who can intervene in severe crises, mediate violent disputes, negotiate and find innovative resolutions for impossible difficulties. But high value is accorded the provider and coordinator of social supports and community resources needed for the client's development and problem-solving adaptation. As resource person and procedural guide the worker actively uses intergroup community processes within the unofficial, natural helping system of the client's social network. Or he deals directly with the official social welfare community and bureaucracies to make available to the client varied social provisions and social utilities such as financial aid, day care, and homemaker and medical care services. The spokesman (advocate) role is one that does not relieve social workers of their obligations to the community and the social welfare institution they represent, but it does call for them to give priority again to the needs and interests of the clients and citizens the welfare community is intended to serve. It also demands that social workers be identified again as social reformers, encouraging changes in values and client participation in social action programs that have both therapeutic and social betterment objectives.

It is as a therapeutic teacher, guiding individual and group learning processes, that the social worker is meeting crucial needs in our society. The current conflicts and dislocations of the urban scene are in part due to processes of vast social migration and mobility; they require extensive social reforms and individualized resocialization-educational programs. Thus social workers help clients acquire the cognitive development, social competence, and the social adjustment or role satisfaction that is also called mental health. They teach clients the skills of deriving maximum benefits from the social security and welfare bureaucratic systems, about which knowledge and skill have become essential for socialization and rehabilitation programs.[35] Still further, they enable the client to learn meaningful personal and social philosophies, live by valid values and standards, and gain viable identities as individual and family members in human communities.

In these therapeutic, integrative, educational, and problem-solving processes, the dynamics of change depend heavily on potent group and

---

[35]Otto Pollak identifies these kinds of skills in "The Outlook for the American Family," *Journal of Marriage and the Family,* Vol. 29, No. 1 (February 1967), pp. 193–205.

situational forces.[36] These influences facilitate the emergence of creative individual and collective adjustment efforts and what Durkheim called a "collective consciousness." In social treatment programs, the social worker can direct his role performances so that they are complementary and reinforcing for new and adaptive role identities and performances on the part of the client and other members of his natural groups. Expectations and mutual aid efforts that operate to effect behavioral and situational changes are activated.

Operationally this means that the social worker does not play Big Daddy to the Baby Boy or rescuer of the sinner, but he does encourage adult, friendly, altruistic relationships and corrective therapeutic experiences. He fosters dyadic and team task performances that move to accomplish concrete tasks and reward effort, learning, self-disclosure, and authenticity for the client and significant others. He enables the collective "interexperience," characterized by a common consciousness of meanings, values, and relationships and a mutual commitment to them.[37] It is through such an interexperience that problems get resolved and support is given to interdependence and individuality, to a sense of personal and social responsibility as well as to the inherent processes of individual and social growth.

Summary and Conclusions

Social treatment is a new-old mode of helping individuals and family groups. Social workers feel comfortable with it because of its old associations yet excited by the new aspects and rich potential for more relevant and effective service to clients.

In current practice social treatment is distinguished by patterns of service that may be said to constitute a new helping method. It is based on a traditional problem-person-situation model for diagnosis and interventive change (also found to be a systems model), for which a variety of theories are useful in an eclectic fashion. Assessment and treatment processes have new aspects in this approach, with a problem-task focus that has important consequences for a more democratic, collaborative relationship between client and worker. There is a renewed emphasis on social situational helping interventions and group leadership by the social worker through role performances that are activist, multifunctional, versatile, and directed toward the accomplishment of both per-

[36]These situational change forces are well discussed by Alan F. Klein, "Individual Change Through Group Experience," *National Conference on Social Welfare, 1959* (New York: Columbia University Press, 1959), pp. 136–155.

[37]The concept and process of interexperience are presented by R. D. Laing, *The Politics of Experience* (New York: Pantheon, 1967), p. 19.

sonality and social system change. Situational interventions can use potent social interactional forces and enable the emergence of a collective consciousness and adaptive experience through which adjustment problems are resolved and individual and group growth are nourished.

Further development of the theory, principles, and procedures of social treatment need direct attention. There is need to determine, for example, how different kinds of problems shape different patterns of services and how differential tasks affect the choice of helping strategies and roles for client and social worker. There is also need to clarify the effectiveness of social treatment programs for specific change in individual behavior and social relationships. Hopefully research about social treatment will again provide, as it did in the past, the hard data about poverty, illness, pathology, and social conditions to support programs of social legislation.

The method of social treatment and the changes in practice associated with it have already stimulated much-needed change in social work education. The delivery of programmatic services and the social work manpower needed for such delivery systems have made for a vast increase in the training of different levels of personnel and for a renewed emphasis on preparation for administrative, program-planning, and evaluative functions. Because it is here that we have allowed unhelpful gaps and vacuums in leadership and service, there is also need to give greater priority to the training of doctorate-level practitioners for front-line service functions and team-leadership roles.

Social treatment appears eminently suitable for the needed structure of direct individualized social work services that can effect behavioral and situational change for clients. As developed during the earlier and the current social reform eras, social treatment gives prominence to the social purposes of the profession and helps social workers recapture the earlier utopian, yet pragmatic, social vision needed today. Hopefully social workers may now be better able to halt the extreme oscillations and establish the balance between the individual rehabilitation and social reform orientations that Mary Richmond and Porter Lee wished for and that have yet to be achieved. With this new-old method of social treatment, social workers can better respond to today's social crises and aid people to achieve both the individual identity and community they so greatly desire.

Professional social work practitioners may use a number of perspectives from which to view unmet needs. Siporin proposes a situational point of view: social situations are identified as the basic unit of all individual behaviors; unmet human needs are then defined as being dysfunctional situations.

Situational Assessment and Intervention

Max Siporin

The term *social situation* is a basic expression and concept in social work theory and practice. The assessment and treatment of social situations are widely proclaimed by social workers to be areas of their expert knowledge and competence. Social work itself has been defined as a social institutional method of "helping people with regard to the difficulties they encounter in their social situations."[1] This point has been much emphasized.

Social work has traditionally not been concerned with the treatment of psychopathology as such but with the task of helping people to meet stress situations. . . . The social worker is trained to look for the reactions of a person in a situation. . . . The social worker may thus be said to have a psychologically informed situational bias.[2]

The ubiquitous use of the term *situation,* especially when it is coupled with the word *reality,* is a characteristic "identity mark" of social workers. The word seems to have magico-ritualistic functions for internal security and client-influencing operations. Thus one rule for social work correspondence is to "add situation to any noun wherever possible: anxiety situation for anxiety."[3]

Such a situational emphasis also distinguishes the cognitive style of the social worker and is a feature of social work thinking. Harriett Bartlett considers this emphasis a distinctive attribute.

The focus of social work . . . is upon the social functioning of persons in life situations, viewed with empathy and considerable objectivity, in terms of the

· Reprinted with permission of the author and the Family Service Association of America from *Social Casework,* Vol. 53 (2), 1972, pp. 91–109.

[1] Helen L. Witmer, *Social Work: An Analysis of a Social Institution* (New York: Rinehart and Co., 1942), p. 84.

[2] Jules V. Coleman, Psychotherapeutic Principles in Casework Interviewing, *American Journal of Psychiatry,* 108:298–302 (October 1951).

[3] M. L. S. Kitchin, Correspondence, *Case Conference,* 10:51–52 (June 1963).

meaning of the situations for the self-realization and growth of individuals, with balanced concern for both inner and outer factors as they affect functioning. . . . The interdependent social work characteristics enable social workers to see the wholeness of personality and situation, to assess multiple factors within the configuration, and to identify the crucial elements calling for intervention —to do all this with considerable effectiveness. . . . The social worker is able to work in moving and changing situations.[4]

In view of this concern with social situations in actual helping practice, it is shocking to realize that the concept itself was long neglected in social work theory. It is only recently that the renewed concern for the social environments of our clients—particularly for those who are poor, disadvantaged, delinquent, or mentally ill—has led to a revival of interest in situation theory, a return to situational diagnosis, a focus on client social situations for planned, purposeful change.

The purpose of this discussion is to help clarify the concept of the social situation in social work theory and practice. Its historical context will be indicated. Social situations are to be understood as functional or dysfunctional, particularly in crisis or disaster states. The characteristics of situational assessment and intervention will then be explored, with attention given to situational change strategies and roles.

Situation theory is viewed here as a generic and basic element in social work theory and practice. It is fundamental to various forms of psychotherapy, group therapy, marital and family treatment, to organizational and milieu, and community work. It is also fundamental for social planning and administration and for institutional change efforts. Situation theory is a part of the indigenous "systems theory" of social work. It deals with personality systems and social systems in their interdependence and in relation to transactional and change processes for both. It supports and validates the emerging new forms of social work helping methodology. In addition, situational assessment and intervention are considered central in the traditional problem-person-situation model of social work practice and focal to the social work ways of helping people with their social problems. They are essential responsibilities and instrumentalities in the social worker's helping efforts with individuals, families, and other social systems, including the social welfare system in our society.

A Historical Note

From their very beginnings as professional helpers to the poor, social workers have been interested in "character and circumstance," in the

---

[4]Harriett M. Bartlett, Characteristics of Social Work, *Building Social Work Knowledge* (New York: National Association of Social Workers, 1964), pp. 1–15.

interaction of personality and environment. The "person-in-situation" perspective has always been characteristic of social work. Until 1917, social work was family centered, and, for both the charity organization and the social settlement workers, the unit of attention for helping was the family situation.[5] In social casework, or social treatment, diagnostic and treatment attention was "situation centered," in contrast to the "personality-centered activity of the later psychiatric era."[6] This largely sociological approach was exemplified in Mary Richmond's conception of the "social diagnosis," as an "exact a definition as possible of the situation and personality of a human being in some social need."[7] She enunciated the problem-person-situation model that has continued to be a viable base not only for casework but for social work practice as a whole.

Although psychoanalytic theory gained increasing dominance after 1917, there was a flowering of situation theory in the early part of the 1920s through the original and seminal contributions of three social workers in the development of major forms of social work practice: Eduard C. Lindeman in community organization and group work, Ada E. Sheffield in social casework, and Mary Follett in social welfare administration. In *Social Discovery,* published in 1924, Lindeman proposed the use of "participant observation" as a way of understanding and then helping to resolve conflicted "group situations."[8] Sheffield, in 1922, 1923, and 1924, described the social caseworker as helping individual and family clients to understand, take control of, and change their "total situation."[9] Follett, in *Creative Experience,* also published in 1924, acknowledged her debt to Lindeman and Sheffield by applying their ideas about social situations to public and industrial organizational administration and in developing her own ideas about "the law of the situation" and "the authority of the situation" as determining factors in administrative processes.[10]

In 1930, there was a historic confrontation between the situational and the newer psychoanalytic approaches in social work. Sheffield presented her famous paper, "The Situation as the Unit of Family Case

[5]Bertha C. Reynolds, Rethinking Social Casework, *Social Work Today,* 5:5–8 (April 1938); and Robert A. Woods and Albert J. Kennedy, *The Settlement Horizon* (New York: Russell Sage Foundation, 1922), p. 396.

[6]Florence Sytz, The Unit of Attention in the Case Work Process, *The Family,* 27:135–39 (June 1946).

[7]Mary E. Richmond, *Social Diagnosis* (New York: Russell Sage Foundation, 1917), p. 357.

[8]Eduard C. Lindeman, *Social Discovery* (New York: Republic Publishing Co., 1924), pp. 177–274. The development of situation theory may be traced in the work of Mead, Cooley, Dewey, Thomas and Znaniecki, as well as in the work of these social work thinkers, with some convergence and reciprocity of thinking taking place.

[9]Ada E. Sheffield, *Case-Study Possibilities* (Boston: Research Bureau on Social Casework, 1922); What is the Case Worker Really Doing?, *Journal of Social Forces,* 1:362–66 (May 1923); and Three Interviews and the Changing Situation, *Journal of Social Forces,* 2:692–97 (September 1924).

[10]Mary P. Follett, *Creative Experience* (New York: Longmans, Green & Co., 1924), pp. 78–178.

Study," at the meetings of the American Sociological Society.[11] She urged the use of "situation-thinking" and the social situation of clients as the primary unit of casework study and treatment. In that same year, Virginia Robinson, in *A Changing Psychology in Social Casework,* sharply attacked the "sociological" and "situational" orientations of both Richmond and Sheffield, and she championed psychoanalytic psychology as the valid theoretical base for social casework.[12] Instead of a productive integration, which then was possible, situation theory was largely jettisoned. Gordon Hamilton, for example, spoke of "situational diagnosis," and gave importance to the use of group processes in helping individual and family clients.[13] The "psycho-social" conception of casework which she helped to develop, however, remained essentially a psychotherapeutic one. The contributions of Pauline Young, Ernest and Harriet Mowrer, and Bertha Reynolds were largely ignored, although they advanced the work of Richmond and Sheffield in elaborating ideas about crisis, conflict, and type situations and about the redefinition of the situation as essential aspects of the casework helping process.[14]

This kind of development away from situational perspectives was paralleled in the history of social group work, community organization, and social welfare administration. During the 1940s, situation theory was extensively explored and advanced, not by social workers but by sociologists, in studies of social crisis situations. It was only after World War II that Florence Sytz and Otto Pollak, among others, called for a renewed attention in social work to the social situations of clients.[15] There was then an explicit development of marriage counseling and family treatment, as well as increasing attention to the sociocultural environment. The return to situational approaches in current social work helping theory and practice has been stimulated by the social crises of our time, by theoretical and research developments in the social sciences, and by phenomenological, existentialist trends in philosophy and psychology. The present concern with primary group

[11]Ada E. Sheffield, The Situation as the Unit of Family Case Study, *Journal of Social Forces,* 9:465–74 (June 1931), reprinted in Ada E. Sheffield, *Social Insight in Case Situations* (New York: D. Appleton Century Co., 1937), pp. 74–97.

[12]Virginia P. Robinson, *A Changing Psychology of Social Case Work* (Chapel Hill: University of North Carolina Press, 1930).

[13]Gordon Hamilton, *Theory and Practice of Social Case Work* (New York: Columbia University Press, 1940), pp. 151, 142, 140.

[14]Pauline V. Young, *Interviewing in Social Work* (New York: McGraw Hill, 1935); Pauline V. Young, *Social Treatment in Probation and Delinquency* (New York: McGraw Hill, 1937); Ernest R. and Harriet R. Mowrer, *Domestic Discord* (Chicago: University of Chicago Press, 1928); Harriet R. Mowrer, *Personality Adjustment and Domestic Discord* (New York: American Book Co., 1935); and Bertha C. Reynolds, *Learning and Teaching in Social Work* (New York: Farrar and Rinehart, 1942).

[15]Sytz, Unit of Attention; and Otto Pollak et al., *Social Science and Psychotherapy for Children* (New York: Russell Sage Foundation, 1952), pp. 27–33.

experience and with situational interventions represents a renewal of the efforts made by the early social workers to aid individuals and families attain that kind of personal self-realization that also helps realize the more democratic, solidary types of human organizations and communities.

Conceptual Considerations

A social situation is the fundamental unit of social interaction and of social behavior. It is a basic social unit for human functioning and experience, for actualization of identity, and for interpersonal relationships. A social situation refers to a social group focalized in action at a certain time and place around some crucially relevant object, person, or goal. It is a combination of people and physical objects in time-space circumstances and events that constitutes a field of meaningful experience.

The *group* may be any type of collectivity in which individuals have some form of active role relationships with others and there is some common focus of attention and action. We are concerned mainly with primary, small groups, but the groups may be informal and large: in gatherings, mobs, and social movements. From the viewpoint of an individual or collective unit, social interaction that is face-to-face is an in-presence situation; and interaction that is not face-to-face is an out-of-presence situation.[16]

A social situation should be distinguished from a social environment.[17] The social environment is a network of overlapping social systems and social situations, including ecological systems, cultures, and institutions. This network influences the individual from outside of the self, and, where there is an internalization of these influences, from within the self. A social situation is an impinging segment of the social environment. It is a segment that has meaning for the individual and that is uniquely perceived and interpreted by him, in which he has one or more status-roles and identities, is a group member, and a role performer. For example, he may function within a family situation as a father, husband, and bread-winner. The aggregate or complex of social situations (in each of which the individual functions as a group member and has a role, identity, and role set) has been termed the *total situation,* according to the older usage of this term by Sheffield, Kurt

[16]Lowell J. Carr, *Situational Analysis* (New York: Harper & Brothers, 1948), p. 21.
[17]Herman D. Stein, The Concept of the Social Environment in Social Work Practice, *Smith College Studies in Social Work,* 30:187–210 (June 1960); Benjamin S. Bloom, *Stability and Change in Human Characteristics* (New York: John Wiley & Sons, 1964), pp. 183–201.

Lewin, and W. I. Thomas.[18] In more recent years, this complex of situations has been referred to as a *milieu*. Milieu therapy denotes the use of an interconnected network of social groups and situations, of which an individual is a member within a treatment organization or within a neighborhood-community, in order to help that person therapeutically.

Essentially, we are dealing with a conceptual construct which makes it possible for an individual to consider himself both as a member of, and also as opposed to, his family situation. Yet, conceptually, a situation is neither a condition, such as a pregnancy, nor a status, an event, or a problem. For example, a social problem, such as marital conflict or delinquent behavior, is a difficulty in social living and social relationships; it is behavior that is reactive to transactions between people and their social situations.

A collectivity, such as a family or work organization, may be thought to have its own situation. For example, a family group may have a church membership role and be highly identified and unified in that role. The church congregation may assign to the family a strong corporate identity, may have a common focus of attention toward it, and may have a common situational definition about its religious activity and functioning. For the sake of conceptual clarity, however, the social field and audience for groups and social systems as entities can be distinguished from a situation and referred to as a milieu or environment.

An individual or group is in action along several dimensions through which a situation can be identified and located in relation to its focus, space, time, boundary, structure, culture, process, and definition.

The *focal dimension* is a primary one. A situational *focus* refers to a center of interest and attention toward which action and relationships are oriented.[19] Generally, a focal object is some form of stress or stressful event, such as a hurricane, the birth of a child, or a death, which alters the situational conditions, structure, and relationships. A hurricane may require the provision of emergency food, clothing, shelter, transportation, and mutual aid within a community. Thus, some kind of resource and some task or issue for members about its input, possession, interchange, or use become the actual focus for interaction,

[18]Sheffield, Situation as the Unit of Family Case Study; Kurt Lewin, *Field Theory in Social Science* (New York: Harper & Brothers, 1951), pp. 238–303; and W. I. Thomas, *Primitive Behavior* (New York: McGraw Hill, 1937), p. 572. On the conception of milieu in milieu therapy, see Maxwell Jones, *Beyond the Therapeutic Community* (New Haven: Yale University Press, 1968), pp. 108–25.

[19]Carr, *Situational Analysis,* p. 11; and Lowell J. Carr, *Analytical Sociology* (New York: Harper & Brothers, 1955), p. 34. For a detailed discussion of situational dimensions, see S. B. Sells, Dimensions of Stimulus Situations Which Account for Behavior Variance, in *Stimulus Determinants of Behavior,* ed. S. B. Sells (New York: Ronald Press, 1963), pp. 3–15; and Daniel R. Miller, The Study of Social Relationships: Situation, Identity and Social Interaction, in *Psychology, a Study of a Science,* vol. 5, ed. S. Koch (New York: McGraw-Hill, 1963), pp. 639–737.

The Individual as Target

adaptation, and change.[20] The attentional focus may vary in object, intensity, or duration, but it reaches a climax of "engrossment," or peak of tension, and then declines in some final point of task frustration or task completion.[21] Usually, a situation is identified and named according to the focal nature or purpose of the group involved: nuclear family, extended family, household, religious, school, work, neighborhood, friendship, racial socioeconomic status, military, and political groups. Some rubrics for situations flow from the groups that have human service purposes: recreational, subway, department store, as well as medical and social agency services.

There is a physical, *spatial dimension,* or a "behavior setting," such as a classroom, a residential apartment, a small lake in a mountain with boats on the water. There are territorial space, facilities, props, and equipment, along with their arrangement and relationships, all of which have important behavior-regulating properties.[22] The *temporal dimension* of a situation consists of interaction units called *episodes* (or *happenings*), containing a program of events, doings, or occasions, as in a school's class hour, a management fight to decide on a company policy, a family outing to the seashore. The episodes are characterized by beginning, middle, and end phases, by a rhythmic pattern, and by a single focus of attention for a central set of participants. The *boundary dimension* has end points in time, space, and membership and in physical or attitudinal barriers which may be elastic but which include participants and exclude outsiders.[23]

According to James Bossard's conception, a situation may be understood also to have a structure, a culture, and a process.[24] There is a *structure* of people ecologically related to a behavior setting, in what is called a scene. Included is a group of people, having a cast of characters, a size, developmental history, and role system. The group may have a full cast, or an unfilled role, as the lack of weakened role of fatherhood in a family. The group's structure itself consists of a role system and of patterns of authority and decision making, affection and support, communication, and task allocation. From the viewpoint of its structure, a situation may be organized, unorganized, or disorganized. There is a *culture* of norm-rules for conduct and engagement, of shared goals, values, traditions, and perspectives, including a sense of place,

[20]This point is suggested in John C. Glidewell, On the Analysis of Social Intervention, *Parental Attitudes and Child Behavior,* ed. John C. Glidewell (Springfield: Thomas, 1961), pp. 215–39.
[21]Erving Goffman, *Behavior in Public Places* (New York: Free Press, 1963), p. 18.
[22]Roger G. Barker, *Ecological Psychology* (Stanford: Stanford University Press, 1968); Edward T. Hall, *The Hidden Dimension* (New York: Doubleday Anchor, 1969); and Robert Sommer, *Personal Space* (Englewood Cliffs, N.J.: Prentice-Hall, 1969).
[23]Carr, *Analytical Sociology,* p. 52.
[24]James H. S. Bossard and Eleanor S. Boll, *Family Situations* (Philadelphia: University of Pennsylvania Press, 1943), pp. 41–68.

a moral order, a group identity, and morale. Culturally, a situation may be one of consensus, difference, dissensus. It may be anomic or solidary, highly or poorly valued by its participants or audience. In addition, a situation has a functioning *process,* in which focused attention and effort are directed toward the achievement of individual and group objectives. Circular patterns of interaction and functioning become habitual and institutionalized through the operation of self-reinforcing and reciprocal reward mechanisms. Courses of individual and collective action thus become programmed and may be ritualized, as in daily family meal. In process terms, a situation may be placid, routine, uncertain, distressed, disturbed, or turbulent. Under stress, a condition that will be discussed in greater detail, a situation may be stressful, troublesome, hazardous, or in a state of crisis, disaster, or catastrophe. The process state of a situation may be an acute or chronic one.

Situational Definition

The definition of a situation by the member-actors or the audience is an important component and also an essential characteristic of the social situation as an entity. It is a mental, symbolic construction of a situation and of its meaning. It consists of the perceptions, explanations, attributions, expectations, attitudes, and feelings about a situational gestalt and its elements: the setting, the people, the interaction, the events, and one's self. The definition is the unique personal meaning, the felt experience and consciousness of a situation. It is formulated on phenomenological, conscious, and unconscious levels of experience in relation to expectations for role performance, rules for interaction, and the utility values of its resources and relationships. Based on the individual's belief-value system, his psychic predispositions, and on social structural, cultural demands, a situation is constructed and labeled by individuals and groups, objectively, subjectively, and inter-subjectively. It may be typified, legitimated, and institutionalized as part of a cultural system in a society.[25]

It is the situational definition or consciousness that influences or calls the actor to action, that guides the selection of stimuli to which one responds, and that cues expectations and obligations for specific role performance and identity negotiation. Symbolic interactionism emphasizes that people relate to each other, interact, and act collectively in relation to their symbolic constructions of a situation. Viewing a child as disappointed, we may feel required to act motherly and comforting. A flood may be defined in terms of self-blame—as punishment for sin —or as caused by some external force, each conception having different

[25]Peter L. Berger and Thomas Luckman, *The Social Construction of Reality* (Garden City: Doubleday & Co., 1966), pp. 50–118.

consequences for our behavior. Where there is blame and self-blame, as in a ghetto riot, a community may respond with repressive and persecutory behavior, rather than respond with altruistic helping behavior, as it does in a natural disaster.[26] As Thomas observed, if situations are defined as real, they are real in their consequences.[27]

The definition of a situation may be conceptual-descriptive, in telling us what is reality, what tasks there are to be assumed, what rules there are to be followed, what roles there are to be played. They may be operational-prescriptive in telling us how to present ourselves, how to relate, and how to act.

One's mental construction of a situation becomes a dynamic for its constantly changing character. Thus, the labeling of a crisis situation as challenging or as threatening may stimulate reverberating chains of reactions and meanings from which new situations emerge. In a marital conflict, the husband's labeling of the wife as a "witch" may result in her perception of him as "irrational," leading her to obtain help from kinfolk and the police to have him hospitalized. The name of the game for the marital conflict situation becomes redefined as a personality problem or "mental illness." Helping in such situations often requires that the situation be redefined back to the interpersonal level of conflict, so that the original conflict in definitions may be resolved.

Interpretations and expectations of life situations need to be objectively accurate and intersubjectively validated through conscious checking and agreements with others, to assure their congruence with situational demands for specific role performance. They also need to be shared and joint products of a "reciprocity of perspectives," of empathic role taking and communication, so as to enable the coorientation and consensus necessary for effective collaborative activity.[28] Certain situations may be rigidly defined, leading the actors to interact largely in relation to their formal roles; or they may be viewed in overpersonalized terms by mentally disturbed people so that the perceptions become unique and nonconsensual, resulting in isolation, alienation, role conflict, and depersonalization.

As an entity a situation may be conceived and perceived as having certain attributes: clarity, potency, consistency, stability, openness, and equilibrium. A situation in crisis is in a state of disequilibrium. A person's death is disturbing to people, yet its immediate influence may be clear, intense, and consistent.

[26]For situational definitions and reactions, see Donald A. Hansen and Reuben Hill, Families Under Stress, in Handbook of Marriage and the Family, ed. Harold T. Christensen (Chicago: Rand McNally, 1964), pp. 782–819; and Peter McHugh, Defining the Situation (Indianapolis: Bobbs-Merrill, 1968).

[27]W. I. Thomas and Dorothy S. Thomas, The Child in America (New York: Alfred A. Knopf, 1928), p. 584.

[28]Thomas J. Scheff, Toward a Sociological Model of Consensus, American Sociological Review, 32:32–46 (February 1967).

A situation may be categorized by its participants or its audience in relation to one of the following types of definitions, as suggested by R. D. Laing.

1. Something is the matter with someone.
2. Nothing is the matter with anyone, but nothing is working properly. The situation is a mess.
3. Something is the matter with everyone, according to everyone.
4. Nothing is the matter with us, or the situation, but outsiders, such as the neighbors or the police, think something is wrong.
5. No one in the situation knows what the situation is.[29]

These constructions of social situations may be internalized by individuals as habitual elements of their personality, as persistent attitudes, expectations, and cognitive-emotional sets toward life and other people. They become part of one's self-identity and life style, one's personality predisposition and character. According to Eric Berne, there are four "life positions" that people develop in regard to life situations: (1) I'm o.k., you're o.k.; (2) I'm o.k., you're not o.k.; (3) I'm not o.k., you're o.k.; (4) I'm not o.k., you're not o.k.[30] These life positions refer to the situational definitions given by Laing. The second, third, and fourth positions are said to lead people into playing hostile and self-defeating games.

People characteristically come to see a situation as trustworthy or untrustworthy, supportive or over-demanding, as a field for one's skill or completely risky or uncontrolled. Julian Rotter presents evidence that people develop a generalized, habitual expectation of internal or external reward (or control of reinforcement) for one's behavior.[31] Thus a person may be internally oriented and believe he can influence life situations and the course of his own life; or he may be externally oriented and feel powerless to do so because he is subject to the influence of others. Persons with a negative "transference" type of expectation tend to be self-defeating and crisis prone. Attitudinal predispositions based on characteristic symbolic constructions of one's life situations are therefore of basic importance in determining behavior and interpersonal relationships.

These kinds of definitions, including that of one's self, give a paradoxical quality to social situations. A situation is objectively and also

[29]R. D. Laing, *Intervention in Social Situations* (London: Association of Family Caseworkers, 1969).
[30]Eric Berne, *Principles of Group Treatment* (New York: Grove Press, 1966), p. 270.
[31]Julian B. Rotter, Generalized Expectancies for Internal Versus External Control of Reinforcement, *Psychological Monographs,* 80:609 (1966).

phenomenologically real. It may be perceived as external to an individual or symbolically internalized within the person. The person's reactions may become a significant aspect of its structure and dynamics. One may step into or out of a situation; one may control or be commanded by it. Within its domain one may be master and victim, object and subject, as an I, and It, or a Thou.

Situations Have
Functions

Social situations serve important purposes for individuals and collectivities. These functions are considered more explicitly here. It is remarkable how pervasively a human being achieves growth, individuality, and personhood in and through social life situations. *Personality* consists of "the portion of the organism polarized toward the situation."[32] It has been defined as a "system of personic tinsits," or "tendencies to act in type situations."[33] A better known definition was given by Harry Stack Sullivan, who thought of personality as the "relatively enduring patterns of recurring interpersonal situations which characterize a human life."[34] One's *identity* is a social situated self. It is formed, maintained, and expressed through social role performances that yield individuation and self-esteem, as well as the acceptance and esteem of others in social situations. *Character,* as Erving Goffman explains, refers to the capacities of the individual to behave effectively and correctly in stressful situations.[35]

Personal adjustment, or optimal social functioning, represents "a goodness of fit between the properties of the person's self-identity and his environment."[36] It expresses a "matching" between situational demands and the personal needs and coping resources of the individual, so that "the resulting transactions contribute maximally to the development of their human potential and to an environment conducive to that development in others."[37] Optimal social functioning is aided by an individual's situational or *interpersonal competence,* which refers to

[32]Gardner Murphy, *Personality* (New York: Harper & Brothers, 1947), p. 883.
[33]Walter Coutu, *Emergent Human Nature* (New York: Alfred A. Knopf, 1949), p. 85.
[34]Harry Stack Sullivan, *The Interpersonal Theory of Psychiatry* (New York: W. W. Norton & Co., 1953), pp. 110–11.
[35]Erving Goffman, *Interaction Ritual* (New York: Doubleday & Co., 1967), pp. 214–39.
[36]J. P. R. French, The Conceptualization and Measurement of Mental Health in Terms of Self-Identity Theory, in *The Definition and Measurement of Mental Health,* ed. S. B. Sells (Washington, D.C.: National Center for Health Statistics, U.S. Department of Health, Education, and Welfare, 1968), pp. 136–59.
[37]William E. Gordon, Fragmentation and Synthesis in Social Work Today, in *Social Work Promises and Pressures,* ed. Sue W. Spencer (Nashville: University of Tennessee School of Social Work, 1968), pp. 1–13.

one's ability and skills in dealing effectively with social situations.[38] These are skills in perceiving, grasping, and defining situations and in having these accepted by, or negotiated with, others. Involved also are skills in enacting one's roles and subidentities, formally and authentically; transacting empathically and acting collaboratively with others; seeking reality feedback, making rational decisions, and maximally utilizing resources. Such competence also includes the effective and appropriate use of situation-coping strategies: to accept, to endure, to fight, to change oneself or influence others to change, to reject and flee to a more positive situation—either temporarily or entirely.

A social situation is a means, a context, a determinant for individual and group action. It is the instrumental life space through which individuals and social systems fulfill their basic needs and actualize themselves as living entities. Kurt Lewin proposed as a basic law that behavior is a function of the situation: $B = f/S$.[39] (Lewin saw the situation as a product of person and environment.) This formula now might aptly be rephrased to state that behavior is a function of the situation as it is defined by its participants.

Current behavior theory suggests that the situation is both a stimulus system and contingency reinforcement system, governing behavior in terms of situational consequences. *Behavior change,* therefore, requires change in a person's situational attitudinal definitions, and interpersonal competence, as well as change in the situational reinforcement system that will expect, reward, and maintain more adaptive behavior. Consistent with such an orientation, *personality change* may be understood to take place in relation to a process of "situational adjustment."[40] This change process concerns a new consciousness and definition of one's life situation, the assumption and enactment of appropriate situational roles and identities, and the internalization of these role attributes and social identities as part of one's self-identity.

It should be emphasized that such ideas about personality, behavior, and their change are in accord with existentialist and humanist ideas about personal choice and responsibility in self-realization and in the construction of personal meanings about one's world. in this view, an essential characteristic of the human person is "the capacity to transcend the immediate situation."[41] Transcending experiences enable

---

[38]Robert W. White, *Ego and Reality in Psychoanalytic Theory,* Psychological Issues, vol. 3, no. 3, Monograph II (New York: International Universities Press, 1963). See also David Mechanic, Therapeutic Intervention: Issues in the Care of the Mentally Ill, *American Journal of Orthopsychiatry,* 37:703–18 (July 1967); and Michael Argyle, *The Psychology of Interpersonal Behaviour* (Baltimore: Penguin Books, 1967).

[39]Kurt Lewin, *Field Theory in Social Science* (New York: Harper & Brothers, 1951), pp. 238–303.

[40]For discussion of this concept, see Carr, *Situational Analysis,* pp. 20–35; and Howard S. Becker, Personal Change in Adult Life, *Sociometry,* 27:40–53 (March 1964). The conception here is adapted from their analyses.

[41]Rollo May, The Existential Approach, in *American Handbook of Psychiatry,* vol. 2, ed. Silvano Arieti (New York: Basic Books, 1959), pp. 1,348–61.

one to explore and actualize possibilities and potentialities in the self and in the situation in order to actualize growth and development in both.[42]

A social situation, therefore, serves (and disserves) people in many ways. It helps answer such existential questions as "Who am I?" and "Where am I at?" It is a social field for a great range and depth of human experience, of stimulus and demand, of opportunity and constraint, of nurturance and punishment, of proaction and creativity. It is a theatre for the dramatic expression and confirmation of self, and schoolroom for the learning of identity and behavior, and a testing ground for social skills and competencies. It is a game and a play in which one takes risks, grasps opportunities, and "makes out" and in which one learns to give performances that are skilled or inept, impersonal or authentic, according to an improvised or foreordained script. It is an arena and an audience for the rituals of love and hate, a battleground for the clashes of interests and reconciliation of differences, a playing field on which one becomes a team member and a citizen in the community of mankind. It is a meeting ground for I-It and I-Thou encounters between human beings.

Functional and Dysfunctional Situations

A social situation may be considered to be *functional* when it meets the needs of individuals and social systems. For individuals, it means enabling people to meet their needs for relatedness and intimate and formal terms, for privacy, stimulation, and rest, for space and place, and for identity and self-esteem.[43] A social situation is functional when it is experienced as livable and favorable, supportive and facilitative of well-functioning human beings and of their environing social and ecological systems. It is within immediate social situations that the demands, needs, and supports of these varied systems intersect, that they are complementary or conflicted. It should be understood that the activity of people is required to actualize these needs and the situational attributes through which they can be met. This understanding underlies such old truisms as that it takes someone to turn a condition into a situation and that it takes at least two people to make a situation.

On the basis of available knowledge, the following appear to be significant attributes of functional situations:

---

[42]Sidney M. Jourard, *Disclosing Man to Himself* (Princeton: Van Nostrand, 1968), pp. 204–28.
[43]For an earlier effort to delineate functional situations, see Werner A. Lutz, Testing the Social Health of the Client's Environment, in *Proceedings, Sixth Biennial Alumni-Faculty Conference* (Pittsburgh: School of Social Work, University of Pittsburgh, 1956), pp. 39–67.

1. The situation is structurally adequate, providing sufficient and well-organized material and people, ecological conditions, and social relationships.

2. It is culturally adequate, in relation to values, meanings, identities, rules, and sanctions, including a moral order, so that specific behavior is expected, tolerated, or disapproved; explicit valued identities are available; and there is scope for constructive, innovative, as well as deviant, types of adaptive behavior.

3. The operational processes of the situation are efficient in that focused action and transactions move purposefully to achieve individual and group goals.

4. The gestalt of the situation is appropriately clear, consistent, potent, stable, yet open to enable adaptive equilibrium and change.

5. It provides needed resources and opportunities for the accomplishment of personal and group tasks.

6. It supplies stimulus and demand, feedback and reinforcement that are relevant, appropriate, acceptable, and valued. Such stimulus and reinforcement systems are neither overly stressful nor overly frustrating in their expectations and rewards for effort and performance and should release human and material potentials.

7. It provides rewards that confirm and enhance a viable identity, self-esteem, and a sense of competence for individuals and collectivities.

8. It promotes predominantly challenging, accurate, helpful definitions of reality and life events, so that it can be experienced as trustworthy, nurturing, and validating, as a field for the exercise of one's skill, allowing some degree of personal control and self—control.

9. It enables its members to have adequate and efficient external relationships, so that there are continuities, consistencies, and interdependencies for people across different situations and within the total situation. This should enable subsystems of an organization, community, or larger social system to act collectively for common goals.

If these kinds of attributes are weak or absent, a situation can be expected to contribute directly to ineffective or inadequate functioning on the part of individuals and social systems and can therefore be *dysfunctional.* Thus, a social situation may be dysfunctional when it is structurally and culturally inadequate or disorganized; is aimless, unfocused, ambiguous, contradictory, threatening, or harmful; lacks needed resources and opportunities; presents unsurmountable barriers; stimulates unacceptable stress or impulses; generates severe interpersonal, role, and value conflicts; requires performance, knowledge, and skills that are beyond an individual's capacity or ability; and does not validate identity.[44]

Severely dysfunctional situations become *crisis situations* when they are so disturbed that the group is unable to cope with them through their accustomed resources and problem-solving patterns. A crisis is

[44]For identification of these kinds of attributes of dysfunctional situations, see Elizabeth G. Meier, Interactions Between the Person and His Operational Situations, SOCIAL CASEWORK, 46:542–49 (November 1965).

produced by the interaction of the definition and meaning of a stressful event, its objective characteristics and hardships, and the coping resources available.[45]

In crisis, both people and situations become "unstuck," over tense, unstable, and even unstructured and out of control. People lose their parts and places; values and identities are threatened or diffused. People and settings become unpredictable, dangerous or "absurd"; expectations of them become ambiguous and uncertain; reactions to them become anxious, fearful, hostile, and rejecting. Anomic, conflict types of crisis situations present behavioral solutions that carry risks of consequent alienation and deviant behavior for individuals and groups.[46] Deviants may embark upon deviant careers and become caught up in social typing processes.[47] Mentally disordered people may have their situational improprieties or offenses labeled as "symptoms" and led through a process in which an "insanity of place," (to use Goffman's term), becomes defined as the "mental illness" of a person.[48] Even such a severe reaction as schizophrenia, Laing says, "is a special strategy that a person invents in order to live in an unlivable situation."[49]

To identify specific models of functional situations remains a difficult matter. Conceptions of eufunctional and dysfunctional situations may vary for different class and subcultural groups because they usually are based on a range of norms that allows much deviation. Otto Pollak presents a helpful model of a eufunctional family group and situation for family diagnosis, although it has been criticized, whether rightly or wrongly, as representing a middle-class value ideal of family life.[50] In addition, as Robert K. Merton has pointed out, what is functional behavior for an individual or one part of a social system may be dysfunctional for other people or social system elements.[51] It may be that such an apparent contradiction expresses social dynamics in necessary, ongoing, adaptive change processes of social systems. Dysfunctional (or maladjusted) situations and people are those that actually are impaired,

[45]Hansen and Hill, Families Under Stress.

[46]Edwin M. Lemert, Human Deviance, *Social Problems and Social Control* (Englewood Cliffs, N.J. Prentice-Hall, 1967), pp. 3–30. For a discussion of anomic situations, see Ann Hartman, Anomie and Social Casework, SOCIAL CASEWORK, 50:131–37 (March 1969).

[47]Max Siporin, Deviant Behavior Theory in Social Work Diagnosis and Treatment, *Social Work,* 10:59–67 (July 1965); and Howard S. Becker, *Outsiders* (New York: Free Press, 1963), pp. 25–39.

[48]Erving Goffman, The Insanity of Place, *Psychiatry,* 32:357–88 (November 1969). For other such discussions, see John Arsenian, Situational Factors Contributing to Mental Illness in the United States, *Mental Hygiene,* 45:194–206 (April 1961); Ernest Becker, *The Revolution of Psychiatry* (New York: Free Press, 1964); Marc Fried, Social Problems and Psychopathology, in *Urban America and the Planning of Mental Health Services* (New York: Group for the Advancement of Psychiatry, 1964); Thomas J. Scheff, *Being Mentally Ill* (Chicago: Aldine, 1966); and Thomas Szasz, *The Myth of Mental Illness* (New York: Hoeber-Harper, 1961).

[49]R. D. Laing, *The Politics of Experience* (New York: Pantheon, 1967), p. 115.

[50]Otto Pollak, A Family Diagnosis Model, *Social Service Review,* 34:19–31 (March 1960).

[51]Robert K. Merton, *Social Theory and Social Structure,* 2d ed. (New York: Free Press, 1957), pp. 19–84.

inadequate, or poorly matched to meet normative requirements for system maintenance in the long run. Optimal functioning and development of human beings and of social institutions require reciprocal and interdependent transactions in which individual and collective societal needs are met. Such reciprocal transactions, marked by synergistic, mutually-benefiting behavior, should identify functional social situations.[52]

Situational Assessment

We have observed that a social situation is the basic operational unit for individuals and social groups in process-action. It therefore is a natural and basic unit for diagnostic assessment and for intervention in helping people with their social problems. It provides a natural lever, both for optimal understanding and as a point of entry and of change, in the life processes of a client or target system, whether this be an individual, family, work organization, neighborhood, community, or social institution. As part of the rationale for helping activity that has evolved in social work, situational assessment and situational intervention have been fundamental concepts, under varied names, in the traditional problem-person-situation model for social work practice.

Within recent years, Harriett Bartlett, Elliot Studt, and others have presented situational assessment as a generic as well as a primary, social work process, relevant for the full range of situations with which social work practitioners are concerned and for any form of social work practice.[53] According to Bartlett, situational assessment involves the application of the common knowledge base and underlies the common problem-solving process within social work practice, with its emphasis on the social functioning of people in social situations. She observes that situational assessment relates people and environment in a way that "leads to a broader definition of social work responsibilities and enlarged opportunities for interventive action." Studt suggests that situational analysis is the first step in case planning, in which there is a focus on helping tasks (viewed as situational activity), and on common goals to be undertaken by a work group, consisting of client, worker, and others in a helping system. For both Bartlett and Studt, a treatment intervention is to be selected as it is appropriate to a specific situation.

Situational assessment is one aspect of a social diagnosis or system

[52]For the concept of a synergistic culture, see Ruth Benedict, Synergy, *American Anthropologist,* 72:320–33 (April 1970).

[53]Harriett M. Bartlett, *The Common Base of Social Work Practice* (New York: National Association of Social Workers, 1970), p. 157 and passim; and Elliot Studt, Social Work Theory and Implications for the Practice of Methods, *Social Work Education Reporter,* 16:22–24, 42–46 (June 1968). For an example of the application of situational diagnosis, see Melvin B. Moguloff, Delinquency Intervention Based on Person and Situation, *Social Work,* 9:42–50 (April 1964).

analysis. It is addressed to understanding one component of the "problem-person-situation gestalt" of the case as a system, of what John C. Whitehorn referred to as "the diagnostic triad" of reaction pattern, personality, and situation.[54] Here, the "person" may be an individual or a collectivity having a corporate identity, such as a work organization, family, or community; it may be the client system or the subsystem experiencing difficulty or the target subsystem that requires change. Neither the social situation nor the other two elements of the social diagnosis can be assessed as pure, discrete entities. Each requires the context and interrelation of the others for a valid knowing. Family diagnosis, marriage diagnosis, assessments of groups, organizations, neighborhoods, and communities are forms of situational assessments.

Clients find it relatively easy and natural to respond to a request that they help us understand their situation. They usually begin with a presentation of their family situations, of their family roles, of their experiences, identities, relationships, and functioning as a family member. They may focus also on a school or work situation in which particular difficulty in performance is being experienced.

A situational assessment is essentially a systematic review of the network of social situations and of the various social systems and primary groups in which the client has a role-status, is an active member, and is a role performer. In addition to the family, other groups need to be examined: kin, work, school, neighborhood, and church. Each situation needs to be explored concerning its ecological characteristics and setting. There should be an explicit appraisal of each group's composition, historical development, its structural and cultural adequacy, and its functioning efficiency in accomplishing its life tasks. There should be an identification of the objectively real and subjectively experienced definition of the situation to its significant members, the meaning and impact of stressful events, and the attentional focus. An important aspect of this system review is an analysis of the wider social organizations and communities, including the social agency situation and the community social welfare situation, with regard for their adequacy and efficiency in being able to deliver—and deliver promptly —needed social resources and services.

The evaluation of a client's situation should indicate its assets, resources, and supports, demand characteristics, obstacles, and liabilities, and reward and sanction system concerning the behavior settings as well as the participant groups and individuals. The analyses should include situational classifications, judgments concerning modifiability of situational elements, prognostic indications, and indications for inter-

[54]John C. Whitehorn, The Situational Part of Diagnosis, *International Journal of Group Psychotherapy,* 13:290–99 (July 1963).

ventive entry and change. These evaluations should be interrelated with the assessments of the client's personality and problems. Treatment plans can then be formulated on the basis of these integrated formulations. Interventive goals, strategies, roles, and tactics are then selected so that they are differentially specific to the case problems, person, and situation.

Although situational classifications do not exist in the form of a systematic diagnostic nomenclature, there are a number of available classification schemes that are used on an ad hoc basis in social work practice. A very helpful set of categorizations for family situations was formulated by James Bossard and Eleanor Boll.[55] Included are such rubrics for a family or home as possessive, overindulgent, companionable, neglectful, impartial, and bickering; mother-controlled, father-dominated, anarchic, child-dictated, and democratic; cooperative, independent, incomplete; snobbish, overly religious, and conventional; inadequately supported, mother-supported, disgraced, and invalid-dominated. Families have also been typed as perfectionistic, inadequate, egocentric, and unsocial.[56] John Spiegel conceived of family role transactions as involving equilibrium in a high complementarity of roles and disequilibrium in a low complementarity of roles, the latter based on types of discrepancies that refer to cognitive, goal, allocative, instrumental, and cultural value aspects.[57] Marital conflict situations have been characterized as masculine-feminine, sado-masochistic, detached-demanding and based on neurotic reactions.[58] Varied classifications are available for types of groups and organizational community situations.

Situations also can be categorized in relation to the games described by Eric Berne, such as the following: let's you and him fight; if it weren't for you; see what you've made me do; kick me; now I've got you; look how hard I've tried; ain't it awful; alcoholic, schlemiel, blemish, stupid.[59] The game, "if it weren't for you," is frequently observed in family conflict situations marked by scapegoating of an individual family member. Such classifications contribute a valuable quality of individualization in understanding the totality of a situation, as well as in identifying the specific aspects that require changing. These classifications, however, should be used as part of, rather than the whole of, a diagnostic statement or analytical formulation.

[55]Bossard and Boll, *Family Situations.*
[56]Alice L. Voiland et al., *Family Casework Diagnosis* (New York: Columbia University Press, 1962).
[57]John P. Spiegel, The Resolution of Role Conflict Within the Family, *Psychiatry,* 20:1–16 (February 1957).
[58]Shirley Gehrke and James Moxom, Diagnostic Classification and Treatment Techniques in Marital Counseling, *Family Process,* 1:253–64 (September 1962).
[59]Eric Berne, *Games People Play* (New York: Grove Press, 1964).

It may be helpful to identify certain assessment principles. A situational appraisal is often best accomplished by the social worker as a "participant observer" within the client's life situations. This appraisal requires home visits and other direct experience with significant life situations in which the client is having difficulty. Patterns of interaction also may be observed by having family and other groups meet jointly in agency or in other treatment settings.

Immediate attention should be given to the identification of situational demands and their meaning, with indications for their relief if they are overstressful, and for the mobilization and provision of needed resources. Problems should be translated into tasks, which essentially are elements of doing in a situation. Objectives should be stated so that they are consistent with client values and are immediate, attainable, and clear. The task program should indicate levels of intervention, entry and change strategies, program activities and resources, with a clear and complementary division and allocation of tasks and roles to be assumed by the members of the helping system—the client, the worker, and others.

A basic principle of the assessment process is that of client participation, that the evaluation can properly be done only with the active engagement and collaboration of the client in a joint worker-client enterprise. To help the client through a diagnostic experience is a basic helping intervention. Situational assessments, moreover, involve judgments about discrepancies between an actual life situation of the client and what is considered normative or appropriate for a well-functioning individual or group at a certain stage of his or its life career. This calls for self-awareness on the part of the social worker and consideration of cultural, class, and other values and criteria being used. Such discriminations and judgments need to be validated in direct discussions with the client.

Another principle of great importance here concerns the priority of situational redefinition. "The first step in the change process . . . is to develop alternative assumptions and beliefs through a process of cognitive redefinition of the situation."[60] Laing argues that diagnosis is a definition of, and an intervention in, a social situation.

The definition of the situation and the call for action are two sides of the same coin. The unique rational strategy of intervention is prescribed in and through the definition of the situation. . . . The way one sees through a situation changes the situation. As soon as we convey it in any way . . . some change is occurring even in the most rigid situation. . . . Social situations are the field

[60]Warren G. Bennis et al., Personal Change Through Interpersonal Relationships, in *Interpersonal Dynamics,* ed. Warren G. Bennis et al. (Homewood: Dorsey, 1964), pp. 357–92.

for the self-fulfilling prophecy. A self-fulfilling diagnosis of the situation may lead to a situation approximating to the situation as defined.[61]

Such situational redefinition may involve relabeling a disaster as a challenging situation or a schizophrenic reaction as a parent-child conflict situation. Crisis situations should be redefined, if possible, as having elements of positive choice, as subject to one's influence and effort.

Mutual diagnostic activity of this kind with a client relieves tension, offers pattern and meaning, and extends a sense of grasp, mastery, and hope. It generates motivation, engagement of the client, and commitment by both worker and client to the change process. Situational assessment, in itself, therefore, is therapeutic in its effect and becomes a powerful stimulus for situational change.

Situational Intervention

Social workers generally operate on the assumption that man is able to make and change his environment. It is also believed that individual and social welfare are so interdependent that changes in both person and situation are usually required for optimal growth and problem solving. Thus Gordon Hamilton conceived of casework as "implemented by attempts: (a) to change or improve the person's situation . . . (b) to help a person change his attitudes or behavior within the social situation . . . (c) or in combination."[62] Social work practice in general is aimed to assist clients or citizens to resolve or prevent social problems, through the improvement of their social functioning, through the improvement of the situational functioning of social structures, and through a readjustment or rematching of personal needs and abilities and situational demands and supports.

In recent years, the social worker's helping activity has been considered an application of an "interventive repertoire" and his specific activity as "intervention."[63] These social work helping interventions are understood as transactional and influential behavior, as procedural activity, directed toward the inducement of change in personality and social systems. Essentially, these interventions are purposeful, goal oriented, task fulfilling and situational. They are situational because their effects consist of alterations in the client's social situation. They may change structural, cultural, and functional patterns in a group, alter the

---

[61]Laing, *Intervention in Social Situations.*

[62]Gordon Hamilton, *Theory and Practice of Social Case Work,* 2d. ed. (New York: Columbia University Press, 1951), p. 239.

[63]Bartlett, *Common Base of Social Work Practice;* and Glidewell, Analysis of Social Intervention. For a different and limited conception of situational interventions, see Werner W. Boehm, Toward New Models of Social Work Practice, in *Social Work Practice,* 1967 (New York: Columbia University Press, 1967), pp. 3–18.

group's focus of attention and effort, and modify its definition of experience and its space-time characteristics. They involve new input, interchange, and output of such resources as love, money, and people and often mean aiding clients to utilize resources in specific task achievement.[64] They create new forms of interaction, identity, or consciousness of a situation. They may cause alteration in the power relations within a family, in a group's interaction pattern, in an attentional focus on the consequences of one's own behavior, and in an attitude toward a family's identity. These alterations and other kinds of tasks are accomplished as a result of the social worker's considerable influence in helping interventions. It should be noted that situational interventions are generally aimed to effect changes in some range of desired, normative behavior rather than aimed at very specific standards of behaviorial outcomes. The client himself should be responsible for determining the specific nature of the outcome behavior.

Situational interventions thus are task procedures that implement a certain strategy or plan of action. The intervention itself consists of a sequence of tactics or techniques. What we call the treatment or action-change process makes use of situational interventions according to two types of strategies: situational entry and situational change. One entry strategy, suggested by Ronald Lippitt, is to use multiple entries, as in working simultaneously with high and low status members or with younger and older generational members of a group in order to terminate pathological interactive processes.[65] Other entry interventions are to demonstrate helping competence, provide research consultation, plug into a power center, carry out a project demonstration, offer desired rewards, induct an individual or group into a new reference group or into the role of clienthood, or gain appointment as group leader. One can take control of a situation by being authoritative, or by giving a valued specific service, or by what Viktor Frankl calls "paradoxical intention" (symptom encouragement).[66] Some of these procedures may be part of a broader kind of entry strategy, which is to motivate the person or group involved to want change, by increasing the dissatisfaction, anxiety, guilt, or cognitive dissonance about the status quo of current behavior or situation, and by increasing the hope, desire, and willingness to adopt new perspectives, attitudes, and behavior.

Situational change strategies may be categorized according to their

---

[64]Glidewell emphasizes this point, and regards the number of interventions as almost infinite. See Glidewell, Analysis of Social Intervention.

[65]Ronald Lippitt, Unplanned Maintenance and Planned Change in the Group Work Process, in Social Work Practice, 1962 (New York: Columbia University Press, 1962), pp. 75–95.

[66]Viktor E. Frankl, Man's Search for Meaning (New York: Washington Square Press, 1963), pp. 193–204.

major change functions and purposes: (1) education-socialization, (2) rehabilitation-therapy, (3) friendship-integration, and (4) problem solving.[67] Because these objectives often are interdependent in the helping process, with greater emphasis given to one or another, the situational change interventions and techniques are applicable for varied purposes. An educational strategy, for example, would give more importance to changing a climate of opinion, whereas a problem-solving strategy would place more weight on the restructuring of power relations in a group. Group psycho-therapy might be considered a form and a strategy of situational change because it provides a new group and social situation in which therapeutic change processes are emphasized. However, it also may utilize interventions of situational redefinition and refocusing of attention. As Whitehorn suggests:

[It] has a special value in disclosing and modifying a patient's propensities for the repetitive creation of characteristically unpleasant situations. In a good group session, situations may be produced, and highlighted, in such a way as to focus the patient's attention upon his biased expectations and attitudes, and at the same time the emotional support from fellow patients in the group may make possible the understanding and acceptance of another viewpoint rather more readily than can be accomplished in the one-to-one interview.[68]

Although there are many others, the following situational interventions are identified as particularly significant for social work helping purposes. The procedures given here are not mutually exclusive. They often are used in varied combinations and sequence within a specific case, as are the tactics and techniques through which they are carried out.[69]

1. Situational Redefinition

This intervention involves altering perceptions, expectations, and meanings, particularly of blame; relabeling behavior, beliefs, and self-concepts; creating or resolving cognitive dissonance; encouraging a more accurate, discriminating, and appropriate situational consciousness (for example, relabeling a disaster as an opportunity).

[67]Max Siporin, Social Treatment: A New-Old Helping Method, *Social Work,* 15:13–25 (July 1970).

[68]Whitehorn, Situational Part of Diagnosis.

[69]For other discussions of situational interventions, see Robert R. Blake and Jane S. Mouton, *The Managerial Grid* (Houston: Gulf Publishing, 1964); Donald C. Klein and Erich Lindemann, Preventive Intervention in Individual and Family Crisis Situations, in *Prevention of Mental Disorders in Children,* ed. Gerald Caplan (New York: Basic Books, 1961), pp. 283–306; and Paul L. Glasser et al., Group Work Intervention in the Social Environment, mimeographed (Ann Arbor: School of Social Work, University of Michigan, 1968).

2. Refocusing Attention

This intervention may involve pointing to significant new factors, to real issues, to an attitudinal discrepancy or dilemma, to self-defeating consequences of a behavior pattern that is misdirected, poorly focused, or inexpressive of good intentions.

3. Stress Reduction

This interventive procedure aims to lessen or remove excess stress, demands, or obstacles, which may be internal or external in relation to a client.

4. Resource Provision

The provision of access to social, community resources, such as financial aid, day care, medical care, as well as varied kinds of social supports and socioeconomic opportunities are included in this procedure. The resources may be mobilized, created, and directly furnished; the client may be advised and counseled in making optimal use of them.

5. Change in Behavior Setting

This procedure may call for different spatial arrangements of people and things, new equipment and facilities, or a new activity program. A completely different behavior setting may be provided, as through a new residential apartment, a recreational center, a different work place.

6. Changing the Climate of Opinion

Clients or a public are led to favor and approve a new policy, program, or course of action. This procedure becomes a way of maximizing motivation and providing needed social supports, including those required for rehabilitation of a deviant individual. Use may be made of such tactics as educational campaign, public meeting, propaganda, or persuasion.

7. Acculturation

Here the worker aids the client and others in choosing and committing themselves to new values, norms of conduct, life goals, and life styles that are adaptive and functional in a given culture.

8. Group Restructuring

This procedure may involve expanding, contracting, or changing the composition or membership of a group. Modifying the patterns of power, communication, affection, and status-role relationships may be accomplished by changing the rules, redefining role concepts, setting limits, or developing indigenous leadership.

9. Group Separation

An individual may be removed or the members physically separated, to allow energy replenishment, relief from prolonged stress, removal of obstructions to group movement, or termination of vicious cycles of pathological interaction. This separation may be effected through institutionalization in a hospital or prison, through foster-home placement, and other measures.

10. Group Disbandment

The group is dissolved, as in the termination of a family group by assisting the parents to give up a child for adoption and then seek a divorce for themselves.

11. Behavior Change

Here sociobehavioral change techniques and socialization-learning mechanisms are used to extinguish maladaptive behavior of an individual or a group in order to aid them in acquiring adequate behavioral repertoires and situational competencies.[70] Essential in this intervention is the creation of new reinforcement contingency systems, of rewarding behavioral consequences, in the form of behavior settings and interpersonal transactions that shape and maintain adaptive behavior. Essential also is the transformation of the client's life situation into an explicit learning situation for its participants.

12. Identity-Role Change

A related intervention is the modification of social, personal, and self-identities of an individual in a more positive direction. Family and other collective forms of identity may also be changed. These modifica-

---

[70]Derek Jehu, *Learning Theory and Social Work* (London: Routledge and Kegan Paul, 1967), pp. 81–111; and Eileen D. Gambrill, Edwin J. Thomas, and Robert D. Carter, Procedure for Sociobehavioral Practice in Open Settings, *Social Work,* 16:51–62 (January 1971).

tions are accomplished through changes in the role-statuses of the group members and in the conceptions, meanings, and behavioral enactments of member roles. A requisite task here is learning to perform competently a valued life role. Competence and the associated satisfaction and self-esteem can reinforce the new identities, such as an effective, responsible mother or a law-abiding, good citizen. The reformulation and relabeling of one's self-concept may be accomplished through official confirmation of status change, as in certifying that a person is no longer a criminal. There also may be a personal reevaluation of one's past life experience that results in a different self-image; for example, from that of a long-suffering martyr to that of a person strengthened by adversity.

13. Ceremonial Ritual

The use of a ceremonial occasion, ritual activity, or official public action to accomplish such purposes as public confession, repentance, or conversion; stigmatization or destigmatization of an individual or group; the casting out or the reinclusion of an individual as a member in good standing in a group.

14. Placement in a Therapeutic Situation

This interventive procedure consists of the placement of an individual or a group in a clearly labeled therapeutic-rehabilitative situation and in a specific role as client (or patient, inmate, parolee, and so forth) within a helping-change system. There is an induction of the individual (or family or other group) into the role identity, rights, and obligations of clienthood. There is an assumption that cooperative performance by the individual in the transitional, helping-system role makes possible the related procedures of behavior and identity change. The situation may involve a psychotherapeutic dyadic relationship, an encounter group, or a milieu therapy organization.

15. Rematching Individual and Group

There is a direct, specific modification of reciprocal demands, expectations, and functions for both an individual and a group or social system, in order to provide a better integration and fit between them. As a result, there may be changes in job requirements, assignment, or retraining for an individual to qualify him for a different work position and work group role.

16. Strengthening the Natural Helping System

This type of intervention means improving the group problem-solving competence of an extended family, union group, or neighborhood social network. The resources of such unofficial, helping, and self-helping systems of mutual aid and social support can thus be made available to the client for current and for future problem solving. The procedure includes steps to strengthen the self-help organizations and the organized or unofficial referral system in a community.

17. Direct Aid in Problem Solving

Direct assistance is given in decision-making, conflict-resolution, and task-completion processes. Use may be made of such forms of decision making as bargaining, concession, persuasion, coercion, compromise, or integrative consensus. The resolution of conflict and achievement of cooperation may be attained through peaceful coexistence, arbitration, confrontation, protest, resistance, civil disobedience.[71]

Intervention Roles and Systems Orientation

Situational change interventions need to be understood as role performances in client-worker helping transactions. Helping roles (as mediator, spokesman, resource person) not only express the application of social work knowledge and values, but also they are responsive to heuristic task demands; they are part of action programs that flow from the logic and authority of the client's life situation and the helping situation. Description and discussions of these situational helping roles may be found in other articles.[72]

The general role of being a work team leader that is carried by the social worker should be emphasized here. Elliot Studt describes the social worker's activity in this role as a strategy planner and as a "strategy guide."[73] He is responsible for identifying and establishing the common base of purpose; providing the conditions, tasks, and working relationships within the work group; and seeing that the client's tasks have priority in the common problem-solving effort. In such activity the

---

[71]Simon Slavin, Concepts of Social Conflict, *Journal of Education for Social Work,* 5:47–50 (Fall 1969); and Roland L. Warren, *Types of Purposive Social Change at the Community Level* (Waltham, Mass.: School of Social Welfare, Brandeis University, 1965).

[72]Max Siporin, Private Practice of Social Work: Functional Roles and Social Control, *Social Work,* 6:52–60 (April 1961), and idem, Social Treatment.

[73]Studt, Social Work Theory and Implications.

social worker often functions as a group discussion leader. It is also the social worker who enables the team leadership to be shifted to different members of the work group, as the changing situation requires, and increasingly to have the leadership role carried by the client.

Situational interventions are usually both people-helping and system-changing. For example, an interpretation to a client that aims to modify his self-concept as a father may also modify his attitudes and behavior toward his son, and thus influence the father-son relationship. Interventions should generalize across different situations, within the client's total situation and within the case as a system. This idea is in accord with the principle of the systems approach that pressure on sensitive points of a system often has system-wide and amplifying change consequences. Explicit steps should therefore be taken to effect system change and to verify that such change is established. Helping an individual to give up hostility-provoking behavior in the relationship with the social worker may necessitate the worker's direct action to intercede in and modify the client's family relationships; in this way the new, nonprovocative behavior may be reinforced and maintained for the benefit of the individual and of the family.

There is also need to understand situational interventions as basic, direct ways of effecting change in all kinds of social systems. They are modes of helping, not only in psychotherapy or social treatment, but also in group, family, milieu, and organizational therapies; in community development and social action; in social welfare policy, planning, and administration. Although some of the names may be different, the functions and purposes of situational interventions are similar in change processes for work organizations, communities, and for governmental welfare systems. Thus the community developer, the social planner, and the social welfare administrator need to act in immediate social situations and to serve as expert troubleshooters, mediators, resource providers, and educators within some type of primary group. They are concerned with common types of social situations that are stressful for general or categorical population groups. These they seek to change through modifications in structural, cultural, and functioning patterns of organizations, communities, and institutions. Even institutional change needs to be accomplished through situational interventions with primary interest groups. Through such groups, new climates of opinion can be forged; support and commitments gained for proposed reforms; consensus arrived at about change methods and plans; programs and policies formulated, adopted, and implemented. It is in life situations that the action is and that social worker actions need to be. Social workers find their common ground and identity as helpers to individuals and to society, in the social life situations of clients or citizens, and in helping them to effect situational change.

Conclusion

We have been concerned here with examining how we might better help with the structure of social encounters and particularly with the socially stressful, crisis situations in which social work clients are entangled. Our inquiry has enabled us to recognize that social work does have an extensive array of theory, knowledge, and skill concerning social situations and also of situational assessment and intervention. These constitute central elements of the common base of social work practice. Competence in these activities is distinctive of social work as a helping profession. Much of this knowledge exists in the form of practice wisdom, much is still in the process of emergence, and much also remains to be discovered and tested.

An explicit and conscious situational perspective enables social workers to achieve a richer and more valid understanding of clients in the context of the social realities of their lives and problems. It gives support to a needed social psychology of personality, to new prefigurings of methodology, and to newly emerging structures of helping practice. There is evident now a rich renewal of development in situation theory and of the situational approach within a comprehensive, eclectic framework for social work practice. Such a development brings social workers in closer accord with the traditional two-fold mission of the profession: to aid people as human beings in real life situations, and to help people improve their life situations so as to achieve authentic, human communities.

One means of defining dysfunctional social situations can be found in social systems theory. Atherton et al. employ role and systems theories to define dysfunctional situations that require interventions. And they present a classification scheme that locates targets for intervention by examining client role performances.

Locating Points for Intervention

Charles R. Atherton
Sandra T. Mitchell
Edna Biehl Schein

One of the most persistent problems for social workers in direct service is the lack of an economical, useful, and generally accepted terminology

Reprinted with permission of the authors and the Family Service Association of America from *Social Casework*, Vol. 52 (3), 1971, pp. 131–141.

that locates a focus for intervention in the life situations of clients without the implications inherent in terms derived from a disease model. Obviously, social workers not wishing to use a disease concept can locate and describe points of intervention in commonplace ways, but this type of communication neither is economical nor has it led to a professional nomenclature for the kinds of problems that social workers confront. This article suggests that a promising alternative can be found by using terms associated with the concepts of social role and social system.[1]

In recent years, considerable attention has been given to the conceptual and descriptive possibilities of "role" and "system" ideas. An abundant and formidable amount of terminology has been accumulated. Although this terminology has generally been used to guide research or theory construction, it can also be used to classify the interactional problems of people with other people, the conflicts between individuals and social systems, and the functional problems of social systems themselves. By this time, a considerable number of social workers have shown an interest in the use of role and system concepts for practice theory, organizational analysis, or the description of professional efforts.[2] This article, in offering an embryo classification of role and system problems, seeks to extend this interest in a form useful to practitioners. Before presenting the classification scheme, it may be helpful to consider some issues.

Preliminary Considerations

The first of these considerations is the inherent value problem in any system of classification of disorders. Someone has to make an evaluation of a given state of affairs and decide whether that state of affairs is "good" or "bad," "functional" or "dysfunctional," "acceptable" or "unacceptable." This decision is not value free. There is no universally known and universally acceptable set of standards to follow in defining

[1]The writers are indebted to Professor Donald Lathrope of the Jane Addams Graduate School of Social Work, University of Illinois, Urbana, Illinois, for his advice, stimulation, and ideas. The work on which this article is based was supported in part by U.S. Public Health Service Grant MH 10652–04.
[2]See, for example, Helen Harris Perlman, The Role Concept and Social Casework: Some Explorations, I. The 'Social' in Social Casework, *Social Service Review,* 35:370–81 (December 1961); idem, The Role Concept and Social Casework: Some Explorations, II. What is Social Diagnosis?, ibid., 36:17–31 (March 1962); Herbert S. Strean, Role Theory, Role Models and Casework: Review of the Literature and Practice Applications, *Social Work,* 12:77–87 (April 1967); Bruce J. Biddle and Edwin J. Thomas, eds., *Role Theory: Concepts and Research* (New York: John Wiley & Sons, 1966); and Henry S. Maas, Behavioral Science Bases for Professional Education: The Unifying Conceptual Tool of Cultural Role, in *Proceedings of the Interdisciplinary Conference on Behavioral Concepts Which Can be Applied to Education for the Helping Professions* (Washington, D.C.: Howard University School of Social Work, 1958), pp. 11–22.

the most desirable state of being for people or societies. Some arbitrariness is, therefore, unavoidable as the social worker examines his client's life situation and tries to evaluate it. The social worker (or psychologist, counselor, or psychiatrist) neither can make his decisions on the assumption that "community standards" of behavior are always definitive of "normal" behavior, nor can he always assume that the client's standards are adequate.

The writers of this article believe that the social worker should assume a somewhat neutral stance and use as a standard the notion that the most desirable state of affairs for people is one that allows maximum freedom of the individual in his personal affairs as long as he harms neither himself nor others. The most desirable society is one whose norms allow freedom and in which whole role performance requirements are clear and acceptable to the individuals in that society, and the society's structure is open so that each individual can realize his legitimate aspirations to the extent of his talent and ambition. This open view permits problems to be viewed as (1) situations in which the individual is hampered, disadvantaged, or prevented from performing legitimate roles, (2) situations in which the individual performs roles harmful to his own freedom and development or to that of others, and (3) situations in which the social system is incompatible with the needs and goals of its component participants.

In other words, the ideal state of affairs would exist when persons live with each other in a state of mutually satisfying interdependence in which these persons are able to achieve the maximum goal attainment and personal sense of satisfaction in their relationships with each other and their institutional systems. This concept, which sees accommodation and interdependence as desirable, does not rule out competition or innovation. There is no intent to see differences and uniqueness of individuals and cultural groups dissolved. This view does, however, reject open conflict as a desirable state on the grounds that it is symptomatic of a breakdown in the basic interdependence of people who should have, in the ideal state of being, legitimate and rational ways of accommodation.

This view of a societal system, then, is the value base from which this scheme is developed. It avoids the implications of disease and narrow morality and focuses on genuine problems of the structure of the social system and the functioning of interdependent individuals on the basis of utility and mutual interests to achieve goals and aspirations that can be legitimated in a free and open society. Thus, behavior is "appropriate" or "inappropriate," "functional" or "dysfunctional" according to a standard that is explicit and can be broadly acceptable. Problems of the society can be evaluated by a standard that is also explicit and acceptable over a broad range of value positions.

The second preliminary difficulty concerns the problem of labeling.[3] By focusing on a label that identifies a faulty role pattern or performance rather than on a faulty personality, the writers hope to avoid some of the negative effects of labeling. This problem may never be resolved satisfactorily, but it is worth the attempt.

The third difficulty involves the vagueness and looseness of the concepts with which the writers are dealing. Although role and system concepts have promise, it is recognized that even the most common terms lack sharp outlines. The writers, therefore, have defined their terms as reasonably and clearly as they can. Where possible, they have borrowed and acknowledged good definitions. In some cases, the definitions represent a synthesis. In other cases, they have supplied original terms or definitions. The writers do not delude themselves by thinking that this set of terms is final and complete. Their chief aim is to provide for the clinician a set of terms and some way of conceptualizing a place to start, based on how things appear to the social worker in the immediate situation he faces.

The Classification Scheme

Any attempt to classify problems is open to question. The writers, therefore, can defend this scheme only on the grounds that it is reasonable and has a certain degree of validity. The notion behind this scheme is that some kinds of problems seem to be centrally located in the individual's immediate, personal relationships, whereas others are located more distantly. There is no intent, however, to order the problems in any hierarchy of importance because a distant problem, such as the closing of a factory one thousand miles away, may be more crucial for an individual than a chronic marital problem. Three major categories will be used: (1) problems related to performance of legitimate and acceptable roles, (2) problematical roles, and (3) problems in the structure of social systems that affect the behavior of individuals. Each of these categories will be defined as it appears; all terms within each of these categories will also be defined.

One additional caution requires emphasis. This classification system does not deal with the question of etiology. It seeks only to describe the way things appear to the practitioner in a particular situation. Much of the terminology is inelegant, partly because the terms available have neither the precision nor the clean distinctions that might be desirable. They are intended only to identify a place or places to start working. For example, *lack of motivation in role performance* is a vague term

[3]See Thomas J. Scheff, *Being Mentally Ill* (Chicago: Aldine Publishing Co., 1966).

at best because the term *motivation* is only a construct for some variables that are not clearly understood. Nevertheless, motivation, whatever it means, may be the basic quality that the practitioner seizes upon as appropriate in his attempt to make an influential contribution to the worker-client relationship. The term, despite its lack of technical precision and refinement, may be useful only as a beginning point.

The writers have agreed to use the following definition of *role*. Role means a set of behaviors expected of an individual in relation to the behaviors of other persons or social objects in a given social situation. The expectation may be either on the part of oneself or others. The point is that there is no role in a vacuum. There are only roles in relation to other social objects.

Problems Related to Performance of Legitimate and Acceptable Roles

In this category, the assumption is that for some clients who use social work services, the major difficulty lies in the performance of a role (or roles) that is legitimate for both the client and the social system. There is little or no controversy about the role itself.

1. Impairment of role performance because of illness.

This term denotes a condition in which the individual is hampered in the performance of a role (or set of roles) because of either an acute or a chronic illness. For the social worker the crucial point is not the cause of the impairment, since that is the physician's focus of interest, but the social implications of the impaired role performance. Some writers use the term "impaired role" or "role impairment." These terms are rejected here because there is nothing wrong with the role—the *performance* is the thing that is impaired.

2. Incapacity for role performance.

This term describes the apparent lack of capacity for performing a legitimate or ordinary role under even favorable circumstances. It is intended to apply to situations in which the individual aspires to or attempts roles that are not within his talents or limits even though he is functioning well. An example of this situation might be that of a very frail boy who wants to be a tackle on the football team but could never make the weight. Care must be taken in using this term because so many people have the potential to achieve almost unbelievable goals, given favorable inputs to their situation.

3. Lack of motivation in role performance.

In this instance, the role is available, clear, and performable. For some reason that cannot be accounted for some other way, however, the individual simply is not willing to achieve the performance of which he is capable. Care must be taken to avoid confusing this situation with one in which the individual is prevented from role performance by some external factor. The term is intended to cover only situations in which motivation simply seems to be the only reasonable explanation for failure in performance.

4. Inadequate role perception.

The problem is that the client is failing to perform a role because he does not understand what is involved in it. If he were aware of the implications he might accept the role (or he might reject it), but he is not really cognizant of the role's requirements.

5. Role rejection.

This familiar term is used to designate a situation in which a client rather actively refuses to play a role that significant others in his social system believe they have a right to expect. The assumption here is that the rejection is something creating a problem that would not exist if the role were accepted.

6. Role abandonment.

Henry Maas considers role abandonment as a mode of adaption and adjustment.[4] It is used in this article, however, to indicate problematical behavior. The definition offered here refers to a passive giving up of a role without apparent anxiety or hostility about it. It differs from role rejection in this sense. Role rejection implies a much more active posture of the individual, whereas role abandonment refers to an extremely indifferent sort of role performance.

7. Inadequate preparation for role performance.

This term describes a problematical situation in which the person lacks the necessary preparation for playing a role that he accepts or wants to accept. There is nothing wrong either with his capacity or with his health. Rather it is simply a lack of adequate social, educational, or

[4]Maas, Behavioral Science Bases, p. 19.

technical skill that causes his unsatisfactory role performance. The use of this term assumes that resources are available either within the person or in the society to remedy the inadequacy of preparation.

8. Deficiency in role performance because of inadequate resources.

Helen Harris Perlman discusses various types of deficiencies that affect a person's ability to perform a role effectively.[5] In this article the term is used to describe interactional situations in which an individual has been unable to achieve satisfactory role performance because his immediate social system lacks the resources to allow him to perform adequately. This condition is hard to distinguish from the previous condition of inadequate preparation but differs in that, in the previous situation, the resources were available but the individual had not been satisfactorily connected to them. In the present situation the immediate lack of resources is the major problem acting as a barrier to role performance.

9. Intrarole conflict.

Intrarole conflict describes the difficulty resulting from incongruent demands imposed by a given role.[6] An example of intrarole conflict might be that of the parental role requiring that one love a child and also discipline him. Sometimes these conflicting demands within a single role contribute to poor role performance. Obviously, this term, like the others, only applies when a perceived problem results.

10. Interrole conflict.

This term denotes the conflict and the resultant problem that occurs when one person is expected either by himself or by others to play two roles that have different norm requirements. An example of this conflict is that of the young man who wishes to be a serious college student and at the same time to be thought of as a very convivial good fellow. This problem differs from that of role separation, described later, in that here the possibility exists that some accommodation is possible.

11. Interposition conflict.

Maas actually uses the term *interrole conflict* in this instance. However, although the writers wish to preserve Maa's definition, they have attached it to a different term. Interposition conflict "is a stressful condi-

---

[5]Perlman, What is Social Diagnosis?, p. 25.
[6]Alfred Kadushin, *Child Welfare Services* (New York: Macmillan Co., 1967), p. 17.

tion for two or more persons in related positions when the expectations for these positions do not complement each other as they should but rather overlap or are at cross purposes."[7] The point here is that the conflict and the difficulty arise because each of two persons has a different definition of the other's position with respect to himself. Maas gives as an example the possible conflict in relations between physicians and other professionals ancillary to medicine in the care of patients. The expectations of one person may be radically different from the expectations of another person for himself.

12. Problem of role separation.

This term describes the difficulty experienced by some people separating two or more legitimate, nonconflicting roles. Unlike role conflict, there is no juxtaposition of norm requirements. Under normal circumstances, the person plays a number of roles satisfactorily. Sometimes, however, one role seems to merge inappropriately with another. For example, a man can be a military officer and a husband at the same time. If, however, he cannot keep these roles separate, he may try to treat his wife and family as quasi-military subordinates—a treatment that would be entirely inappropriate and create a problem in role separation.

13. Incompatible roles.

Maas uses this term to cover situations in which a person is faced with two roles that are mutually exclusive and wholly incompatible.[8] This term is not the same as role conflict because in role conflict the notion is that some norm requirements of the role are mutually exclusive to norm requirements of a second role. In the case of incompatibility, the entire role is diametrically opposed to the other. For example, one cannot be a mother and a virgin at the same time. There is no hint of norm conflict here, as much as it is the totally opposite definitions that are built into the role structure itself. The difference may be academic, but this term is included because it may make a practical difference that practitioners would want to recognize.

14. Problems in role transition.

This term is used to designate those problems that occur when an individual is making a transition from one role to another and is having difficulty in so doing.[9] For example, a wife whose husband is advancing in his business or professional work may discover her situation prob-

[7]Maas, Behavioral Science Bases, p. 16.
[8]Ibid., pp. 16–17.
[9]Ibid., p. 17.

lematical because different role behavior is expected of her in the role "wife" because of the husband's social mobility.

15. Difficulty in role innovation.

This term is employed to identify the difficulty of a person who is attempting to change either the structure or the performance of a given role, but is having difficulty with the actual effort and mechanics of making the change. It differs from the previous term because the motivation for changing is within the person himself. The problem in role transition is caused by the individual's having difficulty because of the change in status or position or performance of a significant other. Role innovation identifies the shade of difference involved when the individual himself is attempting to make a significant change in role structure or performance, such as the difficulty encountered by the alcoholic, not because of his alcoholism, but because of his attempt to practice sobriety.

16. Excessive internalized role expectations of self.

Sometimes people expect more of themselves than they are capable of delivering in some area of role performance. This excessive self-demand creates its own peculiar kind of role problem and failure in performance.

17. Frustrating role expectations.

Although Maas uses this term,[10] the writers' definition of it is slightly different from his definition. It is used here to describe the personal sense of frustration and annoyance that an individual may feel because he is not able to fulfill the role expectations of another; there is no hint here about his capability of performing the role under a different set of expectations. The problem at which intervention is necessary is at the level of the expectations of the other in the case of a person who is sufficiently motivated to perform a role and is capable and prepared to do it under a different set of expectations.

18. Disturbance in role performance because of situational crisis.

This term is designed to cover the situation in which the person is unable to perform as he normally would because of some immediate crisis in his social situation. The term is not designed to include difficulty in role performance because of the person's illness or lack of preparation but

---

[10]Ibid., p. 15.

is limited to the kind of situation in which some critical incident has occurred in his immediate set of social systems or relationships and over which he has no direct control. An example of this problem is that of the person whose role performance is no longer satisfactory to himself or to others because he is out of work because of the failure of the company that had employed him. The crisis does not directly involve the person in its causative aspects, but the reaction is private and personal, because the external incident has occurred. This definition is more limited than the initial description given by Perlman in the article cited.[11]

19. Role confusion.

It is intended here to conceptualize the role performance problem of the individual who is unable to sort out the roles he is expected to play or wants to play. This term is probably deficient in the confusion not of the role but of the individual who seems not to be able to sort out the requirements of a given role.

20. Role performance retrogression.

Role retrogression is the term Maas uses for "slipping back to an earlier and, hopefully, more comfortable role when a current role is stressful."[12] Maas considers role retrogression as a mode of adaption, whereas the writers prefer to consider it a performance problem. It is true that it is an adaptive process, but it is so faulty and so filled with difficulty that it must be regarded as a point for intervention.

21. Role reversal.

This term is used here in a familiar and traditional way to indicate the problem that occurs when two persons in an interaction situation have exchanged roles in an inappropriate manner that creates trouble for them.

22. Role violation.

Here, the intention is to describe on a personal level the violation of one or more prescriptions of a socially legitimate role. It is not intended to regard role violation as a condition in which deviant behavior is present, but rather to limit this term to those situations in which the individual performs a role that is considered legitimate, but does it in such a way that he violates important norm requirements in so doing.

[11]Perlman, What is Social Diagnosis?, p. 26.
[12]Maas, Behavioral Science Bases, p. 20.

For example, the father who neglects to provide for his children according to the generally accepted beliefs and knowledge about the needs of children is performing his role as father, but he is violating the normative concepts of it in such a way to endanger the survival and development of persons dependent upon him. The role of father is not a deviant role, but is, of course, legitimate. The necessity for intervention is created by the violations of the prescriptions of the legitimate role; the father is not following a deviant role.

23. Role shock.

This term is used by Professor Donald Lathrope of the Jane Addams Graduate School of Social Work at the University of Illinois to describe a psychological shock that comes from realizing that one is unable to perform adequately in a specific role. This term thus covers the anxious or disturbed person facing some personal crisis, such as retirement, that will result in the individual's no longer being able to play a desired role and suffering as a consequence.

Problematical Roles

In this category a series of roles that in themselves seem to be problematical will be listed. The difference between this category and the one preceding is that there is not the difficulty of performance of a legitimate role but that a person is confronted with a role that is likely to cause him considerable difficulty. Liberty has been taken with the definitions of the terms in this category. Some of them have been borrowed and are used here in a sense different from that which their originators envisioned. This liberty has been taken simply to suit the convenience of the classification system and cannot be defended in any other way. The writers recognize the danger of this procedure because the terms used may have acceptable and broadly known definitions in another context. The alternative to borrowing a term and not using its original definition would be to create a new term. The difficulty with this procedure is that in the instances used here no other term seems to lend itself to the description of the problematical role being discussed. We have, therefore, taken the more dangerous alternative as the only realistic way to proceed.

1. "Roleless" role or rolelessness.

This term has been used by E. W. Burgess for the role that lacks any definition at all.[13] The lack of a set of norms constitutes a unique role

[13]E. W. Burgess, Aging in Western Culture, in *Aging in Western Societies,* ed. E. W. Burgess (Chicago: University of Chicago Press, 1960).

prescription by itself and certainly the person who is roleless has a doubtful status indeed. An example of rolelessness is the aged person with no significant interactions with his social situation.

2. Inadequate role modeling.

Inadequate role modeling describes a condition in which the client—probably a child or adolescent—lacks a relevant adult role model. The problem is with the entire role identification process for the client. This condition may not seem to fit in this general overall category, but it has been placed here because it refers to a kind of inadequate total role configuration that goes beyond a simple problem in role perform-ance.

3. Anomalous role.

This term is used to refer to persons caught in roles that are poorly shaped and whose norm requirements define a role that is outside the usual and generally satisfying modes of behavior. It probably should be parenthetically explained that this role, like some of the succeeding roles, does not adequately describe the total functioning of the person but centers on a problematical role as a point for intervention. It is the problematical role that the social worker must pay attention to as the focus for effort. It is not implied that everything the person does in some other aspects of his interactive life is faulty. The anomalous role is one that does contain some behavioral norms and expectations, but they are not as clear as they might be, and, as a consequence, the role itself is shaped in a relatively unique way for the person performing it.

The situation of the divorced person in Western society may be considered an example of anomalous role. For this role, norms that can be clearly perceived and followed either do not exist or are so circum-spect that a person cannot always dependably know what behavior is expected of him in social situations. This person is not "roleless" but simply often faces problematical situations because of the varying ex-pectations of performance associated with a role that can only be regarded as an anomaly.

4. Illicit role.

This term describes a role that, although not necessarily illegal, is never-theless clandestine and disapproved of to some degree. It is not inten-tionally implied that the social worker necessarily accepts the social disapproval of this role as a moral imperative, but he must take into account the problems of relationship that are created. Promiscuous behavior is an example of an illicit role.

5. Outsider role.

This term has been borrowed from Howard S. Becker. After considering the alternative of choosing another term, the writers have decided to use Becker's term with redefinition because it suits the notion to be expressed here very well. Becker uses the term to refer to a fairly large category of deviance. In Becker's definition, the outsider is simply a deviant from group rules.[14]

It is used in this taxonomy in a much more limited fashion. The outsider, as used here, refers to those roles of persons who are outside the general norms of a culture but only to those positions to which one must somehow make a commitment of himself. It is not intended to use it in the broadest sense to describe all who are outside the pale but only those whose roles as outsiders involve some degree of personal choice. An example of the outsider is the young person who uses drugs. A case can be made for the idea that any youngster who turns to narcotics does so because of factors in his environment. In this article the writers have rejected an unadulterated behaviorism and have postulated the notion that some degree of choice is present. The individual may have a selection to make among drugs, alcohol, suicide, or some other form of self-destructive behavior. The outsider, in the sense used here, has made a more or less conscious choice to identify himself as a specific kind of violator of customary norms, and in so doing he has accepted another set of norm requirements that he more or less actively follows. This situation is problematical in the relationship of the outsider to significant others. The social worker is agreeable to seeing outsiders, as they are viewed here, at the request of parents, husbands, wives, and other significant others.

6. Deviant role.

The term deviant role is to be reserved for those roles in which the person plays a more severely disapproved role in connection with some significant others than is true for the outsider. The deviant pursues an individual course rather than one adhering to group norms. The deviant also appears to have less conscious choice of his problematical role than does the outsider. Admittedly, the distinction between the two may often appear academic, but it is included in the belief that it may have practical usefulness. The writers consider the voyeur a deviant rather than an outsider because the voyeur behaves primarily as if he were under some compulsion. He also generally operates as an individual rather than as a member of an outside group with a set of norms

[14]Howard S. Becker, *Outsiders* (New York: Free Press of Glencoe, 1963), p. 3.

followed by a number of his fellows. The actual nature of the deviant behavior does not seem important to the writers. There is a certain common element that would be the focus of the social workers' interest; namely, the deviant will have problems with significant others as a consequence of his individual behavior rather than as a consequence of membership in an outsider group. This term is not entirely clear and there might be instances in which it would be difficult to make the distinction. For example, the solitary drinker who consumes much more alcohol than his system can tolerate might be considered a deviant, whereas the convivial drinker who has attached himself to a group that has drinking as a central activity, may, in fact, be an outsider. The writers are not altogether satisfied either with this distinction or with this and the preceding terms; however, they believe they can be useful at this time.

7. Offender role.

This role has been used by a number of writers in an entirely different context. It is the purpose of this article to restrict the use of the offender role to those persons who have more or less permanently adopted a chronic set of norms that have as their central focus the frequent breaking of legal norms. The habitual criminal and the professional criminal are both examples of the role performance elements included in this classification.

8. Stigmatized role.

This term has been borrowed from Erving Goffman.[15] It is used here to refer to that role in which the person senses a great deal of disapproval to the point of revulsion. He recognizes that people are sickened or frightened by his behavior. The behavior may or may not be illegal, but the emotion evoked as a result of the value structure of society is one of extreme distaste. The reason that the writers state this definition in this way is that it would be the stigmatic aspects of the role that would probably be the focus of social work attention. The cause of the problem is the person's image that is reflected from significant others. It is not suggested that the stigma is appropriately placed on this person, for it probably is not. The suggestion is made simply to accept the fact that there are some behaviors or conditions that most people consider so frightening or horrible that they react in a way that makes living difficult for the person possessing the stigma.

[15]Erving Goffman, *Stigma: Notes on the Management of Spoiled Identity* (Englewood Cliffs, N.J.: Prentice-Hall, 1962).

It must be recognized that a number of the roles previously described have some degree of stigma attached to them. However, the difference lies in the ways a social worker would deal with the nature of the problem. For example, in the case of the offender, it is the offensive behavior with which the social worker would try to cope. In the case of the deviant, it is the nature and type of the deviance with which the social worker would deal. In the case of the role that would be considered stigmatized, it is the stigma itself that would receive the major part of attention. In other words, the social worker would be more concerned with the behavior of significant others to the person than he would be with the behavior exhibited by the person in the stigmatized role. As an example of the kind of role that the writers believe should be included here, mention should be made of the mental patient whose symptoms are bizarre and eerie. Social work's primary role would not be to work with the symptoms themselves, but rather to try to do whatever is reasonable to help the individual receive acceptance from his family or his peers and a certain amount of understanding, rather than stigmatization.

9. Ritualistic role.

This term is intended to describe a role that seems to be totally devoid of meaning. There is practically no goal that can be reached by playing the role. Nevertheless, a person seems to continue to play the role as if it had some kind of meaning. This acting is similar to the idea expressed by the term, "ritualistic behavior," used by sociologist Robert K. Merton. An example can be suggested by the rather meaningless kind of role played by the chronically unemployed man who habitually makes attempts to look very busy and very committed to a set of norms that keeps him constantly in motion but produces limited goal attainment. The individual continues to play a very busy kind of part, but nothing ever happens as a consequence.

Problems in the Structure of Social Systems

This category includes various structural problems that seem related to difficulties faced by people in various roles. In some cases it appears that the structural problem mainly affects people as individuals, whereas in others it appears the major effect is on the group life of individuals. It is presumed that if the problem of a client or group of clients can be identified in one of the subcategories in this larger category, then the major social work role is that of advocate, broker, or social change agent. In any case, the reader is reminded that this particular category does not attempt to describe the characteristics of all social systems but only those problematical aspects of structure that seem to have interest and reference for social work.

1. Unfilled status.

This condition exists when a crucial status in a social group is not filled by an occupant. It is assumed that the status in question is crucial for the operation of the group. For example, lack of adequate leadership would seem to threaten the adequacy of a group's functioning and, therefore, a group's lack of an adequate leader would be a problematical situation in a social system.

2. Disapproved group norms.

This category has an elusive "catchall" quality that is not entirely satisfying. It is intended to denote a set of group norms ranging from mildly illicit to destructively antisocial. Sometimes the social worker, particularly one working with groups, needs to recognize that the central fact for some groups is their nonconformity to legitimate cultural norms. Again, the social worker operating from the value position taken in this article, has to decide how harmful these norms are in relation to the freedom and development of the group and its members.

3. Role discontinuity.

Role discontinuity exists when there is an absence of clear and orderly developments in the training or patterning of people within the culture as these people grow into maturity. This term, which originates in the work of Ruth Benedict, is useful in describing the ambivalent position of some adolescents in the industrial society.[16] It probably should be pointed out that this problem is a system problem and therefore is included here rather than in the section dealing with problematic roles.

4. Nonavailable roles.

This difficulty can be seen in those situations where there is a lack of role or status opportunity caused by the existing structure of the social system. Quite obviously, it is crucial for the existence of the social system because no system can operate without providing roles and statuses for the people that comprise it and still remain a system.

[16]Ruth Benedict, Continuities and Discontinuities in Cultural Conditioning, *Psychiatry*, 1:161–67 (May 1938).

5. Excessive role expectations.

This term can be used to explain those situations in which occupants of various statuses within the social structure make excessive demands upon other people, particularly when these demands cannot possibly be met.[17] For example, the extremely domineering wife expects her husband to be a great lover, financially successful, highly intelligent, and handy around the house without recognizing that he lacks the potential to do so. This term corresponds roughly to excessive internalized role expectation of self at the individual level, but it locates the difficulty in a social system itself and does not consider the effect on the individual on whom the excessive demand is made. The social worker, confronted with this situation, has to make a judgment about whether the focus of his intervention is in support of the person with a role performance difficulty or whether he should attack the excessive demands by another person in the client subsystem. If the second decision were made, this term would be descriptive of the problem. If the social worker did not have access to other persons in the original client social system, he would have no other choice than to consider it an individual problem in role performance, thus focusing his interventive efforts on the role performance level, rather than on the level of the system.

6. Damaging role expectations.

This term differs from that of excessive role expectations by suggesting that there are some instances in which the social system or subsystem demands or expects role performance that would be damaging to the person of whom such performance is expected. This damage is not due to an excessive demand, but to the nature of the demand itself. The person can in fact meet these expectations, but it would be damaging for him to do so. A crude example is that of the alcoholic wife who expects her husband to go drinking with her. Although he may be capable of drinking with her, if he is also an alcoholic, the expectation is damaging to him. It seems better to provide this separate category than to have to see this kind of system expectation only as excessive. This category, therefore, has been added to the previous one.

7. Lack of purposive system orientation.

This category includes problems of social systems that occur when a system is dysfunctional because of the lack of a focus that might encourage the commitment of members and enhance group solidarity. One can argue that under these conditions a system ceases to exist. How-

[17]Maas, Behavioral Science Bases, p. 14.

ever, it is preferable to consider it as a disorder of systems on the grounds that, when a social system or group loses its purposive orientation, the system continues to operate for a time, although entropy will probably set in. By the time a social worker views such a group or system, it should be possible to be aware that the group lacks any kind of purpose or goal direction before the system shuts down.

8. Status conflict.

This term refers to conflict within a social system over the occupation of some important status, to the degree that the functioning of the system is seriously threatened. An example of status conflict might be the case of an interacting group whose leader leaves the group and conflict ensues among the other members over the status of leader. Some of this conflict may be healthy, but there is a time when the conflict among members who are seeking status that only one can actually attain will be harmful to the group.

9. Status rejection.

In this case, a social system has reached a state of dysfunction because a member with potential for filling a status within the system actively rejects such a status. The difference between this category and that of unfilled status is that in unfilled status there is no occupant. In this instance, there is a potential occupant, but he has rejected the status actively.

10. System resource deficiency.

This term designates a number of problems in which the social system itself lacks the resources to meet the needs of persons who occupy statuses within the system. It is not implied that resources cannot be created or provided, but at the moment at which the social worker views the situation a deficiency exists. This problem would probably be viewed as a system problem by a community worker but as a role performance problem of an individual by an agency serving individuals.

11. Intersystem conflict.

This condition probably relates more to the subsystems than it does to total systems. It is used to refer to the kinds of problematical situations in which two social systems are in harmful conflict because of differing values or norms. This term is borrowed from Jessie Bernard,[18] but the

---

[18]Jessie Bernard, *Social Problems at Midcentury* (New York: Rinehart & Co., 1957), p. 480.

definition has been altered to suit the purposes of this article. The intention here is to describe the situation in which social movements or interest groups are engaged in a competitive struggle for recognition, domination, or status.

12. Intrasystem conflict.

This term has been coined to cover what Ödd Ramsoy calls normative conflict.[19] Intrasystem conflict occurs when the norms of a given social system are contradictory and persons within the system are forced to make choices of following norms that are in opposition to other norms. An example of this conflict is the case of the man who by law must file an income tax return, but who by custom is encouraged to cheat on it. This problem is not an individual one, but is obviously a difficulty in the structure of the social system.

13. Role rigidity.

Role rigidity is a system problem in which the social system has so narrowly or strictly conceived a role that it can hardly be accepted by people, or it causes problems for them when they do accept it. It is the problem of a system that often establishes some kind of perfect behavior that a person cannot comfortably use as a role model. It could be argued, for example, that the concept of the American mother as a selfless, giving, martyr-like figure is an example of this type of system problem. No woman could possibly meet the norm and yet some women appear to accept this norm as one that they should meet in actual living. The consequent difficulty that they experience in their personal lives, then, is not necessarily a role performance problem, but a discrepancy between the role as the social system conceives it and the actualities of human performance. Role rigidity, therefore, has been classified as a structural problem rather than a role performance problem. When the problem is highly individualized, it would probably be considered one of excessive internalized role expectations of self.

14. Role failure.

This condition involves a role that formerly existed in a social system but is no longer viable or no longer in existence. The condition is not role performance failure, but actual failure in a role to persist in a social system. A commonplace example of role failure would be the techno-

[19]Ödd Ramsoy, *Social Groups as System and Subsystem* (New York: Free Press of Glencoe, 1963), p. 30.

logical unemployment of a young man who chose to be a steam engine mechanic in the early years of this century and now in midlife finds himself completely without a viable occupational status. He has done nothing to warrant this situation, but the invention of other forms of transportation have made the role to which he aspired no longer available in the society. This category is considered different from the non-available role category in which roles have never been in existence in sufficient quantity for persons to occupy them.

Comments

The writers of this article offer this classification system only as a trial effort. They recognize that such a system has a number of difficulties, but believe that this kind of attempt has merit to it if it enhances the abilities of social workers to locate more precise points at which their efforts should be directed. No attempt has been made to determine the kind of interventive strategy that is appropriate, given the offered terms. This determination has to be an additional chore to be worked on at a later time. It is believed that this system is a step—albeit a very small step—in a desirable direction. This scheme has now received a preliminary encouraging test to be reported in the April issue of *Social Casework* [this article follows].

Once dysfunctional role performances have been defined, as outlined in the preceding article, strategies for intervention can be pursued. In this article, Atherton et al. present a tentative scheme for relating these dysfunctional areas to worker actions. A worker must pursue a *variety* of interventive acts, each appropriate both to client needs and to the size of the system in which it is to be pursued.

Using Points for Intervention

Charles R. Atherton
Sandra T. Mitchell
Edna Biehl Schein

In a previous article the writers suggested a way of locating points for intervention in the life situations of clients by using concepts from the

Reprinted with permission of the authors and the Family Service Association of America from *Social Casework,* Vol. 52 (4), 1971, pp. 223–233.

literature on social roles and social systems.[1] The purpose of this article is to answer two questions that may have been raised by the earlier article. (1) How does the points for intervention approach work out in practice? (2) If a point for intervention can be identified, what is the appropriate role of the intervenor?

At this time the writers can give only a partial but encouraging answer to the first question. The material that follows is descriptive data that may be useful to the practitioner. In the latter part of the article a theoretical position concerning the second question is taken—a reflection of the senior author's attempt to link various roles mentioned in the professional literature with the points for intervention classification scheme. It is relevant to point out the tentative nature of this entire effort and to admit the necessity for more intensive research aimed at validation of this approach. The possible directions that research might take will be mentioned in the concluding section of this article.

Using Points for Intervention Material

Space does not permit a lengthy description of the use of the points for intervention material. Several capsulized illustrations are offered, therefore, to show how the material can be used to provide a focus for a practitioner's efforts. These case illustrations describe some of the adolescents in the caseload of one of the authors. Brief descriptions were written of the presenting problems of the caseload to which the writer had been assigned in her second-year field assignment. She then consulted the points for intervention material and applied what seemed to be the appropriate terms. The senior author was then given the same list of original descriptions and he applied terms that seemed appropriate. In all but two cases, the two raters agreed independently on the application of the appropriate terms. In each of the two remaining cases, a five-minute discussion resulted in agreement. This procedure has been described not to offer conclusive evidence of the usefulness of the classification system but rather to suggest that the scheme is ready for a more rigorous test. In the following illustrations, the terms are those that were described in the article, "Locating Points for Intervention."

Alice is a high school student who has been very active in school activities. She wants to be thought of as a leader, but she also wants to graduate. Unfortunately, she has devoted so much time to her activities that she has done poorly in her school work and may not graduate unless she can budget her time more

[1]Charles R. Atherton, Sandra T. Mitchell, and Edna Biehl Schein, Locating Points for Intervention, *Social Casework,* 52:131–41 (March 1971). The work on which these articles are based was supported in part by U.S. Public Health Service Grant MH–10652–04.

The Individual as Target

effectively. Her parents have been no help to her, and the home environment is not conducive to study *(interrole conflict)*.

Betty is an unwed mother. She has no idea of what motherhood involves, and she thinks that she really ought to graduate from high school. She tries to attend school, but her inability to arrange adequate care for her child interferes with her schooling, and she is frequently absent. The social worker's impression is that Betty's chief problem is her complete lack of preparation for the roles she is expected to fill and that she is unable to function adequately in any of them. Perhaps if she could make proper arrangements for her duties as a mother, she might be able to function better as a student *(inadequate preparation for role performance)*.

Dorothy is a young unwed mother who is also attempting to complete her high school education. She used to be in the Emotionally Mentally Handicapped program but is now enrolled in regular classes. She is doing poor work and frequently misses classes. Her major problem appears to be lack of resources to enable her to deal with her situation. She needs a tutor to help her with her class work, and no tutor seems to be readily available. The school has no pool of tutors upon which to draw. Unlike Alice, Dorothy seems to have some support from her parents and seems to be giving her baby good care with her mother's help. Since she had the baby, she has had some difficulty in getting along with her old friends, so her illicit role has complicated her situation (*deficiency in role performance because of inadequate resources* with overtones of *illicit role*).

Edward, fifteen years old, has been repeatedly picked up by police for minor delinquent acts. He refuses to attend class and consequently has been suspended from school. His attitude has made it impossible for long-range plans to be made. Before referral, he spent most of his time in roaming around the halls despite his suspension. His parents have given up emotional support, but they do continue to offer financial support. No employer will hire him because of his age *(anomalous role)*.

Frances is a high school girl whose mother wants her to behave as if she were an adult. The situation is further complicated by the mother's apparent desire to act as if she were her daughter's contemporary. The mother tends to let the daughter do as she pleases and then places a great deal of the blame on the girl if anything happens to go wrong. This mother constantly places unrealistic demands on the daughter and refuses to play the role of mother; consequently, the daughter has refused to attend school and indulges in sexually promiscuous behavior, which appears to be a means of punishing her mother. The social worker thinks that the mother's rejection of an appropriate mother role is at the heart of the problem. If the mother were to play a more adequate role at least in her daughter's eyes, Frances's unacceptable behavior would likely occur less frequently *(role rejection)*.

Gladys is a young high school student who expects too much of herself. She regards herself as a genius and attempts to intellectualize everything that she encounters, but she really does not have the intellectual skill that she thinks she possesses. She performs, however, on a fairly high level. Her parents help support this fiction by reinforcing her types of intellectual behavior but at the same time restricting more ordinary kinds of adolescent behavior. The problem is that as Gladys begins to drive herself to become even more intellectual, she finds herself further away from the ordinary concerns of family life and consequently more distant from her parents than she was before. Apparently she sees intellectual activity as a way to succeed in the world, which is true to some extent. The difficulty is that Gladys does not see any other kind of activity as being of any particular importance, which makes it difficult for her to relate to people who do not share her values and goals *(excessive internalized role expectations of self)*.

Jack is a young person in a difficult situation. He is too young to vote and to assume much responsibility, but he is old enough for the draft. He is part of a group whose norms include cutting class and frequently being absent from school. The norms of this group also include sexual promiscuity and petty thievery. Because the focus of the concern is not the group but the individual student, the social worker is not actively working with the group but rather with the individual student in the school setting. Because the social worker does not have access to the group but only to the individual student, it is necessary to consider this problem mainly in relation to the individual but still in relation to the social system of which he is a part. This student would like to finish school and to mature but is kept from doing so by being a member of a group whose norms are damaging to him. Because the locus of intervention is with an individual rather than with the group, it is necessary to regard the immediate problem that this young man faces in the damaging role expectations of the group. In following these norms he damages other sets of values that he possesses *(damaging role expectations)*.

These examples illustrate the use of the points for intervention material. Although, as indicated in the first article, these categories may lack sharp outlines, they do help the social worker to perceive the problem the client faces and to describe that problem in a relatively economical way.

To show the descriptive power of the points for intervention material, the following illustration is offered. This description is intended not as proof of the superiority of the writer's system but only as illustrative of it.

Case Illustration

Mary T is a sixteen-year-old high school dropout who believes she cannot continue to live at home. Mary lives with her divorced mother, her grandmother, and her great-grandmother. As Mary described her family, it appeared that her mother, Mrs. T, was a weak and fearful person and that her grandmother was really the head of the family. The grandmother was forever berating Mary because of her long-haired friends and had accused her of stealing, drinking, and taking drugs. Mary readily confessed to a variety of sexual contacts and admitted that she experimented with drugs. Although she was a high school dropout, she had participated in radical political activities with some college students. Mary wanted the social worker to contact her mother and persuade her to allow Mary to live with a boyfriend in a commune. The social worker refused to grant this specific request but agreed to discuss with Mary and her mother the general problem of living arrangements. Mary agreed to this plan.

This family structure including four women spanning four generations is relatively unusual even in the Midwest. The home, located in a middle-class neighborhood, is owned by the grandmother. Mary and her mother live in the house for a nominal fee, and the great-grandmother lives with them for at least eight months of the year. Mrs. T has been divorced from Mary's father for eight years.

The great-grandmother is, like many old people in the United States, roleless (rolelessness). In this family, her opinions and ideas are usually ignored. She is sometimes outraged by the actions of Mary and her mother, but this outrage has no effect on the other family members. Like many roleless people, the great-grandmother has lost the power to compel attention.

In many families, the grandmother might be roleless like the great-grandmother. However, in this family she is the strongest adult member and assumes leadership, which creates problems on two levels. First, by strongly defining her major role as that of mother, she creates a role definition problem for her adult daughter who is also a mother. At times family members, particularly Mary, dispute her role as mother and expect her to be a grandmother. The difficulty then seems to be that the grandmother is in some *interrole conflict* between her expectations of being a mother and a grandmother. This conflict seems to have a special meaning for the grandmother psychologically because, if she is forced to abandon the role of mother, she will have to slip into the more roleless role of old age, which she does not want to do.

The mother has a problem of *role confusion*. She is a divorced woman, which is an unclear status in American society. She is a dependent woman living with her wealthy and strong-willed mother. In addition, she has a daughter who demands to be protected from the unreasonable expectations of her sixty-year-old grandmother. Mrs. T's inability to function consistently as either a daughter or a mother results in anxiety and immobility. To the social worker, the mother's major problem is simply that she does not know who she is and is confused about what her role ought to be.

Mary's problem is that there are no clear roles for her in the family structure. She is a granddaughter, but she is growing older. She is a daughter, but her relationship with her mother is apparently not a normal one. Mary, too, suffers from *role confusion*.

Contact with the family was made the weekend after the first interview. Late one night Mary was picked up on a raid by the police as they searched for a runaway. Mary telephoned from the police station complaining of police brutality. (There was no evidence of any, and Mary was not charged.) Mrs. T telephoned the social worker and frantically demanded that the social worker tell her what to do about her daughter. After a lengthy discussion of whether the problem was critical enough for them to meet at lunch Monday or if it could wait until Thursday evening, Mrs. T agreed to Thursday evening. The worker was acutely aware of the degree of the woman's indecision.

Although Mary's original request concerned living independently, the events of the previous weekend focused the first joint session on the late hours Mary was keeping. Mary claimed that she would not be staying out all night if she had privacy at home and could be assured that her grandmother would not harass her. Mrs. T denied that any such harassment existed and declared that if Mary would behave herself there would be no trouble. She also wanted Mary to give her the telephone numbers of the friends she visited during the evening.

Mary refused, saying that when she had given these numbers, the grandmother would call them and threaten to get the police if Mary's friends did not tell her whereabouts. Usually the young people did not know where Mary was and complained bitterly to her about the grandmother's calls. Mrs. T then demanded that the worker insist on Mary's staying home at night. The social worker explained that her role is to help the family solve their own problems and not to force action on one family member or another. The worker then offered suggestions about how trust might be built between mother and daughter so that Mary would let her mother know where she was. Mrs. T became very angry and accused the worker of approving of her daughter's behavior, which Mary denied. The mother then continued by saying the session had accomplished nothing since the worker could not guarantee that Mary would never stay out all night. The worker acknowledged Mrs. T's frustration but stated that the problem had not started in one week, and it would not be solved that quickly either. Mrs. T agreed to return the next week. Mary was visibly pleased with the outcome of the session.

The next session was considerably less painful. Both Mrs. T and Mary seemed to realize the limitations and possibilities of family therapy. Each spoke with some affection for the other. The critical point came when Mrs. T said little could be accomplished without the participation of the other family members. Mary added that it would do little good to make plans with her mother if the grandmother pronounced a final veto. The worker had hoped that by excluding the grandmother, Mrs. T's role as mother might be enhanced. Because the family could not consider this possibility, an appointment with all the family members in the home was made for the following week.

The first session with the entire family clearly was dominated by the grandmother, who spoke at length about Mary's inappropriate behavior and character. She concluded that Mary should be sent to live with her father. Mary and her mother said little, and the great-grandmother only added less vehemently that Mary did not act like any sixteen-year-old she had known.

During the following weeks the great-grandmother did not choose to attend the meetings but watched television. The focus of the sessions was to support Mary's mother in her attempt to play the role of mother more appropriately. The grandmother never saw her actions as having any relation to Mary's. Mrs. T, however, became a little stronger in asserting herself although she always backed down if the grandmother became adamant. Mary's behavior improved so that the family approved of the worker's visits.

During the sessions, the grandmother and mother often brought up Mary's leaving school and asked the worker to influence Mary to return. Mary always said it was impossible to get appropriate courses during the second semester. The worker telephoned the school and learned that appropriate courses were available. When the information was relayed to Mary, her reaction was mixed. She was tired of being a dropout and was delighted at being able to return to school and graduate with her class. However, she also expressed the fear that, once she returned to school, the family would no longer be willing to work on problems at home. Her grandmother would continue to follow her around the house, forbid her to use the kitchen, forbid friends to visit, and force Mrs. T into a dependent position.

Mary's return to school pleased the family immensely. The worker attempted to help the family support Mary in this changed role, but they indicated that once Mary returned to school, the problem would be settled and that the services of a social worker were no longer needed.

Within a week Mary telephoned to say the situation had deteriorated. Mrs.

T no longer even attempted to intervene in her behalf. In addition, the grandmother complained daily about taking Mary to school and the sacrifices she made for her ungrateful granddaughter. She also lectured Mary nightly on how the young girl was the cause of Mrs. T's disturbed behavior.

After two weeks the school and Mrs. T telephoned to say that Mary had left school again. Mrs. T admitted that Mary was being treated unfairly at home and was prepared to try anything to remedy the situation. The school officials were surprised and concerned about Mary's leaving. She had done excellent work in school and was well liked by the students and teachers. Mary also telephoned to say she would like to return to school, but the situation at home was unbearable and she felt she was unable to stay there.

The worker telephoned the school requesting both a staff meeting with Mary's teachers and the principal and a parent conference. The family was asked to attend. Both the mother and the grandmother agreed. Mary was pleased at the news but refused to return to school until after the staff meeting; however, she kept up with her homework.

At the school staff meeting, the teachers were given a role network explanation of the family problem. They were urged to support the positive efforts of Mrs. T and to relate to her as Mary's mother. It was hoped that the teachers could support Mary's ability to play a legitimate role clearly. Although not trained in role theory, they readily grasped the simple concepts and were enthusiastic about the possibilities. The staff meeting lasted about thirty minutes.

The parent conference began by introducing the grandmother and Mrs. T to the staff. Each teacher then told about his experiences with Mary. They reported how Mary worked hard and tried to meet the students and make friends. The most outstanding characteristic was her tendency to stay after class to get to know the teacher, which few of the students did. One teacher remarked that Mary's friendliness and concern had once changed her day. Another commented that in this large high school, Mary was one of the few students he noticed. The grandmother was visibly shocked. Mrs. T was especially pleased when one teacher noted the resemblance between her and Mary.

The discussion then focused on teen-age girls in general and what they needed. One major need mentioned was privacy and independence. The rest of the conference centered on Mary's privacy at home. Mrs. T said that, with family cooperation, Mary could have a room of her own. The grandmother did not object until it was suggested that Mary be permitted to do anything she wanted with the room, including allowing it to be messy, locking the door, and decorating it as she wished. The teachers were supportive, and Mrs. T kept insisting that Mary have these rights; finally the grandmother gave in. Mrs. T seemed to find strength that she had not had before. She brought up the grandmother's shouting at Mary, which she thought was unnecessary. She talked of Mary's need to have friends visit occasionally. It appeared that Mrs. T wanted to talk everything out immediately. She did not appear unreasonable, and she was supported by glances and comments by the teachers. Finally, the grandmother announced she had a previous appointment and excused herself. During the final part of the meeting, the teachers and Mrs. T talked about Mary and child-rearing practices and problems. Mary returned to school the next day.

The worker called Mrs. T and congratulated her for her effective playing of the mother role. Mrs. T was clearly pleased with herself. She suggested that family sessions be held weekly to insure the continuance of the plan.

With a few minor crises, the weekly sessions went smoothly. The grandmother's control decreased until Mrs. T and Mary were the dominant members. Mary continued to do excellent work in school and set up her own curfew.

Although it was a little later than both the grandmother and the mother would like, Mary was consistent and always let them know where she could be reached. Mrs. T began to assert herself more and became increasingly aware of her appearance. She started dressing fashionably—much to Mary's pleasure.

The communication between Mary and her grandmother improved. The great-grandmother began to speak to Mary again although she disapproved of her dress and boyfriends. The worker adopted a less directive and a more supportive role. The sessions became shorter and more jovial. The final decision to be made was whether Mary should go away during the summer to a service camp before entering her last year of high school. Her long-range plan was to attend a state university.

This family was seen for six months. There was a decreased amount of antisocial and disruptive behavior by Mary. Mrs. T improved in her manner of dressing and became a more aggressive family member. The grandmother also was better off because she no longer felt the need to continue to live in a state of *interrole conflict* now that her daughter was successfully functioning as a mother for Mary.

It cannot be proved that this change did not occur as a result of maturation or chance or that it is not a temporary change. Nor can it be proved that all problems can be solved by conceptualizing with role theory. Another method might have been just as successful.

The writers believe, however, that by using role theory, a realistic appraisal of the family could be made. By analyzing the role structure of the family and by identifying possible problematic roles or problematic performance of roles, the worker was able to focus immediately on the problem, and, as a result, keep the clients from premature termination. The time spent in getting lengthy social histories of questionable value was eliminated. The social worker had prevented the clients from wandering about without direction during the sessions. Having a role theory framework, however, did not inhibit client self-determination.

Role theory provides an easily taught way of understanding human problems and can be presented to nonprofessionals (as in the session with the teachers). The use of role theory does not guarantee success in all cases, but, if it is used wisely, it can be effective.

Roles Taken by the Social Worker

The preceding material illustrates the way in which role and system concepts can be integrated into social work practice. It appears to the writers that this type of practice lends itself to finding points at which to begin the intervention process without resorting to a medical model using a disease metaphor. In order to complete the description of the use of the points for intervention material, consideration will now be given to the roles that can be taken by the intervenor once he has determined on a suitable point for intervention.

A number of roles have been attributed to the social worker and offered as if those roles represented the totality of social work activity. It is probably more helpful to speak of the social work "role-set"[2]—a range of role relationships peculiar to the position of social worker. Accordingly, it is assumed that what must be related to the points for intervention categories is a set of roles that the social worker should be prepared to play. The assumption is made here that the social worker should be able to assume any role that is appropriate as he perceives the nature of the presenting problem, rather than to play only one role despite the differences in the presenting problems. It is usually not helpful to a client's problem for the worker always to play the role of psychosocial therapist or always to play the role of advocate. It is not helpful either for the worker to shift between the roles of therapist or social activist.[3] The social worker's role-set includes a wide and varied range of roles.

In the following chart, an attempt has been made to suggest a central role that should be taken by the social worker for each term in the points for intervention scheme. The worker's assuming a particular role does not exclude the possibility that certain facets of other roles would also be called into play. Some of the material may seem to be over-simplified, but it allows a set of rules to be located and made available for discussion. The chart attempts to include all possible roles that can be assumed by any social worker, regardless of setting or field of practice. Clearly, the chart must be read selectively, and the social worker should easily be able to select the roles appropriate to his setting; some imagination, however, may be required.

Conclusion

This article has attempted to carry the points for an intervention scheme further by examining the roles that the social worker might assume in dealing with the problems as presented. The connections between problems and roles are tentative and often uncertain. If the role and system terms are to be of practical use to social workers in the future, there must be (1) clear specifications of the components of the appropriate interventive roles and (2) research that supplies answers

[2]See Robert K. Merton, The Role-Set: Problems in Sociological Theory, *British Journal of Sociology*, 8:111–16 (January 1957).
[3]The writers are deliberately excluding such positions as administrator, supervisor, and social work educator because their focus is on practice.

to the question of whether the assumption of a specific role, depending upon the problem, enables the social worker to offer more rewarding service for the client.

The writers believe, on the basis of their limited evidence, that the specifications of a client's problems in these terms allows a more precise focus for effort. They contend that even this limited specification of the roles in the role-set of the social worker helps the social worker to organize his effort into a more coherent posture than was possible with a dichotomous concept of the social worker as either therapist or social activist.

Problems Related to Performance of Legitimate and Acceptable Roles

Points for intervention	Worker's role	Appropriate activity
1. Impairment of role performance because of illness	Broker (or referral agent)	Refers client to appropriate medical or rehabilitative service as needed
	Interpreter	Interprets (puts in symbols meaningful to client) the social implications of illness or treatment
	Psychosocial counselor	Offers empathy, encouragement, allows ventilation of feelings, and otherwise follows traditional, well-known role of psychosocial counselor
2. Incapacity for role performance	Resource person	Suggests alternative roles that client could perform and helps client find alternative goals that allow him to attain his goals of status, achievement, or performance
3. Lack of motivation in role performance	Sociobehavioral counselor	Shapes appropriate behavior by providing positive reinforcement for behaviors consistent with the person's desired performance (See Edwin J. Thomas, Selected Sociobehavioral Techniques and Principles: An Approach to Interpersonal Helping, *Social Work*, 13:12–26 [January 1968].)
4. Inadequate role perception	Interpretor or Educator	Interprets details and implications of a given role that client wants or is expected to play; teaches role components, such as how to be a good mother
5. Role rejection	Sociobehavioral counselor	Reinforces behavior that increasingly approximates the desired behavioral components of the rejected role
	Mediator	Helps the client find a dignified and minimally damaging way out of the system that expects role acceptance; helps the client explain his role rejection to the family or other group in which he is rejecting the role in terms that they can accept; acts as a mediator (See William Schwartz, The Social Worker in the Group, *Social Welfare Forum 1961* [New York: Columbia University Press, 1961], pp. 146–77.)
6. Role abandonment	Mediator	Acts as a negotiator between the client and the system in which he is unable to participate freely and creatively

The Individual as Target

Points for intervention	Worker's role	Appropriate activity
7. Inadequate preparation for role performance	Educator or Broker	Teaches skills for role performance or refers to appropriate social resource that, through training in skill, knowledge, or art, can prepare the client for the desired role
8. Deficiency in role performance because of inadequate resources	Advocate or Service developer	Acts as the client's agent in trying to persuade or force the community to provide an appropriate resource or, if feasible, to develop the service within existing frameworks (See Mary J. McCormick, Social Advocacy: A New Dimension in Social Work, *Social Casework*, 51:3–11 [January 1970]; and Francis P. Purcell and Harry Specht, The House on Sixth Street, *Social Work*, 10:69–84 [October 1965].)
9. Intrarole conflict	Crisis intervenor	(See Martin Strickler, Applying Crisis Theory in a Community Clinic, *Social Casework*, 46:150–54 [March 1965]; and Martin Strickler and Jean Allgeyer, The Crisis Group: A New Application of Crisis Theory, *Social Work*, 12:28–32 [July 1967].)
10. Interrole conflict	Crisis intervenor	Same as in *intrarole conflict*
11. Interposition conflict	Mediator	Mediates the problem involving two persons with differing expectations of each other's position
12. Problem of role separation	Interpreter	Interprets to the client the inappropriate merging of roles that cause his difficulty
13. Incompatible roles	Crisis intervenor	Same as in *intrarole conflict*
14. Problems in role transition	Crisis intervenor	Same as in *intrarole conflict*
15. Difficulty in role innovation	Crisis intervenor	Same as in *intrarole conflict*
16. Excessive internalized role expectations of self	Psychosocial counselor	Uses the traditional insight development counseling that social workers universally used to apply to all problems
17. Frustrating role expectations	Psychosocial counselor	Relieves the situation by helping to develop insight on the part of the significant other who is making frustrating demands on the client
18. Disturbance in role performance because of situational crisis	Crisis intervenor	Plays an assertive role to give direction and specific help to relieve the problems of client's situation, such as a new job, a place to live, money (See David Hallowitz et al., The Assertive Counseling Component of Therapy, *Social Casework*, 48:543–48 [November 1967]. Hallowitz uses his approach in emotional crisis, but it clearly is adaptable to the situational crisis.)
19. Role confusion	Psychosocial counselor or Crisis intervenor	Clarifies the roles that are confused, allowing the client to make a more informed choice
20. Role performance retrogression	Sociobehavioral counselor	Same as in *lack of motivation in role performance*
21. Role reversal	Mediator	Attempts, through what can best be described as a bargaining process, to induce a reasonable compromise between the parties involved

Using Points for Intervention

Points for intervention	Worker's role	Appropriate activity
22. Role violation	Sociobehavioral counselor	Uses behavioral norms as goals; in the context of family counseling, uses sociobehavioral techniques to help with problems of child neglect, marital infidelity, or some other violation of a legitimate role (See Thomas, Selected Sociobehavioral Techniques; and David Hallowitz, The Problem-Solving Component in Family Therapy, *Social Casework*, 51:67–75 [February 1970].)
23. Role shock	Crisis intervenor	Attempts to cushion the shock by enabling the client to find alternate meaningful roles

Intervention in Problematical Roles

1. Rolelessness	Broker or Referral agent	Helps to find some facility or group in which roleless people can find meaningful roles (For the best resource, see Frank Riessman, The "Helper" Therapy Principle, *Social Work*, 10:27–32 [April 1965].)
2. Inadequate role modeling	Role model or Broker	Serves as a role model himself or refers the client to a facility, agency, or group that offers role models
3. Anomalous role	Catalyst	Uses David Hallowitz's "problem-solving" method as the best approach to the person suffering from the difficulties of an anomalous role (See Hallowitz, The Problem-Solving Component.)
4. Illicit role	Group counselor	Serves as group counselor to offer services to persons ensnared in illicit roles
5. Outsider role	Broker	Refers client to a "helper" group, such as Alcoholics Anonymous and Synanon
6. Deviant role	Sociobehavioral counselor	Same as in *role violation*
7. Offender role	Sociobehavioral counselor	Same as in *role violation*
8. Stigmatized role	Advocate	Represents the client in dealing with significant others
9. Ritualistic role	Sociobehavioral counselor	Helps on the behavioral level, rather than through insight development, those who, according to the old medical model, are classified as character disorders

Problems in the Structure of Social Systems

1. Unfilled status	Catalyst	Same as in *anomalous role*
2. Disapproved group norms	Sociobehavioral group counselor	Adapts Thomas's ideas to working with the group whose norms are causing them trouble

The Individual as Target

Points for intervention	Worker's role	Appropriate activity
3. Role discontinuity	Agent of social change	Focuses attention on the inconsistencies and discontinuities in society; must use creativity to perform the major professional role in a social change or social action framework (For an excellent discussion of the issues and problems involved in this professional role, see Charles S. Levy, The Social Worker as Agent of Policy Change, *Social Casework*, 51:102–108 [February 1970].)
4. Nonavailable roles	Advocate or Change agent	Same as in *role discontinuity*
5. Excessive role expectations	Advocate or Mediator	Gives the client faced with excessive demands support and direct help in defending himself psychologically; relieves the pressure on the client by using mediation techniques
6. Damaging role expectations	Advocate or Mediator	Same as in *excessive role expectations*
7. Lack of purposive system orientation	Catalyst	(For a discussion of the role of catalyst, see David Hallowitz et al., The Assertive Counseling Component.)
8. Status conflict	Crisis intervenor (with group skills)	Uses the methods and strategies usually discussed under the banner of crisis intervention
9. Status rejection	Catalyst	Creates enough tension in the system for galvanizing a potential occupant into assuming the status that he has been rejecting
10. System resource deficiency	Collective bargainer	(For an excellent discussion of the potential of this role, see George A. Brager and Valerie Jorrin, Bargaining: A Method in Community Change, *Social Work*, 14:73–83 [October 1969].)
11. Intersystem conflict	Mediator	Same as in *role rejection*
12. Intrasystem conflict	Agent of social change	Brings conflicts to society's attention and offers means for bringing about change that reduces the contradictions
13. Role rigidity	Agent of social change	Works toward changing the social definition of the problematical roles so that they are not as rigidly defined and consequently hard to play
14. Role failure	Broker	Directs people to other roles or to training that will equip them for other roles

Values and theories of treatment are but two of the many influences upon social work practice with individuals. When these multiple influences are brought together, a model for practice can be developed. Reid outlines one such model that incorporates many of the notions that were spelled out in more detail in the preceding articles in this chapter.

Target Problems, Time Limits, Task Structure

William J. Reid

A group of faculty and students at the School of Social Service Administration has been engaged in developing and testing a particular system of brief, time-limited casework.[1] In this treatment design, the caseworker's interventions are concentrated on helping individuals and families work on specific target problems for which they expressly want help. The course of treatment normally comprises from eight to twelve interviews conducted over a two- to four-month period. The projected limits of treatment are worked out by the caseworker and clients during the first or second interview.

Treatment is organized around a task or set of tasks that the client agrees to try to carry out as a means of alleviating problems. A task represents action the client might be able to take, both on his own and through the caseworker as his agent, to improve his situation. The caseworker's treatment goal is to help the client carry out agreed-upon tasks and his interventions are addressed almost exclusively to that end.

Unlike some brief treatment models, which are designed for use with clients who meet certain criteria, short-term task-centered casework is offered as a "first-line" treatment modality for the great majority of clients in need of casework services. This position reflects our conviction that most clients whom caseworkers have occasion to serve can be given optimal help through planned short-term methods.[2]

This paper will be devoted to a consideration of three sets of theoretical formulations underlying this treatment system: those concerning

Reprinted from *Journal of Education for Social Work*, Vol. 8, No. 2, Spring 1972, pp. 58–68, with permission of The Council on Social Work Education.

[1] This system will be presented in detail in William J. Reid and Laura Epstein, *Task Centered Casework* (New York: Columbia University Press, forthcoming).

[2] This and other positions taken in this paper represent points of view of the writer and Laura Epstein, and not necessarily those of other faculty and students involved in work on the treatment system.

target problems, time limits, and task structure. It is hoped that a discussion of what we have arrived at, and why, in respect to these components will be of interest not only to those with an investment in short-term treatment but also to those concerned about the issues of problem identification, service duration, and treatment strategy in casework theory and practice in general.

Target Problems

Following the work of Helen Perlman, we have taken the concept of "problem" as the means to define the targets of change in our theoretical formulations.[3] In our model, casework intervention is aimed at problem reduction, even though the client's behavior and his situation may need to undergo change in order for the problem to be alleviated.

We have developed a tentative problem typology, one designed to identify the major kinds of target problems to which our model is addressed. Since the model itself is intended for use with most clients who come into contact with caseworkers, the problem typology is broad in scope. However, it lacks certain attributes of an ideal taxonomy; it is not exhaustive nor is it built on well-defined bases of classification. It seemed more sensible to try to conceptualize certain typical problems in a rough but useful way rather than to attempt to develop a more technically perfect but less practical scheme. It is important to keep in mind that we are attempting to classify problems, not clients. Obviously, clients may have more than one problem in this scheme. Also, our interest is in *target* problems, those difficulties to which casework intervention in our model is actually addressed.

We have thus far identified seven major problem groupings. Each category will be described briefly.

1. Interpersonal Conflict

Included in this category are problems of conflict within families (between husband and wife, parent and child, or siblings) and outside of the family context (between teacher and pupil, doctor and patient, employer and employee, and the like). While conflict may have its source in the needs, personality characteristics, role expectations, and behavior of each participant, it cannot be properly viewed in terms of these factors alone. It must be seen as the product of interaction between the participants, of how A behaves toward B which in turn causes B to behave in a certain way toward A, and so on.

[3]Helen Harris Perlman, *Social Casework, A Problem-solving Process* (Chicago: University of Chicago Press, 1957).

2. Dissatisfaction in Social Relations

An individual may not be experiencing conflict with another, yet still may be troubled by certain aspects of his interpersonal relations. A problem of this kind is centered in the individual client rather than between two clients. The client usually perceives lacks or excesses in his interactions with others. For example, he may feel that he is not sufficiently assertive, that he is excessively shy or dependent, or that he is overly aggressive.

3. Problems with Formal Organizations

Problems of this type, like problems of interpersonal conflict, occur between the client and a specified other, although in the present instance the client's antagonist is more properly viewed as an organization rather than as an individual. For example, an organization may not be providing services or resources to which the client thinks he is entitled or an individual and an organization may be in conflict over the fate of someone for whom both have responsibility, as may occur between a parent and a school or a relative and a hospital.

4. Difficulties in Role Performance

If the client's major concern is his difficulty in carrying out a particular social role, then his problem falls in this category. The problem is defined by a gap between how the person actually executes his role and how he would like to. In problems of family relations, it may be hard to decide whether a difficulty is best classified as one of interpersonal conflict or one of role performance, since there may be elements of both types of problems. If two family members perceive a shared relational problem, interpersonal conflict would be the usual classification, since it is unlikely that each would view the problem as a deficiency in his own role behavior. The role performance category is used most often when only one member in a disturbed relation perceives a problem.

5. Problems of Social Transition

Problems associated with social transitions—that is, with movement from one social position, role, or situation to another—are of two types. One concerns dilemmas about potential changes: whether an unwed, pregnant girl will keep or surrender her future child; whether or not a wife will leave her husband. The client's uncertainties about what course to pursue constitute the focus of concern. The other type occurs after a change has been decided upon, as in the case of a patient ready for discharge or an older person who has chosen to enter a residential home. Lack of information and resources, ambivalence about the impending change, and inability to do the necessary planning unaided are among the specific problems that are likely to arise.

6. Reactive Emotional Distress

Anxiety, depression, or other expressions of disturbed affective states may accompany each of the problems that have been described thus far. In problems of reactive emotional distress, however, the client's *major* concern is with his feelings themselves rather than the situation that may have given rise to them. In order to be classified in the present category, his distress must be reactive to a specific event or set of circumstances that can be readily identified, such as the death of a family member, loss of status, financial difficulties, or illness.

7. Inadequate Resources

Target problems in this category arise when the client lacks tangible or specific resources: that is, he is in need of money, housing, food, transportation, a job. Needs of this kind do not in themselves, however, make *target* problems; they become so only if the caseworker is in a position to provide the client with the resources he wants or to help him secure them through systematic effort.

Within these general categories fall the problems to which our model is addressed. In order for a problem to be considered appropriate, however, it must meet three additional requirements.

First, we require that the client himself explicitly acknowledge the problem and express a willingness to work on it. This does not necessarily mean that the client needs to seek out casework help for a well-defined problem. He may come at the insistence of others or may be sought out by the caseworker. Initially, he may not recognize the problems he wishes to solve, but we do require that very soon in the client-caseworker encounter the client recognize a problem of concern to him. A target problem must then be one the client himself perceives as a problem. It may not be the one that a referring organization had in mind, nor the one that the caseworker views as the most important, but it does represent, by definition, some difficulty that the client wishes to alleviate. In our judgment, this quality alone makes the problem worthy of full attention. It is from the problems as expressed by the client that the target problems are selected, with the greatest weight given to that problem of paramount concern to the client.

By taking this position we seek to avoid certain practices that we consider generally unrewarding for both caseworker and client. One such practice consists of fruitless and time-consuming efforts to engage semi-captive clients in helping relationships that they have not asked for, do not want, and probably cannot use.

Another practice we wish to avoid is what we refer to as "double agenda" casework. The client may indeed acknowledge a problem, but the caseworker and agency may see him as having other problems, usually of a graver sort, that are more deserving of attention. Thus, the

problem of concern to the client does not become the target of intervention; the target rather becomes some underlying difficulty that the
client is not aware he has or at any rate has not asked for help with.
The client pursues his agenda, which may call for obtaining a needed
resource or securing help with an immediate problem, while the caseworker doggedly pursues a different agenda, namely one of trying to
get the client to see the "real" problem underneath it all.

A second requirement for a target problem in our model is this: the
client should be in a position to take action to alleviate the problem,
with the caseworker serving as his agent in this task. This requirement
asks that the problem to be dealt with fall within the scope of the
combined resources of the client and caseworker, otherwise there is
nothing with which to hit the target. Very often clients present caseworkers with problems that fail to meet this requirement, and very often
caseworkers seem to act as if they accept such problem definitions. This
is particularly true in problems of family relations, where there is a
general tendency for clients to define problems primarily as difficulties
in the behavior of other family members rather than as problems in their
own behavior. As long as the clients define their problem in these
terms, there is little basis for constructive action on the part of either
client since each regards the necessary action as coming from the
other. If the caseworker gives tacit acceptance to these definitions by
not challenging them, then he is trapped in a hopeless double agent
role.

A common strategy in long-term treatment is to accept such definitions passively until a "relationship is established," then eventually to
try to help the client understand his own contribution to the problem
and to discover ways of acting differently. There is no time available
in short-term work for such a gradualistic approach and, in our view,
this is just as well since we think it is counter-productive in any case.
Until an appropriate target problem has been defined with the client
in such situations, there is little basis for meaningful client-worker communication. Moreover, the caseworker's tacit acceptance of the client's
view that the problem resides exclusively in another person may serve
to reinforce this view, making the job of changing it all the more difficult
later on. We suggest that the caseworker and the client identify a
problem that the client can act on at the beginning of contact, usually
no later than the second interview, and not to proceed further until such
a problem is identified.

What we have said in respect to the second requirement in no way
contradicts our position that the caseworker should give priority to the
target problem as perceived by the client. The second requirement
arises only when the client in fact does not perceive a problem that

constitutes an appropriate target of intervention. Both requirements add up to asking the caseworker to address his efforts to a problem the client both wants to work on and is able to work on.

Our third requirement is that the problem be relatively limited and specific in nature, an essential criterion in short-term models, and, we would suggest, a desirable one for casework practice in general. But such a standard is meaningless unless it can be defined, and this is difficult to do on an abstract level. Perhaps we can convey an impression of our conception of problem scope by considering the two categories—interpersonal conflict and role performance—in which problems are likely to be defined in rather global terms. Problems on the order of a breakdown in communication between husband and wife or inadequacies in carrying out the maternal role are too global to be acceptable in our system. Problems of interpersonal conflict should be specified in terms of particular issues around which conflict occurs, and problems of role performance should be specified in terms of the particular aspects of the role that is affected. Thus, a target problem might concern conflict between husband and wife over the disciplining of their son or the inability of a mother to provide adequate physical care for her sixteen-month-old infant. We are not asking simply for a certain way of recording problems; rather, we are asking that the targets of intervention themselves be sharply limited.

It may seem to some that we are being overly restrictive, if not precious, in our insistence that the target problem be one that the client expresses a willingness to work on, can do something about with the help of the caseworker, and that is of limited scope. We would say, rather, that these requirements reflect the limitations of casework as an agent of change. We assume that casework may be effective with problems so defined, though we have no incontrovertible evidence that this is so. If one wishes to assume a broader range of effectiveness for casework, then the burden of proof is greater, we think. There is certainly little evidence to suggest that casework can bring about significant change with clients who do *not* express a clear desire to work on problems that the caseworker wishes to pursue. If casework has such a capability, one would expect it to emerge in studies in which casework service is offered to clients without self-perceived problems on which they expressly wish to work. Experimental tests of this casework approach, such as those reported in *Girls at Vocational High*[4] and "The Chemung County Evaluation,"[5] have failed to demonstrate its efficacy.

---

[4]Henry Meyer, *et al., Girls at Vocational High* (Washington, D.C.: Russell Sage Foundation, 1964).
[5]David G. Wallace, "The Chemung County Evaluation of Casework Service to Multi-Problem Families," *Social Service Review,* Vol. 41 (December, 1967), pp. 379–389.

Time Limits

Efforts to limit treatment to brief and fixed spans of time have always engendered controversy among caseworkers from the inception of the functional school to the present. In recent years, however, a fairly impressive empirical case for planned brevity has emerged from a variety of sources.

In a study I conducted with Ann Shyne, it was found that families receiving planned short-term treatment limited to eight interviews had better outcomes than a comparable group receiving open-ended treatment of much longer duration.[6] Moreover, a follow-up six months after treatment indicated that outcomes for the short-term cases proved just as durable as those of the continued treatment cases. The findings of this study can be merged with the results of other research in casework and psychotherapy to yield the following empirical generalization: improvement rates for brief, time-limited treatment are generally as good as, or better than, improvement rates for open-ended, long-term treatment.

Data on client continuance suggest that the majority of voluntary clients receiving casework or counseling receive it in short supply. One summary of such data is provided by Fowler:

Despite many sources of noncomparability, the reported rates of nonreturn to a second interview, which range from 15 to 66 percent, tend to cluster around 33 percent. About 33 percent of accepted clientele is lost after two or three interviews, and about 33 percent continue into four or more.[7]

Practically speaking, the twelve interview-four month limit which we suggest seems more than ample for most voluntary clients.

While such data offer empirical support for planned short-term treatment approaches, they provide no theoretical rationale. The lack of a satisfactory theoretical explanation for the advantages of planned brevity has made it particularly hard for many practitioners to see value in brief treatment methods. Practitioners tend to be guided more by theory than research, and prevailing casework theory suggests that adequate help for most clients may require a considerable period of time.

In searching for a theoretical rationale for planned brevity, one turns inevitably to the question of the changes we are trying to bring about through casework. To put this question in terms more relevant to our

---

[6]William J. Reid and Ann W. Shyne, *Brief and Extended Casework* (New York: Columbia University Press, 1969).
[7]Irving A. Fowler, "Family Agency Characteristics and Client Continuance," *Social Casework,* Vol. 48 (May, 1967), pp. 271–277.

purposes: How long does it take to achieve the kind of changes that are possible through casework? Obviously the answer depends on what we conceive our targets to be. If our targets are considered to be, as they are in our treatment system, certain kinds of problems, then our interest is in the change processes that characterize these problems. In general, to the extent that casework is viewed as addressed to problem-solving, then the question of problem change becomes paramount. Casework theory has tended to hold up the problem as the target of change but then to rely on theories of change in personality, attitudes, or behavior rather than to attempt to develop a theory of change strictly pertinent to the presumed targets of our intervention.

The way in which the targets of effective casework intervention have been defined in our system serves as a basis for some formulations about how problems change, either with or without the help of professional intervention. Change in the kind of problems we have defined—when I speak of "problems" I will be referring to these—can be characterized in many ways. We propose that change in such problems has three important characteristics: first, these problems are more likely to undergo change than to remain static; second, change is likely to be in the direction of problem reduction; third, the span of time in which most change is likely to occur is relatively brief, generally not more than a few months.

At a theoretical level these characteristics may be considered reflections of the systemic properties of the human behavior and social environments from which the problems emerge. The individual who acknowledges a problem is in a state of disequilibrium, which leads him to take action to resolve it. This push toward action is a critical feature of the homeostatic mechanisms that are called into play when problems arise. Since our concern is only with those problems that the client is willing to solve, the willingness itself is evidence that he is ready to take corrective action. Since the client's action is in the direction of problem-reduction and since forces in his environment are often directed to the same purpose, most problems do become alleviated. When this happens, the client's own push for change is reduced, since it has accomplished its purpose.

We are suggesting a considerably broader application of system theory to problem change than one finds in crisis theory. Crisis theory seems to require that equilibrium be upset by some identifiable hazardous event that precipitates a pronounced, if temporary, degree of disturbance in the individual.[8] Very often equilibria are upset in subtle

[8]Lydia Rapoport, "Crisis Intervention as a Mode of Brief Treatment," in Robert W. Roberts and Robert H. Nee (eds.), *Theory of Social Casework* (Chicago: University of Chicago Press, 1970), pp. 265–311.

ways and the amount of disturbance resulting may not be readily observable. For example, we are all familiar with the problem-ridden family that seems to be in a perpetual state of disequilibrium, yet on closer examination we usually find that such a family moves in and out of states of temporary equilibrium, corresponding to its movement in and out of social agencies.

What evidence do we have for these suppositions? Unfortunately not much that is directly to the point, since there has been little study of problem change *per se.* Yet the results of casework and psychotherapy research, some of which we have cited in a different context, offer support for our general thesis. First, clients who seek help at social agencies and who generally do not continue beyond a few months might be interpreted to mean that most clients, often aided by casework, experience problem relief rather quickly, at least to the point to attenuate motivation for further help. This interpretation is strengthened by the findings of follow-up studies of clients who terminate after only a few interviews. For example, in a study of 166 short contact cases, which were followed up from three to six months after termination, Kogan found that the majority of clients reported that their initial problems had at least partially cleared up.[9]

Second, studies of the outcomes at closing of brief, time-limited casework and psychotherapy, varying in duration from a few weeks to a few months, also shed light on the question of problem-change. Improvement rates reported by such studies vary from 66 percent to over 90 percent, with a median improvement rate in excess of 75 per cent.[10] Most individuals and families treated were seen either for problems falling within our conception of target problems or for psychiatric problems generally considered to be more intractable. Although treatment may have promoted recovery, it would be naive to assume that

[9]Leonard S. Kogan, "A Study of Short-Term Cases at the Community Service Society of New York" (New York: Institute of Welfare Research, Community Service Society, October, 1957). (Mimeo.)

[10]This statement is based on the combined results of the following studies: John M. Schlien, "Comparison of Results with Different Forms of Psychotherapy," in Gary E. Stollak, Bernard C. Guerney, Jr., and Meyer Rothberg (eds.), *Pyschotherapy Research* (Chicago: Rand McNally, 1966); E. Lakin Phillips and Margaret S. H. Johnston, "Theoretical and Clinical Aspects of Short-Term Parent-Child Psychotherapy," *Psychiatry,* Vol. 17 (August, 1954), pp. 267–275; Leopold Bellak and Leonard Small, *Emergency Psychotherapy and Brief Psychotherapy* (New York: Grune and Stratton, 1965); Louis A. Gottshalk, Peter Mayerson, and Anthony A. Gottlieb, "Prediction and Evaluation of Outcome in an Emergency Brief Psychotherapy Clinic," *The Journal of Nervous and Mental Disease,* Vol. 144 (February, 1967), pp. 77–95; Marjorie K. Hare, "Shortened Treatment in a Child Guidance Clinic: The Results of 119 Cases," *British Journal of Psychiatry,* Vol. 112 (1966), pp. 613–616; Mordecai Kaffman, "Short-Term Family Therapy," Howard J. Parad (ed.), *Crisis Intervention: Selected Reading* (New York: Family Service Association of America, 1965); Edward Murray and Walter Smitson, "Brief Treatment of Parents in a Military Setting," *Social Work,* Vol. 8 (April, 1963), pp. 55–61; Libbie G. Parad and Howard J. Parad, "A Study of Crisis-Oriented Planned Short-Term Treatment, Part II," *Social Casework,* Vol. 49 (July, 1968), pp. 418–426; William J. Reid and Ann W. Shyne, *op cit.,* pp. 96–134, and Robert Shaw, Harry Blumefeld, and Rita Senf, "A Short-Term Treatment Program and Its Relevance to Community Mental Health," paper presented at annual meeting of the American Orthopsychiatric Association, March 20, 1965 (mimeo). Used with permission of author.

it was the only factor. A more reasonable interpretation would be that treatment augmented naturally fast-moving processes of problem change.

Finally, if problems tend to change rapidly and in a positive direction, one would expect to find that the bulk of improvement in long-term therapy would occur during the early portion of treatment. There is evidence that this is so. In their extensive review of psychotherapy research, Meltzoff and Kornreich conclude that: "psychotherapy, when successful, achieves its major gains relatively early."[11] Sachs, Bradley, and Beck investigated client progress after only five interviews in open-ended treatment cases in a family agency. Their evaluation of detailed worker and client ratings led them to conclude that "there was substantial and consistent evidence that progress in problem coping and/or functioning did occur within five interviews in about half the cases."[12] In only one case in ten was the balance of change in a negative direction.

In sum, while there is a lack of research on problem change that is free of treatment effects, the findings of studies of individual and family change associated with treatment suggest that in the majority of cases problem alleviation occurs fairly soon after problem onset. This does not mean, of course, that all problems follow this pattern or that those that do are substantially resolved within a brief period of time. Our central argument is that the greatest amount of problem change is likely to occur early and this amount is usually sufficient to restore equilibrium and reduce the client's incentive for further change.

These considerations have led us to view the function of casework as stimulating, quickening, and augmenting the kind of processes that naturally characterize problem change. With few exceptions, the success of the caseworker's intervention is dependent upon the existence of these processes in much the same way that medical treatment must rely upon the recuperative powers of the body, and education on the student's ability to learn. If the push for change in target problems is short-lived, then the maximum effectiveness of casework intervention is of equally short duration.

Now clients may continue in casework relationships beyond the point of diminishing problem change and of diminishing treatment effectiveness. There may remain some client motivation to work on larger problems, the caseworker may hold out the promise that much more can be accomplished if they stick with it, and the relationship itself may

[11]Julian Meltzoff and Melvin Kornreich, *Research in Psychotherapy* (New York: Atherton Press, Inc., 1970), p. 357.

[12]Joel G. Sacks, Panke M. Bradley, and Dorothy Fahs Beck, *Clients' Progress Within Five Interviews: An Exploratory Study Comparing Caseworkers' and Clients' Views* (New York: Family Service Association of America, 1970). (Mimeo)

provide some psychological comforts to both caseworker and client. In some situations focus for change may be sustained for longer periods of time, accounting perhaps for the occasional very successful long-term case. It is perhaps our gratification with this kind of case that causes us to overlook the vastly larger number of cases in which continued treatment does not lead to progressive gains and to overlook the fact that treatment carried beyond the point of diminishing returns contains certain losses: unrewarded worker and client effort, client dissatisfactions and feelings of failure, and questionable dependency relationships. We also tend to ignore the reality that the client's striving for change is the force that provides the caseworker with the opportunity to stimulate new understandings and action. When this striving comes to an end, the caseworker's technical repertoire soon becomes exhausted as he finds himself repeating once again to his client the same interpretations, the same reassurance, the same advice.

The length of treatment can be kept short, of course, without the imposition of fixed durational limits, which strike many practitioners as arbitrary and restrictive. Why have such limits and, if we need them, how can they be used to the best advantage? The main function they serve in our treatment system, and perhaps in short-term treatment systems generally, is to provide a means of regularizing the length of treatment relationships lacking natural end-points. Even though short-term treatment may be directed at relatively specific goals, it is often difficult to determine when such goals have been achieved to a satisfactory degree, particularly when target problems concern interpersonal conflict or role performance. There is always the temptation to try to push the client a little further. If we assume that what will be accomplished will generally be accomplished within a certain time period, then limit-setting in advance provides the client with protection against the vagaries of open-ended relationships. In general, one expects relationships between professionals and the persons they serve to have fairly well-defined termination criteria. Usually such criteria are derived from service goals, which in other fields tend to be more circumscribed: after the disease has been cured, the house built, the case won or lost, service naturally comes to an end. When goals are not bounded, some form of prearranged limits is usually set. A good example is higher education: the amount to be learned about a particular subject may be limitless, so one takes courses of fixed duration to achieve, in a partial way, certain learning goals related to the subject.

Durational limits have other advantages: they force a concentration of effort on achievable goals, lead to better planning in use of time available, and stimulate both practitioner and client to greater effort. Empirical support for the latter advantage has been summed up by Goldstein, Heller, and Sechrest in their wide-ranging effort to develop research-based hypotheses for therapy.[13] According to these authors, setting time limits introduces a "temporal goal gradient" into the treatment relationship, hence research relating to "goal-gradient" effects becomes relevant. Such research has demonstrated that an individual's output tends to increase as an anticipated end point nears. As these authors conclude, "the effect of anticipation of termination should be to call forth increased patient and therapist effort toward the therapeutic goal, that is patient change."[14]

A final point needs to be made: the use of time limits as a standard method of controlling the duration of service does not prevent the offering of long-term service to clients who have completed a course of short-term treatment and who are motivated to go on. If time limits are established at the onset and if treatment is carried out under the continuing expectation that the time limits, with perhaps some adjustments, will be adhered to, available evidence suggests that few clients will in fact opt for long-term treatment. Such an arrangement would enable us to locate those few clients willing and able to use long-term treatment without attempting to drag entire case loads beyond the point of optimum service duration.

Task Structure

A number of writers, notably Studt, have suggested that the construct of "task" may be useful as a means of conceptualizing social work intervention.[15] In our system this construct serves as a means of structuring the treatment of specific problems within limited periods of time.

In our usage, a task defines what the client agrees to attempt to do to alleviate a problem. More than one task may be worked on simultaneously or in sequence, or shared tasks may be developed in work with couples and families. While "task" connotes an action, as Studt has pointed out, the action can assume a wide variety of forms in our model.[16] We prefer that the client act directly on the life situation that troubles him but we recognize that some clients, because of temporary incapacity or situational obstacles, must act through their caseworkers.

This construct is well-suited to our treatment system for a number of reasons. Most important, it provides a theoretical link between the client's problem and the caseworker's intervention. By definition, a target problem is one that the client can act on directly on his own or

[13]Arnold P. Goldstein, Kenneth Heller, and Lee R. Sechrest, *Psychotherapy and the Psychology of Behavior Change* (New York: John Wiley and Sons, Inc., 1966), p. 281.
[14]*Ibid.,* p. 281.
[15]Elliott Studt, "Social Work Theory and Implications for the Practice of Methods." *Social Work Education Reporter,* Vol. 16, No. 2 (June, 1968), pp. 22–46.
[16]*Ibid.,* p. 23.

indirectly through the caseworker. Furthermore, according to our formulations, the client's actions provide the central means of problem change. Thus it becomes essential to define with the client what course of action might be most effective in resolving his problem. The caseworker's treatment strategy then is directed to helping the client carry out this course of action, which is called the task.

In turn, the view that the caseworker's central function is to help the client achieve his task accomplishes additional purposes. It helps the caseworker focus his intervention on a specific goal, an essential requirement in planned short-term treatment. It also gives the client a sense of self-direction in problem-solving. While the task may have been formulated with the help of the caseworker, it represents action that makes sense to the client, and it is his to carry out. He may make considerable use of the caseworker's help, but he uses this help as a means of accomplishing his own objectives. Finally, the client can get a clear grasp of the purposes and strategies of treatment and of his own role in it, a special advantage for clients who do not readily grasp the means and ends of casework. The task, which he and the caseworker formulate, defines what he is to do and the caseworker's intervention can be expressly related to helping him do it.

We assume, as do most advocates of short-term approaches, that the progress clients achieve in brief, time-limited treatment can serve as a stimulus for further constructive changes after treatment has ended. The concentration of treatment effort on the client's task achievement might be expected to strengthen such after-effects. If the client achieves the agreed-upon task or makes substantial progress toward it, then he has been able to demonstrate to himself that he is able to effect change.

Conclusion

In conclusion, an attempt is being made to develop a set of theoretical formulations to undergird a system of planned short-term treatment designed to serve the bulk of the clientele of casework. Whether or not such a treatment approach becomes widely used will point to some constructive directions for casework practice. The caseworker will have greater impact if he can identify limited target problems and engage clients to work on difficulties about which they want to do something, concentrate his efforts on enabling clients to carry out specific courses of action that make sense to them, and if he can disengage himself after the usually short span of time it takes most clients to accomplish what they deem sufficient to meet the problem at hand.

Selected Bibliography

Briar, Scott, "The Current Crisis in Social Casework," *Social Work Practice, 1967* (New York: Columbia University Press) pp. 19–33. An analysis of the social casework method is presented indicating that if social work intervention focuses directly on needs of individuals and these needs are taken seriously, then an expanded and dynamic conception of the scope and multiple functions of social casework must be undertaken. Several components of an expanded conception are discussed.

Garvin, Charles, and Glasser, Paul, "The Bases of Social Treatment," *Social Work Practice,* 1970, pp. 149–177. The evolution of a social treatment approach to intervention is discussed using earlier modes and theories of social work practice. Analysis is made of social treatment and its relevance to certain types of clients where situational and behavioral change is the goal.

Gyarfas, Mary, "Social Science, Technology and Social Work: A Caseworker's View," *Social Service Review,* 43(3), 1969, pp. 259–273. Changes in social work values, theory, and practice are described as they relate to social work's alliance with social science. Implications for social work in view of technological expansion and resulting social change are examined. Concern is expressed that social work may become primarily a managerial profession unless understanding of and skill in the use of social processes is attained.

Hartman, Ann, "But What is Social Casework?", *Social Casework,* 52(7), 1971, pp. 411–419. The changing identity of social casework as seen by various social work leaders is comprehensively described. The conclusion is that social casework in its various forms represents a broad range of objectives and approaches.

Janchill, Sister Mary Paul, "Systems Concepts in Casework Theory and Practice," *Social Casework,* 50(2), February 1969, pp. 74–82. The basic validity of the person-in-situation concept as the base from which social work practice has evolved is established. Limitations in the social work knowledge base are identified. General systems theory is advocated as a means of understanding the relational determinants of behavior in the person-in-situation configuration.

Meyer, Carol H., "The Changing Concept of Individualized Services," *Social Casework,* 47(5), May 1966, pp. 279–285. The concept of individualized services is examined as it has been altered and reshaped by changes in the structure and function of family life, change in the concept of the unit of social work attention, and new developments in knowledge. Additional changes are inevitable and will further alter social work practice. The ultimate purpose of social welfare programs, regardless of changes, must be service to human beings.

Oxley, Genevieve G., "A Life-Model Approach to Change," *Social Casework,* 52(10), 1971, pp. 627–633. The little-discussed concept of action is selected from other ways in which natural change and growth occur and is considered as an approach to intervention. Action is seen as having therapeutic value when a client is stimulated to action in his own environment. Within a suggested life-model approach, the concept of action is developed in contrast to the concepts of maturation, interaction, learning, and crisis resolution.

Pasewark, Richard A., and Albers, Dale A., "Crisis Intervention: Theory in Search of a Program," *Social Work,* 17(2), 1972, pp. 70–77. By way of critically examining modes of service delivery in the mental health field, crisis intervention is offered as a means of dealing with mental health problems using concepts of primary prevention.

Shoemaker, Louise P., "Giving and Taking Help Individually and in the Group," *Journal of Social Work Process,* Vol. 17, 1969, pp. 127–139. In the interest of assuring better services to clients, the factors of authority, social distance, and communications are discussed in terms of viewing the interrelatedness of giving and taking help individually and in a group.

Sotomayer, Marta, "Mexican-American Interaction with Social Systems," *Social Casework,* 52(5), 1971, pp. 316–322. The need to closely identify, evaluate, and support the socio-cultural strengths of the Mexican-American family is discussed in order to recognize and encourage the self-help process characteristic of this group. Internal family dynamics can be better understood if limitations created by external systems are assessed.

Thomas, Edwin J., "Contributions of the Socio-behavioral Approach to Interpersonal Helping in Social Work," *British Journal of Psychiatric Social Work,* 10(2), 1969, pp. 61-69. To accomplish what are some of the central activities of social work intervention—behavioral change and stabilization—the socio-behavioral approach is considered. This approach is thought promising for its relevance to interpersonal helping, its stronger empirical corroboration, and its ability to afford more concrete action.

4

The Group as Target

It was said earlier that enhancement of individual social functioning involves the interrelationships between the individual and his immediate situation. This chapter is concerned with those circumstances in which an individual has dysfunctional problems that can be best dealt with by means of a group or groups. It will become clear that social workers always engage in interventions with groups and that no one of the three traditional methods is exclusively concerned with individuals.

When a group can be used to meet the needs of the affected individuals better than any other mechanism then it becomes the target for the worker's interventive acts. The purpose may be only to improve the functioning of its individual members—that is, to teach each member how to better interact with other individuals inside as well as outside the immediate group. Or the group may be formed with the purpose of changing some condition or situation that does not touch the group but is in the immediate environment of its members—that is, to cope with a situation that impinges upon individual opportunities to achieve a desired status of functioning (such as the failure of a formal organization to provide its intended services). A third purpose for organizing a group combines the preceding two—for example, the development of a self-help organization: in this instance how members interact would be a concern since this organization would be an ongoing entity; likewise, the environment would be a concern to the extent that the desired outcome of this undertaking is the creation of a new formal organization intended to satisfy some need not presently met by existing organizations. Groups are also essential to clients and workers when their target is an organization or other larger system that is beyond the immediate individual influence of the affected clients. Social action efforts are an example.

In the first reading of this chapter, Schwartz identifies five basic tasks for the generalist involved in any of the above situations, or for that matter in a system of any size. The first task requires a search by the client and the worker for common ground, their goal being agreement on the problem to be addressed, which is the second task. That is, they must agree upon what are the obstacles to that individual's desired outcome. The third task is to make the client aware of ideas, values, and facts—data, if you will—that may help him to deal with his reality. To invest himself in the client's problem is the fourth of the worker's tasks; and to establish a contract that binds the client, worker, and agency to undertake to achieve some agreed-upon outcome is the final task. Schwartz then discusses how these tasks are employed by a generalist who is intervening with a group.

Whittaker relates a five-stage model of the group process to the development of small groups for each of three models: the social goals model emphasizes social change by members of society who know what needs to be changed and who realize the consequences of change; the remedial model stresses treatment for psychological, social, and cultural problems; the reciprocal model, based on systems theory, may focus upon either of the above purposes or a combination of them.

By using systems theory as the basis for an alternative to previous models, Goroff identifies three basic components of any group undertaking: recognition of the interactions among individuals, their subgroups, and the group as a whole; the dynamics operating within the group itself; and the interactions among individuals within the group with their larger social and cultural systems. This view of social group work is based on certain assumptions about reality: man and society are opposite sides of the same coin—neither can exist without the other; the worker cannot help the group realize potentials greater than those that exist within the group itself.

To assess the occurrences within a group, the worker must simultaneously scan each individual's behavior for its clues to his personality, his psychosocial development, how he copes with group situations, as well as how he and the group are related to other social systems. The worker's efforts are always governed by a value system that emphasizes individual rights to self-fulfillment, self-determination, and a realization of the ideals of a democratic society.

Lang observes that models of group work tend to reflect prevailing professional and social concerns. This model begins with the assumption that different orders of groups exist and a different set of interventive strategies is required for each order of group. These strategies range from a highly dependent group, at one end, that requires an active worker to a highly independent group, at the other end, in which the worker becomes, in effect, a member of the group.

Lang's model is based on a developmental rather than a clinical or remedial model of behavior. A way of reconciling some apparent differences between this and other models is incorporated in this particular model as well as a proposed reclassification of practice principles that are not incorporated in other models. Setting considerations and the need to think of goals are omitted in lieu of a recognition of different orders of group and group forms to which worker roles are related. It is assumed that the individual is fully developed but that differing structures, processes, and points of focus require differing levels of involvement on the worker's part.

In summary of this chapter, the generalist is a social worker who at times must intervene with a group to achieve a situation that its members consider a preferred status. The group can have existed before the social worker became involved or can have been created by worker and clients to solve the problem(s) at hand—either when the problem requires that interventive efforts affect the interactions between individuals or when the problem surpasses an individual's ability to solve it and its victims can be formed in a group, or when some combination of these two different kinds of problem holds. Group work rests on the assumption that man is able to grow and develop and on a corollary premise of democratic political theory that individuals and groups must be self-determining to the extent that their decisions do not impinge on the rights of others.

The social work generalist is expected to work with individuals in small groups as well as on a one-to-one basis.
Work with groups is thought to be the most effective
means of dealing with certain kinds of dysfunctional
situations. Schwartz identifies five tasks that are common
to all social work practice, and discusses them in particular relation to work with groups.

The Social Worker in the Group

William Schwartz

Professions have a way of moving periodically through eras of rediscovery in which an old truth comes alive with the vigor and freshness of
a new idea. Such an occurrence seems to be taking shape in social work
practice as we face the realization that the problems of people do not
lend themselves easily to arbitrary·divisions of labor among the various
agencies of social welfare. In fact, this particular truth has been rediscovered several times, cutting deeply, in each instance, into established
forms and calling for new institutional and professional alignments.

This stubborn fact has precipitated a reexamination of social work's
historic system of designating the functions of agencies by reference to
the number of people involved in the client-worker system at one time.
Thus the casework agency, as we have known it, was one which
derived its distinguishing characteristics from the fact that its workers
talked to people one at a time; the group work agency (later called the
"group service agency") worked with people in small, cohesive groups;
and the community organization agency assumed the function of leadership with representative bodies and similar associations.

This typology emerged at an early stage of specialization and has
remained relatively stable over the major course of social work history
—not, however, without a certain marked degree of uneasiness throughout. Group workers have struggled for years with the need to "individu-
alize," wondering whether they were "doing casework" when they
dealt with individual problems, and continually raising the issue of
whether individual or group problems should take priority. The agencies
of social casework have been concerned about the reluctance of workers trained in the one-to-one relationship to carry these skills into·
committee work, multiple interviewing, group consultation, and

From National Conference on Social Welfare: *The Social Welfare Forum 1961,* pp. 146–171.
Reprinted with permission of Columbia University Press.

other group constellations. And the community organization workers have been faced continuously with the vital connection between the tasks that people undertake and the uniquely personal ways in which they approach them.

These vague but pervasive concerns have now begun to crystallize into new conceptions about the appropriate client-worker systems through which agencies carry out their functions. The rapid development of social work services in the institutional therapeutic settings has created a community model which lends itself poorly to a type of specialization based solely on the number of people with whom the social worker interacts at a given time. In these settings, the caseworkers have been pressed into group service, just as the psychiatrists and the psychologists had before them;[1] and the group workers have found themselves involved in a degree of intensive individualization beyond anything they had ever experienced.

In general practice, the developing emphasis on the family as a unit of service has forced both caseworkers and group workers into new modes of activity. The former have been constrained to understand and work with the dynamics of family interaction; the latter, to replace the comfortable aura of friendly visiting with a more sophisticated and focused approach. In both agency types, the traditional forms have been changing, with caseworkers turning more and more to the group as a unit of service and group workers rekindling their old concern with ways of offering skilled individual guidance for those who need it.[2]

In the area of community organization, the picture is less clear. There seems to be little doubt, however, that its conceptualizers are recognizing another old truth, namely, that the only way to work with communities is to work with people, singly and together, and that skill in the helping process needs to be abstracted and formulated into teachable concepts. The newer theoretical attempts lean heavily toward organizing the experience of community workers into concepts that reflect the language and central concerns of social work method. Genevieve Carter, for example, has addressed herself directly to an analysis of the helping process in community organization, and her concept of "cumulative sequence" is an interesting attempt to relate the order of community change to that of individual growth and development.[3]

---

[1]See, for example, "The Psychiatric Social Worker as Leader of a Group," Report of Committee on Practice, Psychiatric Social Work Section, National Association of Social Workers (New York: the Association, n.d.; mimeographed).

[2]See, for example, *The Use of Group Techniques in the Family Agency: Three Papers from the FSAA Biennial Meeting, Washington, D.C., April, 1959* (New York: Family Service Association of America, 1959); "Committee Statement on the Role of the Caseworker in a Group Work Agency" (Chicago: Chicago Area Chapter, National Association of Social Workers, 1958; mimeographed).

[3]Genevieve W. Carter, "Social Work Community Organization Methods and Processes," in Walter A. Friedlander, ed., *Concepts and Methods of Social Work* (Englewood Cliffs, N.J.: Prentice-Hall, 1958), p. 248.

Concurrently, the unification of social workers within a single professional association and the efforts of the social work schools to conceptualize the common elements in practice have dramatized the need to combine the learnings of workers from the various fields and settings into a functional scheme that can be taught and practiced under the name of "social work." Such a scheme would not eliminate specialization but would certainly redefine it; most important, it could create a new integration within which the component parts could be differentiated on a basis more consistent with the facts of life as they actually exist in the community.

The new conceptual framework would be built on the recognition that the function of a social agency is determined more realistically by the social problem to which it has been assigned than by the specific relational systems through which the social worker translates this function into concrete services. It would accept the fact that there is no known correspondence between a function such as child placement, or family welfare, or recreation, or social planning, and the exclusive use of the one-to-one or the one-to-group structure to carry it out. And it would become increasingly clear that any agency should be capable of creating, in each specific instance, that system of client-worker relationships which is most appropriate to its clients' requirements.

A significant corollary would then emerge quite naturally, namely, that the single variable embodied in the number of people one works with at a time is simply not significant enough to be endowed with the designation of "method." Not significant enough, that is, if we reserve the term "method" to mean a systematic mode of helping which, while it is used differently in different situations, retains throughout certain recognizable and invariant properties through which one may identify the social worker in action. In this light, to describe casework, group work, and community organization as methods simply mistakes the nature of the helping process for the relational system in which it is applied. It seems more accurate to speak of a social work method, practiced in the various systems in which the social worker finds himself or which are established for the purpose of giving service: the family, the small friendship group, the representative body, the one-to-one interview, the hospital ward, the lounge-canteen, the committee, the street club, the special-interest group, and many others. Within this frame of reference, the task of safeguarding the uniqueness of the various so-called methods fades before the real problem of abstracting from all these experiences the common methodological components of the helping process in social work.

This is partly why any serious attempt to define a unique entity called "social group work" begins to turn, under one's very hand, into a description of something larger and more inclusive, of which the worker-group system is simply a special case. Having now, after many years of shifting identification, found a resting place in social work function and the social agency network,[4] group workers can indeed make a significant conceptual contribution to the theoretical problems involved in working with groups. But the context has changed, and the moment has passed, for a definition of "group work method." Rather, we must now search for those common elements in social work practice—the very elements which attracted group workers into the social work fold—from which social workers in all settings can draw the specifics of their own practice. The job can no longer be done most usefully by first defining social group work (or casework or community organization) and then trying to fit the description into the general framework of helping theory. The process is now rather the reverse: by laying the groundwork in a social work methodology, we may begin to analyze and clarify the activities of the social worker as he works with people in groups.

To both of these endeavors—building the common model and describing the special case of the group system—those who have been schooled in the traditions of social group work have a rich store of experience from which to contribute. The task is, of course, rendered doubly difficult by the fact that any worker who attempts it must break the bonds of his own training, since he himself has been reared in the ancient fallacies. But, clumsy though these first efforts must be, it seems inevitable that they will be made, and in increasing number;[5] for they represent an indispensable part of the still larger task of conceptualizing the generic framework of the social work profession as a whole. These larger issues are embodied in the Curriculum Study of the Council on Social Work Education[6] and in the work of the Commission on Social Work Practice of the National Association of Social Workers.[7] The present segment of this over-all task deals only with those activities through which the social worker functions in direct relationship with people of established or potential client status; the focus is on the helping process itself and on the factors which determine its nature and its variations. In what follows, we shall not presume to create a compre-

[4]For a more detailed account of the developing integration of group work and social work see the writer's "Group Work and the Social Scene" in Alfred J. Kahn, ed., *Issues in American Social Work* (New York: Columbia University Press, 1959), pp. 110–37.

[5]Although not dealing specifically with the method component, an outstanding effort to develop a foundation for a unifying theory in social work has been made by Gordon Hearn, *Theory Building in Social Work* (Toronto: University of Toronto Press, 1958). See also Joseph W. Eaton, "A Scientific Basis for Helping," in Kahn *op. cit.,* pp. 270–92, and Harriet M. Bartlett, "The Generic-specific Concept in Social Work Education and Practice," *ibid.,* pp. 159–90.

[6]Werner W. Boehm, *Objectives of the Social Work Curriculum of the Future,* The Comprehensive Report of the Curriculum Study, Vol. I (New York: Council on Social Work Education, 1959).

[7]Described by Harriet M. Bartlett, "Toward Clarification and Improvement of Social Work Practice," *Social Work,* III, No. 2 (1958), 3–9.

hensive theoretical statement but simply to highlight a few of the essential components around which such a statement will need to turn.

Let us begin, then, with three fairly simple propositions:

1. Every profession has a particular function to perform in society: it has received a certain job assignment for which it is held accountable.

2. This assignment is then elaborated in certain characteristic modes of activity —certain action patterns designed to implement the professional function.

3. These action patterns are further fashioned and developed within the specific systems in which they operate.

These propositions lead to a working definition of method as a systematic process of ordering one's activity in the performance of a function. Method is function in action.

This line of reasoning thus calls for three major lines of inquiry, each of which carries its own theoretical problems. The first line of inquiry is designed to produce an accurate functional statement which formulates as precisely as possible the particular assignment drawn by the social work profession in the society which creates and sustains it. The second inquiry is designed to convert the functional statement into those patterns of activity through which the social work function is implemented. The third line of investigation is directed to seeking out the specific adaptations of the general methodological pattern in the various concrete situations in which the social worker performs his job.

Requirements for a Functional Statement

The central requirement is to recognize at the outset that the very idea of function implies the existence of an organic whole, a dynamic system, in which the worker performs certain movements in relation to the movements of others. In Parsons's words:

The very definition of an organic whole is as one within which *the relations determine the properties of its parts.* . . . And in so far as this is true, the concept "part" takes on an abstract, indeed a "fictional" character. For the part of an organic whole is no longer the same, once it is separated factually or conceptually from the whole.[8]

And Lawrence Frank, in describing what he calls "organized complexities," speaks of the need for a field concept describing

[8]Talcott Parsons, *The Structure of Social Action* (New York: McGraw-Hill Book Co., 1937), p. 32; italics added.

circular, reciprocal relations . . . through which the component members of the field participate in and thereby create the field of the whole, which field in turn regulates and patterns their individual activities. This is a circular, reciprocal relation, not a serial cause and effect, stimulus and response relation.[9]

This model of a dynamic system which surrounds and incorporates the movements of the worker provides specific clues for our statement of social work function. First, it helps us realize that function is itself *an action concept* and that it cannot be understood as a description of what social workers know, or feel, or hope to achieve. To say, as we often do, that the social work function is to "understand behavior," or "be sensitive to need," or "effect changes," is to beg the functional question entirely. Such statements remain fixed at the level of what the worker may need in order to carry out his function, or what he may envision as a result of having performed it well—they say nothing about the function itself. The social worker's philosophy, social aspirations, attitudes toward people, and even his knowledge about them, are not unique to the profession and do not, in themselves, represent its assignment in society. Properly viewed, these qualities are simply prerequisite to the forms of action through which the profession justifies its social position.

Second, the model illustrates the need for the statement to reflect the activity of the social worker *as it affects, and is affected by, the activity of others* within the system. The failure to understand this feature of the helping system has created great difficulties in both the practice and the theory of social work. The inability to see the system as one "within which the relations determine the properties of its parts" has made it possible to imagine that one may deal with human beings by reference to certain discrete characteristics rather than to their movements within the relational system through which they seek help. To "diagnose" the client, to inventory his "needs," and to recapitulate his life history leave undone the task of understanding how these facts, if such they be, may be moving the client as he acts and reacts within the present field. Where the properties of parts are determined by their relations, the search for discrete characteristics is at best "interesting" and at worst produces a situation in which, in Merton's words, "understanding is diminished by an excess of facts." It should be stated that the uneasy attempt to take over the language and the sequence-of-treatment concept of the medical profession has confused and retarded our own attempts to find terms and concepts which would truly describe the

[9]Lawrence K. Frank, "Research for What?" *Journal of Social Issues,* Kurt Lewin Memorial Award Issue, Supplement Series, No. 10 (1957), p. 12.

helping process in social work. For the helping relationship as we know it is one in which the client possesses the only real and lasting means to his own ends. The worker is but one resource in a life situation which encompasses many significant relationships. And movement, at any given moment, is based on the movement of the preceding moment, as each new event calls for a reorientation of the worker to a new complex of demands for his skill. Such a process is patently different from one in which the function of the person in difficulty is to supply information and the function of the worker is to create action based upon this information, by which division of labor a "treatment" or a "cure" is effected.

The third clue offered by the organic model is the need to represent the *limited field of influence* in which any part of a dynamic system operates. This involves acceptance of the fact that, within such a system, any single part affects only those with which it interacts; and, further, that it affects even these in a limited way, in accordance with its specific function. This recognition can help to scale down the grandiose, cure-all aspirations of any single profession, and to avoid couching its objectives in the language of absolutes—"achieving individual maturity," "fulfilling human needs," and the like.

Fourth, the model points to the fact that, within a dynamic relational system, the interplay of movements of the various actors is in effect an *interplay of functions.* Thus, as the worker is moved by the question "What am I doing here?" so are the others in the situation moved, consciously and unconsciously, by the same question. The worker-client interaction is one in which each needs and uses the other in order to carry out his own sense of purpose within the relational system.

Our next question must then be: What are the systems within which the social work profession in general, and the social worker in particular, derives and carries out the social work assignment?

First, there is the general system of society itself, within which the profession has been set in motion and assigned to a given sphere of influence consistent with its ability to perform certain necessary tasks.

Second, there is the social agency system, within which the social worker translates agency function into concrete services. The agency situation represents a kind of partialization of the larger social system, from which it draws its own special assignment; and the agency creates, in addition, a unique subculture of its own, out of its own mode of living and working.

Third, there is the specific client-worker relationship—one-to-one or one-to-group—in which the social worker expresses both his general function as a professional and his specific function within the agency complex. The client-worker relationship, viewed from a distance, may thus be seen to be a system within a system within a system.

The Group as Target

This is, of course, a simplified version of the relationship of parts to a dynamic whole. It is simplified precisely because we need to choose, from the immensely complex network of relationships in which the social worker finds himself, those which exercise the most significant determining effects upon his movements.[10] We may say that the social worker's movements, within any specific helping relationship, reveal certain constant elements, which he derives from his professional identification, and certain variant elements, which he derives from his agency identification and from the situations in which he operates. The common components of social work function emerge from the social work position within the social scheme; its adaptive components are those which express the specific ways in which the professional function is put to work.

Function: the Professional Assignment

Let us now venture a proposal for the functional statement itself. We would suggest that the general assignment for the social work profession is to mediate the process through which the individual and his society reach out for each other through a mutual need for self-fulfillment. This presupposes a relationship between the individual and his nurturing group which we would describe as "symbiotic"—each needing the other for its own life and growth, and each reaching out to the other with all the strength it can command at a given moment. The social worker's field of intervention lies at the point where two forces meet: the individual's impetus toward health, growth, and belonging; and the organized efforts of society to integrate its parts into a productive and dynamic whole.

More specifically, the social work assignment emerges from the fact that, in a complex and often disordered society, the individual-social symbiosis grows diffuse and obscure in varying degrees, ranging from the normal developmental problems of children growing into their culture to the severe pathology involved in situations where the symbiotic attachment appears to be all but severed. At all the points along this range, the social work function is to mediate the individual-social transaction as it is worked out in the specific context of those agencies which are designed to bring together individual needs and social resources— the person's urge to belong to society as a full and productive member and society's ability to provide certain specific means for integrating *its* people and enriching their social contribution. Placed thus, in Bertha

---

[10]The interdependence of dynamic systems and the problems of abstracting one or another for analysis are discussed in Ronald Lippitt, Jeanne Watson, and Bruce Westley, *The Dynamics of Planned Change* (New York: Harcourt, Brace and Co., 1958), pp. 5–11.

Reynolds's old phrase, "between the client and the community," the social worker's job is to represent and to implement the symbiotic strivings, even where their essential features are obscured from the individual, from society, or from both.

It should be emphasized that this conception is different from that which places the social worker in a sphere of concern known as "dysfunctioning." While it is true that the profession operates in areas where the individual-social interaction is impaired, these areas are only part of the social work field of action. The problems of symbiotic diffusion are inevitable in any complex society and apply not only to social pathology but to the normal, developmental processes and to the ongoing social effort to order the relationship between needs and resources. The concern with developmental tasks has provided part of the traditional preoccupation of the leisure-time agencies, while the ordering of needs and resources has engaged those agencies concerned with social planning and action.

This is obviously only a brief outline of the symbiotic model; its rationale has been elaborated by Kropotkin,[11] Mead,[12] Sherif,[13] Murphy,[14] Bergson,[15] and many others. For our present purposes, the important points are: the fundamental impetus of people and their groups carries them toward each other; this impetus is often blocked and diverted by a diffusion of the relationship between self- and social-interest; where the impetus can be freed to operate, it constitutes the basic motivation, for both individual and social change, with which the social worker engages himself.

This strategic location of social work as a kind of third force implementing the basic identity of interest between the individual and his group creates its own problems when the social worker falls prey to the very diffusion against which his function is set. It is at these times that we hear the controversies about whether he should be more concerned with social or with individual problems, with "content" or "process," "ends" or "means," and so on. This debate disregards the most essential characteristics of social work: that it stands on the meeting ground between the two; that it is inextricably involved with both; and that it sees no contradictions, even where the dualism looms large in the popular mind. The social work function is based on "the recognition of the fact that the individual's normal growth lands him in essential solidarity with his fellows, while on the other hand the exercise of his

---

[11]P. Kropotkin, *Mutual Aid, a Factor of Evolution* (New York: Alfred A. Knopf, 1925).

[12]George Herbert Mead, *Mind, Self and Society* (Chicago: University of Chicago Press, 1934).

[13]Muzafer Sherif, *The Psychology of Social Norms* (New York: Harper, 1936).

[14]Gardner Murphy, *Human Potentialities* (New York: Basic Books, Inc., 1958).

[15]Henri Bergson, *The Two Sources of Morality and Religion;* tr. R. Ashley Audra and Cloudesley Brereton, with the assistance of W. Horsfall Carter (Garden City, New York: Doubleday, 1954).

social duties and privileges advances his highest and purest individuality."[16]

Method: The Professional Tasks

The transition from function to method is essentially a problem in dividing a broad assignment into its component activities. For this purpose, we have chosen the term "task" as an organizing concept around which to gather up the various movements of the worker in any given client-worker system. The implication is that any function can be broken down into a number of tasks necessary to carry it out, and that any specific act performed should come under one or another of these headings. Our emphasis here is on categories of activity rather than on small discrete movements; for the latter may involve us in problems that lie outside the scope of method as we conceive it. While the concern with specific acts is important, the units of activity cannot be so small as to take us either into mechanical prescriptions for worker responses or into problems of personalized style and technique. The tasks are common and are based on a professional method held in common; but many of the helping acts in a given situation are heavily charged with the unique movements and personal artistry of the individual worker.

We envisage the following tasks as those required of the worker as he carries out his social work function within the helping relationship:

1. The task of searching out the common ground between the client's perception of his own need and the aspects of social demand with which he is faced

2. The task of detecting and challenging the obstacles which obscure the common ground and frustrate the efforts of people to identify their own self-interest with that of their "significant others"

3. The task of contributing data—ideas, facts, value-concepts—which are not available to the client and which may prove useful to him in the attempting to cope with that part of social reality which is involved in the problems on which he is working

4. The task of "lending a vision"[17] to the client, in which the worker both reveals himself as one whose own hopes and aspirations are strongly invested in the interaction between people and society and projects a deep feeling for that which represents individual well-being and the social good.

5. The task of defining the requirements and the limits of the situation in which the client-worker system is set. These rules and boundaries establish the context

[16]James Mark Baldwin, *The Individual and Society; or, Psychology and Sociology* (Boston: Richard G. Badger, the Gorham Press, 1911), p. 16.
[17]A phrase borrowed from another context. See Norman Kelman, "Goals of Analytic Therapy: a Personal Viewpoint," *American Journal of Psychoanalysis,* XIV (1954), 113.

for the "working contract" which binds the client and the agency to each other and which creates the conditions under which both client and worker assume their respective functions.

The Social Worker in the
Group

As we move this methodological pattern into the worker-group situation, the first problem is to specify some of the salient characteristics of the small-group system which help create the social climate within which the worker functions.

First, the group is an enterprise in mutual aid, an alliance of individuals who need each other, in varying degrees, to work on certain common problems. The important fact is that this is a helping system in which the clients need each other as well as the worker. This need to use each other, to create not one but many helping relationships, is a vital ingredient of the group process and constitutes a common need over and above the specific tasks for which the group was formed.

Second, the group is a system of relationships which, in its own unique way, represents a special case of the general relationship between individuals and their society. The present group is, in other words, but one of the many associational forms through which its members interact with social values, social objectives, and social resources. More specifically, the cultural climate of the group is drawn from three major sources: Generalized social attitudes about what is good and bad, right and wrong, worthy and unworthy, permeate the group and form a part of its culture. The agency in which the group is embedded has drawn from the general culture its own characteristic and unique constellation of approved attitudes and behaviors. The group itself, by the nature of its central problem, by the activities in which it engages, and by the particular personalities it brings together, creates its own conditions for success and failure.

Finally, the group is, as we have indicated, an organic whole: its nature cannot be discerned by analyzing the separate characteristics of each component but by viewing the group organism as a complex of moving, interdependent human beings, each acting out his changing relationship to society in his present interaction with others engaged in a similar enterprise. In this framework the worker is more concerned with what the member does and feels in the present situation than with what the member *is*. Further, the demands of society can be understood more clearly as they present themselves to the group member in the immediate situation than in abstract, holistic terms like "democratic responsibility" or "social maturity." It is, in fact, this very partialized and focused character of the present enterprise that makes helping and being helped possible and manageable. The implications for the worker himself are that his ability to help is expressed in action and that this action is limited, as in any functional system, to certain areas in which he has some control. He acts to help others act, and the emphasis on new ways of moving, of interacting, is more realistic and productive than the concern with total being, with discrete characteristics, and with totalistic conceptions of change.

With these observations in mind, let us examine the activities of the social worker in the group, following the pattern of the five major tasks outlined above:

1. As he pursues his search for common ground, the worker's movements are fashioned by four major assumptions about the connections for which he is seeking. The first is that the group member's main access to new ideas, new attitudes, and new skills lies through his ability to discern their usefulness to him and to invest affect in the tasks required to make them his own. The second assumption is that such connections —between individual aspirations and social objects—are always present, no matter how obscure they may seem to the members themselves. To conceive of a situation in which the connections do not exist would be to postulate a group in which the members are completely beyond the call of social demands—a situation in which the group itself would be a futile device since its members could exercise no effect upon each other. The third assumption is that these connections are both specific and partial. A gang of adolescents does not rush eagerly toward the ideal of "democratic values"; youngsters in a Jewish Center do not respond quickly to the generalized notion of "Jewish identification"; hospital patients do not invest themselves equally and evenly in the tasks of rehabilitation. In each of these instances, the attraction between the individual's sense of need and the aspirations of society is present and inherent; but it is partial, elusive, and comes into the open only at certain significant points.

The final assumption is that these connections cannot be established in any permanent sense. From meeting to meeting, almost from moment to moment, the group members meet reality on new ground, with new connections constantly to be discovered as each member works at the job of building a bridge between past and present experience.

The worker's search for common ground is expressed in two major forms of activity. One is his efforts to clarify the function of the group and to protect this focus of work against attempts to evade or subvert it—whether by the agency, the group, or its individual members. The other is represented by consistent efforts to point up for the members those areas in which they feel, however faintly, an interest in the social objects which confront them. The clarification of group function represents an active demand by the helping agent that the agency, the group, and its members begin their working relationship with a clear "contract" and a common understanding of the issue: What are we doing here together? All of this is based on the worker's conviction that the search for common ground begins most auspiciously on a field where the members and their tasks have been, so far as possible, brought face to face. The endeavor to uncover and discover connections between individual goals and social realities is rendered infinitely more difficult when the terms of these realities are themselves shifting and unstable; as, for instance, when the worker "builds character" while pretending to teach basketball, or "improves social relations" when the group has enlisted his skill in clay modeling. Further, these attempts to guard the focus of work do not end when the initial statement has been made and the terms of the agreement reached. His activities in this regard persist as he continues to guard the focus of work or, where change in focus is feasible and permissible, he helps the group to consider such changes openly and realistically.

The second complex of activities through which the worker searches for common ground begins with the worker's efforts to seek out the general lines of subject-object connection. This is a kind of internal process whereby he looks deeply into the characteristics of both subject and object to find the elements of attraction and to alert himself to the possibilities of future engagement. What is the attraction between the gang member's hostility toward social norms and society's demand for conformity to these norms? Between the Jewish youngster's desire to be like others and the agency's emphasis on Jewish belongingness? Between the shock of diagnosis experienced by patients in an orientation group and the hospital's need for the patients to move smoothly into the necessary procedures, rules, and routines?

These are, in a sense, "diagnostic" attempts, but such preparatory insights cannot effectively be used to impose a series of prefabricated connections on a ready-made series of events. For the most part, this awareness of the general lines of connection is used in three ways: it enables the worker to be more responsive to subtle and covert requests for help; it compels him to focus on the here-and-now, and to see through the members' evasions and denials to the strengths that lie hidden; and it helps him to structure the situation to favor strength rather than weakness.

2. As the search for common ground continues, the helping agent is constantly confronted with another task which, though it is a corollary of the first, is important enough to be considered on its own terms. This task evolves from the fact that the member's access to social reality is constantly impeded by obstacles which are thrown up in the course of the engagement. The existence of these obstacles is usually obscure to the group member himself. His awareness is limited by his incomplete vision of the common ground and by his own subjectivity, which

makes it difficult for him to recognize his own defenses, to distinguish between internal and external deterrents, and to access his own productivity at any given moment. Thus, a force is needed within the learning group system that will challenge the obstacles as they appear, by calling attention to their existence and asking the group to come to grips with them. This is the second major task of the helping person.

These obstructions stem from many sources and appear in many forms. They originate in past experience and crystallize in the moment-to-moment event of the group situation. They are created by the attitudes of the members, the human image projected by the worker, the nature of the things to be learned, and the function of the agency. The origins of the obstacles are, in fact, so complex and interrelated that it is impossible for the worker to define causation as he approaches them in the context of the group experience.

Fortunately, it is unnecessary for him to do so. What is necessary is that he recognize these phenomena, that he accept them as relevant to his professional responsibilities, and that he offer help with the concrete learning problems they indicate. Whatever its underlying source, each obstacle always takes the form of a very specific struggle between the members and their present tasks: the group has a decision to make, has stressed its importance again and again, but falls into aimless chatting whenever the subject comes up; a member accepts a task with enthusiasm, and repeatedly fails to perform it; a group proceeds, half-heartedly and unsuccessfully, on a course unanimously approved by the members but, in fact, subtly imposed by the worker; another group moves independently, but guiltily, along its "chosen" lines of action.

In these instances, there is an obstruction that lies between the group members and a valued objective, distorting their perception of what is valued and frustrating their efforts to act openly in their own self-interest. There is a path they need to take, and cannot—because its entrance is blocked by taboo. The taboo may be present in the conditions that surround them; often, its complexity is such that it combines several factors. A discussion group may become dull and unproductive because it has built up a fund of resentment against a respected but authoritarian leader. Unable to deal with their need to conform, with the leader's unassailable correctness, or with the general subcultural proscription against self-assertion, the members have no recourse but to express their resistance in listlessness and apathy.

The area of taboo may be painful enough to ward off recognition and remain buried in consciousness as it invisibly directs the actions of the members; or, the group may be aware of its existence but does not dare to enter an unsafe and risky region. Thus, in our example, the members' respect for the leader and their need to be liked by him can be so great that they cannot accept any flaw in him, but can feel only guilt for their own unexplainable lapse of ambition; or they may, on the other hand, feel their resentment against the beloved autocrat but shrink from hurting him or from exposing themselves as rebels.

In either event, the effect is evasion of the obstacle that impedes their path to productivity. Consciously or unconsciously, the members withhold their energies from the task before them. Instead, they devote themselves to movements which reflect no real investment in content, but only their efforts to create the best imitation they can muster.

In the activities designed to carry out the worker's task of dealing with obstacles, he directs himself toward three major forms of endeavor. The first includes those actions in which he reveals the fact that an impediment exists and that this is permissible. His actions here are not "interpretive" in the usual sense; he has no way of "diagnosing" the nature of the difficulty, and no right to ask the members to deal with his causative explanations, even if he were extremely intuitive in this regard. He asks them, simply, to recognize the fact that an obstacle exists, in the form of apathy, evasion, or inconsistency, between them and a desired objective.

The second category includes those movements by which the worker offers support and assistance as the members enter the area of taboo and seek to determine the nature of the impediment. This is to say that the worker helps them to examine the ways in which they are operating against their own interests in this situation. The attempt here is not to exorcise the taboo—that is, eliminate its power for all time—but to help the members identify it and examine its effects. It is important only that they recognize the source of their present frustration and free themselves to determine the direction of their self-interest. In this aspect of the worker's activity, he is asking them to recapture control of their own impetus, and to begin by discountenancing the illusion of work where none exists.

In the third category of activities, the worker moves to keep the function of the group alive lest it be lost in the preoccupation with obstacles. The challenging of obstacles is based on the fact that they come between the member and the social product. When these impediments cease to be regarded as such and become objects of interest in their own right, the analytical process itself becomes an obstacle which needs to be dealt with. This calls for certain movements through which the helping person exercises a kind of "demand for work," an emphasis on performance; he asks the group members to continue with their functional tasks even as they examine the obstacles to their achievement. This is still another way of saying that the examination of obstacles is part of the group function itself and that one does not cease as the other begins.

3. The third task encompasses those movements in which the helping

The Group as Target

agent makes a contribution of data in the group situation. The term "data" is used here to denote any ideas, facts, or value concepts which the members may find useful as they involve themselves within the system. Whether the members' tasks are related to the specific problems of mastering facts and concepts in an established sequence, or to a less tangible complex of attitudes and feelings, the worker has a responsibility to offer what he feels they can utilize from his own store of experience. The worker's grasp of social reality is one of the important attributes that fit him to his function; while his life experiences cannot be transferred intact to other human beings, the products of these experiences can be immensely valuable to those who are moving through their own struggles and stages of mastery.

Thus, nothing can be more destructive to the worker's function than his decision to withhold knowledge on the sole grounds that the member must make his own way. Such withholding is inevitably interpreted by the individual as deprivation, hence rejection; and the result is generally the very opposite of what the worker intends. It is common, for example, to find situations where the group members spend a major part of their energies in straining to find answers which lie hidden in the worker's questions; in this game of educational hide-and-seek, dependency increases as frustration mounts and as the members learn to search for hidden answers rather than to explore the nature of the problem itself.

In providing access to data, the worker is, in effect, providing access to himself. His demand for a culture of work, and for a free sharing of ideas, can best be met if he makes himself available, as he would have them become available to him and to each other. What he knows should be accessible to the members of the group, not after they have tried to proceed "on their own," but in the course of their deliberations so that they may use him in their work. The need to withhold is generally felt by workers whose relationship to the group is too fragile to be sustained in a culture of work. Where the dependence on authority is already great—and not necessarily created by the worker—the reluctance to offer more information to be swallowed whole is a natural one. But the fear of creating dependency must be met in other ways. The worker who finds common ground, is sensitive to the climate in which the subject-object engagement proceeds, and is prepared to challenge the obstacles as they appear, will have no fear that the problem-solving process will be endangered by his assumption of full status as a knowing person in the group system.

As the worker makes his contribution of data, several major considerations guide his movements. The first is his awareness that his offering represents only a fragment of available social experience. If he comes to be regarded as the fountainhead of social reality, he will then have fallen into the error of presenting himself as the object of learning rather than as an accessory to it. Thus, there is an important distinction to be made between lending his knowledge to those who can use it in the performance of their own tasks and projecting himself as a text to be learned. In the first instance, the worker is used in accordance with his function as a mediator of the subject-object relationship; in the second, the worker himself becomes the object.

The second consideration lies in the relationship between the information he shares and the function of the group as this function is understood by the members and by the agency. Often, the worker is tempted to "expose" the group to certain facts and ideas which may, in some future context, be found useful. Such efforts generally serve to confuse rather than enlighten, since there is no frame of reference within which the data assume weight and significance. Where these acts of the worker constitute a series of ideological "plugs," the effect is to breed a vague distrust of the worker's purpose and of his stated desire to assist the group to carry out its own function.

The function of the group may be considered a general frame of reference to be considered by the worker as he selects the data he will share with the members. Even more important as a factor is the specific working context within which he makes his contributions. Again, this assumes the existence of a culture of work, within which the worker's offering is but a single, important ingredient and the worker is but one of many sources of social reality; with his data, as with everything else, the test of utility will inevitably lie in its appropriateness to the demands of the current task. This is the sense in which the old group work injunction that "program is a tool" is important. It is a tool, not of the worker, but of the group and its members; and, like all tools, each fact, idea, or concept must be fashioned to the specific job for which it is to be used.

The final consideration is that, while the worker's own opinions represent important data, they are such only when presented honestly as opinion rather than as fact. There are many occasions where the member is at the mercy of the worker's power to disguise the distinction between the two. The temptation to becloud this distinction is strong, and often unconscious; culture-bound and ego-bound, the worker is himself unclear in many important areas about the difference between reality and his own constructions of it. But the struggle to distinguish between subjective perceptions and external reality is at the heart of all human learning and growing, and the worker who is not engaged in this struggle himself will find it impossible to help others in the same endeavor. As he helps them to evaluate the evidence they derive from other sources—their own experiences, the experience of others, and their collaboration in ideas—so must he submit his own evidence to the process of critical examination. When the worker understands that he is but a single element in the totality of the member's experience, and when he is able to use this truth rather than attempt to conquer it, he has taken the first step toward helping the member to free himself from authority without rejecting it.

4. The responsibility for contributing data is related to the fourth task that expresses the function of the helping agent. This involves those activities through which the worker reveals, frankly and directly, his own hopes and aspirations concerning the outcome of the group experience. Borrowing a phrase used by Norman Kelman in another context, we would designate this task as that of lending a vision to the members of the group.[18]

In these activities, the worker reveals himself as a person whose own aspirations are deeply invested in the interaction between people and society, and who has, through his own struggles, developed a vision of what life can and should be like. In his enthusiasm, his sense of urgency, and his capacity for empathy, the worker demonstrates that his own life experience is involved here, that he has a stake in society, and that he is not here simply to dispense solutions to problems that are beneath him and irrelevant to his own concerns.

More specifically, the worker reveals his emotional involvement in three important ways. The first is his faith in the system itself and in the conditions under which the growing experience takes place. By his movements to safeguard the function of the group, he expresses his respect for the dignity of the group itself and for the reasons which created it. By his refusal to trade identities with either the members or their materials, he demonstrates his faith in the constructive power inherent in the relationship of one to the other.

The second aspect of the worker's personal investment is revealed in his attitude toward the relevant data of the group system. In this respect, the worker's activity reflects something of what the material means to him—its excitement, its depths, and its importance in the human scheme. As the worker shares his own intense involvement with the materials, he projects himself as a living example of their power to attract and intrigue the human mind. It is only in this sense that the helping agent is a salesman; and without the slightest intent to be one but simply by virtue of his position as, so to speak, a pleased consumer. Without this sense of enthusiasm, this vision of immense possibilities, and his status as a model of mastery, the worker's contribution to the subject-object relationship resolves itself into a mechanical questioning

---

[18]*Ibid.* Dr. Kelman speaks of the necessity to "lend our vision to the patient" as the psychoanalytic process proceeds. Although his meaning here is slightly different from ours, his general intent is similar to the one we mean to convey.

and answering; with it, there can be a challenge, a driving curiosity, and a strong motive for work.

Finally, the worker's affect is a strong component in his relationships with the members of the group. The professional relationship can be described as a flow of affect between worker and member, combining the expectations and perceptions of one with the other, as they work together—each on his own tasks—within the group system. Their interaction is based on the circumstances which brought them together; and it is in the work itself that their feeling for each other grows. In this light, the worker's efforts to establish relationship go much deeper than the kind of wooing activity in which he seeks to gain the member's acceptance and approval through the exercise of his personal warmth and attractiveness. The human qualities of the worker, however engaging they may be, should not be used to divert, to charm, or to build personal dependency.

The worker, sensitized by his own need to cope with the complexities of living and growing, has a fund of feeling from which to draw his attempts to understand the member's struggles in detail. This understanding is reflected, not in a generalized "wanting to help," or "giving love," or "accepting them as they are," although these purposes provide an important ideological base from which to operate. Rather, his understanding is communicated in his ability to empathize with the precise feelings engendered in the learner by the demands of a particular task in a specific situation. The worker's ability to call up parts of his own experience, to communicate his feeling, and to demonstrate an active faith in the productive capacities of the member are important parts of the image of vitality that he projects.

In all, the worker's feeling involvement in the group system demonstrates better than words his conviction that the process of growing is complicated and difficult, but also challenging and rewarding if one is left free to conjure with it and to test one's experience under conditions where one can err without failing completely. The worker lends his vision to the members, not in order to exchange it for theirs, but because his aliveness, his faith in productivity, and his stake in work are inherent in his function as a helping person.

5. The agency, the worker, the group, and its members are related to each other by certain rules and requirements imposed upon them by the terms of their agreement. These requirements emerge first in the conditions under which the group is established, its function identified, and its procedures initiated. Later, the rules are modified, amplified, and reinterpreted as their concrete implications become clearer in the events of group life. These expectations are not limited to those imposed upon the members by the agency, or by the worker; they are reciprocal in that each actor imposes certain restrictions and is bound

by others. Thus, while the group and its members are held to certain policies and procedures, the agency and the worker are also limited by standards such as equal treatment, consistency in approach, the members' concept of fair play, and so forth.

To the extent that the terms of the agreement are specific and unambiguous, the participants are free to pursue their tasks within the system in their own characteristic ways. Where the rules are, or become, obscure and vaguely defined, the major energies of both worker and members become diverted to exploring the boundaries and testing the limits of the group situation. This leads us to the final task of the helping agent, in which he calls upon the participants of the learning group to face the necessities inherent in the conditions of their association. This definition of the requirements begins with the worker's first attempts to identify the specific responsibilities that have been undertaken by the agency, the group, and the worker himself; it continues as he monitors these realities and calls for clarification at those points where they become obscure.

The most important aspect of these requirements is that they emerge from the function of the group and the necessities of work rather than from the personal authority of the helping agent. As such, they are parts of a reality which is imposed by the nature of the setting, the conditions of group life, and the purposes for which the group has been assembled. The worker is often frustrated by his "inability to set limits," when his real difficulty arises from his failure to recognize that his task is to explain a situation rather than to create one. Club members find it a great deal easier to accept situational realities and limitations—dress requirements, bans on smoking, and so on—than those imposed by the worker in his own name for reasons which are ambiguous, or moralistic, or designed to build character. Since people do not join clubs to have their characters built, such taboos are not perceived as interpretations of reality, and in fact are not.

Science and Art in the Helping Process

Because of our emphasis on viewing the social worker in action, we have concentrated our analysis on his movements within the group system rather than on the personal and professional equipment which he brings to the job. Most attempts to identify the foundations of professional skill have resulted in an encyclopedic and somewhat frightening inventory of virtues. There is, after all, no sphere of knowledge, no personal strength, and no field of competence which is irrelevant to the responsibilities of the human relations worker. And yet we know that the tasks of helping are not performed best by paragons but by those who want to help, know what they are trying to do, and have sufficient mastery of themselves and of social realities to offer their strengths in the struggles of others. Thus, the central problem for the helping agent does not lie in his nearness to perfection but in the extent to which he can mobilize the powers he does possess in the service of others. In order to find the common ground, he must use certain specific knowledge about human beings; in order to contribute data, to reveal his own stake in society, to define the rules, and to challenge the obstacles in the learner's path, he must be free to share what he has of sensitivity, science, and personal maturity. Where the worker proceeds from a clear sense of focus and function, his own strengths are tools that he uses in the specific tasks that he is called upon to face. As such, his powers are not pitifully inadequate replicas of a formidable ideal but full-blown strengths which he is free to own and to share.

There is nothing in the conception of a professional methodology which denies or subordinates the uniquely personal and artistic component which each worker brings to his administration of the helping function. On the contrary, the concept of a disciplined uniqueness is inherent in the definition of art itself. In a broad sense, we may view artistic activity as an attempt, by someone innately endowed with extreme sensitivity to the world about him, to express strong personal feelings and aspirations through a disciplined use of his materials. The analogy between the helping agent and the creative artist can be struck at several points. In both, there is an emphasis on feeling, on an empathic quality which is cherished as a tool of the craft; both feel a constant need for fresh insights into the nature of things and for new ways to express their view of the world; in both, there is a strong preoccupation with essences and basic principles; there is a high degree of subjectivity, of self-consciousness, which constitutes a major element in their ability to create new vistas and new perspectives; in both, the creativity is nourished by the continuous search for truth and is, in fact, an expression of this search; and both require an atmosphere in which one is free to explore, to err, to test reality, and to change.

If we add to these the powerful urge of both the artist and the social worker to communicate their view of life and to affect the experience of others through their artistry, then the sense in which the helping art is distinguishable from that of the painter, the musician, or the writer lies only in that which they are impelled to express, the nature of their materials, and the processes through which they move in order to carry out their functions.

Systems theory, one theoretical framework for understanding social work practice with groups, calls upon the
worker to become a peer member of the group. Validation for such a point of view is found in democratic
political theory, from which implications for the purpose
of any social work group might be found—the maximization of opportunities for developing the individual to his
fullest capacity.

Social Group Work—An
Intersystemic Frame
of Reference

Norman N. Goroff

Introduction

The increasing proliferation of the use of the group by a variety of
professions in their attempts to help human beings is resulting in considerable confusion as to what differentiates these various group approaches. Evidence of this confusion may be culled from the variety
of names given to the group approach by practitioners. A major factor
in contributing to the confused state is that the names given do not
clearly define what happens in the group nor what the professional does
in them.

It is possible to examine the most recent professional journals and
find the following in the titles of the articles: "Social Group Work,
Group Therapy, Group Counselling, Group Psychotherapy, Group Edu-
cation, Supportive Group Therapy, Group Guidance, Family Group
Work, Family Group Therapy, Cognitive Group Therapy, T-Group,
Group Activity, Group-Analytical Play Therapy, Therapeutic Discussion
Group, Group Case Work, Casework Oriented Group Treatment,
Group Psychoanalytical Therapy, Group Social Therapy, Group Treat-
ment, Group Intake, Group Orientations."

If this is not sufficiently confusing, we can come back to social group
work and find increasing proliferation of settings in which social group
workers are asked to practice. One of the problems resulting from the
diffusion of social group workers has been that the practice of social
group work has been adapted to the settings and inappropriate "models" for the practice of social group work were "integrated." It then
became necessary to legitimatize these changes and the development
of "models" of social group work practice has ensued. Thus we now

Reprinted with permission of *Journal of Jewish Communal Service,* Vol. 47 (3), 1971, pp. 229–
237.

talk about a "remedial" or "restorative model," a "social goals model," a "reciprocal model" with the attendant rise of adherents to each "model" which begins to border on the "cult phenomena."

The "model" building phase takes on the form of post-factum explanations. As Merton[1] points out, the logical fallacy underlying such explanations "rests in the fact that there are available a variety of crude hypotheses, each with some measure of confirmation but designed to account for quite contradictory sets of affairs."

It is recognized that a science can make use of models and model building in the development of its knowledge. The utility of models in the practice professions is questionable. Models are abstractions from reality whereas practice is reality. The danger inherent in model building in practice is that the practice may reflect the model rather than the reality of the needs of the people in the situation. This is particularly true if the criteria for differentiating the models are based on the "population" served, the "specific purpose" the group is intended to have, or the particular activity of the worker.

Social group work in essence must always consider the three basic components; (1) the relationship which exists among individuals, their sub-groups and the group as a whole, (2) the dynamics pertaining to the group itself and (3) the relationship between the individuals and the group and their environing social and cultural systems. Unless there is this simultaneous concern over the links between individual and group, interactions within the groups and the links between the group and significant others we would be hard pressed to recognize the efforts as social group work.

Social group work as defined herein is applicable in any setting with any population whether it is perceived as being primarily concerned with corrective services for social dysfunctions or with "normal growth and development—socialization." It is neither the target population nor the "purpose" for which the social group worker is engaged that is the significant determinant of whether social group work is being practiced. The significant determinant is whether the three basic concerns are present in the consciousness of the worker and if he has explicated these concerns with the members of the group in developing the working agreement with them.

Some Historical Factors

Reissman and Miller[2] characterize the intellectual atmosphere of the 40's and 50's as being taken over by the "psychiatric world view . . .

[1]Robert K. Merton, *Social Theory and Social Structure,* Rev. ed. (Glencoe, Ill.: Free Press, 1957), p. 94.
[2]Reissman and Miller, "Social Change Versus the Psychiatric World View," *American Journal of Orthopsychiatry,* Vol. 34, No. 1, January 1964, p. 29.

which defined almost everything in psychological terms." All kinds of problems were reduced to psychological factors. Thus what Durkheim had cautioned sociologists against, namely the reduction of social facts and sociological phenomena into a psychological framework became the overwhelming orientation.

Social group work as a professional practice succumbed to the prevailing influences of the time. It was during the 40's and 50's that social group workers began to be found in social work settings that were strongly committed to the psychoanalytical conception of personality and to the therapeutic use of the social work methods.

Gisela Konopka[3] describing the use of social group work in child guidance clinics and other institutional settings in 1946 noted that the social group worker needed to sharpen his psychiatric knowledge and diagnostic ability.

The role of the social group worker in treatment settings seemed to be greatly influenced by the hierarchical social structure of the psychiatric hospital in which the psychiatrist was preeminent. This influence is seen in the following statement, "Diagnostic goals for each individual as established by the worker supersedes group goals. . . . Membership is predetermined and diagnostically selected by the worker. . . . He (the worker) is characteristically directive and assumes a position of clinical preeminence and authority."[4]

This view of the social group worker is placed in juxtaposition to that in the statement in "Group Work as We see It"[5] published in 1939 by the Boys Clubs of America which saw the group worker as "setting the stage and providing suitable environment for learning, expression, adjustment and social action based on his understanding of needs of individual members and sensing underlying social purposes of the group."

Social action and social change objectives appeared throughout most of the attempts during the 20's and 30's to define social group work as a method of social work practice.

It is not our intention to bring in the past as a prestigious reason for returning to the founding tradition. Rather it is to recall to our awareness that the early pioneers of social group work recognized the inexplicable interpenetration of the individual and society. It was this recognition that contributed to the emphasis on social action and social change objectives as being an essential component of social group work.

The concept of the interrelationship between the individual and society is equally valid today as it was then. Reissman and Miller note,

[3]Margaret E. Hartford, "The Search for a Definition," *Working Papers Towards a Frame of Reference for Social Group Work,* NASW, 1964.
[4]Pappell and Rothman, "Social Group Work Models: Possession and Heritage," *Journal of Education for Social Work,* Vol. 2, No. 2 (Fall 1966), pp. 66–67.
[5]Hartford, *op. cit.*

"the blinders acquired during the age of psychiatry in the 40's and 50's still limit intense commitment and the search for far-reaching social change."[6] That social work and social group work may still be hampered by these "blinders" seems to be axiomatic.

Frame of Reference

The concept of social group work in its three essences is based on several important views of our "social reality." Man and society are opposite sides of the same coin. One cannot exist without the other. This inextricable relationship between the individual and society requires the social group worker to help the individual and the group to participate actively in the world around them. The literature has viewed this as "citizenship participation in a democracy," "fulfillment of social responsibility," "assuming responsibility for themselves and others" and "to take part in the decision-making process." Rothman and Pappell[7] designate this as the "social goal model." The unfortunate aspect of this designation is to highlight and isolate one of the three interrelated interdependent essences of social group work. The result is to create the impression that the social worker's attempts to help the individual and the group to play a part in those societal aspects which affect them is a unique one called "social action." It seems that social action has become "unique" as social group work incorporated inappropriate role models for professional practice.

Our view of the development of man's nature is based on the theoretical formulation of Charles Horton Cooley—namely, that man develops his basic human nature in constant interactions within a variety of groups—family, peers and neighborhood. We therefore see the individual and the group as being inextricably intertwined in the process of human development. We cannot therefore differentiate between what has been identified as "corrective" on one end of a continuum and "enhancement of growth and development" on the other. We are hard pressed to conceptualize when a "corrective group experience" does not enhance growth and development. Similarly, we do not find it very useful to designate "enhancement of growth and development" as not having elements of a "corrective experience."

The third view is that when a number of people come together to create a group, a social process is set into motion which creates unique group properties which can be utilized by the social group worker in helping the individuals to use the experience for a variety of personal psychosocial needs. It is our contention that these properties can only

[6]Reissman and Miller, *op. cit.*
[7]Pappell and Rothman, *op. cit.*

The Group as Target

be found in a group in its particular form. It is the social group worker's skill in relating to individuals within the context of these group properties that is one of the major characteristics of the professional.

Whatever words we use to try to communicate the essential aspect of the helping process, we return to the "interpersonal relationship" that develops between the professional and the member as being at the core of the process. It follows then that the network of interpersonal relationships established among the participants in the group will materially increase the "power" of the helping process. This recognition of the multiple sources of "potentially helpful relationships" in the group creates a situation which Schwartz[8] has called "a mutual aid society." The concept of "mutual aid" places the worker in the position in which he uses himself to facilitate the operation of the "potentially helpful relationships" so that they become actual helpful relationships. The worker does not bring to the group situation those potentials which do not exist in the group. Rather, he brings knowledge and skill to help actualize the potentials.

A diagram which tries to illustrate the total interrelationship of the individual, group and other systems may be helpful.

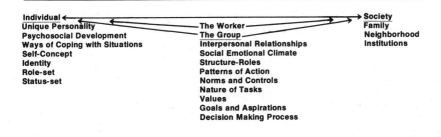

Individual	The Worker	Society
Unique Personality	The Group	Family
Psychosocial Development	Interpersonal Relationships	Neighborhood
Ways of Coping with Situations	Social Emotional Climate	Institutions
Self-Concept	Structure-Roles	
Identity	Patterns of Action	
Role-set	Norms and Controls	
Status-set	Nature of Tasks	
	Values	
	Goals and Aspirations	
	Decision Making Process	

The social group worker in making an assessment of what is happening at any given moment needs to scan simultaneously the possible meaning of the individual's behavior as it reflects or is indicative of his personality, his psychosocial development, his ways of coping with situations within the framework of what is happening in the group situation and how both the group and the individual are linked to other societal systems and how they interpenetrate with each other. It is only as he scans all of these areas that the social worker can make an assessment which encompasses the many factors in a situation. Thus his intervention may be more reflective of the "reality" and hopefully more effective in helping the individual.

[8]William Schwartz, "Some Notes on the Use of Groups in Social Work Practice," mimeo. 1966.

The conception of social group work requires the worker to utilize many frameworks in his assessing process. He needs to understand individual dynamics, social processes in groups, and sociocultural aspects of society. The utilization of any one framework alone may provide the worker with an incomplete and hence distorted assessment of what is happening.

A focus which tends to be limited to a concern with the worker in the group and his activities has led to the development of categories of group influence attempts. Schleidlinger delineates five categories: (1) activity-catharsis-mastery focus; (2) cognitive-informational focus; (3) interpersonal-socialization focus; (4) relationship-experiential focus; and (5) uncovering-introspective focus, all of which are not mutually exclusive nor concerned with the relationship of the individual and group in interaction with significant others.[9] This conception is so narrow that it distorts the real meaning of working with people in groups. There is an underlying assumption about the worker in relation to the group that places too much emphasis on him and not nearly enough on the group members and the group as a whole as crucial contributors to the "helping power of the group."

The intersystemic framework of social group work has a number of important implications for the social worker.

One of these implications is related to the social worker's attitude and perception of people he works with in a group. It is not accidental that social group workers refer to people in groups as members and not clients or patients. There is a connotation to the concept client or patient which has a superordinate-subordinate relationship implication. This hierarchial status relationship places the person seeking help in a dependency position and the worker in a giving position. This is an unequal power relationship in which, whether in reality or fantasy, the social worker can attempt to exert control by either giving or withholding "help." He makes his "resources" available to the person seeking help on the condition that the person respond to him as having some "clinical pre-eminence or authority." He puts a "tax" on his help.

The "mutual aid" concept requires the social group worker to reaffirm his conviction that he is in a partnership relationship with the members of the group. Each participant in the partnership brings his assets and liabilities, his capacities and needs, his ability to give help and take help, his unique personality, his knowledge and skills, and places them at the disposal of the group. Thus, the social group worker must give up his desire to *control* either the process in the group or

[9]Saul Schleidlinger, "Therapeutic Group Approaches in Community Mental Health," *Social Work,* Vol. 13, No. 2 (April 1968), p. 87.

the individuals for "some goals he has developed" in favor of developing a *mutually acceptable* working agreement with the members of the group that will establish the framework for the group members and the social worker to enter into the relationship.

The social group worker, in this endeavor, as in all of his work with people, must be governed by a value system which stresses the inherent right of each person to self-fulfillment, the right of people to be self-determining, the obligation of a democratic society to ensure the constant maximization of opportunities for self-determination and for development of his fullest capacity.

The social group worker must believe in a process of growth and change and in the individual's inalienable right to participate in the decision-making processes which affect him within the group and within other systems. This requires the worker not to do for people that which they should be able to do for themselves. To do for them is to maintain power, control and dependency. To do with them is to share power, control and foster relative independence.

The author has described a technique, called "confrontation with reality,"[10] in which he confronted the group members with contradictions in two areas of overt behavior—verbalization of desires and conduct. The confrontation in the here-and-now reality of the group resulted in some modifications of conduct more in keeping with the verbalized desires. A carry-over of the new behavior into the institutional setting resulted in responses which indicated to the group members the superiors in the institution did not welcome the "new" behavior.

When this reaction was brought to the group, it became clear that the social worker had to intervene in the links between the group members and their superiors. After several weeks of discussions as to preferred strategies, the group members wanted the social worker to intervene on their behalf and the social worker wanted them to meet with the superintendent in a direct face-to-face discussion; the group members agreed to meet with the superintendent.

The social worker had to devise appropriate ways to try to help change patterns of behavior within the institution which were working against the purposes of the group experiences. He had to do it with the members rather than for the members.

Another implication concerns his firm belief in the fact that the basic power to help people in a group resides in the people in the group. People help one another through the process of working through a myriad of group-related and group-generated problems which they

---

[10]Norman N. Goroff, "Confrontation with Reality: A Social Group Work Approach," *Mental Hygiene,* Vol. 51, No. 3 (July 1967).

must continually resolve as they live in the social reality, here-and-now experience we call a group. Tropp[11] said, "people can be helped to help each other: this is the heart of the matter and all else is commentary." For the social worker who has truly accepted this basic truth, there develops simultaneously a greater sense of security for himself in his work with people in groups, a feeling of humility as he *shares* in the process of people helping one another and possibly a sense of optimism as he realizes that the capacity for people to be helped in a group goes beyond those imposed by his limitations.

Increasingly, we find the concepts, "the advocate role," the broker role and "the activist role," being used in social work.[12] The intersystemic framework of social group work has within it these roles for the social worker.

The social group worker is required to become increasingly cognizant of the interplay of the other social system and the group. He must assess the structure and functions of the other system and identify both functional and dysfunctional consequences as they relate to the individuals in the group. The social worker's basic commitment to the well-being of the individual makes it a categorical imperative for him to attempt to effect changes which have dysfunctional consequences for the individual. In order to be effective in this role, the worker needs to develop the necessary knowledge to make the analysis and to formulate strategies necessary to eliminate those dysfunctional consequences. In this process, the social worker must remember that he is working with a group of people who have a stake in the outcome and therefore must be involved in appropriate ways to bring about the change.

Polsky develops a similar theme: "my central point of departure for the discussion of helping social systems is that they serve a function both in society and relative to client needs *and* the two functions are often not complementary. . . . I want to enlarge upon the idea of a system as functional or dysfunctional to its members and the subsystem. I want to approach the idea that in social work, rehabilitation must start with dysfunctional clients and a system functional to clients' dysfunctioning and that both have to change in order to effect a global functional resolution that answers both the positive needs of society as well as its clients. . . . Clients in helping systems need assistance in overcoming the rules that lock them into patient roles so that they can eventually begin to become ex-clients *within* the service system."[13]

[11]Emanuel Tropp, "The Group: In Life and in Social Work," *Social Casework,* Vol. 49, No. 5 (May 1968), pp. 267–74.
[12]Charles F. Grosser, "Community Development Programs Serving the Urban Poor," *Social Work,* Vol. 10, No. 3 (July 1965).
[13]Howard W. Polsky, "Systems as Patient: Client Needs and System Function," presented at annual meeting CSWE, 1968, mimeo.

The Group as Target

Failure to utilize the total framework for analysis will inevitably result in distorted and inappropriate assessments. We have a youngster whom we have diagnosed as being emotionally disturbed. The mere fact of such a diagnosis sets into motion a number of factors which may affect the people working with him. One of these may be what Merton called the "self-fulfilling prophecy"[14] and Goffman[15] called "looping-back onto the patient." In this situation, the child's behavior will be explained by his being "emotionally disturbed" and will provide further evidence of his emotional disturbance. The subsequent behavior of the people working with the child may contribute to the child behavior in such a manner as to in fact fulfill a prophecy.

Redl describes a classic example of this when he discusses a youngster whose behavior in a cottage was extremely difficult for the workers and the residents to cope with. He was highly disturbed and any attempt to work with him within the cottage failed. The staff was ready to conclude that this boy was beyond their capacity to help until the focus was changed from an exclusive reliance on his intrapsychic problems to looking at the individual within the context of the particular cottage. At this point, it became evident that for a variety of factors, namely the composition of the group, this youngster was misgrouped. A transfer to another cottage resulted in a noticeable change in his behavior.[16]

The focus on the individual in isolation from the group resulted initially in a very discouraging prognosis. Viewing the individual within the context of the particular cottage resulted in a shift from the individual to the individual-in-interaction with a group of individuals and hence a different assessment, a modification of the treatment plan—shifting to another group and a more hopeful prognosis.

A focus on the individual in the group without considering the social cultural background will result in inappropriate assessments and hence ineffective strategies for intervention.

In the recent past, when in schools of social work human behavior was taught almost exclusively within the framework of psychoanalytical personality theory and ego psychology, it was rather common for students to make assessments of behavior within that framework. One student, working with a group of eight-year-old boys, made the assessment that one of the boys who didn't want to paint had been "poorly toilet-trained."

After we gathered a supply of old shirts for use as smocks and made

[14]Robert K. Merton, *Social Theory and Social Structure,* Enlarged Edition. (New York: Free Press, 1968) Chap. 13.
[15]Erving Goffman, *Asylums,* (Garden City: Anchor Books, 1961).
[16]Fritz Redl, *When We Deal With Children,* (New York: Free Press, 1966). Chapter 11, "The Art of Group Composition."

them available to the boys, the youngster who had been "diagnosed" as "poorly toilet trained" became involved in painting, clay work and other messy work. The fact that the youngster was from a stable work-ing-class family and came to the center directly from school was not taken into consideration. The student worker discovered that the boy had specific instructions from his mother not to get his "good school clothes" messy.

A focus on the genesis of behavior from outside of the group encoun-ter may hinder the social worker in trying to deal with the particular behavior in the group. However by focussing on the behavior in the "here-and-now of the group" he can begin to try to effect changes by intervening within the appropriate group processses.

Maas describes how he attempted to utilize the group process in dealing with behavior in a group that was reflective of many attitudes which contributed to the problem of the adult patients in a psychiatric hospital.[17] In this group of adult patients and their parents there devel-oped the pattern in which the parents would address each other by the family name, but the adult patients would be called by their given name. The worker intervened in the normative pattern of the group by insisting that every member of the group address each other in a consistent manner, either all would be addressed by their family name or by their given name. This confronted the parents and the patients with the existence of a dual standard which reflected an attitude and a definition of the situation that was debilitating for both parents and patients.

The social worker's strategy in intervening in the group normative pattern had to take into account the effect that this would have on the interpersonal relationship of the group members outside of the group. To intervene without consideration of the possible reverberations out-side the group for the participants does not meet the criteria of group work as viewed here.

A focus on the group without regard for the relationship the members have with the broader socio-cultural environs will provide an equally faulty assessment.

In a city school system, a group of junior high school boys have been referred by the guidance department for social group work treatment because of their exceedingly disruptive behavior.

The academic achievements of the boys are below grade level. They are seen as "dull normal in intelligence, emotionally immature, lacking adequate inner controls which tends to make them impulsive."

As the student worked with them, some very significant facts emerged. Much of the boys' behavior was triggered by being called

---

[17]Philip Maas, "Therapist-Induced Crisis in Group Treatment," *Mental Hygiene,* Vol. 50, No. 1.

upon to perform publicly tasks which were beyond them and therefore doomed them to public failure. These tasks included reading aloud and doing math problems on the blackboard. This meant that the student worker had to intervene within the school setting in order to eliminate the "triggering mechanism" because it was dysfunctional for the pupil, the class, the teacher and for the school in pursuing its educational goal.

The peer culture of the student body was at variance with the behavior of the boys in the group. Yet there were others in the school, who although not as disruptive as those referred, nevertheless did not fit into the overall "peer culture." This resulted in the recognition by the worker of the fallacy of the concept of a monolithic peer culture. There were numerous subsystems of peers within the school. How was this group linked to other subsystems? Was there a reference group with whom they identified?

A gang of high school students, a non-academically oriented self-perpetuating "fraternity" was uncovered. This "fraternity" required a "rep" as a "hardnose" as requirement for membership. The junior high school students were linked to this fraternity in their aspirations. Any potentially successful attempt to affect the junior high students must involve simultaneously efforts to change the high school "fraternity." As long as this particular reference group remains in its present form, the prognosis for change within the junior high school group is poor.

A careful analysis of the community revealed three basic subsystems which were developmental systems. They provided a "career track" for its members who entered the subsystems in elementary school and continued throughout their school career. These subsystems[18] were identified through an examination of the current situation plus some historical information which revealed that these subsystems had persisted over a sufficient period of time for them to have become institutionalized.

The intersystemic frame of reference required the social worker to go beyond the individuals, the specific setting and look for an increasing complex of systemic interpenetration and linkage. The resulting strategies for intervention will involve a variety of groups in addition to the specific boys who were the initial focus of attention.

[18]Albert Alissi, "Social Influences on Group Values," *Social Work,* Vol. 10, No. 1 (January 1965).

As it relates to social work practice, group work theory has been categorized into three general models for practice. Whittaker relates these three models to a five-stage process which is purported to encompass the development of small groups. Appropriate strategies for action and target populations are identified for each of these models and for each stage of the group's development within each model.

Models of Group Development: Implications for Social Group Work Practice

James K. Whittaker

In 1960, Robert Vinter said of the then nascent state of group work practice principles:

Despite the profession's intense interest in methods and techniques of practice, and the large literature on practice, there has been very little analysis of the processes of formulating practice principles. Anyone undertaking this task enters relatively uncharted territory and can be expected to do little more than identify the major peaks and valleys [54:4].

In ten years, the body of group work practice principles has grown so much that, at least in some areas, the group work practitioner is faced with an abundance, rather than with a scarcity, of guidelines for practice. One such well-developed area is that of small-group development, in which a number of different models have been proposed, each with its accompanying implications for practice. The result has been that the group work practitioner often finds himself as disillusioned with the "affluence" of too many practice models—often with overlapping categories and different terminology for the same phenomena—as he was with the "poverty" of too few.

It is the thesis of this paper that the five-stage model for group development proposed by Garland, Jones, and Kolodny represents the most complete statement to date on the subject and contains within its stages the basic elements of the models proposed by the other major contributors to the social work literature in this area (8).[1] The purpose of this paper, then, will be twofold: *(a)* to integrate the other major practice

Reprinted from *Social Service Review,* Vol. 44 (3), 1970, pp. 308–322, by permission of the author and the University of Chicago Press.
[1]See Kindelsperger (16), Maier (26), Sarri and Galinsky (38), and Trecker (49).

formulations of group development into the model suggested by Garland, Jones, and Kolodny, and *(b)* to develop implications for practice for each of the stages of development, on the basis of the three overall models of social group work practice: the social-goals model, the remedial model, and the reciprocal model (31).

Current Models of
Group Development

The knowledge base for group development draws from small-group sociology, social psychology, group psychotherapy, human relations, and social work.[2] Researchers in these areas have provided many studies that illustrate the general cycles and phases through which groups seem to progress. In general, most theorists look upon group development as a series of phases through which all small groups progress, or at least as some sort of recurring cycle of member attraction based on different factors.[3] For example, Bales and Strodtbeck have suggested three phases of development in problem-solving groups: orientation, evaluation, and control, with each of these assuming prominence at any one given point in time (2).

In the literature of social group work, we find a number of studies of group development. Only the more fully developed of these models —those of Maier, Kindelsperger, Trecker, and Sarri and Galinsky—will be considered in terms of how they may be integrated with the Garland, Jones, and Kolodny formulation.[4]

Henry Maier has proposed four phases through which small groups progress: locating commonness, creating exchange, developing mutual identification, and developing group identification. Maier chooses not to look upon termination as a phase of group development, but otherwise his scheme most closely resembles the Garland, Jones, and Kolodny model in its essential components.

Kindelsperger has suggested a six-stage model of group development consisting of the following phases: approach or orientation, relationship negotiation or conflict, group role emergence, vacillating group role dominance, group role dominance, and institutionalized group roles. This formulation, while helpful in some respects, appears to be too inadequately developed to be of any substantial benefit to the practi-

---

[2] For an introduction to the subject see Cartwright and Zander (6), Hare (12), Hare, Borgatta, and Bales (13), Homans (14), Lewin (23), Lippitt (24), Mann (28), Martin and Hill (29), Psathas (36), Redl (37), Scheidlinger (39), and Theodorson (47).

[3] Homans, for example, posits such recurring and reciprocal cycles, with activity, interaction, and sentiment being the essential basis for formation (14).

[4] The author is well aware of the important contributions of Austin (1), Bernstein (4), Northen (30), Paradise (32), Shalinsky (43), and Thomas and Fink (48) to our knowledge of group development, but these materials will not be considered here.

tioner. For example, we are told: "No group ever fits exactly into these categories and all groups do not go through all of the stages," without being told why this is so. Similarly, the author says little about the character of worker intervention at each stage of development and leaves us only with the rather tenuous statement that "it is risky to bypass the stages and to force movement ahead." It is not made clear why this is necessarily so.

Trecker has also proposed a six-stage model for group development that is more behaviorally descriptive than the others. It consists of the following stages: beginning stage; emergence of some group feeling, organization, program; development of bond, purpose, and cohesiveness; strong group feeling—goal attainment; decline in interest—less group feeling; and ending stage, or decision to discontinue the group. Like Bernstein, Trecker suggests a number of key indices which the worker can use in determining the group's stage of development.

One of the best theoretically developed and well-articulated statements of group development has been offered by Rosemary Sarri and Maeda Galinsky. Unlike the other formulations, theirs derives from an analysis of small-group research, primarily in sociology and group psychotherapy. This model of development is congruent with Vinter's conception of the group as both the means and the context for treatment (52). The Sarri and Galinsky model, which rests upon four basic assumptions,[5] consists of seven distinct phases:

1. Origin phase

This phase refers to the composition of the group and is distinguished primarily for analytic purposes, since it is at least a precondition for later development.

2. Formative phase

The initial activity of the group members in seeking similarity and the mutuality of interests is the outstanding characteristic of this phase. Initial commitments to group purpose, emergent personal ties, and a quasi-group structure are also observable.

3. Intermediate phase I

This phase is characterized by a moderate level of group cohesion, clarification of purposes, and observable involvement of members in goal-directed activities.

---

[5] The group is a potent influence system and can be used as an efficient vehicle for individual change. The group is not an end in itself. Group development can be controlled and influenced by the worker's actions. There is no optimal way in which groups develop.

4. Revision phase

This phase is characterized by challenges to the existing group structure and an accompanying modification of group purposes and operating procedures.

5. Intermediate Phase II

Following the revision phase, while many groups progress toward maturation, the characteristics outlined in Intermediate phase I may again appear, though the group generally manifests a higher level of integration and stability than in the earlier phase.

6. Maturation phase

This phase is characterized by stabilization of group structure, group purpose, operating and governing procedures, expansion of the culture of the group, and the existence of effective responses to internal and external stress.

7. Termination phase

The dissolution of the group may result from goal attainment, maladaptation, lack of integration, or previously made plans about the duration of the group.

The writers go on to develop a series of strategies for each of the phases. Despite the theoretical sophistication of the model, it appears to fall short in its description of what is happening to the members in each of the phases, as contrasted to the richly descriptive material offered by Garland, Jones, and Kolodny. In fairness to the authors, it should be noted that their main reason for omitting descriptions of individual member reactions was that several writers in the past had failed to distinguish worker intervention and individual client reaction from the group developmental processes. One wishes that the authors had made such a distinction and then gone on to describe both the group developmental processes and the reactions of individual members, as well as the strategies of worker intervention. In addition, the Sarri and Galinsky model contains no "real life" group-process examples, in sharp contrast to the highly illustrative examples integrated into the Garland formulation.

Finally, the names of the different stages in the Sarri and Galinsky model, while certainly in keeping with the research studies from which they were derived, sound somewhat as if they were contrived strictly for taxonomic purposes. The Garland model, on the other hand, employs, in describing its stages, a rich "central theme" approach which seems to have more overall benefit for the practitioner. Despite these few shortcomings, the Sarri and Galinsky model constitutes a distinct and significant contribution to the group work literature, particularly in terms of its scientifically based descriptions of group structure and processes.

Garland, Jones, and Kolodny: Five Stages of Group Development

This five-stage model of group development was derived from an analysis of group-process records at a children's agency over a three-year period. It is solid in its theoretical underpinnings, well articulated, and richly exampled with group-process materials. It offers the most advanced statement in the literature concerning worker focus at each of the various stages. The authors have identified the five stages in terms of the central theme characteristic of each. They are as follows:[6]

1. Pre-affiliation

"Closeness" of the members is the central theme in this stage, with "approach-avoidance" as the major early struggle in relation to it. Ambivalence toward involvement is reflected in the members' vacillating responses to program activities and events. Relationships are usually nonintimate, and a good deal of use may be made of rather stereotypic activity as a means of getting acquainted.

2. Power and control

After making the decision that the group is potentially rewarding, members move to a stage during which issues of power, control, status, skill, and decision-making are the focal points. There is likely to be a testing of the group worker and the members, as well as an attempt to define and formalize relationships and to define a status hierarchy. Three basic issues are suggested by the power-struggle phenomena: rebellion and autonomy, permission and the normative crisis, and protection and support.

3. Intimacy

This stage is characterized by intensification of personal involvement, more willingness to bring into the open feelings about club members and group leader, and a striving for satisfaction of dependency needs. Siblinglike rivalry tends to appear, as well as overt comparison of the group to family life. There is a growing ability to plan and carry out group projects and a growing awareness and mutual recognition of the significance of the group experience in terms of personality growth and change.

---

[6]This necessarily brief description of the five stages does not do justice to the full and intricate job done by the authors (8).

4. Differentiation

In this stage, members begin to accept one another as distinct individuals and to see the social worker as a unique person and the group as providing a unique experience. Relationships and needs are more reality based, communication is good, and there is strong cohesion. As clarification of power relationships gave freedom for autonomy and intimacy, so clarification of and coming to terms with intimacy and mutual acceptance of personal needs brings freedom and ability to differentiate and to evaluate relationships and events in the group on a reality basis. The group experience achieves a functionally autonomous character in this fourth stage. In freeing perceptions of the situation from distortions of extraneous experience and in creating its unique institutions and mores, the group becomes, in a sense, its own frame of reference.

5. Separation

The group experience has been completed, and the members may begin to move apart and find new resources for meeting social, recreational, and vocational needs. The following reactions have been observed repeatedly in groups in the process of termination: denial, regression, recapitulation of past experiences, evaluation, flight and pleas from the members who say, "We still need the group."

The way in which these different models of group development may be integrated is best represented in tabular form (Chart 1). It should be noted that a relationship of exact equality between the various stages is not being proposed. It is simply suggested that the stages of development in the other models most nearly approximate those offered by Garland, Jones, and Kolodny in the manner indicated. For example, Sarri and Galinsky's "Intermediate I" and "Revision" phases can rather easily be subsumed under the heading of "Power and control." In fact, they add greatly to the description of what is happening to group structure at this particular stage. Similarly, Maier's phase of "Locating commonness" appears to be closest to the "Pre-affiliation" stage in the Garland model. Generally speaking, the stages in the other models continue to run in their normal sequence when placed alongside the Garland model, with some stages collapsed for purposes of clarity.

What is suggested here should in no sense be taken as a complete synthesis of the various models. It is this writer's belief that such a synthesis would create more problems for the practitioner than it would solve, for it would create new stages of group development, which would require, among other things, a new set of terms to describe the various phases. To an area of practice theory already burdened with too much ambiguous terminology, the addition of another set of stages would run counter to fundamental canons of parsimony. What is suggested here is that the other models of group development may be used selectively to complement the Garland model. It can be argued that in specific areas—for example, in descriptions of group structure and proc-

CHART 1. Integrated Stage Model of Group Development

		Parallel Stages of Group Development		
Garland, Jones, and Kolodny	Maier	Sarri and Galinsky	Kindelsperger	Trecker
I. Pre-affiliation	1. Locating commonness	1. Origin 2. Formative	1. Approach-orientation	1. Beginning
II. Power and control	2. Creating exchange	3. Intermediate I 4. Revision	2. Relationship negotiation or conflict	....
III. Intimacy	3. Developing mutual identification	5. Intermediate II	3. Group role emergence 4. Vacillating group role dominance	2. Emergence of some group "feeling," organization
IV. Differentiation	4. Developing group identification	6. Maturation	5. Group role dominance 6. Institutionalized group roles	3. Development of bond, purpose, cohesiveness 4. Strong group feeling—goal attainment
V. Separation	....	7. Termination	....	5. Decline in interest, less group feeling 6. Ending stage: decision to discontinue the group

esses—the Garland model can be significantly enhanced by some of the other formulations—in this case, by the model offered by Sarri and Galinsky. Overall, however, it must be noted that the five-stage model offers the most complete statement in the social work literature, and, far from being contradicted, it is actually supported to a large extent by the other models of group development.

Models of Social Group Work Practice

It is evident that the implications for practice of the five stages of group development will vary according to the overall model for practice utilized by the worker. The author will attempt to show how implications for practice will differ in relation to the three models of group work practice proposed by Papell and Rothman: the social-goals model, the remedial model, and the reciprocal model (31). Only a brief description of each will be outlined here, and the reader is directed to Papell and Rothman for a more complete development.[7]

[7]For an insightful view of the historical development of the three models see Jones (15).

1. The Social-Goals Model

This model of social group work does not exist as a single formulation in the literature, nor does it owe its existence to a central theoretician who has systematically set forth all of its elements. It is, as Papell and Rothman state, a model that has its origins in the earliest traditions of social group work practice. The social-goals model envisages social change brought about by responsible members of groups within society. The principle of democratic group process that is fundamental to this model has become a cornerstone of all social group work practice. Perhaps the leading current exponent of the social-goals model is Hyman Wiener, who states that social responsibility and social identity can be achieved only through scientific projects that must be chosen according to the location of the group worker in the agency, the distribution of power within the agency and community, and the time dimension. Wiener's approach utilizes social-systems theory, and he borrows strategies from Chin and Lippitt in seeking points within society vulnerable to change (56).[8]

2. The Remedial Model

The remedial, or treatment, model of social group work is primarily concerned with the remediation of problems of psychological, social, and cultural adjustment through the use of a selected group experience. The group is viewed as both the "means and the context" for treatment by Vinter, who has outlined five phases in the treatment sequence: intake, diagnosis and treatment planning, group composition and formation, group development and treatment, and evaluation and termination (52).

The remedial model was influenced early by the clinical work of Fritz Redl and David Wineman and by the writings of Gisela Konopka, whose *Therapeutic Group Work with Children* (22) did much to establish group work as a full-fledged clinical modality.[9]

3. The Reciprocal Model

Unlike the other models of social group work, the reciprocal model has been most closely associated with a single theoretician, William

[8]See also Ginsberg and Goldberg (9), Wiener (57), and the early writings of Cohen, Coyle, Ginsberg, Kaiser, Klein, Miller, Phillips, and Wilson. For an excellent view of the values underlying the social-goals model see Konopka (20).
[9]See also Blum (5), Glasser (11), Kolodny (17), Kolodny and Burns (18), Konopka (19, 21), Maier (27), and Vinter (52).

Schwartz. The theoretical base for the reciprocal model derives largely from systems theory and from field theory. Indeed, Schwartz seems to make the point that the system within which the method is practiced should be considered first and that one cannot properly speak of the "group work" method as such. "It seems more accurate," he writes, "to speak of a social work method practiced in the various systems in which the social worker finds himself, or which are established for the purpose of giving service: the family, the small friendship group, the representative body, the one-to-one interview, the hospital ward, the committee, etc." (41).

Since goal-setting is an intrinsic part of the client-worker relationship, it is meaningless, in the view of the reciprocal theorist, to speak about the worker's goals for the client as if they were autonomous, independent entities. Since there are initially no specific social or therapeutic goals, emphasis is placed on engagement in interpersonal relationships. The worker carries out his function if he focuses on the symbiotic interdependence of the client and society and attempts to mediate between the two.[10]

Implications for Practice

To summarize, this paper has attempted to integrate several models of small-group development from the social group work literature with the five-stage model suggested by Garland, Jones, and Kolodny. In addition, a brief outline of the three overall models of social group work practice, as developed by Papell and Rothman, has been provided. The final section of the paper is an attempt to develop strategies of intervention for each of the five stages of group development in relation to the three overall models of group work practice. These strategies of intervention will be consonant with the major requirements for the development of practice principles in social work, as outlined by Vinter (54).

Vinter has identified four major requirements for the development of practice principles in social work:

1. Practice principles must specify or refer to the desired ends of action, the changed states of being in which it is intended that effective action will result.

2. Practice principles must incorporate the ethical principles, commitments, and values which prescribe and circumscribe professional activity.

3. Practice principles should incorporate valid knowledge about the most important phenomena or events with which professional workers are concerned.

---

[10]See also Polsky (34, 35), Schwartz (40, 42), Shulman (44), and Tropp (51). For an introduction to systems theory see Bennis, Benne, and Chin (3), Lippitt (24), and Parsons (33).

The Group as Target

4. Practice principles should direct the professional worker toward certain types of action, which, if engaged in, are likely to achieve the desired ends or goals (54).

Vinter's criticism of the group work literature is that it tends to be valuative and ideological, rather than instrumental. That is, it stresses the larger ends toward which practice should be directed, while it seems relatively uncertain about specific means toward particular objectives. The following implications for practice will, in the main, adhere to the criteria advanced by Vinter, with some slight alteration of the second criterion concerning the identification and incorporation of values.

Jones has analyzed the three models of social group work practice in terms of group purposes, type of service, role of worker, image of group member, activities, requisite worker skills, and theory base (Chart 2). It is the view of this writer that the overall values are implied in the group purposes for each of the three models. Beyond these general statements, the practice implications, or action principles, contain, at

CHART 2. Models of Social Group Work Practice*

	Social-Goals Model	Remedial Model	Reciprocal Model
Purpose of group	Social consciousness and social responsibility	To remedy social dysfunctioning by specific behavioral change	To achieve a mutual aid system; initially, no specific goals
Type of service	Socialization and consumptive services	Integration and adaptive services	Adaptive, socialization, integrative and consumptive services
Role of worker	Enabler	Change agent	Mediator or resource person
Image of group member	Participating citizens and indigenous leaders	Deviants, to at least some degree	Ego vis-à-vis alter
Types of activity	Wide range of activities and tasks, including those of community organization	Use of direct and indirect means of influence, including extra-group means	Engagement of group members in process of interpersonal relations
Requisite worker skills	In programming	In intervention in group process to achieve specified goals	In definition and dialogue
Theory base	Eclectic theory base	Social role theory, sociobehavioral theory, ego psychology, group dynamics	Systems theory and field theory

*See Jones (15).

least implicitly, value components of their own. Put even more simply, what the worker does defines the value orientation and ethical structure he is operating within in relation to his clients.[11] In effect, then, if the social work theoretician has specified the desired ends of the action, as well as the means for achieving those ends, he has, in the very process, made a statement of value preference. Therefore, outside of a statement of the general goals of the group or individual client, and in addition to the set of ethics which the profession holds in common, any further statement of values is superfluous and may even be misleading. In short, one may judge the value component of any practice principle by what it says to do, rather than by why it says to do it.

Action strategies will be suggested for each of the five stages of group development under each of the three overall models of group work practice.

Stage I: Pre-Affiliation

Social-Goals Model

The worker makes a special attempt to identify and involve indigenous community leaders in the group and uses the program for the purpose of acquainting group members with and involving them in the process of democratic participation. This is achieved, for example, in the worker's approach toward resolving decision issues, such as when the group should meet, and where.

Remedial Model

The worker provides an orientation to the group, outlines its purposes, and establishes a treatment "contract" with the members. A well-structured—and a worker-controlled—program allows for distance among the members, while it provides opportunities for exploration and invites trust. Activities that require a high degree of facilitative interdependence are passed over in favor of those that allow for parallel participation of the members.

Reciprocal Model

The worker begins to explore with the group the common elements that bind the members together, as well as those that separate them.

[11] For a further statement of how theoretical orientation influences philosophical outlook see Maier (25).

The Group as Target

The worker may suggest, but not insist upon, various program activities that will help to lay the basis for a mutual-aid system in the group. Through clarification, he helps the group to articulate common needs and explore possible group actions to meet those needs. He is not nearly as directive or controlling as the worker in the remedial model, but he may mediate between the demands of a larger social system (for example, the agency) and the needs of the individual group members.

Stage II: Power and Control

Social-Goals Model

The worker encourages all members of the client group to participate in decision-making but, essentially, he must go along with the group's decision about the leadership structure and work with those leaders who seem to have the support of the majority of the group members. Ideally, if he has been successful in laying the groundwork for democratic participation (in Stage I), then the leaders chosen will most likely be representative of the total group.

Functioning as an enabler, he makes his expertise in social action techniques and strategies available to the group members, but does not attempt to formulate objectives for the group. He may, at times, suggest specific action strategies, which will test the ability of the leadership to muster the support of the members in attempting to secure a specific objective. The task of policy-making, however, clearly rests with the members.

Remedial Model

While allowing for a certain amount of member rebellion and power struggle, the worker acts in his capacity of group executive and controller of membership roles to forestall the crystallization of any power takeover by a particular clique or subgroup. Sarri and Galinsky speak of maintaining the group through the revision stage and, in a similar vein, Garland, Jones, and Kolodny speak of the importance of protecting the safety of the individual members and their physical property. For example, the worker may wish to assign the various roles in activities, choose sides in games, promote low-status members through task assignments, and, generally, exert his influence as group leader to maintain an "open" group structure.

Reciprocal Model

The worker strives to clarify the power struggle and to focus again on the function of the group: to provide a mutual-aid system. In addition, he makes clear that worker, agency, and members are related to each other by certain rules and requirements imposed upon them by the terms of their agreement to come together. Schwartz stresses that any rules for the group should emerge from the function of the group and the necessities of the work, rather than from the personal authority of the helping agent (41). Thus, in terms of his manipulations of the group influence structure at this stage—through direct, personal intervention—the worker's function is considerably less directive than it would be in the remedial model and slightly more directive than it would be in the social-goals model.

Stage III: Intimacy

Social-Goals Model

As the leadership crisis is resolved and the members are more solidly linked together, they will likely raise questions about the worker's role and function within the group. He amplifies his function as consultant on strategy, while disavowing a policy-making role. He also clarifies the growing interdependence among the members and relates this to the ability of the group to attain its stated objectives: "If we stay united, we can achieve success." Finally, he encourages group activities that will reinforce the belief that working together brings results.

Remedial Model

The worker supports the group through the emotional turmoil of increased interdependency; he helps the members to sort out and discuss the positive and negative aspects of increased closeness and works with them to clarify how this group is different from the others (family group, peer group) in which they participate. He is constantly on the lookout for opportunities to entrust the members with responsibility, which in the earlier stages he has reserved for himself. Program is becoming more flexible and is now largely determined by the members themselves. Finally, the worker takes care to allow the group only the amount of program responsibility which it can reasonably handle; specifically, he has some structured activities ready to fall back on if the group seems unable to plan adequately for itself.

Reciprocal Model

In this stage, more than any other, the worker strives to "detect and challenge the obstacles which obscure the common ground between the members." Using clarification and confrontation, he may explore with the members those things that are keeping them from accomplishing their present tasks. While the causes of these obstacles may be fantastically complex, the focus of the worker is on dealing with the specific problems they are presently causing for the group. Through the contribution of ideas, facts, and value concepts, the worker helps the members to "see" what is keeping them from their stated objectives. This process may range all the way from having the members voice very specific complaints: "We don't like the way Joe always butts in when somebody else is talking," to discussions of more intricate and detailed misperceptions, or value conflicts: "If we go with you to the community center, then the rest of the kids on the block will think we're 'goodies.' "

Stage IV: Differentiation

Social-Goals Model

In this stage, the group has resolved most of its power problems and has high mutual support among the members, as well as good communication. The worker helps the group to formulate new objectives (as the original social-action goals may have already been attained) and continues to identify areas of need that might provide a basis for future social action. In carrying out these tasks, the worker takes care not to jeopardize his non-policy-making role. Even in this next-to-the-last stage of the group's development, the worker begins the process of extricating himself from the group, while doing all he can to insure its continued effectiveness by encouraging new members to join and participate.

Remedial Model

The worker helps the group to run itself by encouraging individual members to take responsibility for the planning and execution of program activities. With the increased cohesiveness and the heightened sense of the group's special identity as a separate, meaningful influence system, the worker can begin to direct the group toward projects which involve other groups and agencies in the larger community. He is constantly re-evaluating goals for the individual members and seeing how they may be related to the activities of the group at this particular stage.

He gets the members to begin evaluation of their group experience in preparation for the group's termination. Typically, this may involve discussion of how the members had worked out some of the problems that they had brought with them to the group in the beginning.

Reciprocal Model

With the establishment of a mutual-aid system within the group, the worker helps the members to focus on changes they may wish to make in other systems outside the group. For example, a cottage group in an institution may focus on strategies of intervention designed to get the administration to change its policy on off-campus recreation. The worker uses his skill in definition to make clear when he is operating in his role as group member and when he is functioning primarily as agency representative. The worker aids the group in relating—while not necessarily adjusting—to its environment and helps the group in its effort to provide satisfaction for its members.

Stage V: Separation

Social-Goals Model

In this final stage, the worker aids the group in establishing linkages with other community structures and agencies in order to insure its continued effectiveness after his departure. In short, he tries to prepare the group for the fact of his absence and encourages members to think about new objectives when the original goals of the group have been realized. He may arrange for periodic consultation with the group, but the real test of his success will be made evident when he, literally, has "worked himself out of a job."[12]

Remedial Model

The worker helps the group through the process of termination by encouraging evaluation, recapitulation, and review. He is prepared to deal with nihilistic flight, denial, "separation anxiety," repression, and anger of the members that they are losing the group. Using extragroup means of influence, he helps the individual members plan for the meeting of their needs through other resources after the group has disbanded (55). Program is highly mobile and community-oriented and designed to utilize the skills that the members have learned in the group.

[12]As one group leader recently stated, "I'll know when I have achieved success, when the community group demands my resignation."

Reciprocal Model

The worker helps the members to evaluate the process by which they develop the mutual-aid system and encourages them to think about ways in which they can achieve similar need satisfaction in the other systems in which they function. In addition, he works with the members to define the limits of the external situation in which the client-worker system is set and helps the members to determine how they will continue to operate within those limits (or modify them), once the group has been disbanded.

Discussion

In 1962, Paul Glasser called for group work to broaden its theory base and make use of more concepts from the social and psychological sciences (10). Unfortunately, a recent review of group work literature reveals just how little this suggestion has been implemented (45). While it is undeniably true that group work is both art and science, it is equally true that the literature to date has focused much more on the art than on the science. Though some progress has been made, there are still far too few attempts to integrate knowledge from the behavioral sciences in models of practice and still fewer attempts to validate these practice models through empirical research.[13] The net result is that practitioners are too often left without clear guidelines for practice and are forced instead to rely upon their own intuition in decision-making. Without denying the value of intuition in practice, one can legitimately raise the question: "If intuition becomes the only basis for practice, then doesn't practice itself become so idiosyncratic as to preclude even speaking of any group work method?"

It is suggested that research in social group work should proceed in at least two directions: First, there should be an attempt to integrate existing practice models (as this paper has tried to do in the area of group development) and to develop implications for practice in terms of some overall conception of group work practice. The Papell and Rothman model, despite its limitations, seems best suited for this purpose, especially as it makes the distinction between remediation and social action. The time is past when group work theoreticians can afford themselves the luxury of developing models for practice without taking into consideration what has taken place before.

Second, a concerted attempt should be made to utilize knowledge from the social and behavioral sciences to inform group work practice

---

[13]One recent empirical study in group work was executed by Feldman (7). See also Trieschman, Whittaker, and Brendtro (50) for an attempt to blend psychoanalytic ego psychology, social learning theory, and Redl's life-space theory into a unified model for milieu treatment.

theory. This process should involve not merely the transposition of theoretical models from the social sciences, but their empirical testing as well. While social group workers once viewed themselves as the arbiters of all that happened in groups, it is now sad to note that many group modes currently popular in social work (sensitivity training, family group therapy, and guided group interaction) have developed outside the pale of social group work. Unless, it seems to this writer, group work can look beyond its boundaries and at least attempt to incorporate appropriate strategies and techniques from other group modes, group workers will be in the unseemly position of having convinced only themselves of the efficacy of their work.

The practice implications suggested in this paper are clearly not exhaustive, and it is the intention of the author that they be expanded, modified, or discarded according to their utility. Current formulations of how small groups develop raise more questions than they answer. What, for example, is the relationship between the worker's intervention and the manner in which the group proceeds through the stages of development? Similarly, to what extent should we think of the various stages as mutually exclusive phases, or as elements which are always present in group life to some degree, but achieve prominence only at certain times? These and other questions remain to be answered. Social group work needs not fixed but flexible theoretical models that can incorporate new practice formulations as they are developed. If this brief paper serves as a first step in that direction, then its purpose will have been well served.

Finally, the ever increasing "haziness" between the traditional methods of casework, group work, and community organization makes it all the more urgent to define and develop a scientifically grounded theory for practice—not to rekindle the old arguments over "what" constitutes casework, or "what" is the role of group work, but in order to develop a unified theory of social work practice, which will include the best elements of each.

References

1. Austin, David M. "Goals for Gang Workers." *Social Work 2* (October 1957): 43–51.

2. Bales, Robert F., and Strodtbeck, Fred L. "Phases in Group Problem-solving." *Journal of Abnormal and Social Psychology* 46 (1951): 485–95. Also in Cartwright and Zander (6:624–38).

3. Bennis, Warren; Benne, Kenneth; and Chin, Robert. *The Planning of Change*. New York: Holt, Rinehart & Winston, 1961.

4. Bernstein, Saul. *Charting Group Progress*. New York: Association Press, 1949.

5. Blum, Arthur. "The Social Group Work Method: One View." In *A Conceptual Framework for Teaching the Social Group Work Method in the Classroom*. New York: Council on Social Work Education, 1964.

6. Cartwright, Dorwin, and Zander, Alvin, eds. *Group Dynamics*. New York: Harper & Row, 1960.

7. Feldman, Ronald A. "Group Integration, Intense Interpersonal Dislike, and Social Group Work Intervention." *Social Work* 14 (July 1969): 30–40.

8. Garland, James; Jones, Hubert; and Kolodny, Ralph. "A Model for Stages of Development in Social Work Groups." In *Explorations in Group Work,* edited by Saul Bernstein, pp. 12–53. Boston: Boston University School of Social Work, 1965.

9. Ginsberg, Mitchell, and Goldberg, Jack. "The Impact of the Current Scene on Group Work Policy and Practice." Summary Presentation: Group Work Section Meetings. New York: National Association of Social Workers, 1961–62.

10. Glasser, Paul. "Group Methods in Child Welfare: Review and Preview." In *Group Method and Services in Child Welfare,* pp. 5–11. New York: Child Welfare League of America, 1963.

11. _____ . "Social Role, Personality, and Group Work Practice." In *Social Work Practice, 1962: Selected Papers from the 89th Annual Forum, National Conference on Social Welfare,* pp. 60–74. New York: Columbia University Press, 1962.

12. Hare, A. Paul. *Handbook of Small Group Research*. New York: Free Press, 1965.

13. Hare, A. Paul; Borgatta, Edgar F.; and Bales, Robert F., eds. *Small Groups*. New York: Alfred Knopf, 1961.

14. Homans, George. *The Human Group*. New York: Harcourt, Brace & Co., 1950.

15. Jones, John F. "Social Group Work Method." Mimeographed. Minneapolis, Minn., 1967.

16. Kindelsperger, Walter L. "Stages in Group Development." In *The Use of the Group in Welfare Settings,* pp. 8–12. New Orleans: Tulane University, 1957.

17. Kolodny, Ralph. "A Group Work Approach to the Isolated Child." *Social Work* 6 (July 1961): 76–84.

18. Kolodny, Ralph L., and Burns, Virginia M. "Group Work with Physically and Emotionally Handicapped Children in a Summer Camp." In *Social Work with Groups, 1958,* pp. 28–50. New York: National Association of Social Workers, 1958.

19. Konopka, Gisela. *The Adolescent Girl in Conflict*. Englewood Cliffs, N.J.: Prentice-Hall, 1967.

20. _____ . *Eduard C. Lindeman and Social Work Philosophy*. Minneapolis: University of Minnesota Press, 1958.

21. _____ . *Group Work in the Institution*. New York: Association Press, 1954.

22. _____ . *Therapeutic Group Work with Children*. Minneapolis: University of Minnesota Press, 1949.

23. Lewin, Kurt. *Field Theory in Social Science*. New York: Harper & Bros., 1951.

24. Lippitt, Ronald, et al. *The Dynamics of Planned Change.* New York: Harcourt, Brace & Co., 1958.

25. Maier, Henry W. "Application of Psychological and Sociological Theory to Teaching Social Work with the Group." *Journal of Education for Social Work* 3 (Spring 1967):29–41.

26. _____. "Research Project on Group Development." Mimeographed. Seattle: University of Washington School of Social Work, 1961–62.

27. Maier, Henry W., ed. *Group Work as Part of Residential Treatment.* New York: National Association of Social Workers, 1965.

28. Mann, James, "Some Theoretical Concepts of the Group Process." *International Journal of Group Psychotherapy* 5 (July 1955): 236–46.

29. Martin, Elmore A., and Hill, William. "Toward a Theory of Group Development: Six Phases of Therapy Group Development." *International Journal of Group Psychotherapy* 7 (January 1957): 20–30.

30. Northen; Helen. "Social Group Work: A Tool for Changing Behavior of Disturbed Acting-out Adolescents." In *Social Work with Groups, 1958,* pp. 61–74. New York: National Association of Social Workers, 1958.

31. Papell, Catherine B., and Rothman, Beulah. "Social Group Work Models: Possession and Heritage." *Journal of Education for Social Work* 2 (Fall 1966): 66–78.

32. Paradise, Robert. "The Factor of Timing in the Addition of New Members to Established Groups." *Child Welfare* 47 (November 1968): 524–29.

33. Parsons, Talcott. *The Social System.* Glencoe, Ill.: Free Press, 1951.

34. Polsky, Howard W. *Cottage Six.* New York: Russell Sage Foundation, 1962.

35. _____. *The Dynamics of Residential Treatment: A Social Systems Approach.* Chapel Hill: University of North Carolina Press, 1968.

36. Psathas, George. "Phase Movement and Equilibrium Tendencies in Interaction Process in Psychotherapy Groups." *Sociometry* 23 (1960): 177–94.

37. Redl, Fritz. "Group Emotion and Leadership." In *Small Groups,* edited by A. Paul Hare, Edgar F. Borgatta, and Robert F. Bales, pp. 71–87. New York: Alfred Knopf, 1961.

38. Sarri, Rosemary, and Galinsky, Maeda. "A Conceptual Framework for Group Development." In *Readings in Group Work Practice,* edited by Robert D. Vinter, pp. 75–95. Ann Arbor, Mich.: Campus Publishers, 1967.

39. Scheidlinger, Saul. "The Concept of Social Group Work and Group Psychotherapy." *Social Casework* 34 (July 1953): 292–97.

40. Schwartz, William. "The Classroom Teaching of Social Work with Groups." In *A Conceptual Framework for the Teaching of the Social Group Work Method in the Classroom.* New York: Council on Social Work Education, 1964.

41. _____. "The Social Worker in the Group." In *New Perspectives on Services to Groups: Theory, Organization, and Practice.* New York: National Association of Social Workers, 1961.

42. _____. "Toward a Strategy of Group Work Practice." *Social Service Review* 38 (September 1962): 268–80.

43. Shalinsky, William. "Group Composition as an Element of Social Group Work Practice." *Social Service Review* 43 (March 1969): 42–50.

44. Shulman, Lawrence. *A Casebook of Social Work with Groups: The Mediating Model.* New York: Council on Social Work Education, 1968.

45. Silverman, Marvin. "Knowledge in Social Group Work: A Review of the Literature." *Social Work* 11 (July 1966): 56–62.

46. Slavson, Simon. *The Practice of Group Therapy.* New York: International Universities Press, 1947.

47. Theodorson, George A. "Elements in the Progressive Development of Small Groups." *Social Forces* 31 (1953): 311–20.

48. Thomas, Edwin J., and Fink, Clinton F. "Effects of Group Size." *Psychological Bulletin* 60 (1963): 371–84.

49. Trecker, Harleigh B. *Social Group Work: Principles and Practices.* New York: Association Press, 1955.

50. Trieschman, Albert E.; Whittaker, James K.; and Brendtro, Larry K. *The Other 23 Hours: Child Care Work in a Therapeutic Milieu.* Chicago: Aldine Publishing Co., 1969.

51. Tropp, Emanuel. "Group Intent and Group Structure: Essential Criteria for Group Work Practice." *Journal of Jewish Communal Service* 41 (Spring 1965): 229–50.

52. Vinter, Robert D. "The Essential Components of Social Group Work Practice." In *Readings in Group Work Practice,* edited by Robert D. Vinter, pp. 8–38. Ann Arbor, Mich.: Campus Publishers, 1967.

53. _____ . "Group Work: Perspectives and Prospects." In *Social Work with Groups, 1959,* pp. 128–49. New York: National Association of Social Workers, 1959.

54. _____ . "Problems and Processes in Developing Group Work Practice Principles." In *Theory Building in Social Group Work.* New York: Council on Social Work Education, 1960.

55. Vinter, Robert D., and Galinsky, Maeda. "Extra-Group Relations and Approaches." In *Readings in Group Work Practice,* edited by Robert D. Vinter, pp. 110–23. Ann Arbor, Mich.: Campus Publishers, 1967.

56. Wiener, Hyman J. "Social Change and Social Group Work Practice." *Social Work* 9 (July 1964): 106–13.

57. _____ . "Toward Techniques for Social Change." *Social Work* 6 (April 1961): 26–35.

The activities of a worker with a group are, or should be, prescribed by the stage of development and purpose of the group. Drawing upon systems theory and developmental theory (discussed in more detail in the preceding articles in this chapter), Lang presents a three-stage model for practice with groups that calls for the worker to move from a stage in which the worker is outside of and somewhat above the group to a stage in which he becomes a member of the group.

A Broad-Range Model of Practice in the Social Work Group

Norma C. Lang

Theoretical models of social work practice began to be defined in all parts of the profession when changing problems, needs, circumstances, settings, and goals created the need for new practice modalities (10, 11, 14, 15, 17, 18, 20, 26, 28). The era of model-building in social work reflects the growing complexity of the social work function, as well as the advancement of the profession to new levels of theory formulation. This paper looks in particular at the state of model-building and the existing models of social work practice in the small group, and poses a model that is based on different organizing principles and that has some potential utility for a range of practice foci.

Some Problems of Model-Building

Model-building began in social group work at a time when social work practice in groups no longer seemed to be encompassable within one descriptive framework. As reflected in the writings of Vinter (26, 28), Schwartz (20), Papell and Rothman (14), Tropp (23), and Klein (7) and in the NASW Frame of Reference Statement (6), model-building represented an attempt to acknowledge and deal with problems of complexity and disparateness by ordering the elements of dissimilar practice into separate conceptual frameworks. Creation of the resulting models has constituted a major step in theory formulation, as the models have provided ways of looking at practice differences with a whole-

Reprinted from *Social Service Review,* Vol. 46, No. 1, 1972, pp. 76-89, by permission of the author and the University of Chicago Press.
This paper was prepared for presentation at the National Conference on Social Welfare, Chicago, June 3, 1970.

ness and coherence not possible before the parts were ordered into differing perceptual realities.

Nevertheless, the structuring of practice differences according to various models of practice creates some new problems while it solves others. The relationship between the various forms of practice represented by the models is left unexplored; when disparities become organized into differing frameworks, the tendency is to preserve rather than to examine and reconcile the differences. Furthermore, practice shaped by a given model may suffer from the narrowing or limiting effects imposed by the model.

The possibility waiting to be addressed is that seeming differences in models are in fact facets of a larger, as yet unidentified and unintegrated, model of practice. The components of such a model have been held apart because of premature model-building, or because of some failure of practitioners and theoreticians to differentiate concepts from the settings or circumstances in which they were developed. The disentangling of setting, problem, function, and purpose from the essential components of practitioner activity has been a professional task from the earliest period, a task that seems to require the perspective of time (2, 5, 20).

It can be said that each successive model arose out of the need to delineate some facet of practice not adequately provided for by its predecessor. The failure to integrate the newer dimensions of practice with the old has resulted in the circumstance that separate models of practice may be seen more readily than the connections leading to a larger, synthesized model of practice.

Furthermore, because they are on the order of simple descriptions of practice formulated in relation to such dimensions as goal, function, process, and means of service, existing models tend to carry the imprint of the prevailing societal and professional concerns of the time at which they were developed. For this reason, practice looks different in each of these models, and some commonalities and similarities of practice are obscured.

Problems arise in attempts to compare the models, because they have not all been formulated in the same conceptual terms—the "reciprocal" model, for example, appears to be a process model, while the "social goals" and "remedial" models are goals models (14). The models are not cast in the same defining terms, not expressed in relation to a common supporting theory, and not constructed on equivalent theoretical foundations. The strength of the "remedial" model, best-supported theoretically, is also its limitation—that it rests in part on a sturdy base of research and conceptualization, but is limited by the dyadic interactional unit in which the social science researchers articulated their theory, and by their conception of influence as one-directional (26:20–29).

Development of a New Model

The broad-range model of practice to be presented here has been derived from the same practice descriptions used by other model-builders. It was stimulated by questions generated by their models.

This model was developed in two steps. The first step consisted of reclassifying, on a new framework, the actual descriptions of practice given by a number of writers (1, 6, 7, 8, 13, 16, 20, 22, 23, 26, 29). The results of this recasting of content, which illuminated and made clear some distinctions obscured in previous models, led to the second step of formulation. This consisted of tracing through the implications of some of the findings of the first step and reformulating the model at a different level of abstraction. It is this second formulation that will be described.

This is a compound, dynamic, three-stage model of practice in the social work group. For comparative purposes the model is set forth in summary form in Chart 1, in which the various components are set forth as they appear in three orders of groups.

Previous model formulations have failed to differentiate various orders of group and have assumed all groups to be alike in their group aspects, even though composed of a wide variety of kinds of clients brought together for a range of purposes. This model formulation begins with the notion that there are different orders of group[1] in social work, for each of which a different group form is appropriate. These different orders of group are expressed in the terms "allonomous," "autonomous," and "allon-autonomous" or "transitional."

"Allonomous," defined by Webster as "controlled by stimuli acting on an organism from outside" and as "opposite of autonomous," is here used to signify "other-governed," i.e., governed by the worker. "Autonomous" is here used to mean "self-governed," or, more precisely, "group-governed," with the worker in a more peripheral role. "Allon-autonomous" is a combining term coined to describe a group in which there is some blend of allonomous or worker-directed group functioning and of autonomous group functioning. "Transitional" is used interchangeably with "allon-autonomous" as a less cumbersome designation.

"Autonomous" is a term used in the literature to describe the functioning both of the individual organism and of small and large social

---

[1]Mills (12:59) also uses the notion of different orders of group, which he defines in terms of five levels of interpersonal process, of ascending complexity, through which members of a group pass. Tuckman (24:473) demonstrates in a research study four orders of group system, each having distinguishable characteristics with regard to the nature of group structure and decision-making mechanisms.

CHART 1. The Broad-Range Model of Practice in the Social Work Group

Component	Group Form		
	Stage I	Stage II	Stage III
Order of group	Allonomous	Allon-autonomous (semi-autonomous)	Autonomous
Unit to be worked with	Individuals	Individuals and group-as-whole	Group-as-whole
Focus of service	Individual social development and functioning	Individual social development and functioning; achievement of group social goals	Achievement of group social goals; Individual functioning instrumental to group goal-achievement
Levels of social process addressed	Dyadic, subgroup	Dyadic, subgroup, group-as-whole	Group-as-whole
Form and nature of group	Instrumental socialization medium; immature group form	Instrumental socialization medium and intrinsic social reality; maturing group form	Intrinsic social reality and instrumental task medium; mature group form
Group formation and structure	Agency-constituted, with worker as central constituent; group formation and structure around worker in locus equivalent to indigenous leader; group fully developed in allonomous form	Agency-constituted, with worker as significant constituent; semi-autonomous structure, with worker moving between central and peripheral locus; group fully developed in semi-autonomous form	Agency or autonomously formed, with worker as contributing constituent; autonomous structure with shared leadership, and worker locus peripheral; group fully developed in autonomous form
Nature of worker role	Primary in the functioning of group; surrogation in group processes	Variable, pivotal between surrogation when necessary and facilitation of autonomous functioning when possible	Facilitative of autonomous group functioning and social goal accomplishment
Nature of client	Developmentally, experientially, or circumstantially lacking capacity and skill for autonomous group engagement	Partial capacity for autonomous group engagement, not fully developed in all areas	Capable and skilled in autonomous group functioning
Group processes dealt with	All group processes extensively influenced by worker so that group formation, maintenance, and functioning are possible	All group processes dealt with by worker, with group-directed procedures to the extent possible	All group processes dealt with by worker, indirectly, with emphasis on maximum individual contribution to autonomous group functioning

CHART 1.

Component	Group Form		
	Stage I	Stage II	Stage III
Means of achieving goals of service	Worker-mediated interaction; behavioral conditioning; ego-developmental and ego-strengthening experiences; socialization; worker management of group processes; role-modeling	Worker-mediated interaction; behavioral conditioning; ego-development and strengthening; socialization; worker active in group processes; role-modeling; facilitation of mutual aid	Ego strengthening; role-modeling; worker facilitation of group processes toward goal achievement; task and procedural definition and resource.

units; it is the assumption of the writer that "allonomous" can be applied with equal appropriateness to the functioning of the individual organism and of the small group.

Together, allonomous (worker-governed), allon-autonomous (worker-and-group-governed), and autonomous (group-governed) groups comprise the three orders of group contained in this model.

The prototype of these three orders of group may be found in the family, a group which is first an allonomous one in which the adult, parenting members exert primary degrees of influence and control in a governing capacity. The allonomous group form is appropriate to the personality development and socialization of its young family members, and it is the critical contributor to the subsequent autonomous functioning of its members both individually and in groups.

The normal progression for young family members is from other-directed to self-directed functioning, in stage-successive transition. In tandem with this individual developmental and socialization process, the form of the family group changes, first to a semi-autonomous one, in which the juveniles have a larger voice, and ultimately to a relatively autonomous group form. Since the family group's goals are met in part when the children can function autonomously and independently, the total family unit may not be sustained intact for long in the autonomous form, but may be reconstituted as autonomous pairs when the maturing family members depart and establish new familial units.

It is not suggested that the allonomous group in social work is a symbolic re-enactment of the family, as is held in the psychoanalytic conception of the group. Rather, it is suggested that, for certain people, an allonomous group experience may be a necessary requisite to participation in an autonomous group.

The model is based on developmental rather than clinical and remedial considerations. It is posited that, if the individual is not at a developmental or circumstantial point at which he can maintain a measure of minimal autonomous individual functioning, he will be unready and unable to be a participant in an autonomous group. His lack of readiness for autonomous group participation may stem from age-stage developmental level, inexperience in social groups, inappropriate experience in primary groups, incomplete, faulty, or arrested psychosocial development, incomplete or faulty socialization, or need for resocialization to new circumstances.

Pre-autonomous individual functioning sets limits on the nature of the interpersonal engagement of the members, the readiness of the individual for emotional integration into the group, and the nature of the entity that can be created. For example, in the writer's own practice experience, emotionally disturbed children of latency and preadolescent ages, poorly socialized and arrested in their psycho-social development, had much in common, in their group life, with a group of preschool four- and five-year-olds who were developing normally but on the threshold of primary socialization experiences. Their groups were distinctly similar in some respects; both were allonomous in nature, and both created similar role requirements for the worker. In some of the descriptions of neighborhood block groups organized for social-action purposes, it seems possible that the reported failure of many such groups to move beyond primary group functioning to the assumption of social action goals may be explained in terms of the members' prior need for an allonomous group experience (25).

The Allonomous Group

Unit to be Worked With

In the allonomous group, the individual is conceived of as the unit to be worked with. The service is focused on individual social development and on the social functioning of the individual members.

Level of Social Process

The level of social process (3) addressed primarily is "subentitative"; that is, the necessities of the group life call for dyadic, triadic, and subgroup interactions, in particular, mediated interactions engaging the worker and one or two members at a time. Worker activities with members in interaction are instrumental to the continuance of the group process; they may serve as linking pins between members not able to invest themselves in something as abstract as the group as an entity. This point of engagement with units smaller than the group as a whole is inherent in the need of the group members for a species of support and control for their functioning together which they cannot yet achieve unaided.

Form and Nature of Group

In a sense, this is an immature group form, one in which the entity is a context for interaction and a means for the growth of members' capacity for entitative functioning. In nature, the group is an instrumental socialization medium rather than an intrinsic social reality, although it may take on the latter meaning to its members.

The allonomous group is likely to appear in agencies serving pre-autonomously functioning clients in agency-formed or reconstituted groups, with the worker as a central constituent. Something akin to the allonomous group form may be found elsewhere in society: in the school classroom, where the teacher-centered form of instruction is regarded as efficient for certain kinds of learning; in the interactive play of young children whose interactions call for intermittent mediation by a parent, teacher, or supervising adult; and perhaps in the peer group, which is sometimes characterized by having a fairly controlling, directing, indigenous leader who is more advanced than his peers in developmental level and in capacity for functioning in a group.

Group Formation and Structure

The allonomous group is formed and structured around the worker, who is in the central locus, in a position somewhat equivalent to that of an indigenous leader. The group is fully developed in all its structures and processes, but is characterized by certain evidences of the allonomous form. In particular, the worker may have a disproportionate area and degree of influence in all group processes, and may be singularly active in much of the interaction. Such a structure is the critical necessity of the group. This allonomous structure has been formulated in the remedial model of social work practice with reference to the needs of malfunctioning clients, but without acknowledgment of the nature of the group that such clients are capable of forming. Lack of recognition of the nature of such a group has led to some misunderstanding of the nature of the worker role; it is not caprice or clinical pre-eminence or the need to be controlling that defines a central, directing role for the worker. His actions may be instrumental in maintaining an ongoing life of the group while the members are unable or unready to function autonomously.

Klein (7:123) and Tropp (23:TRP-14E) both argue that the complexity of group life makes it impossible for the worker to be so engaged, but they do not differentiate that they are describing interaction in a more mature social form, the autonomous group, which is capable of an entitative life of its own, regardless of worker activity.

Group functioning and process in the allonomous group are likely to be rather fragmented and episodic, more susceptible to contagion and runaway acceleration of the rate of interaction, and less predictable, less sustained, and less likely to involve all the members in an entitative fashion.

Worker Role

The role of the worker is crucial to the functioning of the allonomous group. A key notion here is that of worker surrogation, a process by which a worker acts to supply missing pieces in the group processes which the group members are unable to contribute. He does so in ways that not only bridge a gap in group process as it is occurring, but serve also as a pattern for future group and member functioning. Through surrogation, certain necessary functions and parts of process temporarily become areas of worker activity, by a process of substituting for missing member interactions and roles, activating and supporting needed group processes, and gradually giving these over to members to perform and manage as they become ready.

Surrogation may occur in relation to individual role performance, interpersonal response, content, group control, group locomotion, group maintenance, group deliberation, and decision-making.

Apart from surrogation in group processes, the worker in the allonomous group is likely to be a great deal more active, directing, and central in the group than he would need to be with an autonomous group.

Nature of the Client

The client is an individual functioning at a pre-autonomous level, lacking capacity, readiness, or skills for participation in an autonomous group.

Group Processes Dealt With

The worker deals directly with all group processes and exerts extensive influence on them so that group formation, maintenance, and function are possible. The worker may be particularly active in the fostering of a sense of commonness out of similar individual goals; the development of interpersonal relationships that are mediated to minimize enmity; the establishment of norms when the members are unable to express these; the selection of experiences that may contribute to the building of cohesion without demanding intolerable amounts of cooperation; and the creation of opportunities for members to become aware of the group as an entity and to experience satisfaction from contributing to and participating in it.

Means of Achieving Goals

Service or worker-defined goals seem to be more prominent in relation to the group that is not yet self-governing and self-propelled. The means of achieving the goals of service are very much shaped by the needs of the client, his developmental level, and the nature of the entity that he can create with others. These means of service in the allonomous group include worker-mediated interaction, ego-developing and ego-strengthening experiences, worker management of group processes, worker role-modeling, behavioral conditioning, and socialization of members through the influence of the group that has been strongly shaped by the worker.

The Autonomous Group

Unit to be Worked With

The autonomous group provides such a marked contrast to the allonomous group that it may be said to be at the other end of a continuum. The group as a whole is seen as the unit to be worked with. The service is focused on the achievement of group-defined social goals in a self-governing unit capable of collective action toward integrated group goals.

Level of Social Process

The level of social process addressed is primarily the group as a whole; the point of engagement by the worker is with the functioning entity rather than with subgroup units. The worker's engagement is not instrumental to the continuance of the group, which is capable of entitative functioning without a worker. The group has no problem in forming and developing a viable entity, but its members may have things to learn and experience in order to shape the group into an efficient and effective tool for accomplishing its collective tasks and goals.

Form and Nature of Group

The group may be thought of as a mature group form, in that it is an intrinsic social reality which processes viable group goals and meets the mutual needs of its members. It will be an instrumental socialization medium in only minor degree; the major socialization of the members has been accomplished elsewhere.

Group Formation and Structure

Whether an agency-formed group or an entity that is self-forming, the group is characterized by autonomous entitative functioning, with the worker as a contributing constituent. The worker is located in the group structure as a participant, in a locus and role distinctly different from that in the allonomous group; his influence in the autonomous group is somewhat more equivalent in extent to that shared by the members.

The group is fully developed in autonomous form, with structures and processes suited to group-governed and group-directed procedures.

Worker Role

The worker role is considerably modified from that appropriate to the allonomous group. The worker serves as the facilitator of autonomous functioning and plays a role in helping the group to develop a suitable entity for efficient handling of selection, processing, and attainment of group goals. A minor part of his role may be short-term, temporary surrogation in group processes in order to facilitate the swift development by group members of an effectively functioning entity. This role is in contrast to that of the worker in the allonomous group, who may be creating tiny samples of limited autonomous group functioning for the members to experience as part of their learning.

Nature of the Client

The client in an autonomous group is an individual who has developed capacity and skill for emotional integration into the group and for functioning appropriately in it.

Group Processes Dealt With

The worker may deal with all group processes, but more indirectly, since his influence is smaller and less pervasive. There will be less need for his engagement in group processes, because of the ability of the group. He may address some of the same aspects of group process that concern the worker with the allonomous group, but the focus of worker actions will be on the better adjustment of the individual and subgroup parts to the group as a whole and the better functioning of the entity. Like the worker in the allonomous group, he is concerned with individual and group functioning; in the autonomous group he works toward the development of maximum member contribution and full group autonomous functioning.

Means of Achieving Goals

Service or worker-defined goals pertain to assisting the group to minimize its entitative functioning capacity, realize the contribution of each member, and accomplish the goals set by the group. Means of achieving these goals include occasional role-modeling, short-lived, temporary or momentary assistance with group processes in an area or moment of difficult group functioning, teaching members how to deal with a particular task, enlarging members' views of goals and the means of proceeding, giving procedural assistance in the management of group processes, making contributions that assist the group in making its own adjustments and adaptations, and serving as a resource in areas in which the group lacks experience.

The Transitional Group

Between these two forms, there is an intermediate form, here labeled "allon-autonomous" or "transitional," which has some characteristics of both the allonomous and the autonomous group and represents a transition between these two. In such a group, the worker, concerned both with individual development and functioning and with the developing entity, the group as a whole, addresses himself to all levels of social process. He focuses on the social functioning of individuals and on the achievement of group-defined social goals. The group is both an instrumental socialization medium and an intrinsic social reality. It is formed with the worker as a significant constituent. It is structured for greater autonomous functioning than is the allonomous group, with the worker moving between a central and a peripheral locus, in keeping with the readiness of members to deal autonomously. The group is fully developed, in semi-autonomous form. The worker pivots between surrogation in group processes, when necessary, and facilitation of autonomous functioning, when possible. The client has some capacity for autonomous group engagement, but his capacity is not yet fully developed in all areas. The means of service may combine worker-mediated interaction, behavioral conditioning, ego strengthening and developing, socialization, worker facilitation of group processes, and worker role-modeling. The worker deals with all group processes; he attempts to create growth-supportive norms, but encourages group-directed processes to the extent possible.

Discussion

The three stages of this model have been developed through the processing and classifying of descriptions of practice of many authors.

As such, it is a derived model leading to a different theoretical formulation.

The model seems to offer a way of reconciling some seeming differences in other model formulations, as well as reclassifying and integrating some practice positions that were set apart in previous models. It omits considerations of setting and eliminates the need to think of models in terms of specific goals such as "social" or "remedial" goals. It adds the notion of different orders of group, different group forms, and distinctly different worker roles related to each. It provides a means of assessing which group form and practice modality will be appropriate for which clients. Additionally, it orders the content of practice descriptions in a way that clarifies some notions about worker role. It affirms what has sometimes been viewed as an inappropriately central and directing role in the remedial model, and distinguishes an appropriate role for the worker in an autonomous group from the present-day reactive cry for status and power equalization of the worker role with that of the client member. The model adds, too, the notion of worker surrogation in a faltering group process.

Furthermore, it makes clear what was uncertain in prior model formulations, namely, that in all three group forms the entity is fully developed, but with differing structures, processes, focus, goals, and worker involvement in each.

Moreover, this formulation brings a dynamic dimension into model formulations that is different from the contribution of phase theory. It offers the possibility of a complete group experience in any one of three group forms (e.g., for some clients the total group experience might have to be allonomous), or of moving, within the life-span of a single group, from stage I (allonomous) to stage II (allon-autonomous), or through stage II to stage III (autonomous), or back and forth in response to the developing capacity and skills of the members for group functioning of an increasingly autonomous nature.

Finally, the model poses an important relationship between the functioning capacity of the individual and the nature of the resulting entity individuals of a given capacity are able to form.

Since this is the first tenuous articulation of this model, it can be expected that it will be developed further and will be altered as more of its dimensions become clear. It should lead to other and sharper definitions than have been possible up to this time. Models are made to be dismantled. They are in terrible jeopardy if, upon being committed to the printed page, they become institutions. A better model can always be built, and successive models should be regarded as steps in a theory-building process rather than as static statements durable for all time.

References

1. Coyle, Grace. *Group Work with American Youth.* New York: Harper & Bros., 1948.

2. _____ . "Some Basic Assumptions about Social Group Work." In *The Social Group Work Method in Social Work Education,* edited by Marjorie Murphy, pp. 89–95. Social Work Curriculum Study, Vol. XI. New York: Council on Social Work Education, 1959.

3. DeLamater, John; McClintock, Charles; and Becker, Gordon. "Conceptual Orientations of Contemporary Small Group Theory." *Psychological Bulletin* 64 (1965): 402–12.

4. Garland, James; Jones, Hubert; and Kolodny, Ralph. "A Model for Stages of Development of Social Work Groups." In *Explorations in Group Work,* edited by Saul Bernstein, pp. 12–53. Boston: Boston University School of Social Work, 1965.

5. Hartford, Margaret E. "Changing Approaches in Practice Theory and Techniques." In *Trends in Social Work Practice and Knowledge,* pp. 132–44. NASW 10th Anniversary Symposium. New York: National Association of Social Workers, 1966.

6. _____ , ed. *Working Papers towards a Frame of Reference for Social Group Work.* New York: National Association of Social Workers, 1964.

7. Klein, Alan F. *Social Work through Group Process.* Albany: State University of New York at Albany, 1970.

8. Konopka, Gisela. *Social Group Work: A Helping Process.* Englewood Cliffs, N.J.: Prentice-Hall, 1963.

9. Loeb, Martin B. "The Backdrop for Social Research: Theory-making and Model-building." In *Social Science Theory and Social Work Research,* edited by Leonard S. Kogan, pp. 3–15. New York: National Association of Social Workers, 1960.

10. Lutz, Werner. "Emerging Models of Social Casework Practice." Mimeographed. West Hartford: University of Connecticut School of Social Work, 1968.

11. McBroom, Elizabeth. "Helping AFDC Families: A Comparative Study." *Social Service Review* 39 (December 1965): 390–98.

12. Mills, Theodore. *The Sociology of Small Groups.* Englewood Cliffs, N.J.: Prentice-Hall, 1967.

13. Northen, Helen. *Social Work with Groups.* New York: Columbia University Press, 1969.

14. Papell, Catherine, and Rothman, Beulah. "Social Group Work Models: Possession and Heritage." *Journal of Education for Social Work* 2 (Fall 1966): 66–77.

15. Perlman, Helen Harris. "Social Work Method: A Review of the First Decade." *Social Work* 10 (October 1965): 166–78.

16. Phillips, Helen. *Essentials of Social Group Work Skill.* New York: Association Press, 1957.

17. Roberts, Robert W., and Nee, Robert H., eds. *Theories of Social Casework.* Chicago: University of Chicago Press, 1970.

18. Rothman, Jack. "Models of Community Organization Practice." In *Social Work Practice,* pp. 16–47. New York: National Conference on Social Welfare, 1968.

19. Schwartz, William. "On the Use of Groups in Social Work Practice." In *The Practice of Group Work,* edited by William Schwartz and Serapio Zalba, pp. 3–24. New York: Columbia University Press, 1971.

20. _____ "The Social Worker in the Group." In *New Perspectives on Services to Groups,* pp. 7–29. New York: National Association of Social Workers, 1961.

21. _____ . "Toward a Strategy of Group Work Practice." *Social Service Review* 36 (September 1962): 268–79.

22. Schulman, Lawrence. *A Casebook of Social Work with Groups: The Mediating Model.* New York: Council on Social Work Education, 1968.

23. Tropp, Emanuel. *A Humanistic Foundation for Group Work Practice.* New York: Associated Educational Services, 1969.

24. Tuckman, Bruce. "Personality Structure, Group Composition, and Group Functioning." *Sociometry* 27 (1964): 469–87.

25. Turner, John B., ed. *Neighborhood Organization for Community Action.* New York: National Association of Social Workers, 1968.

26. Vinter, Robert. "The Essential Components of Social Group Work Practice." In *Readings in Group Work Practice,* edited by Robert Vinter, pp. 8–38. Ann Arbor, Mich.: Campus Publishers, 1967.

27. _____ . "Problems and Processes in Developing Group Work Practice Principles." In *Theory-building in Social Group Work,* pp. 2–16. Workshop Report, Annual Program Meeting. New York: Council on Social Work Education, 1960.

28. _____ . "Social Group Work." In *Encyclopedia of Social Work,* pp. 715–23. New York: National Association of Social Workers, 1965.

29. Wilson, Gertrude, and Ryland, Gladys. *Social Group Work Practice.* Cambridge, Mass.: Houghton Mifflin Co., 1949.

Selected Bibliography

Alissi, A.S., "Social Work with Families in Group-Service Agencies: An Overview," *Family Coordinator* 18 (4), 1969, pp. 391–401. In understanding the family, five sociological frameworks (institutional, interactional, situational, structure-functional, and developmental) are discussed. The emphasis is on practice applications, stressing internal family interactions and external family linkages.

Euster, Gerald L., "A System of Groups in Institutions for the Aged," *Social Casework,* 52 (8), 1971, pp. 523–529. A living and learning program is presented emphasizing work, play, education, and creative endeavor as components of a system of groups to modify and create new patterns of social interaction for older adults.

Feldman, Ronald A., "Group Service Programs in Public Welfare: Patterns and Perspectives," *Public Welfare,* 27 (3), 1969, pp. 266–271. The application of small group knowledge in public welfare settings for use in direct service and administrative tasks is discussed. An analysis is presented of the extent and types of group services provided, and factors associated with the initiation, success and failure of attempted group service programs.

Lawrence, Harry, and Sundel, Martin, "Behavior Modification in Adult Groups," *Social Work,* 17 (2), 1972, pp. 34–43. A small-group approach to short-term treatment of adult problems is integrated with behavior modification principles and procedures. The problems dealt with are child management, anxiety, marital discord, depression, and interpersonal difficulties with family, friends, and coworkers.

Lipsitt, Paul D., and Steinbruner, Maureen, "An Experiment in Police-Community Relations: A Small Group Approach," *Community Mental Health Journal,* 3 (2), 1969, pp. 172–179. Using group discussion, attempts were made to mitigate rising hostility between police and residents of an urban ghetto. The groups met weekly for 12 weeks and resulted in increased awareness of each others' problems and the beginning of cooperation to solve problems.

Schwartz, William, "Social Group Work: The Interactionist Approach," *Encyclopedia of Social Work,* 1971, Vol. II, pp. 1252–1263. In tracing the evolution and development of social work with groups, it is shown that attention is shifting away from defining social group work as a unique social work method and moving toward identifying the various aspects of group work that can help in formulating a general theory of social work practice. An interactionist view is presented to support the generalist trend.

Schwartz, William, and Zalba, Serapio R., *The Practice of Group Work,* New York: Columbia University Press, 1971, Chapter 1: Introduction, "On the Use of Groups in Social Work Practice," pp. 3–24. An excellent current overview and introduction to the use of groups in social work practice, with emphasis on the need to redefine and clarify not only social group work, but all social work practice, and the processes for doing so.

Wilson, Gertrude, "Social Group Work: Trends and Developments," *Social Work,* 1 (4), October 1956, pp. 66–75. A group work classic that identifies basic concepts, principles, and techniques to achieve basic social work aims. The intellectual and practice challenge to the social work profession is outlined within the framework of social change.

Youngman, Louise C., "Social Group Work in the AFDC Program," *Public Welfare,* 23(1), January 1965, pp. 25–31, 59–61. The case for using a group approach in helping AFDC recipients with various social problems is documented. The emphasis is on assisting families to recognize and use their strengths in constructive and healthy growth and development.

5

The Organization as
Target

That body of social work literature devoted to larger systems such as the social welfare system has tended to focus on the geopolitical community. Such a trend is indicated by Moore's review of how the field of community social work practice developed, as it is by Chatterjee's review of how the social scientists conceptualize community. Both authors conclude that this literature has described the community and has not dealt with social work practice theory. An alternative would be to develop a body of literature that has prescriptive implications for worker behaviors but does not neglect the theoretical formulations developing in the social sciences. To this end, Chatterjee calls for social work to become more specific about those areas of the community in which social welfare services are being provided and to begin formulating relevant interventive techniques.

In this chapter, the formal organization—an agency providing social welfare services—becomes the specific target for interventions at the community, or larger system, level. It becomes such a target in one or more of three sets of circumstances: (1) when an organization is requested by an individual or group to provide a service that it is designed to provide but is not providing; (2) when an organization is requested to provide a service that it is not providing although it has the resources to provide it; or (3) when an organization is requested to provide a service it lacks the resources to provide.

The notion that a formal organization is a legitimate target of the worker's interventive efforts has several implications for worker behaviors. The worker is expected to be sufficiently objective to recognize all of the possible contingencies related to a client's situation. This objectivity must permit the worker to identify even his own organization as a possible contributor to a client's situation and therefore a potential target for his efforts at change. The operative value premise is that the worker's responsibility is to the client. Under this premise, the organization must support the worker in fulfilling this responsibility.[1]

A second implication derives from the legitimacy of worker intervention with formal organizations: the worker involved in the direct delivery of services is abler than anyone except the clients to determine how well an organization is satisfying its purpose. The direct service delivery worker is in a position to provide vital information to the decision-makers in his organization. A major criterion of an organization's behaviors should be how that organization is fulfilling its purpose. Clearly, change is usually not required when that organization is fulfilling its purpose, but only when it is not. What must be changed and the directions those changes must follow can be best determined by evaluation of the views of current service recipients and the direct service delivery workers.

In the first article in this chapter, Moore reviews the development of the community organization method in social work practice. He recommends that social workers become more involved in social action. The organization is the primary target for Moore, and groups of social welfare providers and/or consumers are a major vehicle for bringing about organizational changes. Of the three reasons given at the beginning of this chapter for undertaking to change an organization, consumers and providers alike would be involved in all three.

Chatterjee, with Moore, sees the formal organization as the primary target for change when social work is considered. Unlike Moore, Chatterjee emphasizes developing a theoretical base, explicitly stating service delivery objectives of the social welfare system, which in turn helps identify social welfare organizations as a primary target of community change. An explicit statement of these objectives provides a basis for evaluating how well an organization responds to the population it is designed to serve. To evaluate organizational response we need to understand how organizations work, and Chatterjee suggests that social

---

[1]Wilbert E. Moore, *The Professions: Roles and Rules* (New York: Russell Sage Foundation, 1970), pp. 5–6.

science theories about formal organizations are the starting point for such an understanding.

Armitage analyzes how formal organizations now function, and recommends systems theory as an alternative theoretical base for restructuring current organizations to make them more open and responsive to consumer inputs. The analysis identifies different kinds of decisions at different levels in social welfare organizations. The alternative structure proposed here is based on systems theory and offers a model for workers who are interested in making organizations more responsive to client needs. Most significant, this proposed change in formal organizational structure would make the decision-makers more accessible to the organization's constituency.

Setleis proposes that all social work activity must have a political component. Because any formal organization represents a power faction, any effort to change it will require that the would-be agent of change have a power base equal to or greater than that of the target organization. Also, from the premises that clients are *experts* about the reality of their particular situations, and that all client–agency relationships have the purpose of attaining some measure of social justice for the client, it follows that the client is an active participant in the organization's activities, and the "helper–helped" view of worker–client relationships is inappropriate. Setleis is concerned with efforts to change an organization other than that in which the worker is employed. A worker's efforts for change must have the approval of the client who will be affected.

Wax presents an outline of the basic procedures and behaviors that are required to build a power base through which policy decisions— which he sees as the primary means for effecting organizational changes —can be influenced. Although his model is meant for use within the worker's own organization; its outlined behaviors and strategies can be generalized to the larger social welfare system and therefore have general implications for any attempt to effect changes in formal organizations.

Specht indicates how direct service delivery workers can become involved in policy-making decisions within the employing organization. Any sector of society may generate a need for policy change, not just the social welfare system. Specht outlines procedures for identifying this need for involving those segments of society that may be interested in seeing a policy change achieved; he also anticipates the consequences of involving these subsystems. Since it is plain that someone must make policy decisions for social welfare organizations, the issue is who— professional social workers and their clients, or vested interest groups from the larger society.

The Organization as Target   **277**

In summary, among the many situations the generalist must handle in his work with clients and their problems around conditions in the larger society, are frequently the policies and procedures of formal organizations. The generalist must be able to intervene in these organizations to remove these obstacles.

Community organization has evolved from an original concern with overlapping services to a number of more specific areas of specialization including social planning and community development. Moore identifies the formal organization as a primary target for social work practitioners interested in effecting changes at the community level. Both the providers and consumers of an organization should be included in any endeavor for change.

The Practice of Community Organization

Norman R. Moore

This paper is intended to introduce some of the content of community organization as a field of specialized learning and as a form of professional practice. A brief history of the nature of practice in community organization is presented in the first part as a means of providing some understanding of the status and character of contemporary community organization practice. The second part, then, attempts to provide a conceptual orientation to some of the major "elements" of practice (i.e., role process, techniques, etc.) and to some of the broader "contextual aspects" (i.e., social change, community patterns, etc.) in community organization. A number of the basic tenets of current community organization are identified, leading to an effort to unite conceptually the current diversity of community organization.

Some Historical Orientation

This paper shall attempt to present a brief account of the evolution of community organization as a field of practice in an effort to place its current form in the perspective of its history. Much of the history of community organization, of course, closely parallels that of all social work practice. Community organization naturally would claim allegiance to the great social reformers of the early 1900's and their cru-

Reprinted with permission of the author and The University of Tennessee School of Social Work (mimeographed, 1967), pp. 6B–31B.

sades to improve social institutions and social conditions. Many of the events in our social history which influenced the development of community organization also influenced other aspects of social work practice.

A couple of broad points should be made as a way of beginning a discussion of the evolution of community organization practice. These are:

a. Over the past 90 years or so there have been a great many "social inventions" which have contributed to the development of modern community organization. Some of the more important of these social inventions have been identified by Heath and Dunham as follows: the Charity Organization movement; the social service exchange; the community welfare council; joint financing of social welfare agencies, and to a lesser extent, statewide agencies; surveys and studies—particularly broad community social welfare surveys; community development—an international and interdisciplinary movement.[1]

b. Community organization is not the sole product or prerogative of social welfare. In Schaller's view, community organization is like a thread woven from many different strands. Social work, in particular, is the oldest strand, and has produced the most systematic understanding of community organization. Other important contributors to the development of community organization are the institutions of organized labor, religion, political parties, government, and the social experiments in community development, civil rights, and urban renewal. Experience in each of these, Schaller maintains, has produced some lessons, good and bad, for the "art of community organization" as it might be used for a variety of purposes.[2]

In other words, that which has gone on around social welfare in the vein of community organization has had considerable influence on the nature of community organization in social work.

Community organization in social welfare emerged as a necessary extension of the whole pattern of social services, rather than as a distinctively separate movement toward a desired end in social work practice. It evolved from the growth of the whole charity movement, was stimulated by war-time and depression era social needs, was shaped and reshaped by social legislation, was "reformed" by ideological and pragmatic considerations, and, even now, appears headed for still further alteration.

Different students of community organization come up with different ways of classifying the eras of community organization, but most end up with three to five significant eras. We shall use four periods for examining the evolution of community organization.

[1]Heath, Monna and Arthur Dunham. *Trends in Community Organization* (Chicago: University of Chicago, School of Social Service Administration, 1963), p. 60.
[2]Schaller, Lyle H. *Community Organization: Conflict and Reconciliation* (Nashville: Abingdon Press, 1966), pp. 50–71.

1. Charity Organization Societies

The COS's, prominent in the country for about 40 years, are credited with providing the origins for modern social work, particularly with family welfare services, and community organization. The Societies were quite frequently dominated by the wealthy leisure class who were intent upon reforming the "relief system" of their day—for the same reasons as reform is called for today. What concerned the COS's was that a great many agencies were operating with the same functional field, namely, family welfare. They were concerned that the autonomous operation of the relief agencies was leading to the evils of case duplication, client abuse and waste of funds, and of less than possible coverage of need and helpfulness to clients. Their first objective became one of *coordinating the work of private agencies.* To achieve this they developed ways to divide the work, integrate intake policies, exchange case information, and for the central clearance of cases. Out of such developed the practice of the case conference and the social service exchange. The societies also published local directories, and operated information bureaus about charities. These are still common activities of community organization agencies. The COS's were typically authoritarian in their approach, but did meet with some success.[3]

Soon COS's themselves became engrossed in trying to cope with social and economic problems: tenant reform, sanitation, child labor, vagrancy, health, and housing. Part of the effort of COS's was to close gaps through benevolence, legislation, and the extension or creation of organizations. They also began to organize and operate programs, as employment bureaus, day nurseries, wood yards. In these activities, the societies were competitive with existing agencies, if not contributory to the duplication they sought to avoid. More importantly, however, such direct services programming apparently lessened the effectiveness of their original coordinating role. It should be noted that today most community organization agencies try zealously to avoid operating direct services programs for anything more than demonstration. In sum, most students agree that the COS provided the foundations for community organization. In fact, two observe: "The emphasis on cooperation and coordination, on fact-finding and exchange of information and experience, on working on the underlying causes of social problems, have been retained in modern social welfare planning bodies."[4]

[3]Murphy, Campbell C. *Community Organization Practice* (Boston: Houghton-Mifflin, 1954).
[4]Johns, Ray and David DeMarche. *Community Organization and Agency Organization* (New York: Association Press, 1951), p. 85.

2. Federation of Social Agencies

Within a few years, the COS's began to foster councils of social agencies and gradually shifted the leadership for community welfare planning to them. Councils of social agencies began to develop around 1910, the first in Pittsburgh. They were still primarily concerned with *the coordination of programs among the various voluntary agencies.* But councils were intended to have some advantages over a direct-service agency (i.e., the COS), such as objectivity and neutrality, in effecting such coordination.

The early councils themselves were limited in scope and effectiveness. While some attempted, and others showed desire to engage in community planning and social action, councils largely concentrated on the provision of central services and operated as clearinghouses for information, etc. There was *no clear focus interagency planning,* which was a partial consequence of the councils lack of any authority over the standards of service.[5] Much of the reason for this lay in the fact that councils were organized on "delegate body" plans, whereby the council membership was made up of representatives of the agencies. Agencies dominated the councils leaving them without any effective sanctions against the agencies. The initial growth of councils was very slow; by 1917, they existed in only seven cities. The impetus of WWI had brought this number to 20 by 1923.

Another aspect in the federation movement was that of "federated fund-raising." Federated financing originated in England and was adopted in America in 1888, in Denver, and in 1913, in Cleveland, but did not really catch on until during WWI. As early as 1906, principles were being suggested for a "financial clearing house to assume responsibility for the support of local charities" which included *a central budget committee and a comprehensive annual campaign,* both mainstays in our contemporary model.[6] At that time, each agency conducted its separate fund-raising drive which it was reluctant to relinquish, and a period of controversy ensued until WWI. What is now the Cleveland Welfare Organization is considered the first modern community chest. Interestingly, it evolved from some charity policing activities of the local chamber of commerce. This was perhaps the origin for the support as well as control of the business sector so common in United Funds today.

Financial federations expanded tremendously at the stimulation of WWI. "War Chests" developed as if by tidal wave across the country, and were converted to community chests in postwar years. By 1925,

[5]Murphy, *op. cit.*
[6]Heath and Dunham, *op. cit.,* p. 23.

such federations existed in some 250 cities. Chests of this era were typically weak: They had *little authority over the allocation of funds raised or the standards of agencies being supported,* and hence little control over the use of charity funds.[7] Councils of social agencies continued to develop and most affiliated in some way with the chests, for the emergence of the *chest-council concept* in community organization. Some councils exercised some influence over agency allocations through the planning function. Many councils concerned themselves with only the member agencies of their local chest. The characteristic weaknesses of councils throughout the 1920's was that they (a) lacked "community representativeness," i.e., were still dominated by social agencies; and, (b) excluded largely the public services from their planning and coordinating efforts.

McMillen termed these developments as the emphasis in community organization on the *"cultivation of community support,"* as opposed to the earlier emphasis on the *"problems of coordination."*[8] Social agencies consolidated such common activities as fund raising with the chests, and research and interpretation with the councils, in an effort to widen the rather narrow and esoteric bases of support which individual agencies normally had.

3. Advent of Public Social Services

The spread and development of councils were stimulated by social legislation of the depression era. Community chests had experienced another period of rapid growth during 1929–31, as local relief campaigns attempted to meet depression needs in a fashion similar to the war chests a decade earlier. This time, however, they were overwhelmed by the magnitude of the needs. The Social Security Act of 1935 created public services which supplanted the programs of the private agencies. This event ushered in an *era of reorientation and reprogramming* for the voluntary social services.

Councils were pressed into service to aid in planning for this transition within the community social welfare system. This task necessitated *a shift in focus by councils* to the tax-supported programs rather than voluntary ones. This was to become a lasting ingredient for council affairs in the future. Another change typically occurred: The participation of laymen in the work of the councils was greatly expanded. "Citizen participation" was to become a council motto within the next 15–20 years.

World War II produced additional beneficial effects on the develop-

---

[7]Murphy, *op. cit.*
[8]McMillen, Wayne. *Community Organization for Social Welfare* (Chicago: University of Chicago Press, 1945), p. 33.

ment of chests and councils. It ushered in the greatest period of expansion for federated financing, as "war relief" chests became even more widespread than during World War I. Depression relief expenditures diminished drastically, and national revenues were absorbed by the war effort. The War Relief Board organized the National War Fund, modeled after the community chest, and raised large sums of monies for war-related programs. The war fund formation led to the merger of a large number of war-relief agencies which were later converted into community chests—which by 1950 numbered about 1300.

Council development was likewise stimulated through the creation of defense councils and war-service councils under the auspices of the Office of Civilian Defense. The federal government provided funds to create facilities and services to meet social needs in the "war impacted" areas as large influxes of military-related populations created hardships on local communities. Local planning was necessary to cope with these social welfare needs, and defense councils were established. In some cases, existing councils of social agencies were entrusted these responsibilities, in others they were designated for participating roles. Many of the newly created councils survived after the war as community planning councils. By 1950, about 500 councils existed, with nearly every city of 100,000 population having one.

4. The "Problem-Solving" Planning Approach

Community organization experience during the Depression and World War II largely fostered the notion of "planning for the solution of social problems in the community" as the desired direction for practice. Much experience in planning had been gained and community councils were set on a course of developing their modern role. McMillen reported that a shift in emphasis was occurring in the mid-1940's toward efforts by councils "to formulate programs to provide for unmet needs."[9] In this shift, the interrelations of agencies ceased to be of dominant interest. Rather, "problem-solving" became the dominant interest, for which it became more important to arouse citizen concern for community needs.

In recent years, this community organization role emphasis has been sustained by social legislation for the development of public services, by private philanthropy, and the success of fund-raising for health and welfare. For instance, the planning task of community organization has increased tremendously with the passage of federal acts dealing with mental health (1947), housing (1948), juvenile delinquency (1962), public welfare (1962), poverty (1964), and health care (1965), and the

[9] *Ibid.*

many federal grant programs. Since World War II, state and local governments have also expanded their activities in education, recreation, youth services, health, and welfare programs. These actions have made tremendous resources for social welfare available to communities. They have encouraged councils, particularly, to develop ways of directing these resources to social needs in their community—i.e., planning. In the 1960's, it has become rather popular for councils to describe their function as "comprehensive community-wide planning" and to pursue more ambitious social planning projects.

Councils have not, however, given up their earlier function of coordinating social agencies in favor of broad social planning. The nature of a considerable amount of planning is that of resolving problems which are created by the structure of community services itself, or which arise when that structure must make adjustments to stay abreast of changing social needs.

In post-war years, the fund raising task of community organization has also expanded tremendously. Private agencies have proliferated rapidly since World War II, reaching well over 100,000 by 1958. Most of these, particularly the myriad health agencies, have developed outside the structure of federated financing. Early in the 1950's, the "United Fund" movement started to spread to counteract the multiplying number of fund-raising campaigns. The concept of a United Fund was designed to improve the structure of the Community Chests, primarily by widening the scope for voluntarily combined fund drives and by creating community sanctions for controlling the spread of independent campaigns. United Funds have now superseded nearly all except the smaller Community Chests. The problem of multiple campaigns, however, continues to be a struggle. For even today with some 1500 Funds and Chests raising about $600 million, upwards of three-fourths of all voluntary agencies are not participating members. The United Funds have on the whole proven reasonably successful as community organization agencies for "cultivating public support" of community health, recreation, and welfare services. They have tended to develop into rather sophisticated business-like enterprises for financing social welfare.

Later on in the 1950's, the concept of the "United Community Services" agency became popular as a new structure for community organization. The UCS approach combines the United Fund and the Planning Council into a single organization. It represents an attempt to integrate more effectively the functions of financing and planning in community social welfare decision-making. In part, at least, the UCS plan was also conceived as a way to overcome the "friction" which had developed between Funds and Councils in many communities. The United Community Services approach has been adopted rather slowly, but such agencies now exist in a fair number of communities. Whether or not UCS offers superior merits for more effective community organization has not been investigated or generally reported.

Community organization, then, has passed through these stages of development in evolving its current primary functions of community planning and fund-raising for social welfare purposes. In recent years, the interest of most educators, writers, and researchers, as well as many practitioners in community organization has centered predominately on the social welfare planning approach for community problem-solving and program development. A great deal of interest has been generated in such aspects as the process, methods, and strategy in planning, the role of the planner, the non-technical aspects of planning, community influences on planning, etc. At the same time, more attention has been given to certain issues created by contemporary pressures on community planning councils. Planning for social needs has been expanding and proliferating fairly rapidly in recent years. Specialized problem-centered planning (e.g., aging, mental health, recreation, poverty) has been growing as a function of agencies and organizations within functional fields. New social planning structures have come into being and governmental agencies have ventured out further into social planning. The modern scene now contains what Warren calls a "plurality of planning centers" which raises issues and problems for centralized planning.[10]

The central question, then, concerns the probable future role of the community planning councils, and hence the role of organization practitioner. Will other forms of social planning supersede council-type planning, or what will be the new relationships? Some suggest that councils might become "super planning centers" for communities; while others envision councils as agents for coordinating pluralistic planning. Another possible alternative would be for community organization practitioners to work within specialized planning agencies and attempt coordination through their relationships. At the moment, the movement in council practice tends to be toward community-wide planning.

But planning is not the whole of community organization, just as Funds and Councils were not the whole, although it became convenient to think in those terms. There has always been some community organization work directly with the people in their neighborhoods or in similar social problem situations for neighborhood development or social action purposes. The settlement house movement, beginning with the Neighborhood Guild in New York (1886), and the Hull-House in

---

[10]Warren, Roland. "The Impact of New Designs of Community Organization," *Child Welfare*, 44(9): 494–500, 1965.

Chicago (1889), is probably the historical precedent for this aspect of community organization in social work. The settlement approach was a total identification with the disadvantaged neighborhood and its people, and an attempt to elevate socially whole groups of people (e.g., housing, sanitation, education, recreation, medical care). In recent years, there has been a renewed interest within the field in community organization practice at the neighborhood or client level. Much of this interest has been stimulated by the Civil Rights Movement and the War on Poverty of the 1960's. At least a part of community organization practice seems to be moving in the direction of direct organizational work with low-income populations who are not affiliated with the major institutional systems and are not using available services in the community. It would seem that community organization is approaching still another juncture in its evolution.

A Conceptual Orientation

It should be recognized, first off, that there is no "theory for community organization" as a social work method. The literature of community organization does contain a collection of theoretical concepts for guiding practice, but even these are not highly developed nor well-integrated. What are often regarded as "principles" for community organization are usually untested propositions, which might be better described as normative beliefs, traditional assumptions, or the like. In Ross' view, the principles and methods of community organization are "sensitizing concepts" (unvalidated clues) rather than "definite concepts" which have been tested in practice.[11] Later students have been more critical. Morris, for instance, believes that the "global nature" of concepts in community organization renders them of "limited assistance" in dealing with problems in the real world. To Morris, the intellectual task is one of developing practice theory to fill the gap between "philosophy and action" in community organization.[12]

During its history, community organization has been defined by several educators and practitioners, and, yet, has seemed to defy or elude definition at the same time. Currently there is not a universally held or used definition of the community organization method in social work. Nor has there been great continuity in conceiving the objectives of community organization, which, of course, is important to a definition. In the 1920's, Jesse Steiner searched for technology to support a "specific method of social organization" in communities.[13] By 1940, the

[11]Ross, Murray G. *Community Organization: Theory and Principles* (New York: Harper and Brothers, 1955. Revised second edition, 1967).

[12]Morris, Robert. "New Concepts in Community Organization," *Social Welfare Forum, 1961* (New York: Columbia University Press, 1962), pp. 128–145.

[13]Steiner, Jesse F. *Community Organization: A Study of Its Theory and Current Practice* (New York: Century Co., 1930), p. 323.

landmark "Lane Report" had declared the central aim of community organization as a "process" was to secure "a progressively more effective adjustment between social welfare resources and needs."[14] This implied that community organization should be concerned with the "discovery and definition of need," the "elimination and prevention of social needs and disabilities," the "articulation of resources and needs," and the "constant readjustment of resources" to meet changing needs. These functional obligations have continued to be cornerstones in the general conception of community organization.

The Lane Report recognized that "organizing a community" takes place outside as well as inside social work, and a thorough scrutiny was needed before "the field in which the community organization process operates" could be accurately circumscribed. But, it stated, what distinguished community organization in social work from all others was the social welfare nature of its objectives when "coupled with its general content and setting." Here the Report made a key statement, saying "the justification of the community organization process is improvement in the coverage and quality of service to clients which the community is enabled to provide." This kind of orientation has been particularly strong in the thought and practice of community organization. In later years, the emphasis was to stress that the *practitioner enables the community* to provide improvement in services as the concept of "the community as the client" began to emerge.[15]

By 1954, Murphy viewed community organization as "a set of processes and skills" and "a field of activity." For Murphy, the *field* was largely comprised of those agencies which specialized in community organization. These were the "coordinating agencies" (planning) and "promotional agencies" (fund-raising, educational) which had reached high peaks of development. It was these specialized agencies which constituted the primary *setting* for practice. The *skills* of community organization were those of the social work method (e.g., using self and relationships, diagnosis) and rested on the same body of values and principles (e.g., acceptance, self-determination). The practitioner was essentially in an "enabler" role, using what Murphy termed "professional discretion." The *processes* were those of social change through democratic procedures which seek to unite rather than divide groups, and to plan "with" rather than "for" people. Here Murphy upheld one of the basic tenets of community organization, saying it "is not the work of a directive few; it is a matter of representation and participation by all concerned." Murphy's orientation is well summarized in his own words, which underscore the "community as the client" concept, as follows: "Community organization practice attempts to meet the com-

---

[14]Harper, Ernest and Arthur Dunham (eds.), *Community Organization in Action* (New York: Association Press, 1959).
[15]Murphy, *op. cit.*

munity where it is, to help it determine its own needs, to move at its own pace, and decide its own solutions." The similarity of this conception to that for other social work practice is apparent.[16]

In the most complete theoretical treatment of the community organization method, Ross in 1955 challenged much of the existing theory. For Ross, neither *setting* nor *content* determined the nature of the community organization *process.* Ross conceptualized almost entirely free from any agency referents, such as Murphy had done, so that the notion of a "field of activity" was unimportant. Community organization to Ross was a "distinctive pattern of work" which had "wide application" in community work, including the fields of community development and community relations as well. What was essential was the process itself, and its end product—which must always be to enhance "community integration." By "integration" was meant the community's "capacity to function as a unit in solving its own problems." Integration constituted the "process goal" of the community organization method, and always took precedence over the "content goals" of any specific project or endeavor. Community organization, then, as Ross defines it, was:

. . . to mean a process by which a community identifies its needs or objectives, orders (or ranks) these needs or objectives, develops the confidence and will to work at these needs or objectives, finds the resources (internal and/or external) to deal with these needs or objectives, takes action in respect to them, and in so doing extends and develops cooperative and collaborative attitudes and practices in the community.[17]

Ross differed little with Murphy with respect to role and method. Community organization has a "unique frame of reference" which was a composite of the "particular value orientation" of social work philosophy, a "particular conception of community problems," and "certain assumptions influencing methods." Ross was particularly emphatic about the latter, saying they constitute the "foundation of community organization," i.e., its nature, its methods, its principles. For instance, a couple of Ross' assumptions were that "communities of people can develop the capacity to deal with their problems," and that "people should participate in major changes in their communities." Communities of people, Ross held, will change their ways only if forced or highly motivated to change. Community organization must be committed to "indigenous plans" in preference to "externally imposed plans," since communities do not develop problem-solving capacity when there is imposition rather than desire.[18]

Ross, in 1955, apparently saw no need to restrict community organi-

[16]*Ibid.*
[17]Ross, *op. cit.*
[18]*Ibid.*

zation to social work practice nor to narrowly construed social welfare concerns. His concern was "community integration" rather than the achievement of a preconceived social welfare program, and in this reflected the considerable influence from the field of international community development. In 1956, however, Ross attempted to "distinguish community organization in social welfare from all other approaches to community work." The concept of community organization lacked clarity with respect to the "essentials of a social work process" and the "discipline of method, including the relation of ends and means." Ross reasoned that the "reform" and "planning" orientations to community work were not *per se* social work processes, and therefore not the whole of community organization. The "process orientation," however, did meet the criteria of social work, but was probably only appropriate for use within the social welfare community. In his words, "the planning council within the welfare community should be committed to the use of the community organization process, to the end that there may be movement toward a strong, cohesive welfare community with increasing capacity to plan and act." The welfare community in seeking objectives in its geographic community, however, does not have to rely on the "slower and gentler methods" of community organization, but may use any approach appropriate to the endeavor.[19]

The foregoing, I believe, is the essence of the traditional conception of community organization in social work. Much of it seems to have been fairly well captured in the 1959 Curriculum Study: While community organization is "only beginning to be considered a 'basic' method of social work" it is increasingly "conceived to be a direct service method" whose aim is "to provide services to community agencies for the enhancement of community life and the functioning of community groups, and thereby indirectly contribute to the enhancement of the social functioning of individuals."[20] Social work literature contains several works directed at the twin questions of whether community organization is a "method" and whether it is "social work." All would require that it embody the "core" values, goals, knowledge, and methods common to casework, and group work to be part of the "social work practice family."[21] Newstetter, for instance, wrote that the "social process" of community organization becomes a social work process when "it has social work objectives" and it is "consciously effected" by a person whose professional role is primarily that of "bringing social work knowledge and methods to bear on the solution of a problem."[22]

[19]Ross, Murray G. "Conceptual Problems in a Community Organization," *Social Service Review,* 30(2): 174–181, 1956.
[20]Boehm, Werner W. *Objectives of the Social Work Curriculum of the Future,* Vol. 1, Curriculum Study (New York: Council on Social Work Education, 1959), p. 136.
[21]Carter, Genevieve. "Practice Theory in Community Organization," *Social Work,* 3(2): 40–57, 1958.
[22]Harper & Dunham, *op. cit.,* pp. 179–191.

The Practice of Community Organization   **289**

Beyond this basic qualification, Carter held that it was the use of the "core elements" of the social work method in a "problem-solving process" with phases which produced "a system of ordered activities" for the community organization method. The core elements were identified as "social study and diagnosis" which leads to shared goals; "a change process" directed toward social change for better functioning; and "evaluation of the changed situation" for accountability to the profession and the public. The phases of the problem-solving process, on the other hand, were the "reconnaissance phase" in which the problem's treatment feasibility is assessed; "the diagnostic phase" in which an approach or strategy to the problem is formulated; the "planning phase" in which the change process is initiated, the problem analyzed, alternative solutions developed, and a group decision reached; and the "implementation phase" in which a plan of action is formulated, strategic and tactical factors considered, action is completed and social change is evaluated. Carter and others have maintained that the method of community organization is limited to "project-centered activities" where the problem-solving process has "a recognizable case beginning and termination."[23] Ross, as we have seen, does not share this view. Others, notably Newstetter and Pray, have maintained that the quality of social relationships between the people and groups engaged in the community organization endeavor is just as important as the goals pursued. Both agreed that the primary role of the practitioner was to enable people to find and use constructive and satisfying social relationships in the intergroup process, and this is the social work function. Both the "project-centered" and the "social relationships" positions have become strong tenets in practice. Practitioners have sought to create cooperative, integrative, harmonious, "consensus-type" relationships within a problem-solving process focused on a particular situation in the community.[24]

Another fundamental belief in community organization is that it is a *process of social change.* In its simplest definition, such as Schaller uses, it may be nothing more than "a method of effecting social change."[25] Even Boehm, in social work language, has said that community organization "attempts to help collective man change his common environment to permit better social functioning of individuals."[26] Enlarging on her 1958 article in Friedlander's book, Carter stated that the practice of community organization involves "(a) social work intervention in a given situation, which (b) initiates or guides (c) a movement or change process toward (d) a goal."[27] A number of key concepts guide and

[23]Carter, *op. cit.*
[24]Harper & Dunham, *op. cit.,* pp. 179–191.
[25]Schaller, *op. cit.*
[26]Boehm, *op. cit.*
[27]Friedlander, Walter A. (ed.). *Concepts and Methods of Social Work* (Englewood Cliffs: Prentice-Hall, Inc., 1958), p. 240.

influence this practice, including those of goal movement, enabling community readiness, representativeness and need. In oversimplified form, these concepts may be interpreted as follows: a community, itself, (1) must recognize that a social need exists, for it to be a real need, and (2) it must focus on some specific attainable goal, (3) toward which the worker facilitates the work of a group, (4) which is representative of the interests affected by the problem, (5) through activities geared to the readiness to move of the people involved and the community, (6) which must result in some progress toward the goal. These are not sequential steps in a change formula, however, but rather are factors which must be occurring or in evidence almost simultaneously. These are a few of the things which the literature tells us of social change with respect to the community organization method.

But the questions arise: Who shall change and who shall be changed?, and What shall be changed and how shall it be changed? Traditional community organization has, since World War II, premised that the "leadership" in the community shall decide, plan, and activate social change. In the last several years, there has been a particularly strong emphasis on "lay" or "citizen" leadership, as opposed to that of professionals or officials in social welfare. The attendant assumption has been that community social welfare policy should be under lay control. Citizen participation and decision-making should precede any change in the community's policy and provisions for social welfare. In this approach, community organization functions to organize people as "providers" of social welfare goods and services for the community.

With the momentum of the Civil Rights Movement and the War on Poverty in the 1960's, however, has come a rather spirited interest in community organization practice on the neighborhood or community sub-group level. The idea of neighborhood organization is by no means new, although its context and thrust seems to be changing. Previous neighborhood organization has had various orientations, such as "planning" (District Welfare Councils), "action" (The Woodlawn Organization), "common-interest" (tenant associations), "special problems" (juvenile delinquency, voter registration), "development," etc. Current neighborhood and sub-group organization seems to combine the action and common or special-interest orientations with a stronger commitment to action, a stronger ethic of participation and a bolder set of tactics (e.g., conflict, protest). It emphasizes the role of the indigenous people or sub-group members and the task of influencing the larger community to act in ways beneficial to the people represented by the organization. In this approach, community organization functions to organize people as "consumers" of social welfare goods and services in the community.

The "providers" and "consumers" approaches represent opposite bases for community organization practice. One could probably find other bases in between, such as "neighbors" for neighborhood development, which would have some characteristics of either pole base. But the basic question would seem to be: Can the pole bases be reconciled for community organization in social work? They can, if we take *social change for social welfare* as the primary objective and essential property of community organization practice. In the writer's view, social change through deliberate efforts using competent methods is the key to the refinement of community organization. In order to reconcile the pole bases, then, we would need a conceptual framework something like this:

Community Organization: A *Method* of Effecting *Social Change* in All or Any Part of a Community through the Modification of the *Behavior of Its Institutions* and Its *Ways of Using Resources* in Social Welfare Matters

People may be organized as:	Providers	Consumers
	Of social welfare foods & services Around some social value (s)	Of social welfare goods & services Around some material objective (s)
To work through:	**Decision-makers, in:**	**Needs-makers, in:**
	Service-systems (health, housing, welfare, recreation) Institutionalized systems (political, economic, religious) Socio-economic systems (status, role, power)	Recipient-groups (housing, welfare, education) Institutionalized systems (churches, settlements, schools) Neighborhood social systems (clubs, organizations, friendship & leadership)
On the institutional & resource problems of:	**Scarcity**	**Scarcity**
	Creating new resources Expanding present resources	Demanding new & expanded resources Creating & expanding own resources
	Allocation	**Allocation**
	Rational pattern of use Planning & organization of use	Equity in distribution Reorganization of use patterns
	Delivery	**Delivery**
	Agency coordination Policy integration Program operation standards	Rights of beneficiaries Participating in policy control Changes in policies & program

This framework obviously strives only to be conceptually complete, and not exhaustive of all concrete manifestations in community organization. An instructive word is perhaps needed here. The elements in the above chart may be read in several different combinations. For example: People may be (1) organized as (a) providers of social welfare goods and services around some social value to (2) work through (b) decision-makers in a particular service system (3) on an institutional and resource problem of (c) allocation to obtain a more rational pattern of resource use. Similarly, the elements identified in the "consumer" column may be linked in various combinations to describe the essence of a community organization effort. What the chart indicates is that while the elemental content of community organization with providers and consumers may obviously and necessarily vary, the essential characteristics of the process and objective need not vary.

An orientation such as this is useful in several ways. First, it calls attention to the fact that the problems in the community social welfare system are related to the supply and utilization of resources. One aspect is the scarcity of resources, and hence the problem of discovering, developing, expanding or creating resources. Another is the pattern of resource allocation to the community's various programs and services, and hence the problem of securing the most rational and equitable distribution for maximizing community social welfare. A third aspect is resource utilization, and hence the problems of delivering social welfare goods and services in accordance with social needs and community capabilities.

Second, it suggests that these problems of resources may be approached by community organization efforts on two levels in the social welfare system: Those with the "providers" of social welfare, and those with the "consumers." This is so because the general problem is one of effecting change in one or more of the aspects (scarcity, allocation, or delivery) of social welfare resources. Many resource problems may be, and some should be, approached on both levels, either in joint or separate efforts for change.

Third, it suggests that a community's resource problems are frequently related to the nature and behavior of its institutions, since they control the major social welfare resources in the community system. "Lag" occurs whenever institutional behavior is not in accord with the current social needs or conditions of the community. Community organization efforts must be oriented toward reducing "institutional lag" in social welfare, and this is a focus on social change.

What the foregoing suggests is not a radical departure in community organization. In important ways, community organization has long been concerned with the need for deliberate social change, and the problems of resource supply and utilization and of institutional lag and behavior.

What is suggested as needed is a sharpening in its focus on the problems of social change in the community, and the development of concepts, methods and skills more adequate for dealing with those problems in a professional practice. This doubtless would be a difficult goal to realize. For one matter, it would imply that the practitioners role repertoire should be expanded (e.g., to include the roles of "advocate," "activist," etc.) as well as his ability to use a wider variety of social processes (e.g., competition, adversary, conflict). For another, it would imply that the practitioner should have a broader foundation for understanding, using, and dealing with community "dynamics" (i.e., social forces, elites, politics, economic dominance, etc.). In this respect, community organization would need to draw more heavily on the social sciences. It is somewhat difficult to tell exactly where community organization is in its thought and practice and the direction in which it is moving. In the writer's estimation, these few pages represent the status of its development and its efforts toward greater sophistication in its methodology.

Sociology and political science have supplied much of the theory used by social work practitioners who have engaged in community organization and social planning. But for social work these theories suffer from a lack of prescriptive implications for practice. Chatterjee identifies a need for theory that is more prescriptive in nature, particularly in relation to formal organizations identified as targets.

"Community" in Social Science and Social Work

Pranab Chatterjee

An examination of the lacks and linkages between the concepts of community in the social sciences and community organization in social work and other fields entails the following procedures: outlining of social science theory as diagnostic or analytical tools; utility of theory toward intervention techniques; and use of theory in determining the unit which may be referred to as community under given conditions. This paper undertakes the tasks outlined above.

Chatterjee and Koleski developed a typology of schools of theoretical approach in the social sciences to the unit idea of community.[1] This

Reprinted from the *Indian Journal of Social Work,* Vol. 31, No. 2, 1970, with permission of the author and the Tata Institute of Social Sciences.
[1]Pranab Chatterjee and Raymond Koleski, "The Concepts of Community and Community Organization: A Review," unpublished paper accepted for publication in *Social Work,* in press.

five-fold typology classified the Social schools of approach to community as follows: *regulatory, integrative, ecological, monographic,* and *political-stratificational.* To discuss the lacks and linkages in the concepts of community and community organization, it is now necessary to discuss the adequacy of these various schools to community as *diagnostic or analytical tools* for the practitioner in community organization.

Social Science Theory
as Diagnostic or
Analytical Tools

The regulatory approach[2] of community is useful to the practitioner in helping him understand the nature of the principal institutions themselves. It may be possible that many practitioners do not conceptualize about their unit of service, i.e., their community, in terms of *gemeinschaft* and *gesellschaft* or mechanical and organic solidarity. However, many practitioners do conceptualize their unit of service in terms of rural and urban or agrarian and industrial. It may thus be suggested that the practitioners also do conceptualize their service unit *in terms of the principal institutions themselves,* but perhaps at a different level of abstraction. Thus community organization in the Appalachian region entails an understanding of the attributes of a *gemeinschaft*-type entity, whereas community organization in a major American metropolitan area entails an understanding of the attributes of a *gesellschaft*-type entity.

The regulatory approach to community, thus, helps the practitioner understand his community in broad and generic terms. No specific or detailed understanding is fostered by this approach for the practitioner.

The integrative approach,[3] when operationalized from Parson's paradigm, helps the practitioner understand his community in somewhat more—though in unspecified degree—detail. Thus, if a practitioner knows that he is working in an Appalachian region (conceptualized as a *gemeinschaft*-type entity according to the regulatory approach), then an understanding of the process whereby the four institutions of occupational structure, political jurisdictions, communication complexes, and residential patterns are integrated is fostered by the integrative approach.

---

[2]The regulatory approaches are those social science approaches which "delineate in terms of *the principal institutions themselves.* It is imperative in this approach that the principal institutions 'regulate' the character of community." *Ibid.,* p. 3.

It is to be noted that Toennies' *gemeinshaft* and *gesellschaft* typology, is an example of the regulatory approach.

[3]For a detailed discussion of this approach, see Talcott Parson's, *Structure and Process in Modern Societies* (New York: The Free Press, 1960), pp. 250–79.

The ecological approach[4] to community fosters the practitioners' understanding of distributory patterns in specified geographic units. This school of approach to community seems to be quite useful for the community organization practitioner, since this approach defines given problems areas (crime rate, delinquency patterns, solidarity of ethnic groups, zone and gradients, etc.) *in relation to a geographic community.* Thus perhaps an older theoretical approach such as the ecological school to the study of community needs revival for social work practice in community organization.

The monographic approach[5] has many variations within itself. Lipset and his associates define a functional community with a monographic approach;[6] Dollard's monograph is a combination of social science and psychoanalysis;[7] and the Lynds' works on Middletown are a monograph on class structure in an Indiana town.[8] The benefit that a practitioner may derive from this approach is when the community he serves is very similar to those studied by scholars with a monographic approach. However, in such a case the attainment of comparability between the practitioners' community and a community described by a given scholar in the monographic approach remains the burden of the practitioner himself.

The political-stratificational approach[9] is narrower in scope, since it proposes to study only the distribution and development of power and influence in given communities. As a topic, this approach is indeed useful to the practitioner, since he has to deal with various levels of power sources in the practice of community organization. Whether such practice is city-wide planning, coordination, and fund-raising, or development of a grass roots organization in a ghetto, the practitioner needs to know and clearly identify the sources of power and influence. However, the problem for the practitioner is that there is hardly any agreement among theoreticians on the way the source of power is measured. It is not clear from the writings of social scientists on the subject of community power (and its relation to national power) as to whether there are certain types of power elites, and also which type

[4]For a detailed discussion of the ecological school, see Milton M. Gordon, *Social Class in American Sociology* (New York: McGraw-Hill Co., 1963), pp. 21–51.

[5]Pranab Chatterjee and Raymond Koleski, *op. cit.,* p. 5.

[6]Cf. Seymour Martin Lipset, Martin A. Trow, and James S. Coleman, *Union Democracy* (New York: The Free Press, 1956).

[7]Cf. John Dollard, *Caste and Class in a Southern Town* (New Haven: Yale University Press, 1937).

[8]Cf. Robert S. and Helen M. Lynd, *Middletown* (New York: Harcourt Brace and Co., 1929); and *Middletown in Transition* (New York: Harcourt Brace and Co. 1937).

[9]For interesting discussions on the reputational and the pluralistic models of study of power distribution in communities within the political-stratificational school, see Arnold M. Rose, *The Power Structure* (New York: Oxford University Press, 1967); and Nelson W. Posby, *Community Power and Political Theory* (New Haven: Yale University Press, 1963).

The Organization as Target

of power exists in what type of community. Thus the practitioner, if he wishes to utilize the political-stratificational approach to community, is left with a two-fold burden: identification of issues in his community which are similar to those dealt with by social scientists in this school; and concurrent identification of structures which are also similar to those dealt with by social scientists.[10]

The most difficult problem for the practitioner is outlined in his dilemma with the political-stratificational approach. He needs to know not only the sources of power in a given community, but also often the relationship of such power sources to the national structures of power. Perhaps the resolution of this dilemma for the practitioner lies in his understanding of economic and political institutions. In that case, however, a theory such as the political stratificational school serves merely as a guide rather than a diagnostic or analytical tool.

The foregoing discussion examines the existing schools of approaches in the social sciences toward the unit-idea of community and their adequacy for community organization practitioners in various fields. One specific social science approach to the community which was not outlined in the review[11] is that approach which views the community as a socialization agent. There seem to be three major sociologists who have outlined the community primarily in terms of socialization agents. These three authors are Seymour M. Lipset and Reinhart Bendix, and Philip M. Hauser. Lipset and Bendix in their notion of "community of orientation" point out the possibilities of intra- and inter-generational mobility.[12] Hauser viewed the community as a socialization (and in the case of geographically mobile populations, possible resocialization) agent.[13] While the notion of these two social scientists did not seem to constitute a "school of approach" (and therefore not summarized in the review of concepts of community), it may be worthwhile considering the lacks and linkages of this type of formulation with the method of community organization.

It would seem that the notion of "community of orientation" as

[10]All the methodological debate of the early 60's on community power notwithstanding, there seem to be recent trends to take C. Wright Mills and his economic-elite dominance hypothesis seriously. Those who oppose the economic-elite dominance thesis point out that many community decisions—as in Edward Banfield, *Political Influence* (New York: The Free Press, 1961)—are *not* made by economic notables, raising the following question: are these issues of any interest to the economic-elite? Thus it may be possible that the economic elite do not decide certain issues *because the elitist interests are not involved* in those issues.

[11]Pranab Chatterjee and Raymond Koleski, *op. cit.*

[12]Cf. Seymour M. Lipset and Reinhart Bendix, *Social Mobility in Industrial Society* (Berkeley: The University of California Press, 1962), pp. 203–226.

[13]Cf. Philip M. Hauser, *Population Perspectives* (New Brunswick: Rutgers University Press, 1961). It is to be noted that the angry comments of Silberman on the "beer can in the cotton patch" are in response to Hauser. Cf. Charles E. Silberman, *Crisis in Black and White* (New York: Random House, 1964), pp. 36–67.

formulated by Lipset and Bendix may serve as an excellent *diagnostic or analytical tool* for community organization practitioners[14] in such areas as planning and rehabilitation of various types of population groups. Hauser's theoretical formulation may also be used for the same purpose. Thus, for instance, a community organization effort in developing more employment opportunity for some minority groups may face three important tasks. First of these would be the creation of more employment opportunities. The second task faced by such an effort would be to socialize (or resocialize) some parts of this population to undertake training for various types of employment, to function in large formal organizations, to develop work habits which are in accord with the norms of the community, etc. Third, the Lipset and Bendix and Hauser formulations may help in setting realistic goals (both short and long-term) for such a community organization effort, since *such theoretical formulations help determine the extent of social mobility possible within a more or less specified period of time.* Thus Lipset and Bendix and Hauser, while not constituting a specific "school" of approach to the community within the discipline of sociology, may yet serve as useful analytic or diagnostic tools to practitioners.

Utility of Social Science
Theory as Intervention
Techniques

The foregoing discussion makes it clear that the five schools of approach to community are, at their best, only relevant to the practitioner as primarily descriptive and sometimes as analytic or diagnostic tools. None of the schools outlined above are adequate to formulate theoretically relevant intervention techniques. However, since power, resources, and high levels of decision-making are in the hands of large formal organizations, it would seem that social science conceptualizations on formal organizations should be helpful to the practitioner planning interventions. In addition, perhaps the basic assumptions of different types of social science theory building (like structural-functional

[14]At this point it is necessary to note that the term "community organization" has different meaning to theoreticians and practitioners. Thus to many social scientists the term community organization has a general and specific meaning. The general meaning is somewhat of an all-inclusive concept that denotes the organization or the structure of a given community. The specific meaning is to denote all forms of formal organizations that are developed within the community for promoting or discouraging one or more given issues in the community.

To social workers, the term community organization is understood as a method, primarily toward the goal of improvement and coordination in the field of social welfare. Only recently have social workers shown concern in fields not directly related to traditional social welfare such as health, education, housing, employment opportunities, etc. With such recent concerns, however, such terms as community action have been added to the social work vocabulary. Traditionally, community action meant social action or social reform. It is a rather recent trend where the two are being viewed as the same. In this paper, community organization denotes a social work method unless otherwise stated.

type *vis-a-vis* conflict-orientation type) are also helpful in developing intervention techniques.

Negotiation or bargaining with large formal organizations—and in some cases confronting them—is the task of organizations developed for that purpose rather than individuals or small groups. The point may be illustrated by using the foregoing example of a community organization effort toward developing more employment opportunity for some minority group. It may be shown that such community organization effort has to *bargain* and *negotiate* with, or in some other cases, *confront,* other such large organizations as industrial, business and service concerns and various levels of government for the purpose of enhancing *opportunities* for employment. On the other hand, the same community organization effort may yet negotiate and bargain with or confront various parts of the educational, recreational, and other such systems *whereby patterns of socialization may be changed.* The essential point is that whatever the need, it would be necessary to have a large organization to attempt to solve them. Von Hoffman, who may be considered a commentator on practitioners, has suggested that the chief need for a ghetto ("a natural area," according to the ecological school) is to build "an organization that wields power."[15]

Alinsky himself, after announcing the "health and welfare councils, neighbourhood councils, Mobilization for Whosis, Operation Whatsis, or Task Force Whereis" as "nice, ineffective, non-controversial do-gooder innocuous phenomena totally unrelated to the world as it is," declared that the chief need of these urban pockets is to build an organization "broad enough so that it attracts and involves most of the groups in the community."[16] Theoretically, then, it would seem that Alinsky groups have a justified goal, since in a formal organization oriented urban community it may be necessary to build a strong power-wielding organization. There already are sociological statements demonstrating that organized power is only balanced by counter organizational power.[17] Sherrard and Murray, in a recent article, doubt whether such a conflict based community organization is "realistic" and "honest."[18] Actually, there seem to be two essential differences between Alinsky-style community organization and community organization as a social work method. First, Schaller points out that the basic dividing line between Alinsky and his critics is on the values of right to dissent in a community, despite "the argument that the

---

[15]Nicholas Von Hoffman. "Hard Talk on Organizing the Ghetto," *Renewal,* February, 1966, p. 13.

[16]Saul D. Alinsky. "Citizen Participation and Community Organization in Planning and Urban Renewal," (Chicago: The Industrial Areas Foundation, 1962, mimeographed), pp. 3–10.

[17]Cf. Seymour M. Lipset, *Political Man* (New York: Doubleday and Co., 1963), pp. 6–8.

[18]Thomas D. Sherrard and Richard C. Murray. "The Church and Neighborhood Community Organization" *Social Work,* 10, July, 1965, p. 9.

Alinsky methods banish the apathy and the indifference of the lower classes remain to be proved."[19] Second, it seems that Alinsky-style community organization proceeds under the older axiom of American politics which can be summarized as "Go fight City Hall and everyone else;" while social workers have increasingly become aware of the need for their "planned participation" in the public sector, to "deal with, involve, plan with, bring pressure upon, or even to cause changes in local and state governmental bodies."[20]

Thus, Von Hoffman's commentary on and Alinsky's prescription of a powerful organization have been questioned as to usefulness. These questions are raised, for the most part, by practitioners. Theoretically it seems to be acceptable that a powerful organization is necessary, since only powerful organizations can negotiate with, bargain, or confront the established systems of a formal organization oriented urban structure. The issue here in the examination of theoretically relevant intervention techniques is neither the apathy of the lower classes nor the inculcation of a norm that suggests conflict with all existing institutional systems—for these doubts raised by the practitioner would not ordinarily be those of the social science theoretician—but it is *whether or not such an organization would become oligarchical.* It would seem that the social scientist would be satisfied to see the development of powerful organizations in the ghetto, where the control is in the hands of the members of the community. The problem of the social scientist is how the powerful organization, being a quasi-political organization,[21] may be prevented from becoming an oligarchical organization (which dictates the community). Existing social science theory would suggest that such oligarchy is very likely.[22] If such oligarchy does occur, then the democratic goals of community organization are defeated. Social scientists have only one model to offer which prevents the development of oligarchy in quasi-political organizations. This model is a deviant case study of the International Typographical Union.[23] The three sociologists who studied the ITU discovered most of the reasons which prevented the development of oligarchy in it. Some of the important reasons were that the union was so structured that the leadership positions could not be monopolized by a few.[24]

[19]Cf. Lyle E. Schaller. *Community Organization: Conflict and Reconciliation* (Nashville, Tenn: Abingdon Press, 1960), pp. 103–109.

[20]Alfred J. Kahn. "Trends and Problems in Community Organization," *Social Work Practice,* 1964 (New York: Columbia University Press, 1964), p. 9.

[21]The criteria for quasi-political organization are: at least a pretense of representative leadership; and use of bargain in its various forms with other organizations. Labor unions, for instance, would also be classified as quasi-political organizations under these criteria.

[22]Cf. Robert Michels. *Political Parties* (New York: Dover Publications, 1959), pp. 365–392.

[23]Seymour Lipset, Martin Trow, and James Coleman, *op. cit.* It is to be noted that the ITU has been perceived by these authors both as a functional community (discussed earlier as part of the monographic school) and as a quasi-political organization which has turned out to be democratic.

[24]*Ibid.*

Thus the ITU, from the point of view of the social scientist, may serve as a model for organizations to be developed or built for community organization work. However, this whole area seems to be one where there are more lacks than linkages between social science theory and social work (and related) practice. The discussion above points out areas where attempts toward linkages may be made.

Yet another item where the utility of theory towards intervention techniques is lacking is in the process determining the type of strategy needed under different conditions. Depending upon the type of conditions that may prevail in a given community, a wide range of strategies may be outlined. These strategies are: planned *cooperation* for egalitarian distribution of resources, *bargain* towards more uniform distribution of given resources or development of new resources, *confronting* those in power for some desired change, and *conflict* chosen to strip some groups from power. All such strategies may be considered as a part of intervention techniques. However, theoretical presumptions on the structural components and characteristics of community may also determine, or at least influence, the type of intervention used. Thus, the notions of structural-functionalists would help the practitioner to work toward the ends of maintenance, co-ordination, and distribution of resources under the present systems. However, the ends of social change seemingly cannot be pursued with the acceptance of the structural-functionalism. Change entails some form of conflict beginning from bargaining and negotiation to confrontation and some form of coercion.[25]

Thus theoretical presumptions stemming from a structural-functional orientation would probably call for cooperation or bargain, whereas those emerging from the conflict orientations of Coser and Dahrendorf are likely to call for confrontation and conflict as strategies.

The dilemma outlined above may be solved if one extracts the goals of a given community organization effort. *Such goals may be said to fall in two principal categories: change of given social systems; and pattern-maintenance in given social systems.* Thus proper identification of goods of any given community organization effort may turn a lack between social science theory and social work practice into a linkage, since intervention techniques toward pattern-maintenance may be developed from the notions of structural-functionalists, and those toward change may be an application of the notions of conflict theo-

---

[25]Cf. "The extent to which the social system model has influenced even our thinking about social change and has marred our vision in this important area of problems is truly remarkable. Two facts in particular illustrate this influence. In talking about change, most sociologists today accept the entirely spurious distinction between "change within" and "change of societies," which make sense only if we recognize the system as our ultimate and only reference point." Ralf Dahrendorf. "Out of Utopia," *The America Journal of Sociology,* LXIV, p. 125.

rists.[26] The problem in accepting a premise such as Dahrendorf's, is that most social workers lack the knowledge or the experience in the use of social conflict. Further, conflict that does not deviate from the "social work value base, is hard to define,[27] since *it is hard to isolate values that are unique to social work and not inherent in the social system in general. Instead of using such ubiquitous terms as "social work values," perhaps social workers need to clearly outline what may be termed canons of practice.* Nevertheless, use of conflict and concepts of social work value base constitute a major area where utility of theory toward intervention is problematic.

Use of Theory in
Determining the
Community as a Unit

A final item where there are both lacks and linkages is in the determination of appropriate units. For what is delineation of community boundary to social scientists, is the proper choice of service area to social workers. Both social scientists and social workers are concerned with the non-primary community as a unit-idea in social science and service unit in social work. The task is simple for both disciplines when the interactional patterns are contained in a small geographical unit, as in the case of small rural communities or "natural areas."

Community as a unit—both in the social sciences and in social work —has often been determined in terms of political jurisdiction, geographic convenience, ecological groupings, interest groups, formal organizations, etc. What remains problematic is the understanding of the relationship between *community as a unit as it may be theoretically defined* versus *community as a unit as it is chosen as a service area.* Thus, for instance, social science theoreticians may define an entire metropolitan area as a community (on the basis of existing political boundary) or a neighborhood as a community (on the basis of shared institutions), whereas social workers may be involved in community organization work in the total metropolitan area through a health and welfare council, at the neighborhood level (ecological grouping) through a block club concerned with local issues, at the level of a formal organization such as an association for the parents of mentally retarded children, etc. A problem of adequate conceptualization is apparent,

[26]The notion of change is perhaps best enumerated by Dahrendorf in the concept of interest group conflict. Such formulation is a theoretical reinstatement of the axiom known to the 19th century English nobility: "There are no permanent or temporary alliances; there are only permanent and temporary interests."

[27]For a statement on community organization practice being guided by social work values, see National Association of Social Workers, "Defining Community Organization Practice," (New York: National Association of Social Workers, 1962, mimeographed), pp. 5–15.

TABLE 1. Units and Sub-Units of Various Communities

Units Political and/or	Small Community	Large Community	Metropolis
Sub-Units	1. Ecological groupings	1. Ecological groupings 2. Interest groups	1. Ecological groupings 2. Interest groups 3. Formal organizations

since all of the service units mentioned in the foregone discussion may also be termed as communities by social science theoreticians. This problem may perhaps be avoided if the unit is delineated in terms of its size, and corresponding possible service areas are clearly outlined as sub-units. Such an attempt has been made in Table 1.

It is clear that the major units may be chosen by the conventional definitions stemming from political and/or geographical boundaries. However, as the size of the political or geographical boundary increases, it becomes increasingly necessary to find functional sub-units. As one moves one's attention from the small community to the expanding metropolis, the number of sub-units tends to increase. Further, it is to be noted that the sub-units may overlap, only if seen from the viewpoint of aggregate number of persons covered. Thus in the metropolitan unit, the residents of a blue-collar neighborhood (ecological grouping) with similar ethnicity and shared institutions (interest group) may be primarily employed in a nearby light industry or vote for the same political candidate (formal organizations).[28] This would be the case where the functional units would overlap. However, the dimension of the functional units is still larger in the metropolis, since such perfect overlaps of functional units would be more of an exception than a general rule in today's metropolitan communities. In general, however, the functional sub-units in Table 1 lend toward the construction of a Guttman-type scale.

The units and sub-units of the Guttman-type scale in Table 1 encompass small, expansive, and functional communities in relation to each other. Community organization practice may be both possible and feasible in one or all of these units and sub-units, if the goals of such practice are clearly identified. Identification of such goals, it would seem, is the burden of the practitioner.

[28]Thus we may note that agencies practicing community organization in the metropolis may engage the citizen or actor in a variety of institutional settings; he may be involved in the delivery of service to his family where he lives: he may be involved in decision-making through his concern for developing mental health services throughout the metropolis; and he may fight for adequate street lighting or schools within the political sub-division wherein he lives; he may be involved as a contributor to the financing of services where he works. Thus the multiplicity of roles of the actor or participant living in the metropolis affords expanded points of intervention and engagement for the community organizer.

"Community" in Social Science and Social Work

Summary and Conclusions

Five schools of approach to the unit-idea of community were examined for their adequacy as diagnostic or analytical schools for the community organization practitioner. It was found that these schools of approach are primarily helpful for the practitioner for more or less descriptive purposes. A sixth approach to the unit-idea of community developed by social scientists Lipset, Bendix, and Hauser where community is seen as a socialization agent, was suggested to be the most helpful diagnostic or analytical tool for the practitioner.

In discussing the utility of social science theory as useful for intervention purposes, it was suggested that basic theoretical orientations in the social sciences such as the structural-functional school or conflict theory is more helpful for the practitioner for the purposes of pattern-maintenance or social change, respectively.

Also, social science was found to be helpful in delineating the boundaries of community. Since a community organization practitioner needs to identify and work with small, expansive, or functional communities, it was suggested that boundaries of community delineated in this paper in the form of a Guttman scale would help in identifying the appropriate service units.

When formal organizations are unresponsive to the groups they were intended to serve, changes in their rules and regulations are a legitimate target for the social work generalist. Armitage outlines the more traditional forms of organizational structure and suggests an alternative based upon systems theory. He identifies targets for the generalist at different levels of decision-making within any formal organization.

A Structural View of Welfare Organizations

W. A. J. Armitage

The study of organizations has centred on the task of designing and controlling them so that they pursue clearly defined goals. Conversely, in evaluating organizations, it has been standard practice to judge to what extent the organization is achieving its goals.

The goals of welfare organizations are usually stated either in the form

Reprinted with permission of the Canadian Association of Social Workers from *The Social Worker,* Vol. 37 (3), 1969, pp. 171–176.

of an attempt to solve some particular problem, e.g., narcotic addiction, or in the form of the adequate provision of some service, e.g., day care. When evaluated by these stated goals it is often found that welfare organizations are inefficient and ineffective. Inefficiency and ineffectiveness in obtaining goals affect other organizations as well and have been considered as characteristics of all organizations. In truth, most organization goals serve a symbolic rather than a substantive purpose. The rare organization that achieves its goal, e.g., the Polio Foundation, usually immediately seeks a new goal for itself.

The "Systems" Model of an Organization

For these reasons members of the "structuralist" school of organizational analysts suggest[1] that the usual type of "goal model" for the study and analysis of organizations has some inherent disadvantages. They propose that a "systems model" be substituted for the "goal model." Such a model consists of a statement of those relationships necessary for an organization to exist and operate. Two major sub-types of a model may be specified. The survival model constitutes a statement of those relationships necessary for the organization to exist. The effectiveness model constitutes a statement of those relationships that would make the organization most effective in the service of a particular goal.

The systems approach to organizational analysis serves to liberate our understanding of organizations and organizational behavior and serves to prevent it from being distorted by learning that, in relation to stated goals, organizations are ineffective. The organizational "goal" approach to understanding organizations tends to suggest that organizational resources used for the maintenance of the organization are misused, that all resources should be directed towards goal attainment. The systems approach suggests that the organization must seek the optimum distribution of the resources between maintenance and goal attainment objectives.

The organizational "goal" approach centres all attention upon the organization's accomplishments. Important as these are as subjects for evaluation, it is important also to study the network of relationships which connect the organization to its environment and the relationships which connect the parts of the organization together. A study of the competing forces acting in these relationships adds depth to the understanding of the ways in which organizations behave, and hence assists the executive task of directing the organization's activities towards achievable goals.

[1]Amitai Etzioni, *Modern Organizations,* Prentice-Hall, p. 16f.

Relationships in a Public
Welfare Organization

Welfare organizations, in common with all organizations, exist within a network of relationships. These relationships are between the organization's personnel, the sources of sanction for the organization's existence—including the source of funds, and the constituency of persons served by the organization.

Let us examine how these elements relate to one another in the case of the welfare organization administering public assistance. The individual who applies for public assistance contacts an organization which makes numerous decisions affecting his welfare. These decisions are affected by three principal considerations:

1. The requirements of those that provide the money. These are usually governments and their actions are affected by political pressure, existing legislation and the terms under which welfare costs are shared between municipal, provincial and federal levels of government.

2. The requirements of those that receive the money. The clients of public welfare agencies aspire to the consumption standards of the affluent population.

3. The requirements of those that distribute the money. The interests of the social workers, accountants, clerical staff, etc., who obtain their income and work satisfaction within the organizations established to administer public assistance.

It is obvious that the interest and requirements of these three groups are not convergent. Clients prefer large grants, governments wish to restrict welfare costs, and social workers like to be able to use their professional judgement as to what will be given to whom. Thus the public assistance organizations exist in the midst of conflict. This conflict results in the organization being subject to criticism from all sides —clients protest, governments disparage and staff resign.

Faced with these conflicts it is not surprising that many public welfare organizations tend to adopt a "survival" type model. This includes a primary identification with the interests of the source of finances, an avoidance of all controversy, an unwillingness to innovate or establish precedents, and an attempt to manipulate the clients so that they are contented with ("adjusted to") the standard of living provided by the organization. However, such a "survival" type model cannot be accepted as the best model by the administrator who is committed to social work values.

The goal of public welfare organizations is rarely the solution of the problem of financial dependency. The goal of the public welfare organization is usually more modest—for example, the service of its clients. With this as the stated goal, relationships within organizations can be studied to assess what effect they have on goal accomplishment, i.e., what contribution they make to this organizational "effectiveness" model.

For example, a common answer to the problem of attaining the service goal of the organization is that the organization employs staff who are sensitive to the clients' needs. The organization thus learns of the clients' needs and adapts to them by internally channelled changes.[2] The systems approach illuminates two serious weaknesses of this approach:

1. Contact with clients is limited to the lower ranking personnel of the organization who are least able to produce change in policy. Furthermore, organizational policy in effect, if not by intent, tends to discourage sensitivity to the client. Promotion, for example, means that the social worker takes a step away from the client and a step deeper into the organization. The best candidate for such promotion will be the worker who is interested in the organization rather than in the client. Hence the promotion structure discourages client-centredness,[3] and this in turn discourages the worker from articulating client-centred interests.

2. As mentioned earlier, the interests of social workers and clients are not always convergent. For example, in asking that welfare payments be based upon the social worker's judgement of the client's needs, the social worker is asking for freedom to make this decision on the basis of professional competence rather than on the basis of administrative regulations. To most social workers this would appear a desirable change, but the client might well prefer decisions based on administrative regulations. The regulations that restrict the social worker offer the client a chance to understand the basis on which the decision was made and hence to appeal when he considers himself unfairly treated.

Thus the study of relationships and conflicts within the organization, and between organization and client population, show the administrator those points requiring special attention if the effectiveness goal of the organization is to be reached by the proposed model.

Common Sources of Conflict in Organizations

Conflict within organizations frequently occurs at the following points:

1. Between those sections of the organization directly engaged in obtaining the organization's goals and such organizational divisions as statistics, accounting and operations research. These latter divisions serve to collect information on

[2]This method of achieving the organization's "effectiveness" goal does not endanger the organization's "survival" goal as it keeps change within the organization and hence does not involve exposing the organization to external criticism. This contributes to its popularity.

[3]This is not inevitable. The organization can attempt to distribute the symbols of success and the structure of money rewards in such a way as to encourage client-centredness rather than organization-centredness.

the work of the line personnel dealing directly with the organization's clients or customers. It is usual for the line personnel to regard provision of this information as a form of spying on their work, and hence as an undesirable imposition.

2. Between professional and administrative personnel. The correctness of a professional decision is judged by the professional's peers on the basis of the information available and the ethics and values applied to the decision. The correctness of an administrative decision is judged by its agreement with written rules and past precedents.

3. Between the interests of the organization and the interests of the group or groups it is supposedly serving.

4. Between those with power to direct the work and the rewards and sanctions given or applied to others, and those affected by such decisions.

The Effectiveness Goal
of Welfare
Organizations

The application of the systems model to welfare organizations raises issues beyond the increased clarity it provides for organizational analysis. The examination of organizational relationships and processes suggests the formulation of a different type of "effectiveness" goal for welfare organizations than that usually adopted today.

Business organizations have long since abandoned a product type effectiveness goal for themselves. Few businesses now conceive of themselves as being organizations that primarily produce a product such as refrigerators, or boxes, or furniture. Instead the organization is conceived of as a collection of assets that, subject to sufficient time being available, can be routed in any profitable direction. New products can be introduced, new staff recruited, the organization can relocate in another community, etc. Hence the form and appearance of the organization can change radically over a period of time.

Welfare organizations have not adopted such an open-ended conception of themselves. The services provided by existing organizations are almost exclusively determined by the impetus that originally created the organization. New services are usually introduced by the formation of new agencies or organizations. As mentioned earlier, the "effectiveness" goal of most welfare organizations is the solution of some problems or the adequate provision of some service. Where the goal is defined as the adequate provision of some service the organization's task is severely circumscribed and obviously self-serving. Where the task is defined as the solution of some problem the organization has a "product" type goal that is usually so global in scope as to be unobtainable. Thus both service and problem solution goals fail to provide the organization's personnel with a sense of purpose.

Welfare organizations would benefit immensely by adopting a more open-ended "effectiveness" goal for themselves. A goal that would correspond to the corporation's goal of "profitability." The most economic solution of "partialized" social problems would be a goal of this type.

Benefits accruing from such a goal would include:

1. Liberation of the welfare organization from any conception of itself limited to a single problem or single set of services. It would provide the personnel of the organization—and particularly the executives of the organization—with a concept of the welfare organization's task that is flexible and open-ended. This in turn would encourage the organization to search out new challenge for itself. Bower[4] writes that in an organization "a symptom of declining vitality is the inability to define new goals that are meaningful and challenging."

2. Welfare executives would be encouraged to ask which problems out of the total array of social problems could be solved and at what cost. At present the growth of too many potentially able executives is stunted by their feeling that they have responsibility for social problems so global in scope as to be insurmountable. An effectiveness goal for welfare organizations that caused them to seek out surmountable problems would serve to liberate and develop their abilities. For example, it is usual for a section of most large child welfare agencies to be concerned with services to unmarried mothers. Solution of the whole problem of unmarried parenthood is too global a goal and the continuing provision of services is a goal that lacks challenge. Service provision is the goal of an organization that reacts to its environment rather than affects that environment. An executive looking for a surmountable problem in this area might settle upon reducing the rate of repeat unmarried parenthood as a challenge. Such an effectiveness goal would encourage the executive to seek criteria for determining those clients likely to have further illegitimate pregnancies and then to provide such additional services, e.g., adequate birth control information, as might reduce the rate.

Today, welfare organizations experience clear, unambiguous success far too seldom for their own health.

3. Encouragement of horizontal integration between voluntary social agencies. As compared to business, the voluntary welfare field is characterized by a large number of small organizations, rather like the grocery business prior to the growth of the large supermarket chains. The large numbers of small organizations result in many inefficiencies of operation. Larger organizations offering a more diversified range of services would reduce the need for clients to use the services of several agencies and hence reduce the need for interagency coordination—a very expensive and time-consuming process in itself.

Another advantage offered by the larger diversified organization is that such functions as purchasing, accounting, research, personnel and public relations can be shared by all branches of the organization. This leads to greater efficiency and economy in their performance.

It is anomalous that there is much more vertical integration in the private welfare field, (i.e., local organizations have linkages to provincial and national bodies), than horizontal integration. Horizontal integration would seem to offer

[4]Martin Bower, *The Will to Manage,* McGraw-Hill.

the greater benefit to clients and the greater efficiency of operation; its virtues are stressed by the community organization theorists,[5] but, apparently, to little effect.

4. Finally, the open-ended goal for welfare organizations would be congruent with the recognition of the institutional, rather than residual, nature of welfare organizations. When the task of welfare services was defined in limited, residual terms it was not surprising that the organizations offering these services adopted limited concepts of their role in the society. Today there is a growing recognition that the welfare services provide an essential component to our society. Consequently welfare organizations may adopt a more confident concept of their role. Their energies can be freed from the task of apologizing for their own existence and employed in the larger task of grappling effectively with social problems.

A Different Concept of
the Welfare
Organization

The insight provided by the "structuralist" analysts demands a different attitude of mind towards the organization's task by the organization's executives and personnel.

The welfare organization is seen as a device for making things happen. A device capable of mastering its environment, rather than a device that at best reacts to its environment.

The primary resource that the welfare organization has to accomplish this purpose is its own personnel, particularly its own executives. The central maintenance task of the welfare organization is a personnel task, the selection of executives, the development of their potential, the determination of their mutual relationships and their motivation to best advantage.

At present far too many social workers regard organization and administration as synonymous with red tape. They are a hindrance rather than a help in accomplishing what they see to be "their" goals.[6] This state of affairs is testimony to energy and ability being wasted in frustration and confusion. It is apparent that the concept of organization suggested by the structuralist school is more congruent with the goals to which social workers aspire than were earlier concepts of the welfare organization.

[5]R. L. Warren, *The Community in America,* Rand McNally, p. 267f.
[6]A recent M.S.W. thesis showed that social workers had different goals for their work than the goals of the organization employing them. Armitage, Beck and Sprong, *Community Work in Public Welfare,* M.S.W. thesis, University of British Columbia, 1966, p. 72.

Earlier in this book the value premise was presented that the social work profession can find one of its purposes in democratic political theory. Related to this was the premise that social workers must be as concerned with the human rights aspects of social functioning as they have been with the human need aspects. Setleis describes political practice as a legitimate area for social work practice wherein the professional practitioner moves from the "helper-helped" relationship into a peerlike relationship and the employing organization must restructure itself to become more open to client input.

Social Work Practice as Political Activity

Lloyd Setleis

The spirit of revolt which has taken hold of public assistance clients and university students, among others, represents in no uncertain terms a clash between individuals and established social institutions. Fundamental to the growing battle is the more pervasive struggle of people to find in society's institutions an essential relevance and responsiveness that are crucial to personal and social fulfillment. The poor, the young, and all who lack political, economic and social power feel keenly a sense of impotence in affecting established institutions. The anguish of recent assassinations and the pain of war, both so close to daily living, impede any effort to capture the reality of what we are about.

Yet along with the national discontent, there is a vital and hopeful movement toward changing that which is unfair and unjust. The creation of welfare rights groups by public assistance clients for the purpose of developing needed power represents a socially useful form of engagement with institutional forces. Student insistence in sharing in the administration of university life is another illustration of a growing movement to affect those social institutions which play an essential role in the lives of young people.[1] The ferment of the urban ghetto signifies a restless and often violent effort to enhance human dignity and establish the principle of human rights.

At this point in social work development, it is necessary to ask how

Reprinted with permission of the University of Pennsylvania Press from *Journal of Social Work Process,* Vol. 17, 1969, pp. 141–153.

[1]For an elaboration of this student-university relationship see Lewis B. Mayhew, "Changing the Balance of Power," *Saturday Review,* August 17, 1968; Steven Muller, "Thoughts on University Government," reported in *Current,* August 1968. Also, an analysis by Fred Hechinger of the resignation of President Kirk of Columbia University, *New York Times,* August 24, 1968.

professional social work is responding to this pervasive struggle. Social work as an institutional profession is integrally related to the struggle for institutional relevance and responsiveness. The options for social work are: it can become an instrument for maintaining the status quo; it can participate in a revolutionary effort to overthrow present social institutions; or, social work can participate in the orderly transformation of social institutions within the framework of democratic processes.

It is the purpose of this article to suggest a concept of practice that will enable social work to participate in the transformation of social institutions, so that they can become more relevant and responsive to individual and social need.[2]

Social work has been firmly based in its activity to facilitate processes of individual, group, and community relationships in connection with institutional arrangements. The major emphasis of its efforts has been toward enabling people to make use of the institution for the enhancement of themselves and society. The concept of individual dysfunction, while not held by all social workers, has become ingrained in social work activity. In this view, the major burden for change has been placed upon the individual. Social work methods have reflected and have been directed toward this purpose. At this time social work needs to enhance its relevancy and responsiveness to changing individual and social need.

The historical development of social work clearly indicates that in each era of significant growth, social work has responded to changing needs and demands in terms of the normative principle that was operative within the society. At different times the concepts of "sin," "economics," "sociology," and "psychology" have provided the framework for a meaningful social work activity. In the last several years, the concept of the "social" has held sway, so that the purpose of social work methods has been to facilitate interactional activity between individuals, groups, and communities in relation to institutional arrangements. It is now apparent that the present concern is with the form and structure of the institution. It is possible to respond to this concern consciously through understanding the meaning of contemporary institutional conflict.

At this point in social development, the struggle has gone beyond enabling people to find an institutional *connection* in order to enhance individual and social development. The relationship between people

[2]This article grew out of a study conducted by Mr. John Main and the author during the summer of 1967. The study, entitled "A Study of the Social Services in Public Assistance Directed Toward Definition of the Elements of Training Required for Personnel Offering These Services," was sponsored by the Department of Public Welfare, Pennsylvania. It was supported by the Bureau of Family Services, U.S. Department of Health, Education and Welfare. Of major importance to the development of a political concept of practice was the author's experience as a consultant to the New York City Department of Social Services during the summer of 1968.

and institutions now involves the process of institutional *transformation*. In this process, the issue of institutional relevance and responsiveness has some basis for resolution.

For social work to have a rationale for its activity in the process of institutional transformation, it is necessary to understand that the normative principle which is currently operative within society is "political." Political activity occurs when individuals have the power to participate along with others in directly determining the character and quality of an institution in terms and conditions that are consistent with individual and social needs. People need to be involved more directly in a wider array of functional relationships which affect the decision-making processes that attend the ongoing activity of particular organizational forms. In a real sense, each person is "expert" with reference to his own interest and stake in the specific organization, and thereby in the larger institution. The direct involvement of people in institutional change makes possible a transformation of the institution to represent the widest range of community interest. This includes and incorporates the client's group.

The view of the client as "expert" in the reality of *his* situation requires that the basis of the client-agency relationship be rooted neither in charity nor pathology but in justice. Justice means that there is an essential worth and value that inheres in a person by virtue of his being a human being. When justice prevails, an individual has the right to make those claims upon a society that exist for all members of society. His existence is not dependent upon the beneficence of some or the love of others, or his utility to any segment of the society. A just society provides in its institutions the necessary protection against any force that violates the basic humanity of a person. Justice provides the person with the opportunity and the means to fulfill the potential that he may have as a human being. The translation of this concept into operational terms leaves much to be desired.[3]

Each era of social development has given rise to the creation of criteria which have been derived from the prevailing normative principle and used to selectively limit the participation of people in the mainstream of American life. In the case of the Afro-American, the limitations have been gross.[4] The "worthiness" of the poor as a basis for help still permeates American values. In a just society the mother of illegitimate children does have the right to public assistance, and the issue of illegitimacy is irrelevant to her right to decent and humane

---

[3]A particularly good collection of papers dealing with the concept of social justice is Richard B. Brandt (ed.), *Social Justice* (Englewood Cliffs, N.J.: Prentice-Hall, Inc., 1962).

[4]James L. Curtis, M.D., "Effects of Racism and Poverty on Negro Child Development," presented at the Downstate Medical Center Seminar: "Psychiatry Looks at Today's Problems of Youth," May 26, 1968.

Social Work Practice as Political Activity

treatment. This means not that illegitimacy is either encouraged or condoned, but that the right to live decently is a matter not of beneficence or love but of justice.[5]

The concept of social work practice as political activity can further provide a framework within which there can be a new synthesis in practice, of the "treatment or reform" issue. The polarization of this issue has been with social work from its earliest inception as an organized and accountable social activity. Social work practice as a political activity means that the social agency must have a broader view of its function. Our literature has not dealt amply with the direction of an agency's function. For example, is a particular function directed toward the rendering of a service that is rehabilitative, or preventive, or provisional? Specifying these directions adds clarity to the broader institutional significance of agency function, and, in addition, gives form to specific patterns of agency organization and methods of providing a service.

Much confusion and struggle have occurred in rendering public assistance, for example, because of the value conflict that inheres in the issue of whether public assistance is a provisional or a rehabilitative service. This issue has become exacerbated further by the attempt to use casework as the method through which public assistance is provided. If it is a rehabilitative service then we presuppose that the client is in some way deficient in the ability to function as a responsible person. Little if any responsibility is assumed for the institutional dimension of client deficiency. The burden is placed upon the client for change in behavior, for casework as a method has as one purpose the effecting of individual change in relation to a social reality. If the service is provisional, then the expectation for behavioral change is neither explicit nor implicit. What is of concern is that the provisional service be given in a way that is respectful of the recipient. But when the service is provisional and the method is geared toward behavioral change, the client becomes enmeshed in a hopeless struggle.

When there is clarity about a specific direction of a particular function, functional objectives can be fulfilled in a way that embraces and incorporates the "treatment-reform" aspects of service. Social agencies offering services to the family, to children, and to the mentally ill, to name a few, have concentrated on the rehabilitative aspect of service. The encounter with institutional inequities and irrelevancies in the in-

[5]The concept of the client as citizen was advanced by the author in "Civil Rights and the Rehabilitation of the A.F.D.C. Client," *Social Work,* IX (April, 1964).

See also Chief Justice Earl Warren, writing for the United States Supreme Court in *Smith vs. King,* as published in *Current,* August, 1968.

dividual life of the client has been directed toward enabling the client to cope with these forces. Efforts to deal directly with institutional issues have been perceived by social agencies as social action, a form of practice that has been left to community organization.

It is necessary to emphasize that social agencies offering services to individuals have in their practice dealt directly with institutional forms in the interest of the individual. Family, psychiatric, children's agencies, and the like have in their practice always maintained connections with those forms of institutional arrangements which have been of significance to the individual client. However, these involvements have sought institutional accommodation. The concept of a political practice on the other hand, requires institutional transformation.

The introduction of the community mental health concept has provided many mental health centers with a rationale for dealing directly, and with the involvement of patients, in the problems of racial discrimination—in employment, in insufficiencies in housing, and in the educational system.[6] These are institutional dimensions of patient conflict. This broader view of agency function facilitates greater client involvement in the activity of the agency. The agency becomes (for the want of a better word) an "arena" for institutional transformation. The agency itself becomes more responsive and relevant as it lends itself to this kind of direct involvement with other institutional forms.

Practice that is politically conceived requires the agency to assume a position of advocate for the individual client in relation to the necessary institutional change that the client's situation demands. Reference to advocacy in social work has been generally limited to the activity of the worker. The basic issue is not whether a worker shall or shall not be an advocate, but whether the agency is committed to this aspect of practice in its purpose, its representativeness of community concern, and its organization.

The social agency, public and private, has evolved from a period when social institutions were not so directly challenged. For the most part, agencies have represented specific institutional values. When the major social issue is the transformation of institutions, however, the social agency is committed to a more militant role if it is to have social usefulness as an instrument of individual and social change. Highly organized institutional forms require at the most practical level of operation a skillfulness in negotiating. The pattern and structure of institutional arrangements contribute to the loss of connection with those individuals whom such institutions are designed to serve. Thus, a means must be

[6]Brewster M. Smith and Nicholas Hobbs, *The Community and the Community Mental Health Center,* American Psychological Association, June, 1966, p. 9.

created for the individual to act in his own interest. In this regard, the ombudsman is an illustration of how an institution (government) can create the means to respond relevantly to the individual. In assuming the advocacy aspect of practice, the agency acts to identify those human conditions which necessitate appropriate institutional response and involvement.[7]

The social agency must broaden its involvement with the wider community, especially in identifying with diverse groups, all of which share a stake in a particular institutional issue. Board membership should reflect the widest range of community opinion and power. This statement includes the creation of structural mechanisms that bring clients and client groups more directly into the agency system for the purpose of policy formation and participation in decision-making.

The client's active participation in the creation and development of a service makes the "helper-helped" relationship no longer viable. The agency does not then represent in its purpose or organization the "have" group of society helping the "have-not" client group. The present position of social services within the political, economic, and social structure has not fully reflected the participation of those who use these services. Within the context of contemporary social life, the direct involvement of people in those institutions which determine the bounds of their individual experience is a social imperative.

A practice that is politically conceived offers the client an opportunity to fulfill his roles in broader terms than may be the case in a psychologically or socially conceived practice. For example, the parent of a brain-damaged child in need of an unavailable service fulfills his role as parent when he participates with the agency in the creation of the needed service. This kind of involvement opens for the client new possibilities. His own situation can take on new meanings as the base of action is extended. The agency, through its relationship to the wider network of institutional involvements, provides a mechanism for action. This client-agency relationship forms a strengthened base for effecting institutional transformation. The client's growth emerges from the discovery of the institutional dimension of his role. Direct engagement with institutional forces for the purpose of achieving greater relevance represents, too, a further development for social work, since the major portion of its activity has been directed toward helping people deal with the effect of institutional impact. The client who loses a job because a company decides to leave the community and a youngster whose particular

---

[7]The correspondence between Elaine Rothenberg and George Brager, *Social Work,* July 1968, pp. 3–5, in reference to Brager's article on advocacy, "Advocacy and Political Behavior," *Social Work,* April 1968, is most illuminating. Neither writer, however, deals with *the role of an agency in advocacy.*

ability in learning cannot be developed because the educational system does not provide the necessary conditions are both illustrations of individuals in need of help.

The support and facilitation of a political practice depends upon the internal organization of the agency. The pattern of an agency's organization reflects its values, defines relationships, and determines the nature of its activity. Agency organization has followed the traditional pattern of the inverted pyramid. At the top is the board, then the executive, the supervisors, and then the workers, who are interlaced with the client "somewhere down at the bottom." The authority "drips down." The vertical organization suggested in this inverted pyramid represents a hierarchy that limits an agency's ability to be responsive to itself, to the community, and to the client group. The gap between the top and the bottom impedes the vital communication that is essential for the provision of significant and meaningful service. The vertical structure by its positioning of personnel creates antagonisms that are inherent in the positioning, rather than in the functional roles they may have. The further down the inverted pyramid one goes, the narrower is the range of opportunities and the weaker the power to affect institutional transformation. While the problem of agency organization becomes more acute in the larger public agencies, the structure based on the inverted pyramid is the prevailing one.

A political concept of practice requires a more horizontal organization: all on the same plane, each representing a different point on the organizational spectrum, each having direct access to each other in the vital decision-making processes. The opportunity for all personnel, board members, and clients to participate more directly in policy formation and decision-making enables the agency to become more responsive to itself. Horizontal organization does not eliminate functional responsibility; rather, it allows for a greater and more realistic exercise of responsibility because people are not boxed into a hierarchal structure that severely limits the range of what can be functionally creative and expressive. To put this simply, an administrator's direct engagement with a worker or a client does not limit his functional responsibility. On the contrary, such an engagement yields rich social data with which he can administer more relevantly to those who are on the line of service.

Living has become highly interdependent and human need at all levels more intensified. Change is the constant, and the struggle "to make it" as a parent, a worker, a student has become more eruptive and external than it is internal. There is just so much that an individual can do himself without the support, the encouragement, and the opportunity that a society must offer.

When public assistance clients present their grievances and demands in an organized form of protest, the expectation of help this action represents requires from the agency a response that is just. Hundreds of clients demonstrating and taking over a welfare center can be overwhelming and dangerous. But this movement toward confrontation with high-level administrators characterizes an engagement with institutional forces. The psychology of such action is one of control and self-direction rather than of defeat and failure. This can be a most disturbing experience for a worker. His apathetic client of yesterday is a negotiating member of a committee today. Workers have felt "loss of control" and even anger at the client for behaving in this way. It is necessary to point out that the clients are not attempting to overthrow the system. To be able to take over one's life and to act in one's own interest, is this not an objective of social work? What is so striking is the sense of oneself that comes through as an individual is able to feel that he is part of a larger movement. The demand for individual service does not decrease, but the client is able to participate more fully with the caseworker because of his involvement with a group that shares his interest. In a real sense, the client does not feel at the mercy of the system. He's "got friends outside."[8]

In a politically conceived practice clients will need to join with other clients in dealing with the institutional dimension of their situation. This activity must be considered as part of rendering an individual service. Whether clients being with an agency as an organized group or whether they need help in becoming organized, institutional transformation cannot be brought about without the involvement of many. In this effort, the agency and the clients have the same goal and objectives. The practice is based upon social work principles, but the principles take on a significance that is consistent with the social reality. For example, in this kind of practice time as a dimension is more insistent; the action is now! Again, the involvement of people is essential. It is interesting to note the concern of many social workers as to who does what in practice—the worker or the client? The fear of taking over a client's life is a real concern, but in a politically conceived practice no one person or no one agency can take over. Where such an effort is made, the process will at some point break down. There are too many involvements, too many individuals and groups whose interest and stake in specific action are affected and motivated by other considerations. Underlying the practice is the commitment to a democratic process that evolves through legal means.

With the client group participating more fully in the activity of the

---

[8]These observations of worker response to client demonstrations are based upon the author's work with the training supervisors, New York City Department of Social Services, during the summer of 1968, when client demonstrations were held at the city's welfare centers.

social agency, the stance of the agency shifts to one that more accurately represents the client group as an integral part of the community. When social life is understood in institutional terms all segments of society are affected, in different ways perhaps, but affected nevertheless. The community can no longer be seen as divided between "haves" and "have-nots"—"we" and "they." The transformation of social institutions requires political processes. Unless this is understood, there can be little hope for people to find the kind of relevant responsiveness they seek from social institutions.

The social work generalist will find it necessary to pursue changes in any formal organization—including that which employs him—that is unresponsive to the consumer population that organization was designed to serve. In the preceding article, Setleis outlined a strategy for bringing about changes in organizations through political strategies. In this article, Wax outlines a strategy for bringing about changes within the worker's own organization.

Power Theory and Institutional Change

John Wax

It is hard to know just when in our history power became a dirty word. Perhaps it started with Lord Acton's famous maxim, "Power corrupts, and absolute power corrupts absolutely." Woodrow Wilson described strong-armed international diplomacy as "power politics," and Lincoln Steffens associated power with big-city political bosses. This nation's nearly hysterical reaction to the term "Black Power" attests to the fact that the word "power" still triggers our flight-or-fight reflexes. Among social workers, the commitment to democracy, dignity, and self-determination produces an especially negative reaction, and it was not until the recent resurgence of interest in social change that the concept of power became respectable—perhaps even fashionable.

Definitions and Types of Power

The classical sociological definition states that power is the ability to influence the beliefs and behaviors of others in accordance with a wish

Reprinted from *Social Service Review,* Vol. 45 (3), 1971, pp. 274–288, by permission of the author and the University of Chicago Press.

or a plan. Another somewhat more interactional and controversial definition states that power increases as the power-holder exercises increasing influence over others, while they exercise decreasing influence over him. Two other definitions for our purposes are *(a)* Power is the control of a resource or resources which are essential to the functioning or survival of an individual or an organization. *(b)* Power is the ability to influence behavior through the use of rewards and penalties. The most clear and succinct definition is the colloquial: "Power is the ability to make things happen."

Floyd Hunter (3) was an important factor in the development of the popularized notion of a power structure. Actually, the notion of a power structure may be simplistic and misleading. It implies a fixed and monolithic system of decision-making, which controls the entire community or institution. The oligarchs of Dallas or the combination of merchants and ward bosses of Chicago may aspire to this kind of control, but most communities, institutions, and organizations are too large, varied, and complex to be decisively and comprehensively controlled by a single power structure. We would do well to discard the notion of a power structure and replace it with the concept of relevant power.

Power is kaleidoscopic, in that it appears in innumerable forms and in an infinite variety of combinations. Power flows from many sources. The following list of power sources is intended to be illustrative rather than exhaustive: money, votes, laws, information, expertise, prestige, group support, contacts, charisma, communication channels and media, social role, access to rewards, position and title, ideas, conceptual and verbal skills, ability to gratify important needs, monopoly of essential resources, coalitions and alliances, energy, conviction, courage, interpersonal skill, and moral conviction.

Each social unit—family, hospital ward, mental health center, union, school board, or city—has its own unique constellation of power sources and its own unique ways of distributing power. As power is distributed, relevant types of power accumulate in specific areas, which we may think of as power centers. Power centers overlap and interpenetrate. City hall is a center of political power. The chamber of commerce and central labor council are centers of economic power, which penetrate into the centers of political power. Relationships among and between the various power centers may be stable, but they frequently shift with issues, personalities, and social change. Management and labor groups may be basically antagonistic, but may join forces in the United Fund appeal. The mental health society and the Catholic social agency may work closely on most issues, but part company on the matter of abortion legislation. The ward team may find its efforts supported or undermined by another power center—the informal or underground patient government. The enormous complexity and fluidity of the sources and distribution of power will be complicated by the fact that a society which is expanding in population, wealth, and social institutions is constantly generating more power of all kinds for us to assess and organize. Our task is to determine which constellation of powers is relevant to a particualr social objective, and then to mobilize those powers to work toward the attainment of that objective.

Power is not confined within a power structure. It is located or latent at every level of society. We have all seen highly educated community organizers go down to abject defeat at the hands of neighborhood militants, many of whom were dropouts. Until recently, many highly trained public health physicians were reduced to hopeless frustration by the practitioners of folk medicine in some areas of the American Southwest. Even the so-called powerless have discovered that they have power. The ghetto poor do not appear to have political, economic, or social power in the usual sense. What resources do they control that the community requires—especially if they are not in a position to withhold their labor? They have learned that they can withhold their children from the schools, their meager dollars from unscrupulous merchants, and their participation from unrepresentative Office of Economic Opportunity programs. As a last resort, they can withhold their acquiescence to the community's standards of law and order and social control (8). So, power is where we find it, where we develop it, where we mobilize it, and where we focus it.

There is another frequently used distinction between types of power. Power may be "ascribed," as in formal delegation or job title, such as "executive director"; social role, such as "father"; education and degree, such as "Doctor of Medicine." Power may also be "achieved." Power is achieved in a great variety of ways, for example, through competence, ability to meet organizational or community needs, force of personality, etc. In a clinical organization ascribed power is largely concentrated in the hands of physicians. Nurses, social workers, administrative personnel, and other paramedical personnel rely heavily on achieved power. The constant, dynamic tension between ascribed and achieved power is a major factor in the complexity and the turbulence which characterize the hospital as a social system. The other major factor behind the complexity and turbulence of the hospital is the fact that power is highly decentralized. Each department head exercises a near monopoly over a specialized resource or skill (X-ray, psychology, social work), without which the hospital cannot function. Department heads in the various specialties are in extremely short supply; hence they are in a very strong bargaining position. Add to this the professional worker's traditional insistence on his professional autonomy, and it becomes clear that the hospital is a network of interlocking power centers or empires, each of which is struggling to preserve its autonomy and maintain its own boundaries, while at the same time it is attempting to increase its own share of institutional resources, space, money, etc., and to increase its influence upon policy-making.

In a community, as in a hospital, both ascribed and achieved power are distributed unevenly, and each power center seeks to expand its influence over the distribution of resources and rewards. The various power centers enter into coalitions or alliances; they trade power, they contract and discharge obligations. As the hospital or community is bombarded by changes, and as decisions must be made which differentially affect various power centers, new coalitions are constantly formed and dissolved. Any given policy decision can be viewed as an expression of the distribution of power in the system at a given point in time. Any initiated change will affect the existing power arrangements. Or, to state it in reverse, it is only as power is redistributed that change takes place (6).

As we have struggled to produce social change in accordance with social work knowledge and values, social workers have relied heavily on achieved power. We would do well to remind ourselves of Webster's definition of the word "achieve": "to obtain by exertion." "Exertion" is the key word for us. Power does not come to the passive, the timid, the indolent, the defeated, or the obsequious. The development and exercise of power is a strenuous business, which requires energy, conviction, courage, resilience, and cool pragmatism.

Social workers bring to health programs certain ascribed powers by virtue of their organizational roles and titles and professional training, prestige, and expertise. Achieved power comes from a variety of sources, i.e., methods and techniques, interpersonal skills, understanding of social and psychological dynamics, information about community needs, conviction about human needs, and a relentless determination to improve social institutions. Given the above as a power base, the following strategies may be employed for augmenting social work power in health systems.

Sources of Power

The keystone of power in a professional environment is competence. Until and unless we command respect for our mastery of our own body of knowledge and skill, the question of power is irrelevant. Until the social work base is sound and our own house is in order, we are in no position to change other parts of the system. It is especially important to fulfill the original contract. If, for example, a clinic is established by a community with the expectation that it is to provide treatment service, confidence in the quality of that service is a necessary prelude to branching into consultation, education, or prevention programs.

The social worker must have good interpersonal skill in the usually accepted sense of the word. He must also have good social insight, an awareness of how his beliefs and behavior affect the people with whom he is interacting. He must express, but not preach, his convictions. He must not presume to moral superiority. In recent years it has become fashionable to speak of social work as the conscience of the community or the conscience of the institution. This notion is presumptuous, objectionable, and unwarranted. Social workers have no monopoly on virtue, and a "holier than thou" attitude is always inappropriate. Another important aspect of interpersonal skill is the ability to earn trust. Integrity and credibility are vital as the social worker negotiates, trades, promises, offers, and asks. Most of the "contracts" he enters into are not written or even sealed with a handshake, but they are understood, and they are binding. Credibility, reliability, and loyalty are constantly evaluated.

The social worker should understand and respect the dominant value themes of the organization or community. He has to know the game and play the game before he can change the game. When trying to produce change from inside the system, the social worker must maintain contact ideologically with the basic values of the significant others, or he becomes a psychological outsider or a social deviant, and neither of these roles is conducive to social influence.

As the social worker understands and associates himself with the dominant values of the organization he becomes responsive to the needs of the organization and endeavors to fulfill those needs beyond the ordinary call of duty. Such an effort may well call for a redefinition of social work functioning and involve assuming risks associated with organizational innovation. For example, in a hospital social workers can move into the management side of the hospital operation by mediating disputes between supervisory personnel and aggrieved members of minority groups. Social workers can teach supervisory concepts and skills to supervisors, from the business offices to the diet kitchen. Social workers can offer consultation to the personnel officer and other department heads concerned about how to deal with the distressed employee. Social workers attentive to the social processes of the hospital can help management personnel understand and cope with problems of excessive turnover, poor morale, communication breakdowns, etc. The social worker who views the entire organization as his client is able to inform and advise management personnel about the social strains in the organization, such as problems between racial or ethnic groups, and problems associated with social stratification, for example, strife between registered nurses and nursing assistants. Thus, the social worker becomes an essential administrative resource, as well as an indispensable clinical resource. Since we have defined power as control of a resource which is essential to the functioning of the system, we can now develop the following formulation. The more indispensable social service becomes to the people with the greatest power, clinical and administrative, the more power social service commands by virtue of its control of a scarce and vital resource.

Development and use of Power

As indicated above, social work role and function can be redefined and renegotiated in the clinical, administrative, and community areas. The process of definition and negotiation is continuous. The social worker is the only person fully qualified to define social work competence, and he should define it in ways that will bring the best, the newest, and the most inventive qualities of social work to bear on the needs of the organization and its clientele.

The development of conceptual and verbal skill is important to the development of power. As indicated above, the ability to define the problem, the ability to explain a definition of the situation, the ability to establish the definition of the relationship are central to the ability to influence the course and outcome of a social process. Skill in verbalizing social work concepts of psychological and social processes is crucial in helping others in the system accept our definitions and ideologies. Good command of the literature; rich vocabulary; ability to abstract, generalize, and particularize; ability to manipulate words and ideas; and the ability to be at home in the world of the intellect are all required of those who expect to influence the beliefs and behaviors of highly educated professional colleagues.

As case aides and other subprofessional workers become more available, and as the more pedestrian functions can be delegated, it becomes feasible as well as desirable to redefine and renegotiate social work functioning at increasingly high levels of responsibility, versatility, autonomy, and authority.

Using the Informal Structure

Another way of developing power is to understand and use the informal organization of the hospital or community. Many decisions ceremonialized at the conference table were made days before at the coffee or bridge table. The grapevine, the leak, the trial balloon, the inside joke, the buddy system, and the fix are all nourished in the informal organization. To be "in" in the informal organization is to be at the hub of the communication network and to have access to the decision-making process before it becomes a conscious process.

The Organization as Target

Trades, deals, coalitions, and an endless stream of sociological games flourish in the informal organization. To be one of the boys or a member of the club is one of the surest and most effective ways to develop or enhance social power.

The social worker should understand how power is distributed and develop his power by plugging into the system at the points at which power is concentrated. While the doctor may nominally be in charge of the ward, it is likely, especially in teaching and psychiatric hospitals, that the nurse really runs the ward. In a state mental hospital, the real power may lie with the chief attendant or with a clique of patients. A social worker wanting a successful group on such a ward may seek the doctor's concurrence and the nurse's cooperation, but without the active support of the underground patient government the program will not really develop. The worker must locate and influence the groups whose power is relevant to the social work objective.

Forming Alliances

Plugging into the sources of power described above has a very important set of variations which may be described as the formation of alliances. There are two types of alliances—standing and ad hoc. The standing alliance has continuity from time to time and issue to issue. It is usually based on ideological, methodological, and personality similarities. In a hospital, psychology and psychiatry, because of their humanistic ideology and prescientific methodology, are often standing allies of social work. On the administrative side, the personnel department, with its concentration on dealing with people, is a likely ally. In the community our most likely standing allies are mental health societies, community welfare councils, some labor and ministerial groups, professional societies (APA and NASW), and some civic groups (the League of Women Voters and the Association of University and Professional Women). These standing alliances, which are always reciprocal, provide a high level of emotional support and a variable level of political support, depending on the issue at stake. A standing alliance is something like a credit card. A person can borrow power, within reason, as he needs it, to add to the power he has to get what he needs. The more standing alliances he can form, the stronger his position becomes, because he not only has allies when he needs them, he also has a group of allies who need him. He is strengthened as much by their need for him as he is by his ability to call on them.

The other type of alliance is the ad hoc alliance, which is transient (unless it develops into a standing alliance). The ad hoc alliance is formed to combine power to attain a shared goal. Once the goal is attained or lost, the alliance is dissolved. The ad hoc alliance can be extremely useful and effective, precisely because it may be so unusual and special. The Child Welfare Committee of the American Legion may be interested in a health program directed specifically at children. Civil rights militants must be our allies in the establishment of storefront clinics in black neighborhoods. The police should be our allies in the programs for identification and proper management of psychiatric emergencies. Any project of real organizational or community significance will ramify into the spheres of influence of other interest groups or power centers. The use of alliances provides a broad enough power base to produce adequate support and, where necessary, to neutralize the opposition.

Giving and Withholding

Power employed is power believed. Power is not acquired for its own sake, but rather because it is instrumental in implementing knowledge and values. Once we have assessed how much intellectual, political, social, and psychological power we possess, we must use that power appropriately and judiciously in a variety of situations. One aspect of the use of power which we are often reluctant to discuss is the use of rewards and penalties. The ability to reward and punish is a basic requisite of power. The power to give or withhold may operate in subtle, low-key, almost imperceptible ways, such as in a person's readiness to give loyalty and maximum commitment or mere technical obedience.

The power to give or withhold may also be used in an open political manner with educational intent. Any director of social service must deploy his staff on the basis of several criteria, such as patient need, organizational need, worker job satisfaction, political pressures, etc. One major criterion has to do with the extent to which various assignments do or do not allow for the maximum play of social work competence. It is not only good economics to invest social work time where it is best used, it is also good educational practice to make clear that social work participation is a scarce resource—one of the goodies that the system has to offer. It is offered generously to physicians, departments, or programs when the social worker is treated as a professional co-worker with maximum responsibility and autonomy. The doctor who attempts to prescribe and proscribe social work functioning in such a way as to restrict professionalism and perpetuate handmaidenism should be penalized by getting as little social work participation as the needs of patients and hospital permit. Similarly, in a community it may be necessary to threaten to withhold or actually to withhold a service if other interest groups, less committed to social goals, threaten the quality or proper development of the service. This type of open, explicit exercise of power is not always endearing, but it is usually effective. At those times when it is more important to command respect than to be a nice guy, power is indispensable.

Using Group Process

Another way of developing and employing power is through skillful use of group processes. Much decision-making takes place in groups, and the group member who times his interventions in terms of the phases of group life has a distinct advantage. If a group is in a period of intense conflict, a proposed solution may be wasted because it will not be heard. When the group is quite anxious about the conflict and signs of desire for reconciliation appear, a proposal that can serve as a rallying point for reconciliation may be received eagerly. To know the signs of readiness for closure is to know when to call for a vote— or a recess. It is also possible to employ group pressure as a way of moving a recalcitrant adversary, and it is possible to use a group as a vehicle for creative conflict resolution. There are five ways in which a group can handle conflicts between members:

1. A member or members may be expelled.
2. A member or members may be subjugated, i.e., forced to abandon a position in order to "be a good team player" or to avoid being labeled as grossly deviant.
3. Alliances may be formed to outnumber and overpower a member or faction.
4. Differences may be compromised by taking parts of the contending solutions.
5. An entirely new formulation or solution may be created out of a redefinition or reconceptualization of the interests and needs of the contestants.

Obviously, the last method is the most sophisticated and productive, and the most likely to assure group satisfaction and cohesion. The social worker who can help a decision-making group operate at this level and who can actively participate in the redefinition of the problem will be making the sort of contribution from which respect and power flow.

To have effective power, one must understand the unwritten, and usually unspoken, rules of the power game in a given institution or community. Considerable self-awareness and self-control may be required to stay within the rules. To compete for a share of scarce resources is expected. To be thought of as a competitive person is unfortunate. To succeed is desirable. To succeed at someone else's expense may be negatively sanctioned. To advance one's cause is approved. To do so by attacking a competitor explicitly is often disapproved. Competition within the organization may be healthy. Competition that degenerates into conflict may be very dangerous to the professionalism and interdependence of the contestants. While some conflict may be allowed, an open break which would threaten essential cooperation may not be tolerated. Conflict may be tolerated when well-developed organizational techniques assure reconciliation and resolution. Conflict may be expressed by attacking an adversary's assumptions, data, or conclusions. Personal attack is usually taboo. Conflict must be modulated and impersonal, and hostility is best expressed in the guise of humor or "kidding on the level." To win is good—to gloat is bad. It is best to be graceful and modest in victory and to help an adversary save face. The rules of the game consist of local ground rules and general rules of interpersonal skill. To play the game without knowing and respecting the rules can be very costly.

The skillful use of crisis intervention can facilitate the development of power (4). When an individual, a family, or a social system is in a state of crisis, it is by definition in a state of disequilibrium. The parts of the system change in relation to one another. Defenses are weakened and subject to shifts. Anxiety, dependency, and suggestibility levels are high. Perhaps this is what the Chinese had in mind when they defined the concept of crisis as the combination of two other concepts—danger and opportunity. We have long been aware of the dangers in crises, but we are just beginning to be aware of the opportunities created by the heightened susceptibility to intervention caused by loosening of defensive patterns, increased dependency, etc. The opportunity to help the system establish a new equilibrium at a higher level of social functioning (following resolution of the crisis) is an opportunity we must grasp. Many hospitals and communities are facing a series of crises as we attempt to adjust to new social arrangements for distributing medical and mental health services. Many will look to social workers for help in redefining relationships with recipients. Many social work values will have new meaning for physicians and health administrators, and social work knowledge will have increased utility for all health personnel (1). As we turn to face the crises which lie ahead, social workers, along with all our co-workers, will be mindful of the dangers, attentive to the needs, and sensitive to stress reactions. Above all, we must be oriented toward and energetically responsive to the opportunities, for these opportunities make it possible for us to make the contribution to health care which we have long sought to make.

Negotiating

Another essential aspect of power development is negotiating skill. Negotiation is essentially a process for securing the most favorable distribution of resources, services, rewards, authority, and other goodies. We negotiate for such things as money, space, status, role definitions, "turf" (people outside of the field of community organization call it jurisdiction), treatment philosophy, access to sources of power, or for acceptance of our conceptualization of the problem, situation, need, or opportunity. Negotiation is a highly reciprocal process of trading, seeking concessions, making concessions, assessing and making threats in order to attain the most favorable possible agreement. Negotiation is a process that requires acute sensitivity to the needs, resources, power, and determination of the opposition; a careful assessment of our own needs, resources, power, and determination; and a careful attention to the timing of requests, demands, concessions, threats, and closures. Timing is based on being able to diagnose what is negotiable and what is fixed in concrete, when the opposition is uncertain or weakening, or when it is firming up a position. Attentiveness to nonverbal cues, such as fatigue, tension, or impatience, is extremely important.

The good negotiator conveys an image of confidence, conviction, controlled flexibility, endurance, patience, respect, and a desire for limited victory, rather than unconditional surrender. He is knowledgeable about the issues and the facts that undergird the issues. He has prepared in advance a series of positions to which he can retreat when necessary, and he works hard to assess and predict what, when, and where the opposition can withdraw. He uses his verbal and conceptual skill in an effort to define the facts and issues in a way that is most consistent with and acceptable to the value system that impels his opposite number. He attempts to influence by persuasion and by emphasis on rewards. He is not afraid to use implicit or explicit threats when necessary, but he adheres to the principal of "minimal force" so that the loser is spared loss of face, bitterness, a commitment to retribution, or a need to break off the relationship.

Negotiation is of three types: The adversary type of negotiation is seen in some aspects of international diplomacy, labor-management disputes, and divorce, personal injury, and other arenas in which attorneys are the gladiators. In the adversary type of negotiation, the stakes and risks are high, the anxiety level is high, aggression is not sublimated, but, rather, may be expressed as open hostility. There may be heavy reliance on threats, such as war, embargo, strike, lockout, law-suits, resignations, etc. The central characteristic of this type of negotiation is explicit conflict (7). Both parties know that the outcome may be the destruction of their relationship, or at least heavy damage to that relationship.

Happily, in most social work practice, the adversary type of negotiation is the exception rather than the rule. Occasionally, we see a power struggle between department heads, or other power center leaders, which culminates in the resignation of the loser, or the termination of a program, but, for the most part, we are spared explicit and destructive conflict and rely on the other two types of negotiation.

The second type is the semiadversary type, which is characterized by competition which we keep from degenerating into conflict. This is the most common type of negotiation for us. Social workers compete with other professional groups for establishment of treatment ideology, clinical and policy decision-making power, etc. In so doing, they spend much time negotiating definitions of roles, functions, values, and influence.

Various program elements compete for funds, staff, space, and turf. Various agencies compete for funds, board members, community support, etc. Since they must go on working together, and since their negotiations are not usually bound by international or civil law, and their negotiators are not trained to be gladiators as attorneys are, social workers have a different style of negotiation. Emphasis is placed on persuasion and rewards (Program X can do more for the community than Program Y). Threats are rarely used and are carefully modulated, e.g., "Such a small budget allocation will impair the effectiveness of our service." In this type of negotiation, competitiveness is expected and explicit. Anxiety and aggression are present, but are sublimated into a desire to do a good job. Both parties compete without wanting to be viewed as competitive—an evidence of their desire to protect the relationship from undue strain, which would impair later collaboration.

The third type of negotiation is nonadversary, and so low key that we might question whether it is, indeed, a negotiation process. Its central characteristic is cooperation. It occurs in clinic teams, agency staffs, community committees, and other groups which have worked together long enough and well enough so that they have a common value system, comfortable role definitions, and clear, common, stable, communication styles. Threats are virtually nonexistent, and explicit demands are rare. The emphasis is on implicit but understood expectation of reciprocal support, effort, and sharing of tasks and goals. What gets negotiated here is the meeting of members' needs so quickly, quietly, smoothly, and gladly that cooperation is not allowed to develop into competition.

It is important to be mindful of the distinctiveness of the three different negotiation styles and to be able to use the appropriate style. The use of explicit threats in a nonadversary meeting might destroy the group or make the threatening person a group outcast. To use the nonadversary style to face an attack by the John Birch Society might "turn away wrath," but it might be viewed as weakness.

Understanding
Decision-Making

Another type of knowledge essential for the person who wishes to be influential is knowledge of decision-making. Decision-making is the source, focus, goal, and outcome of power. The social worker must be able to identify and appraise the relevant decision-making apparatus.

Obviously, the making of decisions varies from group to group, place to place, and level to level. But formal decision-making process does have some general characteristics which social workers would do well to understand.

A decision-making process takes place in a framework which has five sets of limits which define, direct, and regulate both the process and the content. They are: *(a)* the limits of permissibility, i.e., laws, charters, etc.; *(b)* the limits of resources, i.e., funds, personnel, space; *(c)* the limits of time; *(d)* the limits of previous binding commitments; and *(e)* the limits of available information. Because of these strictures, organizational decision-making attempts to be highly rational, sharply focused, goal-directed, practical, empirical, and predictive.

The process itself consists of seven stages, the first and third of which are especially crucial. The first stage of the decision-making process is the definition of the problem. This stage is loaded with opportunities to influence the course of the process. To define the problem is to locate the problem. If, for example, the problem is located in the patient, the decision-making process would be very different from what it would be if the problem were located in the institution.

The problem may be defined in a judgmental, projecting manner, or in a nonjudgmental, self-examining manner. The problem may be defined in terms of racial, class, or ethnic stereotypes, or it may be defined in terms of knowledge of sociology and ethnology. If we define it judgmentally, our solution may be punitive. It we define it psychologically, our solution may be more psychological than social. Hence, the most decisive point at which to influence the decision-making process is at the point of defining the problem.

The second stage of the process consists of enumerating the existing alternative solutions to the problem. The third stage consists of an effort to expand the range of alternative solutions. At this point we have another excellent opportunity to contribute alternatives which flow from social work knowledge and values. Having defined the problem and arrayed the full range of alternatives, we enter the fourth stage, which is an effort to predict the extent to which the various alternatives will produce the desired or intended consequences. The predictive effort grows more difficult as we enter stage five, which is an effort to forecast the unintended or undesirable consequences of the various alternatives. Frequently the unintended consequences flow from the sensitivity, subtlety, and intimacy of the relationships of various organizational elements. We are often perplexed by the manner in which elements which we did not consider are affected by the reverberations of change in another part of the system.

The sixth stage involves the complicated and difficult process of assessing the alternatives on the basis of a predictive weighing of the intended and unintended consequences.

Stage seven is the selection of the alternative or combination of alternatives which has the most favorable ratio of intended consequences to unintended consequences.

Clearly, we have all been party to decision-making activities that did not proceed in such logical and orderly sequence; or we may have gone through the process without having conceptualized it. We may have gone through various stages without being aware that we had moved from one stage to another. However, the more important the decision is, the more important it is that it be reached in a logical and orderly sequence, and the person who can help decision-makers think their way carefully through each stage will render an important service.

Decision-making is more than process; there is important content, also. The content in decision-making involves two types of material. The overt, conscious, or explicit material consists primarily of information, plus judgments and predictions about the meanings and uses of that information. This material produces what we may call the factual premises in decision-making. A premise is an alternative course of action and a social consequence linked together in a cause-effect relationship. A factual premise is based on reasonably hard data, experience, and good ability to manipulate the alternative. For example, if we increase the heat (the cause) this will make (cause and effect) the molecules move faster (the effect). Or, if we increase caseloads (cause) we can (cause and effect) reduce the waiting list (effect). Factual premises appeal to decision-makers because they appear to be neat, objective, manageable, and, above all, if you will forgive the redundancy, based on the facts.

The second type of content in decision-making may be covert, unconscious, less visible, and less discussable, or it may be explicit, philosophical, ethical, and ideological. It may be based on various types of material:

(a) Material that is known and consciously withheld or suppressed. (This is sometimes referred to as the hidden agenda. An example is seen in a committee, or other decision-making group that goes through the motions of decision-making when the top man has made up his mind and arranged things so that the committee is merely ratifying a decision, rather than making a decision.)

(b) Material from the psychological unconscious, such as dependent yearnings, sexual wishes, transference reactions, competitive and destructive impulses, etc.

(c) Material from the social unconscious or preconscious, particularly role prescriptions and value commitments which infuse and direct our behavior without our being fully aware of their impact.

(d) Strong, clear value commitments.

All four types tend to be expressed in what we may call the value premises (2). An example of a value premise is as follows: As we provide more professional stimulation (alternative), we expect (cause and effect link) higher staff morale (consequence). The value premises are usually somewhat vague, subjective, difficult to manipulate, and highly charged emotionally.

Physicians and managers are oriented toward hard data and inclined toward factual premises. Social workers, perhaps because of our lag in research and our intensely humanistic orientation, have been contributing more value premises than factual premises to the decision-making process. We are painfully aware of this state of affairs, which accounts for some of our diffidence about our ability to influence medical decision-makers. However, we will become less diffident with the passage of time because of the rapid growth of research and other rigorous intellectual pursuits in social work. Another reason for reduced diffidence among social workers is that, as we observe some of the medical and managerial decision-making with a more practiced eye, we see that the separation between facts and values is not as clear or as strict as we may have been led to believe. Factual and value premises are often combined, for example: "We can move more patients out of our mental hospitals (a factual alternative) and they will be much better off in the community" (a value consequence). Or a value may be stated as a fact, for example: "A mental patient is better off in the community than in a mental hospital."

The point of all this is that when a social worker seeks to understand a decision-making process in order to influence that process he must be able to distinguish between facts and values. He should be able to identify clearly which values are impelling the decision-makers so that he will know when and how social work facts and values can most effectively be brought to bear on the decision-making process.

Being Aware of Organizational Factors

We must take pains to understand the power differences in differing systems, such as formal organizations and communities.

The formal organization provides a reasonably clear, tidy, and manageable distribution of power. Central direction and budgeting, clear geographical, legal, and functional boundaries, well-defined hierarchies, regulations, procedures, and disciplinary arrangements, in short, all of the accouterments of bureaucracy act to distribute and manage power in an orderly and predictable way (9). One has only to look at a table of organization to get a quick, clear picture of where ascribed power is located.

By contrast, the power distribution in a neighborhood or city is chaotic. Innumerable power centers, based on every conceivable source of power, are actively and single-mindedly pursuing their own interests. Since there is no central direction, no system of regulation or discipline, no commitment to a single mission, no binding interdependence, and no established communication network, each power center is autonomous, sometimes to the point of isolation. Competition easily degenerates into conflict, for example, as different racial and ethnic groups struggle for control of such resources as housing, recreational facilities, or jobs (5).

To mobilize community power relevant to a specific social objective, a variety of techniques are available, only a few of which will be briefly mentioned (10):

(a) Appeal to the enlightened self-interest of the various power centers affected by the objective.

(b) Relate the power centers to the objective in such a way as to maximize their participation and investment.

(c) Develop an interdependence among the power centers by emphasizing the desirability of the objective and the importance of each power center to the fulfillment of that objective.

(d) Establish some new reference groups for members of power centers by establishing committees composed of members of various power centers.

(e) Encourage members of power centers to also join other power centers, producing interpenetration and overlapping of power centers, thus reducing their isolation, increasing their interdependence, and broadening the power base for the objective.

(f) Out of the objective, develop a terminology and value position specific enough to serve the objective and general enough to be transferrable to subsequent objectives.

(g) Use group work methods to develop cohesion, standards, controls, leadership, a sense of mission, dedication, and optimism, forming a new, larger, composite power center, focused on wider objectives.

Summary

Social workers are committed to democracy, dignity, and self-determination. They are also committed to inducing and producing social change, which they can do only by developing, mobilizing, and applying relevant power. They must, once and for all, disabuse themselves of the notion that there is some sort of incompatibility between the two sets of commitments. There can be no democracy without an equitable distribution of powers. There is little dignity for the powerless, and there is no self-determination without alternatives and the ability to act on those alternatives. Lord Acton may be right. Power may tend to corrupt. This is most likely to happen when it is highly concentrated, when those who use it are not held publicly accountable, and when it is not possible to develop countervailing power. Social work is concerned with the broad distribution of power, with making power-holders increasingly accountable to their constituents, and with developing countervailing power among previously low-power groups in our society.

References

1. Dorfman, Albert, M.D. "The Role of Medical Schools in Community Health." *Social Service Review* 42 (June 1968): 207–15.

2. Frankel, Charles. "Social Values and Professional Values." *Journal of Education for Social Work* 5 (Spring 1969): 29–35.

3. Hunter, Floyd. *Community Power Structure: A Study of Decision Makers.* Chapel Hill: University of North Carolina Press, 1969.

4. Parad, Howard J., ed. *Crisis Intervention: Selected Readings.* New York: Family Service Association of America, 1965.

5. Pruger, Robert, and Specht, Harry. "Assessing Theoretical Models of Community Organization Practice: Alinsky as a Case in Point." *Social Service Review* 43 (June 1969): 123–35.

6. Rein, Martin. "Organization for Social Change." *Social Work* 9 (April 1964): 32–41.

7. Slavin, Simon. "Concepts of Social Conflict: Use in Social Work Curriculum." *Journal of Education for Social Work* 5 (Fall 1969): 47–60.

8. Specht, Harry. "Disruptive Tactics." *Social Work* 14 (April 1969): 5–15.

9. Stein, Herman. "Administrative Implications of Bureaucratic Theory." *Social Work* 6 (July 1961): 14–21.

10. Warren, Roland. "The Interaction of Community Decision Organizations: Some Basic Concepts and Needed Research." *Social Service Review* (September 1967): 261–70.

The ability of a practitioner to deliver social services, to work toward the amelioration of unmet client needs, will be directly influenced by the policies of the organization in which he is employed. Specht outlines an eight-stage model for evaluating organizational policies. He describes a set of tasks and roles for the worker to pursue and identifies resources within the organization for him to use in undertaking to influence and change social policy.

Casework Practice and
Social Policy Formulation

Harry Specht

Gordon Hamilton continuously stressed the relationship between casework practice and social policy formulation. In 1952 he wrote:

One cannot successfully solve problems of interrelationships without a sound economic and political structure, but it is also true that one cannot solve—and this is less readily granted—economic problems without profound understanding of human behavior and psychodynamics. These two complementary areas must be integrated for policy and program . . . social workers must find more successful ways of bringing their insights into social legislation. . . . Informed social action can proceed only on deepening knowledge of the personality which determines and is determined by its society, as well as on the more familiar and accepted data of political and related science.[1]

The need for social workers to play a more direct role in the formulation of the social policies that guide social service institutions increases as these institutions grow larger and more complex.[2] Too frequently, though, the charge to the practitioner is delivered in oversimplified cliches that ask professionals to "get into the political arena" or learn to deal more effectively with the "community power structure."[3] In general, the call is for more social action and a more aggressive professional stance in policy formulation. However, the demand for this new

Reprinted with permission of the author and the National Association of Social Workers from *Social Work,* Vol. 13, No. 1 (January 1969), pp. 42–52.

[1]"The Role of Social Casework in Social Policy," *Social Casework,* Vol. 33, No. 8 (October 1952), p. 317.

[2]Social policy refers to the goals of social transactions in private and public institutions serving human needs. "Goal" is used as the major referrent of policy because it suggests that concepts of organization, structure, economics, and administration be viewed as independent variables that affect policy, but are not themselves policy since goals remain constant, whether or not they are actualized. For a differentiation of social policy and economic policy, see Kenneth E. Boulding, "The Boundaries of Social Policy," *Social Work,* Vol. 12, No. 1 (January 1967), pp. 3–11.

[3]Alan D. Wade, "The Social Worker in the Political Process," *Social Welfare Forum, 1966* (New York: Columbia University Press, 1966), pp. 52–67.

stance can be demoralizing to professionals, particularly such practitioners as the social worker in a hospital or family counseling agency. At best, a general call to arms without more specific instructions about which arms to use or how to use them is only temporarily inspiring and, at worst, likely to leave many feeling inadequate.

This inadequacy occurs in part because, as Donald Howard puts it, ". . . of the failure to stress social policy formulation as a process rather than in . . . exclusively substantive terms."[4] That is, there is a tendency to conceive of participation in social policy formulation as requiring expertise in a major area of service, a comprehensive and extensive knowledge of a field. But if policy formulation is recognized as a process that can be taught to *all* in a profession, and if it is seen as a process that entails many different tasks and roles, then all professionals can learn to utilize the process so that they can contribute to it in ways most appropriate for them.

A second reason for the practitioner's sense of inadequacy in dealing with social policy formulation is that it is not as well defined as other professional tasks. In casework, for example, the actual doing (counseling) and the units with which one does it (cases) are relatively clear. Many of the methods used in direct practice allow professionals to work within a series of fairly well-defined roles that usually have a high degree of consonance and frequently can be filled by one person. However, as shall be explained in this paper, the process by which policy is formulated involves a wide range of roles that often strain against one another and must be filled by several people. In addition, the caseworker must see these roles in the context of the societal forces that necessitate change in social welfare institutions. Therefore, the author has provided a brief review of the major forces generating change in this society before moving on to a discussion of the policy formulation process.

Forces Generating
Change

The first of these forces is the combined effect of automation and an expanding labor force, both of which produce an overabundance of goods and a shortage of jobs. Increasingly, it will be in the human services that much of society's work remains incomplete—the health, education, social welfare, recreation, and other professions—where society can and should use its surplus manpower. This, of course, will necessitate great change in the organization of social welfare services.

[4]"Social Policy Formulation as Process" (Los Angeles: UCLA School of Social Welfare, February 1965). (Mimeographed.)

There are not enough professionals to meet present demands and there is little likelihood that this situation will change in the near future. Therefore, a reexamination of professional functions and the development of a more creative use of subprofessionals and workers in new careers, to do much of the work the professionals may be doing unnecessarily or for which there is not the professional manpower, will be necessary.

The press for civil and social rights in this era will make further demands on the service professions. Society will need to speed up the creation of new mechanisms to meet needs, such as a guaranteed minimum income; the separation of income maintenance programs from social services, as suggested originally by Gordon Hamilton; and the whole host of noneconomic services presently being experimented with in the Office of Economic Opportunity and Model Cities programs.[5] Increasingly, social work will require programs that encourage self-help and allow for citizen participation so that clients, rather than being passive recipients of services that often do not meet their needs, may participate in designing and implementing programs that do.

These problems will demand a more enlarged role of government in meeting social needs than do the already burgeoning and complex programs. New forms of government to deal with the problems of metropolitan areas and joblessness and to coordinate and humanize public services will be called for. The problems encountered in policy formulation must be assessed in light of these forces generating change.

Social Policy
Formulation Model

In this paper the various stages of the policy formulation process, the tasks involved at each stage, the institutional resources needed to carry out these tasks, and the professional roles required at each stage will be identified. Following this, the strategic points at which the caseworker can play a role in policy formulation will be considered. By utilizing the model, the gaps in role sets of professional groups concerned with policy formulation may be found.

Many authors have developed models of policy formulation along similar processual lines to the one proposed here.[6] The purpose of this paper is to identify the different professional tasks and roles relevant

[5]Gordon Hamilton, "Editor's Page," *Social Work*, Vol. 7, No. 1 (January 1962), pp. 2, 128.
[6]See, for example, Elizabeth Wickenden, *How to Influence Public Policy* (New York: American Association of Social Workers, 1954); and Robert E. Agger, Daniel Goldrich, and Bert E. Swanson, *The Rulers and the Ruled* (New York: John Wiley & Sons, 1964).

The Organization as Target

at the several stages of the process. It is this notion of *difference* that is most important for understanding the relationship between practice and policy formulation.

Table 1 identifies all the elements mentioned. The process may be summarized as uncovering both incipient and unmet needs and blazing a trail of advocacy toward new methods of meeting those needs. It might take place in a variety of settings—in one small agency, in one department of a large agency, or in a nation-wide bureaucracy—or the different resources and subsystems of only one institution or a wide variety of institutional resources and organizations might be involved.

The reader should bear in mind that the model only suggests the various stages through which policy moves; it does not take into account the question of *who* generates interest in and takes initiative for carrying the process forward. The force generating change might be the practitioner, the professional association or another voluntary association, the administrator, or an interested citizen. Regardless of where the desire for change originates, all these elements are part of the process once it is started.

Whether someone introduces a policy goal from outside the institution or it originates from within, it must at some time become the preference of a person within the decision-making structure to become a part of the process. Otherwise, it will remain stillborn in the mind of its originator.

The following two case examples will illustrate the process. One concerns a caseworker in a city welfare department. The worker's interest in policy stemmed from an administrative ruling that transferred the authority to grant funds for "special needs" from the line supervisor to the senior supervisor. As a result, clients had to wait for unnecessarily long periods to receive funds. These amounts, although usually small, were often needed for family emergencies. The worker questioned the policy at a lower-level staff meeting and was told the issue was settled and closed to further discussion. This response revealed a second policy issue—one relating to administration—the absence of means by which the professional staff could participate in policy formulation. Clients were, of course, emphatically excluded from any participation. These practices resulted in the agency's having policies that were frequently rigid, unyielding, and unresponsive to client needs.

The other example involves a caseworker in a voluntary agency that frequently dealt with runaway children who was distressed by the physical mistreatment of children in the county probation department's residential institution, which was operating with poor facilities and insufficient funds. Finding the institution's administrator defensive and unwilling to bring these problems to the authorities' attention, the worker sought counsel from other social workers. This small group

TABLE 1. Stages of Policy Formulation

Stage	Tasks	Institutional Resources	Professional Roles
Identification of problem	Case-finding, recording, discovery of gaps in service	Agency	Practitioner
Analysis	Data-gathering, analysis, conceptualization	Research organization (e.g., university)	Researcher
Informing the public	Dramatization, public relations, communications (writing, speaking)	Public relations unit, communications media, voluntary associations	Muckraker, community organizer, public relations man
Development of policy goals (involvement of other agencies)	Creating strategy, program analysis	Planning bodies, voluntary associations	Planner, community organizer, administrator
Building public support	Developing leadership, achieving consensus	Voluntary associations, political parties, legislative and agency committees	Lobbyist, community organizer, public relations man
Legislation	Drafting legislation, program design	Legislative bodies, agency boards	Legislative analyst, planner
Implementation, administration	Program-organizing, administration	Courts, agencies	Administrator, practitioner, lawyer
Evaluation, assessment	Case-finding, recording, discovery of gaps in service, gathering data	Agency, research organization	Practitioner

The Organization as Target

informed the social action committee of their local NASW chapter, which helped organize a broadly based citizens' group to deal with these problems.

First Stage: Identification
of Problem

The basis for institutional policy change is in some problem identified as an unrecognized or unmet need in the community, a need the originator of the policy goal believes the institution is responsible for meeting. The perception of the problem and the institution's responsibility are related to the political, economic, social, and institutional forces that come to bear on the perceiver; what is perceived to be a problem will depend on the institutional position of the initiator. So, for example, it is possible that concerns for institutional maintenance might guide the perceptions of professional administrators more than their feelings of responsibility for providing better service to clients. (The welfare department caseworker was concerned about his client receiving benefits promptly; the administrator was interested in keeping the costs of the special needs program as low as possible.)

Tasks that must be completed during this stage are case-finding, recording examples of unmet needs, and discovering gaps in services. The institution itself is the resource to be utilized during this stage, and the practitioner role is most important. Gordon Hamilton noted that skill in determining how family functioning, personality development, and intergroup relations are affected by policy is the most important contribution the caseworker can make in this endeavor.[7]

It is in their functions as advocates and social brokers for their clients that caseworkers will most likely be involved in the policy formulation process. Scott Briar has discussed these functions as part of the caseworker's professional role, pointing out that caseworkers bring to them ". . . a substantial body of knowledge with which to understand the dynamics of the welfare system and its constituent agencies."[8]

However, to use such knowledge in this process requires a professional orientation that views service to one's client as the foremost professional responsibility. The welfare department caseworker's colleagues, for example, felt he had "betrayed" the department when he pressed his criticisms of department policy. Because discussion was foreclosed at the staff level, he presented the issues to the mayor's commission on welfare in co-ordination with an NASW representative,

---

[7]Hamilton, "The Role of Social Casework in Social Policy," p. 319.
[8]Scott Briar, "Dodo or Phoenix? A View of the Current Crisis in Casework," *Social Work Practice, 1967* (New York: Columbia University Press, 1967).

urging its members to intervene in the department's handling of the matter.

Many social workers will ask at this point: How does one weigh the importance of working within the agency structure as against going outside the system as the welfare worker did? But a too narrow view of the system prejudices the case against workers who take action on their clients' behalf. These workers view the agency as part of—really only an agent of—a larger system of state and federal government. The worker *was* working within the structure, just as Benny Parrish and Harold Supriano were working *within* the system when they conflicted with their welfare departments.

Benny Parrish, a caseworker for the Alameda County Department of Social Services, refused to participate in a mass morning raid on the homes of recipients of AFDC grants (then called Aid to Needy Children) to find out if there were any "unauthorized males" present because he believed that such a raid was in violation of the recipients' privacy. For this reason he was discharged for insubordination in 1964. Harold Supriano, a caseworker for the San Francisco Department of Social Services, was discharged shortly before completing his probationary period for several reasons, including his after-hours participation in a community organization that encouraged low-income residents to organize to protest police brutality abuses.[9]

As it turned out, the courts made it clear in the Parrish and Supriano cases that it was the agencies who were out of line—who were not working within the system—and whose behavior was illegal. Professional social workers will be able to help clients obtain their rights only when they are able to absorb the strain and conflict that occur when they mediate the interests and rights of clients. The profession, through its educational institutions and professional association, must provide the mechanisms to help its members do so.

Practitioners, then, can play an important role in the policy formulation process and must be alert to the potential for change in certain aspects of their practice. As a case in point, there are many problems that practitioners regularly confront in their day-to-day work to which these new conceptions of services are relevant. For example, new career concepts can be useful in dealing with problems of overly large case loads, hard-to-reach clients, waiting lists, staff that are hard to reach because of turnover and personnel shortages, and apathy and alienation in the community to be served.

[9]In *Parrish* vs. *Civil Service Commission of the County of Alameda,* 35 U.S.L.W. 2583, Cal. Sup. Ct. (March 27, 1967), the court decided in favor of Parrish. In April 1967, the judge of the Superior Court for the City and County of San Francisco, before rendering his decision in *Harold Supriano and the San Francisco City and County Employee's Union, Local 400* vs. *San Francisco Department of Social Services* (Case No. 566214), called the city's attention to other recent court decisions involving workers' rights and urged the city to settle the case out of court.

Second Stage: Analysis

Having identified a problem, it is necessary to develop some factual data about the number of people who are affected and a clear-cut statement of how the problem is actually being measured. Gathering data may not require highly scientific and formalized research procedures. For example, the caseworker at the city welfare department figured the cost to the agency in manhours of implementing the less desirable special needs policy and how much time clients had to wait for funds. An $8.00 special needs grant for one client, he found, cost the agency over $100 in staff time, and the client was kept waiting for an unnecessarily long period—over six hours for a transaction that could have been completed in a few minutes. When his research was presented to the mayor's welfare commission, its members were horrified and immediately took the matter under consideration.

In the other case illustration, the citizens' group concerned about the probation department set up meetings in various sections of the city to which it invited all youths who had been at the institution and wanted an opportunity to speak about their experiences and grievances; scores of youngsters came. These meetings provided much of the raw data for the citizen committee's work.

The kind and quality of the information-gathering function will change as the process evolves. The citizens' committee used a fairly informal procedure in their early work. Later on, as some of the issues became clear, the committee directed its energies toward bringing in a highly respected professional standard-setting agency to evaluate the community's probation program.

From a processual point of view, the knowledge required is *how* to move from an expression of concern about unmet needs to an organized (and frequently complicated and/or expensive) program of information-gathering. The institutional resource is a research operation —consultation with an agency research department or a university research center; the professional role is that of researcher.[10]

Third Stage: Informing the Public

The public is the various subsystems in the institution or general community that must be informed of the problem. The size of the public —as big as the community at large or as limited as the administration of an institution—depends on the nature of the problem or the stage of

[10]By "professional roles" is meant those roles that must be filled in the policy formulation process. The concern here is to identify the tasks with which professionals in the institution to be changed must be prepared to deal , whether or not the roles are actually filled by professional social workers.

the process. The task is to present the problem in a form that will capture the interest and attention of the public by use of appropriate media.

The institutional resources are these media. They might be channels within the institution (public relations department, staff meeting) or outside institutional resources (the press and television). Although the form of action may vary, this is the stage at which counterdemands will essentially determine the extent to which activity in the following stages is to be consensual or conflicting.

For example, the welfare worker only asked the mayor's commission to consider the impact of the special needs policy on clients. His reasoned presentation to the commission was sufficient to spur them to work for changing the policy. Although a local newspaper did print the story, that was not a scheduled part of the worker's plan. But the citizens' committee was attempting to demonstrate the inadequacy of the funds allocated by the county for probation. To do this required its challenging the entire system's functioning. That is, the departmental administrators, the juvenile court judge, the juvenile justice commission, and the county officials all recognized (but not publicly) that the probation department's financing was inadequate. However, they did not want to take responsibility for bringing this to the public's attention since they would then have to demand additional funds. Thus, the citizens' committee intentionally sought and received widespread coverage by the news media.

The necessary professional roles differ from those previously mentioned. The muckraker, community organizer, and public relations man (each with different roles) bring the institutional problem to the public's attention.

This step precedes the next stage—developing policy goals—because while the parties who are initiating change may have specific policy goals in mind, they will have little meaning to the relevant public until it is aware that a problem exists. For example, the mayor's commission could not become interested in rearranging responsibility in the welfare department until it understood the problem; the citizens' committee could not begin to suggest changes in policy until it had persuaded the public there was reason to examine present probation policy. One further reason for this order is that the parties who participate in seeking policy change will want to be involved in shaping goals. Anyone who initiates change without this realization is likely to find himself without the support he will need later on.

Fourth Stage: Involving
Other Organizations in
Developing Policy Goals

Many solutions will be offered for dealing with the problem, all of which must be sifted, analyzed, and shaped into a strategy so that the goal will actually provide a solution to the problem. Essentially, a strategy is a set of program goals based on a theory of the problem's origins.

Different voluntary associations and planning bodies are likely to participate at this point, including those that function within and outside the institution. This is the point at which the professional association, as a voluntary organization, can become most actively engaged in policy formulation.

Alan D. Wade's case history of the NASW Chicago Area Chapter's fight against Governor Kerner's attempt to slash the welfare budget in 1962 illustrates the important role of voluntary associations in policy determination.[11] In that undertaking, the chapter made extensive use of a wide range of other organizations at several stages of its effort. Another instance, reported by Marjorie D. Teitelbaum, illustrates that much of the effort of an NASW chapter's attempt to influence standards used in selecting a state social welfare director went into working with other organizations.[12]

The important role of voluntary associations in the determination of social policy cannot be overestimated. It is through their associations with others that Americans make their needs known in political life. The classic theoretical view of the operation of a political democracy is somewhat misleading in this regard.[13] In that view, it is the direct relationship between the legislator and the voter that is the chief determining factor in policy formulation; such intermediary mechanisms as interest groups, political parties, lobbies, and pressure groups are viewed invidiously, as "selfish interests."

However, in reality direct relationships with legislators through elections or their letter writing are not effective simply because elections deal with too many issues to be considered conclusive debates on any one issue. While the town meeting view of government is worth cherishing as part of the past, it is not a helpful model for contemporary government.

Generally, legislation is handled through a complex committee sys-

---

[11]"Social Work and Political Action," *Social Work,* Vol. 8, No. 4 (October 1963), pp. 3–10.

[12]"Social Workers in Social Action: A Report from Maryland," *Social Work,* Vol. 9, No. 4 (October 1964), pp. 100–107.

[13]Betty H. Zisk, "Formation of Public Policy: Constitutional Myths and Political Reality," in John H. Bunzel, ed., *Issues of American Public Policy* (Englewood Cliffs, N.J.: Prentice-Hall, 1965).

tem and the factors of time, distance of the central government from the local community, and largeness of government make it next to impossible for the individual to affect policy. It is through organizational interests of all sorts that the interplay between claimants and decision-makers takes place. Any movement for change, whether for reform or reaction, that fails to take account of this fact of American political life cannot succeed.

Professional roles required are those of planner, community organizer, and administrator. But it would be well to bear in mind that strategies must change as goals change. For example, policy issues relevant to new careers programs might move from (1) the viability of using the poor to serve the poor in selected, specialized communicating roles, to (2) using the poor to assume some responsibility carried by professionals in all aspects of service, to (3) utilizing the re-examination of the staffing patterns in social services as a mechanism for broadening community participation in designing and implementing programs. Each of these policy goals is vastly different and will require the work of different people in their formulation.

Fifth Stage: Building
Public Support

Many different subsystems of the institution and the community will have a stake in policy formulation. The originator of the policy will have to find those groups in the system that can support the goals described in the previous stage and translate them into instruments for action. That is, a consensus must be achieved among those groups who can support the policy.

Compromises may be made at this stage and the processes of bargaining, exchanging, and persuading will be used. The welfare worker, for example, gained sufficient support for his position by working only with an NASW representative who attended welfare commission meetings. Their posture before the commission was worked out quickly and with relative ease. On the other hand, the citizens' committee decided at the beginning of its activities to seek the support of many civil rights groups and local child care agencies because of the difficult political route it was attempting to navigate. The committee worked many weeks before coming to an agreement on tactics and a position that was acceptable to all members. In Chicago, Wade reports, the battle to resist cuts in the welfare budget required mobilization of forces throughout the state, and much of their work was directed toward co-ordinating the thinking of the many groups and organizations involved.[14]

[14]Wade, "Social Work and Political Action."

The Organization as Target

The culmination of this stage is the creation of a platform by the group supporting the goals, whether it is a political party or the administration of an agency setting forth a general statement of direction. As Teitelbaum notes: ". . . the basic position statement of the [NASW] chapter . . . served as the framework for the position taken by the other groups . . . whose support was enlisted."[15]

Major tasks involved at this stage are the cultivation of leadership for the coalition and utilization of skills for negotiating a consensus among the supporting groups. Thus, the citizens' group, in dealing with the probation department, selected independent, aggressive leadership rather than the reasoned professional approach used by the welfare department worker. Its previous experience in dealing with the probation department in a co-operative and nonthreatening manner had been unsuccessful; its members believed their energies would be sapped in further delay if such an approach were attempted again.

The history of the development of social policy in medical care for the aged demonstrates that leadership and coalitions change as issues and goals change.[16] In the 1930's the issue was whether medical insurance of *any* kind was acceptable; major leadership was provided by professional groups using fact-finding and educational methods. In the 1940's, when both hospital and medical insurance on a voluntary basis were well established, the issue was the adoption of a national system and whether it should be compulsory or voluntary; the labor movement and the American Medical Association became the chief opponents and provided the leadership. In the final stages of the fight, in the early 1960's, the question of federal sponsorship was settled; the issue was which mechanism: social insurance, public assistance, or some other scheme? The major leadership, in addition to labor and the AMA, was political.

Voluntary associations, political parties, legislative committees, and committees of boards of directors are the institutional resources most likely to be active. The professional will be called on to fill the roles of lobbyist, community organizer, and public relations man.

Sixth Stage: Legislation

The program must be formulated in statutory terms, whether it is written as a law for consideration by some legislative body or as a statement of program to be considered by an agency board of directors. Legislation must be drafted that will describe the allocation of responsi-

---

[15]Teitelbaum, *op. cit.*
[16]Eugene Feingold, *Medicare: Policy and Politics, A Case Study of Policy Analysis* (San Francisco: Chandler Publishing Co., 1966).

bility for the program and, to a greater or lesser extent, will deal with organizational structure, financing, and program operation.

Gilbert Y. Steiner, in his analysis of the politics of social welfare, points out that specific knowledge of both social welfare and political science is required to negotiate the legislative policy-making process.[17] The legislative analyst and social planner are the professional roles required in this stage.[18]

Seventh Stage: Implementation and Administration

Depending on how detailed the legislation is, a large part of the process of policy formulation may be left for this stage, when the concrete policies of program may be established by practice, precedent, and experimentation. A good example is the Economic Opportunity Act of 1964, in which the policy referring to "maximum feasible participation" of the poor was quite vague; the practical details of implementation were left to the program administrators.

Policy formulation may take place informally within the structure of government without fanfare or public proclamation when formal changes in the law are not required, but rather a demand is made for an altered pattern of action within the law. In the cases of the welfare worker and the citizens' committee, no changes in law were required to put the policies they supported into practice. The tools needed to implement their policy goals were already within the administrative discretion of the agencies. The citizens' committee did, later on, win the support of a state assemblyman who developed legislation that gave the state youth authority increased power to investigate the kind of conditions being protested.

Also, it succeeded in presenting the problem to the county board of supervisors, which debated the feasibility of a study by an independent organization. Afterward, the grand jury, social planning council, bar association, and many other agencies became involved. The citizens' committee seems to have lost in their effort to have an outside national agency do the study. However, the community is now committed to a study by *some* social agency, and even if it is not the one selected by the committee, the community has learned a good deal in the process.

[17] *Social Insecurity: The Politics of Welfare* (Chicago: Rand McNally Co., 1966), esp. chap. 10, "Relief Policy Reconsidered."

[18] Wilbur J. Cohen, "What Every Social Worker Should Know About Political Action," *Social Work,* Vol. II. No. 3 (July 1966), pp. 3–11.

The chief tasks at this point are administrative and programmatic, getting the program organized and policy clarified. The institution and the courts are the chief resources for determining policy; the primary professional roles are administrator, practitioner, and lawyer.

The courts become a major significant institution for determining policy because it is by establishing a system of rights and guarantees through appeals and judicial precedents that a body of administrative procedure and law evolves for any social program. Thus, social service personnel must be able to utilize the skills of lawyers in determining how policy goals can be effected through legal mechanisms such as appeals, rulings, and litigation.

Eighth Stage: Evaluation and Assessment

In a sense, the goals of social policy are ever receding. New programs create new expectations and needs and uncover additional unmet needs. Programs themselves become a major element in the "demand environment" of policy. For example, the passage of the Medicare bill has created the need for a vast increase in the number of nursing homes; this new need has given rise to many other questions of social policy regarding private agencies, standard-setting policies, and financial arrangements.

This stage requires an assessment of the impact of policy and an evaluation of how effectively the policy meets the problem. Actually it is the first stage all over again, for the process of policy formulation is ongoing and has neither a discreet beginning nor an end.

Implications for Casework

The model of the process should draw the attention of caseworkers to the series of roles professionals fill in the formulation of policy. Several gaps may exist. If professionally trained social workers are not prepared to undertake these tasks, their assignment will fall to other professionals who may not be fully able to represent the interests of the profession. Therefore, the profession must be concerned about whether educational preparation of professionals helps to build both a basic knowledge about the social policy formulation process and specialized training for roles that are not presently being filled (e.g., carrying out the legal tasks in policy formulation). Or, in the absence of professionals who can fill such roles, means of teaching the skills required to work co-operatively with other professionals must be devised.[19]

The past decade of ferment, change, and achievement in civil rights has exhilarated all people who are dedicated to serving others. As the country now enters a period of political reaction, social workers must develop knowledge by which to use their professional skills and must consciously capitalize on all that has been learned in these last years to participate actively in, illuminate, and enhance the policy formulation process in this revolutionary era.

Gordon Hamilton believed this was the difficult responsibility and the exciting challenge of casework:

> Political democracy and civil liberties must fight every inch of the way and one can expect no easier road for social welfare. . . .
> In short, everyone wants welfare until it is made clear what it means to socialize the inner drives and the real wants, to accept ourselves and not only our neighbors but those "outgroups" which comprise other nationalities, races, and classes.[20]

[19]The inability of many social workers and lawyers to communicate with each other is a good example of this kind of knowledge gap. See Homer W. Sloane, "Relationship of Law and Social Work," *Social Work*, Vol. 12, No. 1 (January 1967), pp. 86–93; and Paul E. Weinberger and Peggy J. Smith, "The Disposition of Child Neglect Cases Referred by Caseworkers to a Juvenile Court," *Child Welfare*, Vol. 45, No. 8 (October 1966), pp. 457–464.

[20]*Theory and Practice of Social Casework* (2d ed.; New York: Columbia University Press, 1951), p. 10.

Selected Bibliography

Chatterjie, Pranab, and Koleski, Raymond A., "The Concepts of Community Organization: A Review," *Social Work*, 15 (3), 1970, pp. 82–92. The concepts of community and community organization are examined in terms of their historical development and changes as reflected in the literature. Five approaches are presented to the concept of community, along with a working definition of community. The rapidly changing concept of community organization is analyzed on the basis of ideas of various theorists and activists.

Gil, David G., "A Systematic Approach to Social Policy Analysis," *Social Service Review*, 44(4), December 1970, pp. 411–426. A definition of social policy as a concept is discussed along with a proposed general framework for systematic analysis of specific social policies. The elements of social policy are identified in addition to key mechanisms through which social policies operate as well as the main tasks of policy analysis. A highly usable outline is included in the appendix.

Hunter, David R., "Social Action to Influence Institutional Change," *Social Casework,* 51(4), 1970, pp. 225–231. The scope and knowledge of social action to influence institutional change is viewed from a practical standpoint. Basic suggestions on proceeding with social action are reviewed in terms of appropriateness and concern with changes in basic and important problem areas rather than peripheral side issues.

Levine, Rachel A., "Consumer Participation in Planning and Evaluation of Mental Health Services," *Social Work,* 15(2), 1970, pp. 41–46. Underutilization and rejection of social agency services by hard-to-reach individuals and groups is examined in light of the absence of options open to them. Illustrations of their involvement in the choice of specific services and subsequent evaluation of the results indicate that they will accept and profit from these services.

Paull, Joseph E., "Social Action for a Different Decade," *Social Service Review,* 45(1), 1971, pp. 30–36. The dynamic developments of the decade provide the basis for viewing social action. It is not now a matter of whether social action is appropriate, but which strategy, including direct action, is best. Social action activities now include factors within the social work delivery system, with advocacy a major component in bringing about internal change.

Perlmutter, Felice, "A Theoretical Model of Social Agency Development," *Social Casework,* 50(8), October 1969, pp. 467–473. In order to understand and evaluate change, and determine the relevancy of social work effort to major social problems, a model of social agency development is presented that traces three stages of agency development from self-interest to professionalism to social interest.

Scheidlinger, Saul, and Sarcka, Anne, "A Mental Health Consultation-Education Program with Group Service Agencies in a Disadvantaged Community," *Community Mental Health Journal,* 5(2), 1969, pp. 164–171. In an attempt to achieve institutional change, attitude change of individual service providers, and promotion of new skills, a consultation-education program was initiated with community group service agencies. The approach included a planning body for administrators, a consultation service for individual and group problems, and training workshops for agency staff.

Thursz, Daniel, "The Arsenal of Social Action Strategies: Options for Social Workers," *Social Work* 16(1), 1971, pp. 27–34. Various social action strategies and ethical boundaries are presented to use in careful planning for attaining specific goals. Desire for social change must be translated into an action orientation with administrative rule-making or the election process as possible targets.

Wasserman, Harry, "The Professional Social Worker in a Bureaucracy," *Social Work,* 16(1), 1971, pp. 89–95. The dilemma a social worker faces in a public welfare bureaucracy between his professional self and the demands and constraints of the employing organization is examined. The bureaucratic manipulation, sense of powerlessness, and emotional and physical fatigue that workers encounter are discussed for their effect on how clients and their needs are viewed.

Weeks, Silas B., "Involving Citizens in Making Public Policy," *Journal of Extension,* 8(4): 1970, pp. 40–45. Facilitating effective citizen participation in public policy making and institutional change through small decision-making groups or committees is proposed. The factors contributing to reduced citizen involvement are identified along with general rules for reversing this trend.

6

Individual, Group, and Organizational Systems as Target

The *generalist approach* to social work practice has developed from the experiences of practitioners; these experiences have demonstrated that social conditions are a source of many of the stress conditions that bring clients to social welfare agencies. The stress condition may be due to some quality of the client's—say, blindness—that makes general social expectations unrealistic for his unique situation: society is geared to the sighted person. Or the values of the larger society—for example, the work ethic—create requirements that are similarly incongruent for segments of society—the unskilled and uneducated, mothers without husbands, etc. Institutional racism provides still another set of obstructing social conditions. In total, there is a multitude of similar sets of obstacles to social functioning for many segments of the population. In short, the private troubles of individual clients are often symptomatic of public issues.

This is not to suggest that private troubles be neglected in favor of an emphasis on public issues, for individuals are *the* major concern of social work practice and the enhancement of individual social functioning is *the* primary purpose of social work practice: symptoms of social obstacles to functioning must be attended to by the practitioner; individuals, singly and in groups, need assistance to cope with areas of dysfunctioning. The point is that alternative theoretical frameworks, such as systems theory, must be a part of—if not the base for—reconceptualizing practice theory. Clearly, practice theory must be more closely aligned with the realities of client situations, rather than with some preconceived notion about the way things are.

Thus, in the term "generalist approach," *approach* emphasizes a view that transcends current connotations of method. While "method" suggests a predetermined sequence of steps for diagnosing and solving problems of dysfunctioning, "approach" suggests flexibility in diagnosis and solution. This perspective represents a value position held by generalists, but the generalist perspective of a systemic relationship between the individual and his environment is also based on knowledge. There is also a belief that systems theories offer insights about these relationships that have yet to be fully explored.

One major thread runs through all of the articles in this chapter: the interlocking relationships between individuals and their larger environment. Systems theory is consistently the theoretical framework that most clearly permits the social worker to identify and understand these relationships and to choose actions by which to intervene in those relationships. Intervention in only one part of a network of relationships is shown to have little or no impact on client goals.

The preceding chapters described situations in which the obstacles to functioning were conditions that were either outside the client or inside the client or both. The premise of the generalist approach to social work practice is that a worker must intervene in all of the systems that are affecting a problem. Changing behaviors in one part of a system cannot be assumed to relieve any obstacles in its other parts. On the other hand, changes in one part of a system *may* have some effect on other parts. The effect—if any—is an unknown quantity unless an effort is made to influence the direction of that change. These factors must be taken into account as the client and worker plan interventive strategies.

Each article in this chapter uses one or more of the factors discussed above as a rationale for the generalist approach. Schneiderman notes that the social welfare system is, in reality, a subsystem of society and, as such, has been charged with three major objectives: system maintenance, system control, and system change. These objectives may be in conflict with the purpose of social work—enhanced social functioning, "a product of a transactional process between person-in-situations and not as an expression of the intrinsic properties or attributes of individual actors." The professional social worker must balance these potentially conflicting demands so that the target population's hopes and aspirations for social equity and justice are reconciled with society's need for security and order. The worker is the fulcrum of this balance.

Auerswald proposes an ecological systems approach as a theoretical framework for organizing social work practice theory. These terms "systems" and "ecology" reflect a way of thinking and a style of operation at the present time. That is, systems theories and ecological systems theories do not offer the social work practitioner prescriptive behaviors. These theoretical formulations do require the practitioner to think of interactions among various units in a system. They also suggest that no single professional discipline can cope with most problems that confront social workers. In short, the social work practitioner must examine a variety of factors that may impinge upon a given situation and consider alternative approaches for resolving these situations. The ecological systems approach, for example, emphasizes points at which systems come into contact with each other, which permits the use of any number of theoretical models for understanding interactional processes. A mechanism is then available for use as a bridge between various disciplines which may be working together on a given case. This approach requires a planning process that realistically determines with more clarity those areas in which the client (individual, family, group, organization) needs assistance to more effectively alter existing conditions.

Hoffman and Long present a case illustration of how professionals employ this ecological systems approach in an interventive effort. This case clearly illustrates many of the notions outlined in the General Introduction, and embodied in the case illustration included there. The worker begins with only the individual as a target. As the case progresses, the individual client, his immediate family, and several organizations are all at the same time targets of intervention. "How to redress an imbalance of power when dealing with disturbed people in poor families when the presence of powerful helpers is one of the factors contributing to the imbalance in the first place is the problem as it is conceived by a 'systems' worker."

The unique problems of families are the topic addressed by Riley, who describes family advocacy as a service designed to improve the conditions of people through a commitment to action which has changes within formal organizations in the geopolitical community as a major outcome. Advocacy is an integral part of the social work process in which a worker is seen to move freely from direct service with a client to interventions in other systems such as formal organizations that are influencing that direct work and then back to direct interventive efforts. Influencing those obstructing conditions then permits the client and worker to concentrate on enhancing client behaviors.

In Taber's discussion of intervention strategies, the group becomes a medium for individual and system change when society's institutional values obstruct social functioning. An ecological systems approach delineates the interactions that have created such problems as poor self-concept and feelings of powerlessness. Successful completion of intervention strategies becomes a key to correcting these conditions. Tasks are related to an interlocking network of variables including a person, his immediate family, his community of reference, and the larger community (environmental system) within which he functions.

Fantl, along with Purcell and Specht, present situations in which a variety of strategies were pursued to make a social welfare system more responsive to the population it was designed to serve. In both articles, formal organizations are primary obstacles to functioning for the client/target populations. In each instance it is decided that it is fruitless to attempt to change client behaviors without effecting a major change in one or more formal organizations in the community to which these target populations are directly related. A network of interlocking relationships required the workers to intervene with all of these systems. To do otherwise is shown by Auerswald to be a waste of time and energy on the part of all systems whether they are directly or indirectly related to the client.

The conclusion seems clear. Interventive efforts must be predicated upon the generalist frame of reference, which is that the aspirations and level of commitment to the client must be served. Otherwise one must reject Schneiderman's recognition of a need for balance in a system that is more concerned with system control than system change. Such an objective is inevitable if the enhancement of individual social functioning is accepted as the *purpose* of social work practice and if society's institutions and organizations are acting as barriers to the realization of that purpose.

The social work generalist carries the primary responsibility to assure that individual needs and aspirations are related to the resources for satisfying them. Schneiderman sees this responsibility as threefold: system maintenance, system control, and system change. The social work practitioner is obligated to maintain a balance among these three dimensions, with highest priority being to satisfy unmet client needs.

Social Welfare, Social Functioning, and Social Work: An Effort at Integration

Leonard Schneiderman

The goal of social work as a profession can be stated as the "enhancement of social functioning wherever the need for such enhancement is either *socially* or *individually* perceived."[1] To fully comprehend the goal of "enhancement" for both the *individual* and the supporting *society* one must see social work in the larger social welfare context of which it is *one* part.

The social welfare system is a sub-system of the larger society which sanctions and supports it. Social work's position within the social welfare system depends upon its capacity to perform specific functions, at acceptable levels of effectiveness and efficiency, which are seen as important to the achievement of system objectives. Efficiency and effectiveness are themselves variables which are dependent upon the changing levels of importance assigned to each system objective (the goal mix) at different times and places.[2]

I Social Welfare Objectives[3]

Social welfare is an organized activity that aims at helping towards a mutual adjustment of individuals and their social environment. (United Nations)[4]

Reprinted with permission of the author. Mimeographed, 1969.

[1]Boehm, Werner, *Objectives of the Social Work Curriculum of the Future,* Vol. I, Council on Social Work Education Curriculum Study, 1959.

[2]Schneiderman, Leonard, "Can A War On Poverty Be Won?", *Public Welfare,* April 1968.

[3]This section of the paper draws upon: Leslie, Gerald, *The Family in Social Context,* Oxford University Press, New York, 1967; *Services For People,* Report of the Task Force on Organization of Social Services, U.S. Department of Health, Education and Welfare, October 15, 1968; Grosser, Chas., "Changing Theory and Changing Practice," *Social Casework,* January 1969.

[4]*The Development of National Social Service Programs,* United Nations, 1960.

The welfare state is a modern democratic Western state in which the power of the state is deliberately used to modify the free play of economic and political forces in order to effect a redistribution of income. (Charles I. Schottland)[5]

Social welfare is a device for maintaining or strengthening the existing social structure of an industrial society. (Martin Wolins)[6]

Western society was driven to welfarism by the most powerful and stark of all motives: fear. It became evident early in our century that any government that rejected responsibility for the welfare of all its citizens would forfeit the loyalty of those whom it neglected. It was the overwhelming need to bribe the masses into remaining loyal—not sentimental idealism—that created the welfare state. In the last analysis, welfarism is a form of social Machiavellianism designed to prevent the population from being harried by insecurity, poverty, and despair, into the arms of Fascists or Communists. (Arthur Schlesinger, Jr.).[7]

About all we can suggest as a general principle is that a society must become a welfare state to the extent necessary to prevent disintegration and conflict over the question of distributive justice. (Wallace Petersen).[8]

The redistributive welfare state is not simply a mindless response to democratic pressures; it is a necessary condition of democratic stability, and its importance grows the closer a democratic society approaches its ideal of careers open to the talents. For precisely to the extent that a democracy opens opportunities to all comers and succeeds in making individual character, ability, and performance the key to social position and power, it makes life steadily harder for the underdog. Despite comforting illusions to the contrary, it is generally easier for men to bear defeat when they think they have been beaten unfairly. The sense that the world is unjust, like the belief in heaven, is enormously consoling. It allows men to keep their self-respect and to live in hope, and is probably a necessary condition for psychological survival. In consequence, if a successful democracy is to endure its good fortune, it must find ways of easing the exacerbated feelings of those who find themselves at the bottom of the pile. (Charles Frankel).[9]

Taken together these, and other comparable statements, suggest three major objectives for the social welfare system; i.e. system maintenance, system control, system change. These objectives are reflected in some degree in all social welfare programs. They are separable only artificially and for the reason of analysis.

A. For the purpose of this discussion *system maintenance* as an objective is taken to include preservation and perpetuation of existing societal norms and arrangements including those related to; (1) definition of the meaning and purpose of life; (2) motivation for individual and group survival; (3) norms for age-sex role performance; (4) norms related to the production and distribution of goods and services; (5) norms of conflict resolution, etc. In the social welfare system activity

---

[5]Chas. I. Schottland, editor, *The Welfare State,* Harper Torchbooks, 1967, (p. 10).
[6]Martin Wolins, "The Societal Functions of Social Welfare," *New Perspective,* Spring 1967.
[7]*The Welfare State,* op. cit. pp. 119, 120.
[8]*The Welfare State,* op. cit. p. 134.
[9]*The Welfare State,* op. cit. p. 210.

to achieve such an objective could include; (1) activities designed *to socialize* members to acceptable norms; (2) increasing *accessibility* to existing resources and opportunities through provision of information, advice and guidance (e.g. maximizing the utilization of existing resources by the *general population,* facilitating ad hoc transfers, etc.); (3) *compensation,* on a residual basis, for system deficiencies; (e.g. supplementing or replacing other social arrangements such as the family, the market place, the education system, the health system, etc.) while leaving basic social arrangements essentially unchanged. This activity includes compensatory fiscal policy to ensure maintenance of the overall economy (e.g. relief and social security payments whose objective is to increase purchasing power and spur the economy).

B. The objective of *system control* is to bring behavior which is out of conformity with, and seen as threatening to, existing societal norms, under effective control. Social welfare activity to achieve such a goal includes; (1) Intensification of the maintenance functions of *compensation, (re)-socialization,* and *accessibility* for population groups manifesting high levels of "deviant" behavior (e.g. youth and racial minority groups), in order to promote self-control (e.g. through meeting legitimate grievances, cooptation, coolingout, etc.); (2) Manipulation of legal procedures and restraints to promote external controls of "deviant" behavior, (e.g. the mentally ill and retarded, neglecting and abusive parents, suicide prevention, crime and delinquency, etc.); (3) Some combination of (1) and (2).[10]

C. The *system change* objective of the social welfare system is to promote change in the direction of increased system effectiveness for all members. The social welfare system attempts this by being an instrument for the removal of obstacles to; (1) fuller and more equitable participation in decision-making; fuller and more equitable distribution of resources; (3) fuller and more equitable access to the system's opportunity structure.

Some mix of all of these objectives is to be found in all social welfare programs.[11] The goal mix will vary through time depending upon the relative strength of each objective's constituency and the performance demands made upon the system by the larger society.[12] These objectives, this context, and the temporal variation in goal mix all have very

---

[10]Wineman and James make the point that a juridical principle is now evolving in the courts which asserts that "when government (society) deprives a person of his right to liberty, that person is entitled through constitutional protections to prompt treatment so that his chance to regain the freedom of community life is maximized." *Social Work,* April 1969, pp. 23–32.

[11]Economic security programs, community development programs, employment, mental health, family and child welfare, etc. all are directed to achieving maintenance, control and change goals.

[12]Spect, Harry, "Casework Practice and Social Policy Formulation," *Social Work,* January 1968, pp. 43, 44.

Social Welfare, Social Functioning, and Social Work　　　　　　　　**359**

obvious and very direct implications for social work practice. (Is social work a cause or a function? Is the social worker a therapist, policeman, or reformer? Such questions are not resolvable in terms purely internal to the profession.)

II Social Work—Social Functioning

The *connection* between social work's macro-concerns and obligations to the larger society and its micro-concerns and responsibilities to the welfare of individual persons is made through the concept of social functioning. The piece of the empirical world we call social functioning, (which constitutes social work's conceptual field of action), is understood to be represented by the total constellation of social roles through which persons participate in significant relationships. It includes also the total constellation of social, cultural, physical and psychological variables conditioning those relationships. The social functioning of any human being can be understood only in the context of the total personal and material situation into which his personality functions are integrated. Social functioning is viewed as a product of a transactional process between persons-in-situations and not as an expression of the intrinsic properties or attributes of individual actors.

The clearer conceptualization of these processes as a result of the incorporation of new insights from the social and behavioral sciences has necessitated serious reconsideration of the traditional organization of social work practice.

The notion that practice could be so conceptualized as to generate distinctive approaches to intervention with "individuals," "groups" and "communities" has come to be regarded as inconsistent with the greater theoretical clarity developed. One simply cannot comprehend the "individual" apart from the network of social roles he occupies. All social roles require the existence of one or more reciprocal roles with which the individual interacts in a complex transactional field. All social functioning, then, must concern itself with people in groups.

Roles exist at different levels of social and cultural meaning and at different levels of intensity when viewed in terms of their relative importance to the total psychic economy of the individual. What we have referred to as intervention at the "individual," "group" and "community" levels is perhaps more adequately understood as intervention into different, but closely interrelated, "role clusters."

"Individual" services have in the past concerned themselves primarily with those group involvements essentially unique to the person, such as his family role as father, husband, son, etc. and his interpersonal relationships to significant, but unique, others.

Intervention at the "group" level has involved that role cluster concerned with problem-focused identity roles, such as among the mentally ill, the aged, delinquents, alcoholics, drug users, etc. as well as with persons facing common maturational tasks, such as in work with specific age-sex groupings.

Intervention at the "community" level has concerned itself with the individual's position in the larger society, as citizen, as resident of a ghetto, as member of an ethnic, or racial grouping.

The point to be made here is that the logical consequence of our use of social functioning as a core organizing concept in practice theory is the conclusion that social workers are always involved in intervention at the group level and that no one of the three traditional methods is exclusively concerned with the "individual." The group worker's concern with individual participants in the group process, the community organizer's concern with the individual functioning of the committee chairman, the committee member, etc. are all cases in point.

Social functioning and social dysfunctioning are understood as expressions of an interaction between the *individual's* needs, aspirations and functional capacities on the one hand and *situational* expectations, opportunities and resources on the other. Social dysfunctioning implies an imbalance in this relationship. The enhancement of social functioning, that is, the establishment or re-establishment of a workable balance in the person-situation interaction may therefore be achieved by using any one of the following approaches:

1. Modification of functional capacity so as to bring it within the range of situational expectations, opportunities and resources; that is, helping the person to function more adequately within the limits imposed by his reality situation.

2. Modification of situational expectations, opportunities and resources so as to bring them within the range of individual functional capacity and need, that is, changing reality in a direction which promotes the well-being of people.

3. A combination of these two.

Achieving *balance* in the person-situation interaction is not in itself the ultimate goal of the social work profession. A qualitative consideration, introduced by the value commitments of the profession, mediates this process and determines the *goals* of professional intervention as well as its methodology. Social workers are not simply in the professional business of improving the adjustment of people to their reality situtations, though this may be one important and appropriate proximate goal in particular situations. No one ought to be permanently well-adjusted to such conditions as living in a slum, having inadequate supplies of food, clothing, shelter and medical care or being the victim of punitive, restrictive and unresponsive public policy. Such conditions are inherently dehumanizing and "pathological" and demand change. Such demands are, of course, not easily won and may lead to conflict.

Social workers are used to dealing with conflict. Conflict between individuals, members of families, between community groups are all common in practice. The profession's efforts at conflict resolution have been largely characterized by a very few basic assumptions. These assumptions have been built upon the proposition that conflict is a consequence of (1) inadequate understanding, (2) failure in communication, and, (3) apathy and disinterest on the part of the adversaries. It follows logically from such a conceptualization of conflict that if people can be helped to "understand" themselves and others, if they can be helped to "communicate" effectively and if "interest" and concern can be aroused and apathy overcome, then conflict will be largely resolved.[13]

Whether dealing with parent-child, or, marital relationships, or, with group relationships and community problems, the traditional operating principles in social work have been essentially the same. They are, (1) help people to understand themselves and others, educate them, help them to gain insight; (2) get them together to talk out their differences, organize a meeting or plan a family interview; and (3) arouse interest, arouse concern so that people will be aware of and motivated to address themselves to their problems.

We have learned, perhaps too slowly, that people who "know," that people who can "communicate," and that people who are "interested," do not always agree. While some conflict is explainable in these terms it is also true that what are often the most divisive, the most important, the most potentially malignant conflicts which confront the community are not the consequence of too little "understanding," or of ineffective "communication," or of inadequate "interest." They are, in fact, often conflicts between persons who are vitally interested, fully informed and able to communicate but whose life experience, whose world view, whose self-perception, whose fundamental value assumptions are so basically different as to lead to totally different evaluations of and sets of conclusions drawn from the same set of facts. This realization has required social work to move beyond the employment of practice methods designed exclusively to achieve consensus to the utilization of non-consensual forms of conflict resolution.

These non-consensual strategies of conflict resolution are based upon the confrontation of competing interests and the temporary setting aside

---

[13]Warren, Roland L., *Types of Purposive Social Change at the Community Level*, University Papers in Social Welfare, No. 11, Florence Heller Graduate School for Advanced Studies in Social Welfare, Brandeis University, 1965; Schneiderman, Leonard, *Political Functions of Social Work Practice*, School of Social Work, Ohio State University, Mimeographed, March 23, 1969.

of the desire for agreement in favor of a wish to prevail over, rather than to achieve agreement with, one's adversary. Such strategies of conflict resolution are commonplace in our society, in our courts, in our politics, in our organizational and group life. They are essential to the operation and stability of our society. They represent additional tools, needed by the profession, in order for it to participate more meaningfully in the resolution of contemporary social issues.[14]

III Social Work Functions

What models of the social-worker-in-action have been, or can be, defined to express the full range of the profession's societal functions?

What follows is an effort to respond to this question. All of the functional models described are inextricably bound together. They are not new. The reader will recognize that many of these are now performed by social workers and have been so for a very long time. Others have been talked about but less fully implemented; they stand in need of development and of substantially more supporting practice theory and skill. What is sought here is a full articulation of models of direct (as opposed to administrative) practice which may be employed in achieving professional objectives. The position taken is that much existing practice theory and much of our practice skill can be incorporated within the proposed models. What we know and have tested, if not in research, then through the trial and error selection processes of practice, is not to be discarded, but reformulated for greater clarity in a practice system which will at the same time open up additional opportunities for professional impact. It should be clear that the social welfare system includes many actors in addition to social workers. What follows is an effort to enumerate social work functions, only.

1. The Clinical Model
(Treating)

The goal of clinical practice is the restoration, maintenance or enhancement of adaptive capacity; facilitating optimal client *adjustment* to current social reality.

The goal is achieved through provision of services on an individual or group basis which provide emotional support, generated through an enabling relationship to the social worker (and group members); through support given to those strengths in perceptive, integrative and executive functions (understanding-insight, organization, skill, etc.), as

---

[14]Specht, Harry, "Disruptive Tactics," *Social Work,* April 1969, pp. 5–15.

well as to those material and relationship resources in the environment, which facilitate adjustment. Specific techniques include purposive listening, reassurance, persuasion, direct advice, teaching, guidance, suggestion, logical discussion and exercise of professional and/or legal authority.

Group participation may be employed to provide an experiential base for the restoration, maintenance or enhancement of client adaptive capacity. In clinical practice the "problem" to be worked, the "program" undertaken with groups, the "project" around which community effort is organized are all viewed as *instrumental* to the personal growth and development of participants. Successful change in social reality, as a consequence of the participation in group effort, is viewed as secondary to enhanced adaptive capacity achieved through personal change.

2. The Direct Provision Model
(Providing)

The goal of this model is the enhancement of client social functioning through the direct provision of material aid useful in eliminating or reducing situational deficiencies.

The model involves the *direct administration* of existing programs of material aid (e.g., income transfer, health care, housing, employment, training, family care, etc.). Such provision involves any one or all of the following activities: (1) case-by-case involvement of the client in the study and evaluation process (determination of need and of forms of need-meeting); (2) a determination of eligibility within the administering agency's terms of reference; (3) a judgement that the provision of the service or benefit will promote the client's best interest (that it will not have counter-productive consequences which might be overlooked by the untrained observer); (4) recruiting, selecting, training, supporting, collaborating with personnel offering direct care (e.g., homemakers, foster parents, adoptive parents, health personnel, trainers, day care workers, etc.).

3. The Mediator Model
(Mediating)

The goal in this model is the enhancement of social functioning through activity designed to bring persons with unmet needs and existing resources together. The point of departure for the model is the reality of a social service system that is now, and is likely to continue to be, characterized by multiple and often conflicting goals and a complex proliferation of services organized in a highly fragmented way. Negotiating the service system is a difficult and complicated task, frequently beyond the functional capacities of the average citizen, (especially so when functioning in an already stressful situation). Within the mediator model the social worker is concerned with the individualized needs of his client. His point of intervention is the representation of his client's needfulness to the agencies controlling needed resources.

The function performed is that of mediating the social distance between the client and the needed service or benefit (e.g., money, child care, substitute relationships, job training, etc.). He offers help to the individual in finding his way to the needed service, in obtaining the service, in protecting his rights, and in finding a response to his complaints. The mediator may lack any formal administrative relationship to agencies other than his own. The ultimate source of his authority in such cases may be his knowledge of the social welfare system, his knowledge of the client situation and the authority of the client's "right" to expect a response to his need. Mediating functions require a very substantial knowledge, skill and capacity to work within and between bureaucratic structures. In mediating the distance between his client and the social service system the worker's activity may range from the simple giving of information, facilitating communication, completing eligibility requirements and arousing agency interest in his client (consensual approaches) to the utilization of non-consensual strategies, such as, direct confrontation, administrative appeal, and the use of judicial and political systems, as appropriate. The mediator is the partisan advocate of his client's interest.[15]

The mediator function is, in an important sense, a conservative model of action since it represents an effort to maximize service delivery within existing social service structures. It may have some potential for broader institutional change as the cumulative impact of ad hoc adjustments in particular cases become systematized into more permanent revisions in the service delivery system.

4. The Change-Enabler Model
(Changing-Enabling)

The focus in this model is upon the motivation and mobilization of the client system itself for the purpose of achieving specific changes in social reality. This model is contrasted with the clinical model described above on the essential point that it is change in social reality which is

---

[15]The role of "mediator" defined here includes the "social broker" and "advocate" models discussed elsewhere in the literature (Briar, Grosser, etc). The position taken in this statement is that "social broker" and "advocate" tasks represent different aspects of the mediator's effort to bring people and needed resources together. "Social broker" and "advocate" tasks vary in their relative reliance upon consensual (developing understanding, communication and interest) and non-consensual (confrontation, adversary proceedings) strategies of action in extracting resources. As noted, the mediator role includes both. The term "advocacy" is used, with a different intended meaning, later in this paper.

sought, and which is primary, rather than growth in the adaptive capacity of participants. Such a distinction is, of course, artificial. Nothing is more therapeutic and growth enhancing than success. This model, however, intended to make a sharp distinction between functions performed with groups which are focused primarily upon situational change and those in which "program" is primarily the vehicle for the growth of member participants. Criteria for outcome evaluation will differ sharply in each case. While growth is inevitable in the process of enabling change to take place, the primary goal of this model is upon motivating and enabling change in some aspect of social reality defined by the client system itself as offensive and unacceptable. The gains reported in many of the "activist" programs developed in recent years have been measurable primarily in terms of the increased growth and development of participants. In this sense they are primarily clinical. This model focuses attention upon the full exercise of the rights and responsibilities of citizenship and upon the politicalization of the client role, including the utilization of a full range of consensual and non-consensual approaches to conflict resolution.[16]

5. The Documenting Model

By far the largest segment of social work practice is in the service of translating agency *programs* into *services* to people. Programs are designs of action to achieve socially sanctioned *policy* goals and purposes. The social goals and purposes to be achieved through program implementation are themselves incomprehensible except in the context of prevailing conceptualizations of the social problem to be solved.

Problem⇌policy⇌program⇌service form an interacting, interpenetrating system. Direct service practitioners most often comprehend the system best at the agency *program* level (child welfare, family service, probation and parole, mental hygiene, etc.). Given the program design they are employed to occupy a specific position within the agency organization. From that vantage point the service practitioner is in a position to undertake meaningful analysis of social welfare policies and programs.

This social work function is based upon the assumption that each client served, (in any agency program), in addition to presenting a completely unique constellation of factors, is also a member of a population group of persons with many common attributes and concerns. Each client contact is viewed, in this context, not only as an opportunity for service, but as an opportunity *to document* the present level of

---

[16]Miller, S.M. and Rein, M., "Change, Ferment and Ideology in the Social Services," *Proceeding of the Annual Meeting of the Council on Social Work Education,* 1965.

adequacy of existing policies and programs for such population groups (e.g., the unmarried mother, the delinquent, the unemployed, the dependent and neglected, etc.). The inadequacies in social welfare policies, programs, and services, which the social worker daily confronts in his practice, can be documented and reported to the larger community in terms of their consequences in the lives of persons directly involved.

The practitioner makes (documents) an accounting to the supporting community not only of direct *services* rendered, but also, of what he has learned from his experience about the present adequacy of *program* design, its feasibility and functional relationship to articulated *policy* goals, and the adequacy and implications of existing *problem* conceptualizations. The right of the supporting community to know, to be educated to a fuller comprehension of its needs and problems, cannot be met if practitioner experience is stored away in case-oriented agency files. Practitioners who have had the privilege of learning at first hand about the personal lives and experiences of their clientele exercise the professional obligation to use that experience and knowledge to stimulate corrective community action.[17]

If anything can be said to distinguish the problem-solving efforts of a professional person, it is that he does not stop his work upon the completion of direct service tasks; he takes responsibility to go beyond them; or sees to it that others do so, to translate the experiences gained into improvements in the services themselves and the policies of agency, community and nation that underlie them.[18]

6. The Analyzing–Planning Model

Going beyond the documenting tasks of the direct service practitioner, this social work function includes analysis of: (a) the prescriptive implications of the theoretical and value framework within which social problems are conceptualized, (b) the process of generating social policy goals (e.g., who are the problem definers, the interest articulators, etc.), (c) the feasibility of translating alternative program designs into services delivered, (d) the relatedness of program design to the goals sought, (e) the continued appropriateness of the goal and the anticipated consequences of its attainment, etc.

The analyst-planner needs also to study the distribution of social

[17]Schneiderman, Leonard, "A Social Action Model For The Social Work Practitioner," *Social Casework,* October 1965; and *A Case Illustration,* School of Social Work, Ohio State University, Mimeographed, December 6, 1965.
[18]Weissman, Irving, *Social Welfare Policy and Services in Social Work Education,* The Social Work Curriculum Study, Council on Social Work Education, New York, Vol. XII, 1959 (p. 57).

problems in the general community. He needs to call attention to the fact that the non-random distribution of problems within a population, (the existence of differential levels of vulnerability among persons of different races, social classes, social-physical environments, for example) suggests that etiological factors other than those common to all men are at work and need to be accounted for in the conceptualization of the problem and in planning the policies and programs which are to be generated to cope with it.

7. The Advocacy Model
(Advocating)

The advocacy model is based upon the notion that the social work profession, as an indentifiable, corporate entity, has vital professional commitments of its own. It is based upon the notion that the goal and purpose of social work, its guiding value system, the responsibilities which emanate from its knowledge of the human situation, necessitate that social work undertake the political task of attempting to influence *problem* definition, *policy* making and *program* development at the highest levels. This advocacy function is distinguished from the "change-enabler model" outlined above. There is a difference between *advocacy* and *enabling*. In the change enabler model the social worker is involved as a catalyst for action by others, for *enabling* the organization of client resources to find solutions to those problems of the social reality which clients have defined for themselves. The advocacy model involves something different, for it is not in the pursuit of goals *necessarily* enunciated by particular client systems, as such, that the social worker acts within the advocacy model. The point of departure in this model centers upon the vital interests and commitments of the social work profession itself which necessitate that it act, out of professional conviction, in its own behalf. These distinctions are important to make. It is as an "enabler" of group action and not as a "member" of the group that the social worker acts in the change-enabler model. Conversely, in advocacy it is as a member of the professional group itself that the social worker advocates and pursues change through both consensual and non-consensual approaches.[19]

Advocacy needs also to be distinguished from mediation. The advo-

---

[19]The N.A.S.W. Ad Hoc Committee on Advocacy distinguishes between two forms of advocacy: (1) "one that pleads the cause of another," and (2) "one who argues for, defends, maintains, or recommends a cause or a proposal." The second definition, according to the Committee, incorporates the political meaning ascribed to the word in which the interests of a class of people are represented; implicitly, the issues are universalistic rather than particularistic (p. 17). As used in this paper the term "advocacy" is reserved for the second definition. The concept as used in the first definition belongs to the "mediator" role. "The Social Worker as Advocate," Report of the N.A.S.W. Ad Hoc Committee on Advocacy, *Social Work,* April, 1969, pp. 16–22.

Individual, Group, and Organizational Systems as Target

cate seeks *change* in policies and programs. The mediator seeks optimum performance within *existing* policy and program commitments. The objectives sought are very different. The means employed to achieve change, and to extract services, may have much in common in their use of non-consensual strategies of action.

IV Conclusion

Some system of shared objectives is a prerequisite to the existence of any society. The *maintenance* of such a system, (and the norms which it generates), is essential for the provision of the social supports on which human beings are uniquely dependent for their survival and development.

The social welfare system (including social work as one component part) performs such a set of system maintenance functions. In social work practice these functions are founded upon the premise that human social functioning is a product of a person-situation exchange; that behavior cannot be comprehended except in the situational context in which it is manifest. The fundamental inseparability of individual and social systems leads directly to efforts to assure system maintenance through the channeling of behavior into acceptable norms of expression, and, to efforts to change existing social arrangements when they are responsible for obstructing personal growth and development.

System maintenance, control and change are all legitimate goals of professional practice. They are themselves interrelated and present in some degree in all social welfare activity. They are in tension with each other. That tension needs to be held in balance in order to assure a "goal mix" which balances recognition and response to the hopes and aspirations of the citizenry for equity and justice, and, society's need for security against disorder. Excessive concentration upon "maintenance-control" threatens the use of professional resources to perpetuate system inequities which freeze people into a rapidly solidifying social caste system and out of a full share in the larger society's opportunities and resources. Excessive concentration upon change from "what is," to an as yet defined future, runs the risk of so overwhelming existing institutional norms as to leave them replaceable only by an authoritarian system which equates power with morality.

The vertical axis on the accompanying grid represents an effort to enumerate social work functions which can be employed to achieve system maintenance, control, and change goals. There has been an extended and highly productive effort within the profession to define these functions. Much debate has taken place concerning the place of consensus and confrontation, individualized service and social change, in professional practice.

Relating Social Work Functions to Social Welfare Objectives—Practice Tasks

Social Welfare Objectives

		System Maintenance	System Control	System Change
Social Work Functions	Treating			
	Providing			
	Mediating			
	Change-Enabling			
	Documenting			
	Analyzing–Planning			
	Advocating			

Less well developed has been the problem of assuring balance (goal mix) in existing practice methods, (the horizontal axis on the accompanying grid). What, for example, is the system control potential of "change-enabling"? What is the system change potential of individualized clinical practice?

This last point deserves special attention because of the tendency to see individualized service as part of the profession's "conservative" past and to assume that meaningful change will come as individualized services decline in importance within the profession. The social change potential of individualized services may be suggested by several questions.

What, for example, is the place of the individualized service as a future counter-force to the bureaucratization and dehumanization of life in our schools, hospitals, government, factories, churches, labor unions, etc.? Will we need more or less individualized service?

What is to be the place of the individualized service in a society tending more and more to deal with people as categories rather than as persons, as students, the aged, the poor, the black, the establishment, the disabled, the welfare mother, etc. etc. etc.? Will we need more or less individualized service?

What of the need to respond to the individualized hurts of people; to recognize other people's humanity, and to express our own, by experiencing others at a very personal level of *caring?* Will we need more or less of such concern?

Social workers, it seems to me, must be in the forefront of advocacy for the extension of such social services and not join in the current tendency to lose sight of *persons* in *systems.*

Social work is part of the larger social welfare system. Its impact upon that larger system needs to be felt as it acts to achieve an effective balance in the social welfare system's overall output, and as it maintains good balance in the goal mix reflected in its own practice. To succeed in such a role will require that social workers have full awareness and understanding of the range and interrelatedness of all system objectives and skill in executing a wide range of professional functions.

Recent developments in systems theories now make it possible to look at human services from a systems theoretical framework. One school of thought, ecological systems, is presented here "as a way of thinking" rather than as a formal theoretical framework that is directly applicable to social work practice. A case example illustrates that this way of thinking leads to a style of operation that recognizes a variety of intersystemic relationships between individuals and their social systems.

Interdisciplinary versus Ecological Approach

Edgar H. Auerswald

The explosion of scientific knowledge and technology in the middle third of this century, and the effects of this explosion on the human condition, have posed a number of challenges for the behavioral sciences that most agree are yet to be met. The overriding challenge is, of course, the prevention of nuclear holocaust, but such problems as crime and delinquency, drug addiction, senseless violence, refractive learning problems, destructive prejudice, functional psychosis and the like follow close behind.

Practically all behavioral scientists agree that none of these problems can be solved within the framework of any single discipline. Most espouse a putting together of heads in the so-called "interdisciplinary approach." The notion is not new, of course. The "interdisciplinary team" has been around for some time. Some new notions have emanated from this head-banging, but there have been few startling revelations in the last decade or so.

However, a relatively small but growing group of behavioral scientists, most of whom have spent time in arenas in which the "interdisciplinary approach" is being used, have taken the seemingly radical position that the knowledge of the traditional disciplines as they now exist

Reprinted from *Family Process,* Vol. 7, No. 2, September 1968, pp. 202–215, with permission of The Family Institute and the author.

is relatively useless in the effort to find answers for these particular problems. Most of this group advocate a realignment of current knowledge and re-examination of human behavior within a unifying holistic model, that of ecological phenomenology. The implications of this departure are great. Once the model of ecology becomes the lattice-work upon which such a realignment of knowledge is hung, it is no longer possible to limit oneself to the behavioral sciences alone. The physical sciences, the biological sciences, in fact, all of science, must be included. Since the people who have been most concerned with constructing a model for a unified science and with the ingredients of the human ecological field have been the general systems theorists, the approach used by behavioral scientists who follow this trend is rapidly acquiring the label of the "systems approach," although a more appropriate label might be the "ecological systems approach."

These terms are currently being used metaphorically to describe a way of thinking and an operational style. They do not describe a well formed theoretical framework as does the term "general systems theory." It is with the former, the way of thinking and the operational style, that I am concerned in this paper.

The two approaches described above differ greatly. Let us examine why the difference is so profound. The ongoing accumulation of knowledge and its application to practice follows a well known sequence. This might be broken down into steps as follows: the collection of information or data, the ordering of that data within a selected framework, analysis of the data, synthesis of the results of analysis into hypotheses, the formulation of strategies and techniques (methodologies) to test the hypotheses, the construction of a delivery plan for use of these strategies and techniques, the implementation of the plan, and the collection of data from the arena of implementation to test its impact, which, of course, repeats the first step, and so on.

The key step in this sequence is the second one, the ordering of data within a selected framework, because it is this step, and this step alone, that gives structure to the rest, all of which are operational. Not only does the nature and outcome of subsequent steps depend on this structuring framework, but so does the prior step, the collection of data. What data among the infinite variety of available natural data are considered important, and are, therefore, collected in any given arena, will depend on the conceptual framework used. It is here that the difference between the two approaches is to be found.

The "interdisciplinary" approach maintains the vantage point of each contributor within his own discipline. While it has expanded the boundaries of the theoretical framework of each discipline to include concepts borrowed from other disciplines, only those concepts which pose no serious challenge or language difficulties are welcomed. More importantly, I think, the interfaces between the conceptual frameworks of different disciplines are ignored, and, as a result, the interfaces between the various arenas of systematic life operation (e.g., biological, psychological, social or individual, family, community) represented by different disciplines are also ignored.

The structural aspects and the clarity of context of the data collected are lost as a result. The precise source, pathway, and integrating functions of messages passing between various operational life arenas in the ecological field cannot be clearly identified. Analysis of such data depends almost entirely on the *content* of these messages, and much distortion can and does take place.

The "systems" approach, on the other hand, changes the vantage point of the data collector. It focuses precisely on the interfaces and communication processes taking place there. It begins with an analysis of the *structure* of the field, using the common structural and operational properties of systems as criteria for identifying the systems and sub-systems within it. And by tracing the communications within and between systems, it insists that the structure, sources, pathways, repository sites and integrative functions of messages become clear in addition to their content. In my opinion, this, plus the holistic non-exclusive nature of the approach, minimizes the dangers of excessive selectivity in the collection of data and allows for much more clarity in the contextual contributions to its analysis. And the steps which follow, including prescription and planning of strategies and techniques, gain in clarity and are more likely to be rooted in concrete realities.

There are some very practical advantages that accrue as a result of the above. At the level of *theory,* for example, the ecological systems model, by clarifying and emphasizing the interfaces between systems, allows for the use of a variety of theoretical models which have to do with interactional processes and information exchange. These models form bridges between the conceptual systems of single disciplines. Information theory, crisis theory, game theory, and general communications theory for example, represent some of the bodies of research and knowledge which become useable in an integrated way.

Knowledge that has been accumulating from the study of specific ecological systems, such as the family and small groups, the development of which lagged until recently because the systems did not fit neatly into the bailiwick of any one traditional discipline, can also be included without strain. And the developmental model of the life cycle of the individual man and of various larger human systems as they move through time in the ecological field of their environment assumes meaning in a larger context.

In addition, the use of this model in planning has demonstrated its many implications for the design and operational implementation of delivery systems, especially for community programs (e.g., "comprehensive community health" programs). The ecological systems approach insures that the entire process of planning for a community is rooted in the realities and needs of that community. The organized identification of the ecological systems making up a target community allows for the planned inclusion of information collection stations in each key system and at primary interfaces which provide feedback to the planning arena, thus setting up a servo-system which assures that planning will remain closely related to changing need. Over a period of time, as a picture of a target community emerges from such data, it will emerge as an idiosyncratic template of the structural and operational configurations of that community. It will not, as in the "interdisciplinary" approach, emerge as a predetermined template of the theoretical structure of the dominant discipline.

As a result, program designs constructed in this manner are deeply imbedded in the target community. They will develop as another ecological system among the many, thus greatly clarifying the context in which any program can be integrated into the life of the community as a whole. Furthermore, the delivery organization itself becomes viewed as a system with assigned tasks made up of sub-systems performing sub-tasks including intra-organizational tasks. This allows for more clarity in the selection of staffing patterns, in the definitions of staff role functions, in the construction of communication systems and data collection (record-keeping) systems, and of the assignment of tasks within the organizational structure to staff members best equipped to handle them. Of special import to community programs is the fact that with the clarification of specific tasks to be performed comes the increased possibility of identifying those tasks that can be carried out by staff members or volunteers who need relatively little training.

At the *operational* level the strategies of evolution and change can be more clearly designed. More important, perhaps, use of the ecological systems approach allows for the development of a whole new technology in the production of change. Many techniques have, as a matter of fact, already appeared on the scene, largely within organized movements aimed at integration in its broadest sense, such as the Civil Rights Movement and the "War On Poverty." Some community organization and community development programs, techniques using economic and political pressure, and techniques which change the rules of the game such as the non-violence movement, all represent a new technology, and all have their relevance to the broadly-defined health needs of socially isolated individuals, families, and groups.

In service programs working with individual people and families this new technology is also emerging, more slowly perhaps. Many new ways of coping with familiar situations are being developed. Techniques of treating families as systems, for example, represent one advance. In particular, an emphasis which stresses the organization of events in time and traces the movement of the developing infant-child-adolescent-adult-aged individual's degree of participation versus his isolation in relation to his family and to the flow of surrounding community life—such an emphasis makes it possible to determine with much more clarity in what life arenas the individual, the family, or a group of individuals needs assistance, and thus to more effectively combat the anomie and dehumanization characteristic of our age. The result is that the targets of therapeutic activity are much clearer and therapeutic work is more clearly focused on forces and situations that are truly etiological in a given problem situation. Techniques of producing therapeutic change can be brought to arenas much larger than the therapy room or even the home. I think that a single story will serve to illustrate more concretely what I mean.

In the story I wish to tell, two therapists, one a "systems" thinker, the other a member of an "interdisciplinary" team, became involved in the case of a runaway girl.

To give you some initial background, I should explain that I have been involved in designing and implementing a "Neighborhood Health Services System" for provision of comprehensive biopsychosocial care to a so-called "disadvantaged" community. The main aim in setting up this unit was to find ways to avoid the fragmentation of service delivery which occurs when a person's problem is defined as belonging primarily to himself, and he is sent to a specialist who is trained to deal primarily with that type of problem. The specialist naturally sees the problem not only as an individual matter, but defines it still further according to the professional sector he inhabits. He is not accustomed to looking at the total set of systems surrounding the individual with the symptom or to noticing the ways in which the symptom, the person, his family, and his community interlock, and he is often in the position of a man desperately trying to replace a fuse when it is the entire community power line that has broken down. Furthermore, the specialist's efforts to solve the problem are apt to be confined to arbitrarily chosen segments of time called "appointments." And finally, there is that unfortunate invention, the written referral, a process of buck-passing that sends many a person in trouble from agency to agency till he finally gives up or breaks down. As a beginning we decided that we would have to pilot some cases in order to gain some experience with the different approach we felt was needed.

At this point, a case providentially dramatizing the points we had in mind fell into our hands. (We have since found that almost every case that falls into our hands providentially dramatizes these points.) One of our psychiatrists was wandering about the neighborhood one day in order to become better acquainted with it and to explore what sort of crises and problems our neighborhood program must be prepared to serve beyond those we already anticipated. I should say here that this psychiatrist,[1] by virtue of several years of pioneering work with families, including the experimental use of game theory and games in diagnosing and treating them, was particularly well qualified to handle the situation I will describe. His explorations that day had brought him to the local police station, and while he was talking to the desk sergeant, a Puerto Rican woman arrived to report that her twelve year-old daughter, Maria, had run away from home. This was apparently not the first time. She described the child to the police, who alerted their patrols to look for her and assigned two men to investigate the neighborhood. Our psychiatrist, whom I will refer to from now on as our "explorer," was intrigued and decided to follow up the situation himself.

He first identified himself to the mother as she left the police station and asked if she would be willing to allow him to help her with her current difficulty. She agreed. He learned that she lived a few blocks away with her now absent daughter and another daughter, aged 14. Her own parents lived nearby, and she had a paramour who also lived in the neighborhood. The father of her two children had long since deserted his family, and she was uncertain as to his whereabouts. The exploring psychiatrist learned also that the runaway girl had been seeing a psychotherapist at the mental health clinic of a local settlement house. In addition, he ascertained the location of her school.

He then decided that his behavior might appear unethical to the child's therapist, so he proceeded to the mental health clinic, a clinic which prided itself on the use of the "interdisciplinary" team approach. The original therapist turned out to be a social worker of considerable accomplishment and experience, who agreed to cooperate with him in his investigation after he explained what he was up to and that he had the mother's permission. He read the child's case record and discussed the girl with the therapist at some length. He learned that at a recent team case conference, the diagnosis which was originally assigned to the girl, that of childhood schizophrenia, was confirmed. The team also decided that in the light of repeated episodes of running away from home, her behavior was creating sufficient danger to indicate that she be placed in a situation where that danger would be alleviated while her therapy continued. For a twelve year-old Puerto Rican girl in New York City, especially one carrying a label of schizophrenia, this almost always means hospitalization in the children's ward of a state hospital. Accordingly, the arrangement for her admission

[1]Dr. Robert Ravich. I am indebted to Dr. Ravich for the case material reported.

to the state hospital covering the district had been made and was due to be implemented within a few days.

The next stop for our explorer was the school, where Maria's teacher described her as a slow but steady learner, detached from most other children in the class, vague and strange, but somehow likeable. The guidance counselor reported an incident in which she had been discovered masturbating an older boy under the school auditorium stairs. This behavior had led the school authorities to contemplate suspending her, but since they knew her to be in treatment they decided to hold off, temporarily, at least.

The exploring psychiatrist also learned at the school that Maria was involved in an after-school group program at the settlement house. He returned there and got from the group worker a much more positive impression of the girl than he had previously encountered. She participated with seeming enthusiasm in the projects of the group and got along very well with the other children. The group worker, by way of providing evidence that Maria had much potential, showed the therapist a lovely and poignant poem she had contributed to a newspaper put out by the group. It was never ascertained whether the girl had written or copied the poem. She had, nevertheless, produced it, and there was general agreement that its theme of isolation was one which was expressive of her.

Back at Maria's home, our explorer talked to Maria's sister, who at first grudgingly, but then with some relish, admitted that she knew where the girl had gone during her previous runaway episodes. She was the sometime mascot of a group of teenage boys with whom she occasionally traveled for two or three days at a time. The sister did not know where she went or what she did during the junkets, but she suspected that sex was somehow involved. She also volunteered the information that neither she nor her mother had ever found it easy to communicate with her sister, and that if the therapist really wanted to talk to someone who knew her, he should talk to her grandfather. So off to the grandparents' apartment he went.

The grandmother turned out to be a tight-lipped, highly religious Pentecostalist who was at first unwilling to say much at all about the girl.

The grandfather, however, was a different kettle of fish. Earthy, ebullient, jocular, bright, though uneducated, his love for Maria was immediately apparent. He spoke of her warmly, and bemoaned the lack of understanding that existed in her home. Remembering a passing reference in the case record at the mental health clinic to a suspicion that the grandfather may have engaged in seductive play with the girl, if not open sexual activity, our explorer raised the issue of the girl's emerging adolescent sexuality. This brought an outburst from the hitherto silent grandmother that confirmed the mutually seductive quality of the grandfather's relationship with the girl, followed by a return blast from the grandfather who revealed that his wife had refused to sleep with him for several years. He readily admitted his frustrated sexuality and the fact that he was at times aroused by his budding granddaughter.

I have presented only a sparse picture of the rich amount of information collected by our explorer up to this point. In a continuous five hour effort, without seeing the absent Maria, he was able to construct a picture of her as a child who had grown up in relative isolation in a home where she received little support and guidance. Communication between herself and her mother had become more and more sparse over the years, most likely because of efforts of her older sister to maintain her favored position in the home. She had turned to her grandfather, who, feeling frustrated and himself isolated in his own marriage, brought his sexually-tinged warmth willingly into a relationship of mutual affection with her. Furthermore, it seemed clear that with someone like the group worker who liked her and who, because the group was small, could spend time with her, Maria could respond with warmth and exhibit an intelligence that otherwise remained hidden. But, and this was, of course, speculative, the tools she perceived as useful in her search for a response from others would most likely be limited to infantile techniques of manipulation developed in early years prior to the need for verbal communication or, based on the relationship with the grandfather, some form of seduction where the currency of acceptance was sex. And, at the age of puberty, having been shut out of the female world of her mother and sister, she was using this currency full blast in the world of boys.

The next day our explorer talked again to the mother, who told him that the girl had been found by the police on the street and had been hospitalized at a large city hospital on the adolescent psychiatric ward. Before visiting her, he briefly questioned the mother about her paramour. It turned out that the subject of marriage had come up between the two of them, but because he earned a limited income, both he and the mother had decided against living together or getting married. Either action would result in loss of the support the mother was receiving from the Department of Welfare for herself and her two children.

All that had been predicted the day before was corroborated when our explorer visited the girl in the hospital. Her behavior with him, and, as it turned out with the resident physician on the ward, alternated between childish manipulation and seductive behavior of a degree which appeared bizarre in a 12 year-old. But she was, at the same time, a lithely attractive girl with a lively wit which blossomed once she felt understood. She was ambivalent about the alternatives of going home or of going to a state hospital, mildly resisting both.

Our exploring psychiatrist then returned to the mental health clinic to discuss what he had observed with the child's therapist and the consulting psychiatrist. He suggested a plan of action as an alternative to hospitalization. By targeting on key issues in various systems surrounding this child, it seemed theoretically plausible that the conditions which held her fixed in a pattern of behavior that had been labeled as sick and crazy might be changed, thus freeing her to accept new coping patterns which she could be helped to learn. An effort to re-establish communication between the child and her mother, who had shown with her other daughter that she could raise a child with relative success, would be one step. It might not be feasible to work with the grandparents' unsatisfactory marriage, but an explanation to the grandfather, who had already tentatively understood his contribution to the girl's dilemma, might be useful. If the Department of Welfare were willing, and if the boyfriend's income could be enhanced by at least a little supplementary public assistance, the mother and her boyfriend might be induced to marry. Teacher and guidance counselor could be helped to understand the girl's behavior more fully and might cooperate on a plan for helping the girl learn new ways of relating in school. The group worker's investment in the girl could be used to a good effect in this joint effort to help her grow. And the original therapist, instead of concerning herself with defense systems and repressed conflict could concentrate on helping the family provide the maximum of support and guidance possible, or, if she wished, could still work with the girl herself. With these suggestions, our exploring psychiatrist bowed out.

A month later, a follow-up visit to the mother revealed that the girl had been sent to state hospital on the recommendation of the resident on the adolescent ward who agreed with the diagnosis and felt that, since she was "a schizophrenic," she should be in a hospital. No one had made any counter-move and contact between all of the helping people except the state hospital doctor and the girl's family had been terminated. This outcome had occurred *despite the fact that the mother and her boyfriend had, after a conversation stimulated by our therapist-explorer, presented themselves at the mental health clinic and expressed their willingness to marry if it seemed wise, their wish to have Maria come home, and their hope that someone at the clinic would help them learn what they must now do for her as parents.*

I have, I realize, presented an unusual situation. Reasonable question could be raised, I suppose, as to how often this sequence could occur. And my own bias is obvious in the manner of my presentation. But I think the case illustrates the radical difference between the two approaches under discussion. The approach of the therapist from the interdisciplinary clinic and that of our exploring psychiatrist are not merely two points on a continuum of techniques. The "ecological systems" approach literally changed the name of the game. By focusing on the nature of the transactions taking place between Maria and the identifiable systems that influenced her growth, it was possible for the "systems" psychiatrist to ascertain what strengths, lacks, and distortions existed at each interface. Two things happened when this was done.

The first was that Maria's behavior began to make sense as a healthy adaptation to a set of circumstances that did not allow her to develop more socially acceptable or better differentiated means of seeking a response to her needs as a developing child. Thus, the aura of pathology was immediately left behind.

The second was that the identification of lacks and distortions in the transactional arena of each interface automatically suggested what needed to be added or changed. Thus the tasks of the helping person were automatically defined. Rigidity of technique in accomplishing these tasks could not, under those circumstances, survive. Flexibility, ingenuity, and innovation were demanded.

The implications of what can happen if this approach is used universally are obvious. If proper data is kept, it seems inevitable that new clusters of data will occur to add to our knowledge, and a new technology of prevention and change develop.

The case of Maria has a certain uniqueness that separates it from most similar cases across our country. The uniqueness is not to be found in the "interdisciplinary" approach used, but rather in the quantity of skilled people who were trying to help her. Despite their dedicated efforts, all they managed to accomplish was Maria's removal from the only system that could be considered generic in terms of her growth and socialization—her family—and her removal from the school and community which should provide the additional experience she needed if she were to become a participant in the life of her society. In addition, they succeeded in stamping a label on the official records of her existence, a label which is a battleground of controversy among diagnosticians, but which means simply to the lay public that she is a nut.

By chance, Maria wound up in a mental hygiene clinic where her behavior was labeled as sick. She might just as easily have joined the many girls showing similar behavior who wind up in court and are labeled delinquent. Either label puts her in a category over which various members of "interdisciplinary" teams are in continued conflict. The needs of the girl, which are not clearly apparent, in either arena, become hopelessly obscured. Decisions made by those charged with the task of helping her are likely to be made without cognizance of those needs, since they depend for their outcome too often on the institutionalized procedures and momentary exigencies in the caring organization or person.

As a final point, let me explore the nature of the communications breakdown that occurred between the two therapists.

In his explorations, our "systems" psychiatrist collected a good deal of data that was not known to the "interdisciplinary" therapist and team in order to insure that he understood the operations that had been going on at each interface in which he was interested. This additional data only supplemented the data previously collected and agreed with it in content. Thus the two agreed substantially as long as they confined their communications to content and to inferred construction of the internal psychodynamics of the persons involved, Maria and the individual members of her family. And, as it happened, this was all they discussed until the exploring "systems" psychiatrist returned for a final chat. At that time, having ordered his data in such a way as to clarify the transactions which had been taking place at the interfaces between Maria and the various systems contributing to her growth, his suggestions flowed from a plan designed to affect those interfaces. The "interdisciplinary" team, including the original therapist, had not ordered the data in this way. Since the dominant disciplinary framework used in their arena was psychiatric, they had ordered the data around a nosological scheme for labeling illness. The outcome of their plan of action, therefore, was to apply a label signifying the nature of Maria's illness, and to decide, reasonably enough within this framework, that since treatment of her illness on an outpatient basis had not been successful, the next step was hospitalization, a decision backed by the assumption that her runaways were dangerous.

It was literally impossible, at the final meeting, for the suggestions of our "systems" therapist to have meaning to the "interdisciplinary" team. They fell on ears made deaf by a way of thinking which could not perceive them as meaningful. They came across as a dissonance which had to be screened out. Communication between the two approaches thus broke down completely.

This instance of breakdown is characteristic of efforts of communication between people from the two arenas. Conversations I have had with a variety of people who take the ecological systems view, backed by my own experience, seem to add up to the following:

There seems to be no serious problem of communication between the systems thinker who emphasizes structure and the experimental behavioral scientist who does basic research in his laboratory or even the researcher who is attempting to deal with a wide range of natural data. Such researchers have selected and defined the structure of the theoretical framework in which they wish to work and are the first to admit that the outcome of their research carries the label of validity within that framework alone.

The clinical scientist, whose emphasis is more on the content of his data, is for the most part a different animal. Most clinical theorists, planners, and practitioners, regardless of discipline, seem caught in the highly specialized sequence of their own training and intradisciplinary experience, upon which they seem to depend for the very definition of their personal identity. Generally speaking, a situation seems to exist in which the integration of the cognitive apparatus of the clinician is such as to exclude as a piece of relevant data the notion that his intradisciplinary "truths," which he carries to the interdisciplinary arena, are relative. He most often will hear and understand the notion when it is expressed. But, again speaking generally, he treats it as unimportant to his operations, as peripheral to the body of knowledge he invests with meaning. Why should this be?

I think it is because the clinician is a product of the specialized fragmentation of today's world of science. To him, admission of this fact would mean that he would have to rearrange his cognitive style, his professional way of life, and, all too often, his total life style as well, if he were to maintain a sense of his own integrity. Not only would he have to renounce his idols, but he would have to go through a turbulent period of disintegration and reintegration. He would have to be willing and able to tolerate the fragmentation of identity boundaries such a transition entails. He would have to leave the safety of seeming truths, truths he has used to maintain his sense of being in the right, his self-esteem, his sense of values, and his status in the vertical hierarchies of his society. He would have to give up the games he plays to maintain his hard-won position in his discipline, games such as those which consist of labeling persons from other schools of thought as bright but limited, misguided, or insufficiently analyzed. More often than not, he would rather fight than switch.

I imply, of course, that he should switch. Thus the question must reasonably be asked: Why should he? Why should he attempt such a fundamental change? After all, he can point with pride to the many accomplishments and successes of his discipline and his own work within it.

But to rest on his laurels, in my opinion, is to abdicate responsibility. It is like crowing over the 70% or so of juvenile delinquents who become law-abiding citizens, and ignoring the 30% who do not. The major responsibility of today's behavioral scientist is to those who don't or won't make it, not those who do, to Maria, not to Little Hans, whom he already knows how to help.

The least he can do is examine his labels and how he uses them. In the life-space of Maria's world, there is a serious question as to which system deserves the prefix, *schizo.*

The social welfare system was contrived for the express purpose of meeting the unmet needs of people in our society. Hoffman and Long relate a case illustration in which the actual functioning of this system creates a dysfunctional situation for a client. Then an ecological framework is used to illustrate an alternative approach that makes the system more responsive to client needs. Service delivery workers are shown to be as involved in policy changes as in the delivery of services to the client, and these two activities are seen to be interdependent.

A Systems Dilemma

Lynn Hoffman
Lorence Long

Introduction by Edgar H. Auerswald

The current shift of interest, reflected in public policy, from the production of goods to the provision of services, has caused a major re-examination of the nature of the services the individual can expect from his society. This re-examination is producing a number of insights, some of them shocking. In particular, we are learning that many of the systems we have created to deliver services are, in the name of "progress" and "civilization," contributing to the conditions of human distress they were designed to alleviate.

Much has been written lately about how service systems of one kind or another subvert their announced goals—how a welfare system perpetuates poverty, or how the medical profession creates iatrogenic illness. There has not been very much written, however, about how several systems inadvertently combine in their day to day operations in such a way as to frustrate each others' activities, and how, in so doing, they destroy in varying degrees the lives of people, or render it difficult for them to improve their lives. We have all been much too tightly locked in our own niches by training, experience, and various types of private interest to see this kind of interlock. It comes into sharp perspective only when one studies the problems of a single person in terms of his total life space, his "ecology."

This paper represents an effort to describe one such situation in a family as viewed from a community health

Reprinted from *Family Process,* Vol. 8, No. 2, 1969, pp. 211–234, with permission of The Family Institute and the authors.

services program designed to approach human crises as ecological phenomena, and to explore and respond to them within this framework. We have found that the best way to organize our view of the environmental field people move in is according to the diverse systems which make it up, so we have labeled our theoretical base "ecological systems theory." (1) What is of particular interest to the behavioral scientist in the situation described is that neither individual nor family diagnosis, nor the contributions of the larger systems (in this case a housing system and a system of medical care) will, if viewed separately, explain the state of the man in question. Only when the contributions of all of these systems are made clear, and their interrelationships explored, do the origins of the phenomena described begin to emerge.

This study investigates the context of a man's breakdown. In the first part of the story, evidence about the social systems in which he moved will be presented, in order to trace out factors that may have contributed to his collapse. The second part describes an attempt to intervene in some of these systems in order to get him back on his feet. A single person is the focus of the study, but the entire ecological field—individual within family within wider social network—is the area under consideration.

A special interest of this paper has been to document the peculiar nature of communications in this area. These communications were characterized by dissonances, self-contradictions and confusions, and may be seen as part of the scapegoating process which pushes individuals and their families, especially if they are poor, into positions of increasing powerlessness.

Finally, the question will be asked: does this "systems" way of looking at individual dysfunction bring with it a different way of dealing with it, or is what we shall be describing merely traditional social work?

The central character of our story, Charles Johnson, is a fifty-two year old black man who worked for eleven years as a chef in a proprietary nursing home. His wife, Bernice, works in a home for brain-damaged children, and before he quit his job, they made enough to keep their 15 year old daughter, Lorna, in private school, and their 19 year old daughter Gail, in college. Mr. Johnson was brought to the attention of the social services department of a neighborhood health center on New York's lower East Side because of the following dilemma:

Mr. and Mrs. Johnson's combined income was above the limit for the low-income housing apartment which they had occupied for 17 years, and the New York City Housing Authority was trying to evict them. The neighborhood was in the throes of a severe housing shortage, so that there was little prospect of finding decent housing at a rent they could afford. Mr. Johnson had for some years been subject to dizzy spells, in addition to drinking a sizable amount of liquor each day, and twice he had fallen while at work. The second time, three years before, he was taken to Bellevue, and his wife was told he was an epileptic. He had been having dizzy spells more frequently in the past months, and this prompted the Housing Authority agent, who wished to help the Johnsons, to suggest that he get a statement from a doctor saying that the spells were serious enough to put his working future in doubt. This would allow him to quit work and collect disability payments, and at the same time, the family's income would be sufficiently reduced to enable them to stay on in their apartment.

Mr. Johnson agreed with the Housing agent that this might be the best thing to do, and his wife supported this opinion. Unfortunately, the drop in income would mean that the family could no longer continue to keep the two girls in school without extra financing. Quitting work would also seriously undermine Mr. Johnson's status both outside of and within his family, particularly in regard to his wife.

Mr. Johnson was thus in a peculiar situation. It is the type of situation in which a person is punished by the social system on one set of grounds for functioning and on another set of grounds for not functioning. Mr. Johnson is being a good husband and father and is obeying society's rules for upward mobility by providing for his family and by giving his children an education which will guarantee them more opportunities than he had. However, to continue to provide these opportunities, he must depend to some extent on government subsidies, such as low income housing. To keep this housing, he must now fulfill the requirements of being a poor person by reducing his income and lowering his ambitions. Thus he is caught. If he persists in being the model American father who works, he throws his family into the streets. If he gives up his job and accepts disability payments, he continues to provide for his family but at a cost of personal dignity and a diminution of hopes for his children. One is reminded of Gregory Bateson's classic image for paradoxical systems (applied here to the Russellian logical paradox):

A mechanical model of such an oscillating or paradoxical system may be of use to the reader. Such a model is the ordinary electric buzzer or house bell. This machine consists of an electro-magnet acting upon an armature (a light metal spring) through which the current which activates the magnet must pass. The armature is so placed that the circuit is broken whenever the magnet is active and causes the spring to bend. But the current is re-established by the relaxation of the spring when the magnet ceases to act. We may translate this system into logical propositions by labeling that position of the spring which closes the circuit as "yes"; and labeling the contrasting position which breaks the circuit as "no." The following pair of propositions can then be stated:

1. If the spring is in "yes," the circuit is closed and the electro-magnet operates; therefore the circuit must go to "no."

2. But if the spring is in "no," the magnet is not operating, and the spring must therefore go to "yes."

Thus the implications of "yes" involve "no"; and the implications of "no" involve "yes." The model illustrates precisely the Russellian paradox, inasmuch as the "yes" and "no" are each of them being applied at two levels of abstraction. In Proposition I, "yes" refers to position, while "no" refers to direction of change. The "no" to which "yes" is an answer is therefore not the same as the "no" which is an answer to "yes."

This matter of the paradoxes is here discussed at some length because it is impossible to go far in thinking about communication and codification without running into tangles of this type, and because similar tangles of levels of abstraction are common in the premises of human culture . . . and in psychiatric patients (2).

In studying paradoxical systems in human affairs, the usual emphasis has been on the conflicts between levels of messages exchanged by persons in ongoing relationships, mainly families (witness the large "double-bind" literature) (3). This is too narrow a view when one starts to look at lower class city families which, being poor, uneducated, isolated, and often from an alien culture, cannot go through the smallest life crisis without becoming encrusted with parent-like figures who represent the acculturation and controlling systems of the wider society. These systems seldom act collaboratively, and are more often than not in conflict with one another. As a result, a person may be caught in a paradoxical situation in a family which is in turn caught in paradoxical situations within the systems designed to help the family or person.

It could also be observed that at this point in the history of American benevolence, helping institutions have begun to carry out a coercive function beneath a genuinely charitable intent (4). Our national welfare system has become notorious for legislation whose covert policy seems designed to break up or weaken poor families and place their members into self-perpetuating cycles of helplessness. Thus an attitude of benevolence is itself beginning to be a self-contradiction in many of our helping settings. If the proponents of the double-bind theory are right, in a situation where one party is extremely dependent on another, an action which is supposed to help the weaker party but has a punishing result can be particularly devastating.

With these thoughts in mind, it might be useful to frame our narrative in terms of the many contradictory messages (if not truly paradoxical in Bateson's double-level sense) received by Mr. Johnson from persons in various systems during the period after the Housing Agent suggested he stop work. Of course, one must not forget that the receiver of a message is also collaborating with, or even eliciting the message. In addition, our arbitrary picking out of particular messages is a reduction of what in real life is a much more complicated, many-messaged affair.

It was in mid-October, 1967, that the Housing Agent contacted the social services department of the Health Service for advice in locating a doctor who would certify Mr. Johnson too ill to work. A social worker was assigned to the case and talked to the Housing Agent about it. He then called the Johnson's home. Only Mrs. Johnson was in, but she was glad to speak to the worker. His case report states:

> Mrs. J. spoke anxiously of her husband's condition. She equated him with the brain-damaged children with whom she works. His drinking complicated the seizure problem, and it seemed to be getting worse. He had been missing work more lately. Worker arranged for Mr. and Mrs. J. to meet with him.

The Housing Agent and the wife were both contributing to the original dilemma, but for different reasons. Mrs. Johnson saw her husband heading for collapse, where the Housing Agent seemingly saw him as capable of working, but in a position where the best strategy would be for him to opt out, claiming the "seizures" as an excuse.

The social worker now met with the couple together for the first time. His impression was of the well-known team: "dominating" wife and "passive" husband. During the interview, the wife took over as spokesman for the husband. The matter of what to do in relation to the eviction threat was discussed, with Mr. Johnson saying that he had thought of quitting his job so as to bring the income level down. Mrs. Johnson then suggested that she could quit instead. The worker asked them how they would decide who should quit work, and remarked later in his notes: "There seemed to be no answer." Mr. Johnson next turned the subject to his dizzy spells and how they affected his working. The worker asked him to tell the full story of his illness to the doctor the Housing Agent had arranged for him to see at the Health Service, because the medical opinion could help to stave off the impending eviction. He stressed that Mr. Johnson should tell his own story, not let his wife tell it for him.

At this point, Mr. Johnson took his leave, explaining that he had to baby-sit for their pre-school youngest daughter, Maureen. After her husband had gone, Mrs. Johnson again expressed anxiety about his "seizures" and his increased drinking, and said that he slept most of the time when he was at home. She preferred his sleeping, because when he was awake, he would often explode over nothing, and his "grouchiness," as she termed this behavior, was hard to take. Sometimes he would even try to hit her, but she claimed she was the stronger and got the better of him in any physical fight. Thus the message from Mrs. Johnson seemed to be: stay at home and sleep and we'll have less trouble. On the other hand, it was Mrs. Johnson who was most committed to seeing that her daughters got a good education, and if this commitment were to be fulfilled, she could not afford to let her husband stay at home and sleep. There were contradictory aspects to her attitude too.

Up to now, Mr. Johnson had not talked very much for himself. However, during an interview with Mr. Johnson alone, just before the appointment with the doctor, the worker was able to uncover points of pride in Mr. Johnson's opinion of himself. He was proud of his skills as a cook and proud of his position of responsibility as supervisor of a large and busy kitchen where complicated diets for sick people had to be adhered to. He had held the same position for many years. He was naturally disheartened by the increased frequency of the dizzy spells and unnerved by the fear that one more "seizure" at work might cause him to be fired. Caught in the grip of a self-fulfilling prophecy, in that his fear of having the seizures was part of what provoked them, Mr. Johnson would clearly be vulnerable to messages from others confirming these fears. As an example of Mr. Johnson's easily crumbled sense of personal rights and gloomy expectations, here is an excerpt from the worker's account of the interview:

Worker said, Your wife said the other day that you had had two seizures on the job, and that one more would mean the end of the job. Is that so?

Mr. J. said, Yes. Worker said, Who made that ruling? The insurance company? (Wife had previously mentioned the insurance company in that connection.) Mr. J. said, No, well, you see when I had the last seizure at work—when I had my head injury—as the Hospitals Department inspector was coming in the door, I was going out on a stretcher. My boss told me that the inspector said that one more seizure and he'd have to let me go.

Worker asked, Is that just the inspector's idea, or is that a ruling by the Department of Hospitals? Mr. J. said, I don't know. Worker asked, Exactly how did your boss tell it to you? Mr. J. said, He said the inspector said, if a man falls out like that, you can't keep him, can you?

Worker said, Would you like me to try to find out if there really is such a regulation, or if this was just an off-hand remark by the inspector? Mr. J. responded, I'd be delighted.

The next chapter of the story concerns Mr. Johnson's visit to the doctor. A new set of opinions now fell out, containing a new proliferation of contradictory meanings. Mr. Johnson had been coming to the Health Service since 1964 for physical complaints, and in the course of his first work-up, the doctor learned and noted down that he customarily drank up to a quart of liquor a day. A look at the medical chart reveals that the statement "chronic alcoholic" is written at the bottom of every subsequent entry in the chart, no matter which department in the clinic Mr. Johnson came to, or for what reason. In discussing his "drinking problem" with the social worker, Mr. Johnson said that he usually kept whiskey by him on the job, "because if I feel shaky, I take a drink and then I'm usually all right." However, Mr. Johnson's doctor had told him that "anyone who takes a drink before six o'clock in the evening is an alcoholic." The medical record converts this opinion into a disease syndrome by analogy with other biological diagnoses found in medical charts. Yet no doctor proposed a treatment plan. There is a confusion here between explicit moral disapproval of drinking on the one hand, and exoneration of alcoholism as a medical condition on the other. The opinion of it as a medical condition is kept in the chart and not made explicit.

This confusion reappears, with a new twist, in the encounter with the different doctor who examined Mr. Johnson at the time of the referral to the social service department. The worker had sent this doctor a long memo explaining the importance the medical opinion would have in regard to the family's housing. Initially, the worker had accepted the request from the Housing Agent: "Certify this man as unable to work." But the conversation with Mr. Johnson raised doubts in the worker's mind about the advisability of removing the support that work represented to him, and the memo reflected the worker's ambivalence. The following statement was issued by the doctor:

Apparently patient is a lazy, indifferent, passive immature, dependent, inadequate personality who cannot maintain a responsible position for any appreciable length of time. He prefers alcohol to anticonvulsive medications and indeed, at times, his convulsions may be merely "rum fits" or delirium tremens. Apparently the best that can be expected with this individual is that he can be productive on occasions as long as he is "mothered" by his wife and society. I would suggest that he not be moved from his present apartment since his present income is likely to vanish at any moment of stress.

The worker feared that his memo had sounded too protective to the doctor, and had called forth this anti-mothering response. He phoned Mr. Johnson, expecting him to be upset. On the contrary, Mr. Johnson said that his interview with the doctor had gone very well. The doctor had behaved in a kind and benevolent manner to him and had told him that he wouldn't have to worry about being moved after the Housing Authority read what he was going to write in his statement.

The worker then called the doctor, who said that he was only willing to sign a statement that Mr. Johnson was a chronic alcoholic. The worker called a lawyer at an anti-poverty agency, who told him that to show this diagnosis to the Housing Authority would not stop the family's eviction; on the contrary, it would ensure it. The worker then appealed to a doctor further up the clinic hierarchy, who issued a diagnosis of "chronic seizure disorder and labile hypertension," and stated that Mr. Johnson should be permitted to remain in his present apartment as the stress of moving at this time might prove harmful. The wording here was important, as it did not tie the Johnsons' continuing occupancy of their apartment to Mr. Johnson's decision about work.

The worker was just about to mail this statement to the Housing Authority when he learned that Mr. Johnson had just had a bad dizzy spell at work and had decided to quit for good. In view of his situation as we have described it, this event was not surprising. There were many conflicting pressures for and against his continuing to work, both within the circle of Mr. Johnson's immediate and daily relationships, and within the circle of helpers around the family. The explanation that a human being cannot continue to function under the strain of this kind of bell-buzzer fibrillation may be as reasonable a way to see his collapse as to trace it to a single aspect, whether this be a "dependent personality," a "dominating wife," the "over-mothering of society," or some mysterious physical condition such as "chronic seizure disorder."

Whatever its cause, Mr. Johnson's decision to quit his job, which occurred a little more than two weeks after the Housing Agent first called the Health Service, created a new configuration. Now, not loss of housing but a far more difficult loss to repair came into question: a man's loss of executive function and social place. In particular, a shift in the relationship between husband and wife had taken place, leaving the wife on top and the husband on the bottom. This shift had been hanging in the air for a long time, but it was only now, when the outer social systems finally got into the act, that it became sanctioned and fixed. Three doctors, a Housing Agent, Mrs. Johnson, Mr. Johnson, possibly his boss, and to some extent the case worker, all became implicated in a process which caused Mr. Johnson to accept, and/or provoke, a label of helplessness.

Now a two-fold job presented itself: first, to get Mr. Johnson out of the sick man's seat and back on his feet; second, while this was being attempted, to work out the changed economics of family life now that Mr. Johnson no longer contributed an income. This second task alone meant endless case work time that had to be devoted to dealing with a multitude of institutions and agencies. A list of these institutions will give an idea of the forest of helpers that had sprung up around the Johnson family: the Health Service, with its various departments; O.E.O. Legal Services; the Housing Authority; Mr. Johnson's union; the Veteran's Administration; Workmen's Compensation; a private loan company; All Saints Parish; Franklin Settlement; and Southern College.

Rather than describe in detail how the worker helped the Johnsons to deal with all these agencies, one single example will be presented: the raising of funds so that the oldest girl could finish the year at Southern College, where she was now a junior. Neither Gail nor Lorna were doing too well at school, and Mrs. Johnson said she had never tried to look for scholarship aid to Gail, "because my daughter is not the brightest person in the world." It seemed that Gail had been in a subdued struggle with her mother for some time. The main issue had become the low-status black college in the South that Gail had chosen to go to, which affronted the mother's school and social expectations for her. Two years before, the girl had begun to get migraine headaches, and the psychiatrist she saw commented to Mrs. Johnson that they might stem from the mother's feelings about Gail's college. The mother denied this, but the headaches stopped after this suggestion was made, and Gail was allowed to attend the college. The worker, sensing the importance of keeping Gail in school, offered to help Mrs. Johnson find a source of scholarship funds. What was done in the work around getting the scholarship was to build on the upward-bound motivation of Mrs. Johnson, which required her to keep her daughter in college at any price. The alternate current in Mrs. Johnson—let daughter fail and come back home to reconstitute an unhealthy family triangle—was strong, and all the more so because it was not recognized. Insight therapy was not particularly suited to this family and it seemed more logical to strengthen the conscious drive toward achievement by off-spring.

In order to give an idea of the number of fund-raising operations that took place over a two and a half month period between four persons and seven systems, a list is appended (see Appendix) telling what each of these transactions consisted of in chronological order. Multiply this sequence many times, and you begin to see how much time and energy of persons and agencies has to be poured into the vacuum left when even an unassuming cook like Mr. Johnson relinquishes his share of the social burden.

The last part of this story will describe what was done to reverse the machinery which had created an invalid out of Mr. Johnson. The worker had already been consulting with a psychiatrist at the Health Service about the case and now asked him to meet with Mr. and Mrs. Johnson. This psychiatrist looked at the situation through two sets of glasses: the medical one, which would support the assumption that Mr. Johnson suffered from some physical condition, epilepsy or alcoholism or some combination of both, and the "ecological" one, which would widen the focus of the investigation to include non-biological factors. What he found tended to support the hypothesis that social and environmental factors rather than purely physical ones were at work.

First of all, he discovered that ever since the "seizure" three years before, Mr. Johnson had been taking large dosages of Dilantin and Librium (tranquilizers) and Phenobarbital. It was only *after* this time that the dizzy spells began to manifest themselves. On seeking further medical advice, Mr. Johnson was told that they were preludes to seizures: "aura." Because of the dizzy spells, his dosages were increased. He was now constantly feeling dizzy and constantly terrified that another seizure was coming on. He found that a drink of whiskey would dispel the dizziness for a while, and gradually upped his liquor consumption to about a quart a day. The dizzy spells continued, now augmented by the large amounts of medication and the large amounts of drink. Further visits to doctors brought increased dosages of drugs which brought on more dizziness which prompted him to drink more. There was also some doubt as to the nature of Mr. Johnson's seizures. The psychiatrist summed up his opinion on the medical aspects of Mr. Johnson's condition thus:

In a review of the chart, and on careful questioning, I can find no evidence that Mr. Johnson has ever had a seizure since the first one that brought him to Bellevue. There is a notation that he had a couple of blackout spells which turn out, on questioning both Mr. Johnson and his wife, to be fainting spells, not seizures. These can be reasonably explained as resulting at least in part from the combination of sedative and anesthetic (alcoholic) drugs he was taking, as can his dizzy spells. His EEG is normal (slow, but this is compatible with sedation).

The psychiatrist pointed out to Mr. Johnson the possibility that far from helping him, the drugs were in part responsible for the dizzy spells. A few days later, an incident occurred which helped Mr. Johnson to see that he could do without medication. Mrs. Johnson interpreted a vague remark on the part of her husband, mistakenly as it turned out, as a suicide threat. She took away the store of medication he had amassed, fearing that he would overdose himself with pills. Mr. Johnson reported to the worker that while he was deprived of his usual medication, he had no serious dizzy spells.

At the same time, the psychiatrist looked at the family factors which might be contributing to Mr. Johnson's difficulties. He learned that the onset of Mr. Johnson's heavy drinking coincided with the birth of his youngest daughter, six years before, at which time his wife stopped having sex relations with him. His drinking was opposed by Mrs. Johnson until he had his second "seizure." After that, he was able to defend his drinking on the ground that it kept him from having his spells. At the same time, Mr. Johnson was accepting more and more the position of a sick and disabled one. This at least brought him concern from his wife. She also seemed to be more comfortable in a situation in which she held the reins.

The psychiatrist presented his over-all impression of the case as follows:

In my opinion, Mr. Johnson is a passive dependent man who has gradually accepted the role of an epileptic individual provided for him by those about him. There is no evidence that he is epileptic. He is an alcoholic. But even his alcoholism seems to be secondary to his sense of exclusion from his family resulting from his wife's sexual withdrawal and what seems to be a coalition of females (wife and three daughters) who find it easier for him to be powerless than to deal with him as the head of the household. Secondary gain is provided for him as the result of the actions of the Department of Public Housing and his wife's provision of mothering for her "sick" husband (child).

The psychiatrist recommended to Mr. Johnson's doctor that he withdraw all sedative drugs and suggested that the worker confront the family with the dynamics which were placing Mr. Johnson in the invalid role and work to re-establish Mr. Johnson's status as man of the house. He stressed particularly the need to get Mr. and Mrs. Johnson back together as a married pair.

At this point, a disagreement arose between the psychiatrist and the social worker. Acting on a cue from Mr. Johnson, who had said he wanted to get "dried out," the worker suggested that he be hospitalized for this purpose. This would also allow Mr. Johnson's physical condition to be assessed in a setting where his intake of both drugs and alcohol would be controlled. The psychiatrist argued that hospitalization might reinforce the label of invalid which was already hanging over Mr. Johnson's head. He also feared that a new set of medical authorities might pick up and re-affirm the old label of epileptic from Mr. Johnson's previous hospital record. For these reasons, he felt it would be best to hold off on hospitalization. Until, as will be seen, Mr. Johnson himself broke the stalemate, the worker continued to see the family every week, and the question of hospitalization remained open.

For the next two and a half months, an uneasy stasis prevailed in the family, perhaps related to the uneasy stasis between the psychiatrist and the worker, who still differed on the subject of hospitalization. Mr. Johnson lay around the house and continued to drink, and Mrs. Johnson complained to the worker about his drinking but continued to supply him with his daily allotment. Even though she also complained about the fact that Mr. Johnson's drinking cost her forty dollars a week, it was clear that she had a stake in keeping alive the idea that her husband needed to drink. Once, for instance, in the period just after Mr. Johnson had quit work, the worker called and was told by Mrs. Johnson that they had had a terrible weekend. Mr. Johnson had accidentally spilled the bottle of liquor she had bought him to last the weekend, and she had no money to replace it. She said he had been in great pain, which was hard on her too, as she couldn't bear to see him suffer. Also, he was difficult to handle when he couldn't get his liquor. During his next meeting with the couple, the worker asked Mr. Johnson about what had happened. Mr. Johnson said that he had knocked the bottle onto the kitchen floor. "I washed the kitchen floor with gin," he said. "I felt real bad about that." The worker asked, "How did you feel without your liquor?" Mr. Johnson said, "Lonely." Otherwise, he had apparently got through the weekend quite well.

Mrs. Johnson also preferred to have her husband stay at home, drinking or doped up, because she had less trouble keeping the upper hand. In a later interview with the worker, she said (the interview record is being quoted):

One thing that has been better since he's been home is that we've had fewer arguments. We used to argue all the time. My whole married life has been nothing but arguments. . . .

Worker asked, These arguments, who wins them—half and half, or do you win most, or does he? Mr. J. said quickly, She wins them all. Mrs. J. said, Well, there's never any agreement, so nobody wins. Worker said, But usually you do what you feel must be done, whatever happens about the argument. Mrs. J. said, Yes.

During this time, the worker kept pushing on a number of fronts, all designed to move the see-saw that had locked with Mrs. Johnson in the up position and Mr. Johnson in the down one. During an interview in mid-February, the see-saw started to loosen. Among other things, the worker was trying to get Mr. Johnson to think about going back to work. If he had part-time work, it would not affect his housing eligibility. Mr. Johnson countered by describing all the panicky feelings and dizziness he was getting whenever he ventured out. Mrs. Johnson moved in too, saying that work was out of the question until Mr. Johnson stopped drinking. Her fear was that Mr. Johnson would get a job, they would lose their housing, he would collapse, and they would then be left without sufficient income to pay for more expensive quarters. She brought up hospitalization again and said with some feeling that she would like to see progress. The worker said that in his opinion progress for Mr. Johnson was tied to two things: working and having sexual relations with his wife. The couple started talking about the difficulties they had in being intimate together, a subject which they were not accustomed to airing and which put the wife on the spot for a change. The worker put her on the spot again by bringing up her failure to register their youngest child for a Headstart program, an intention she had expressed in the first interview, months before. Of course, her not having done this meant that her husband, who was now at home all the time, was perpetually baby-sitting. Mrs. Johnson promised to try to register the child, but ended the meeting by complaining about her husband's growing resentment at having to baby-sit.

The meeting seemed to have broken some kind of dam. The next day, Mr. Johnson had another "seizure" as he went out to buy some liquor. He was taken to the Health Service, where a doctor gave him a prescription for sedative drugs and sent him home. The worker came to see him as soon as possible; he felt now that not talk but action was required, and pushed for hospitalization. Mr. Johnson seemed genuinely eager to go ahead. He said that he seemed to be going down the drain and he wanted to prevent that. Mrs. Johnson for the first time began to show signs of doubt about hospitalizing her husband, but the worker said that he would go ahead and make plans, because Mr. Johnson had said he was ready. The wife called the worker several days later and said that if Mr. Johnson did not stop drinking, she herself was going to have to quit work; she had come home that evening and found him asleep when he should have been taking care of the little girl. It was an interesting message: "I want my husband to stop drinking so that he can baby-sit for me better," but it seemed her way of supporting the decision to go ahead with hospitalization.

The worker now turned his efforts to finding a hospital which would allow the clinic some measure of control over Mr. Johnson's case. The hospital he found was satisfactory in this respect to the psychiatrist, who now supported the plan. However, the psychiatrist still wished to guard against the danger that the wife might interpret the move as a further proof that her husband was sick and thus offset any good it might do. Before Mr. Johnson went into the hospital, the psychiatrist had one more meeting with the couple. In it he pointed out that Mrs. Johnson, by supplying her husband with liquor, helped to incapacitate him, both as a breadwinner and a bed-partner. He was particularly concerned to expose the wife's share in the problems of the husband, which both preferred to define as belonging to the husband alone. He did this, not by telling the wife all the ways in which she was dominating or babying her husband, but by putting her on the other end of a fulcrum. If Mr. Johnson was willing to give up drinking, as well as the benefits of the invalid position, Mrs. Johnson must make some concessions which would prevent him from lapsing back and would help to restore his sense of worth as a husband and head of the house. This particularly meant sex, as the psychiatrist emphasized strongly.

In a subsequent interview with the worker, Mrs. Johnson said that she could understand why the psychiatrist had criticized her, but that she didn't give Mr. Johnson liquor to hurt him, only because it was easier for her when she did so. She thought he ought to be strong enough to resist it. She also brought up the question of sex, which the psychiatrist had pushed her on; she said she didn't want to seem uncooperative, but she could not promise to begin sleeping with Mr. Johnson because she didn't want to promise anything that was not going to happen. The worker said that it was not so much a matter of sleeping or not sleeping, but if she was going to work at keeping him a nonparticipant in family life, then this whole effort would be for nothing. If, on the other hand, Mr. Johnson was going to be helped to regain his place in the family, then they could work with his being hard to get along with. Mrs. Johnson seemingly got the point and agreed, but the worker did not feel her heart was in it.

The evening of Mr. Johnson's departure for the hospital did not go very smoothly. Mrs. Johnson kept postponing their leaving, even though Mr. Johnson and the worker, who was accompanying them, were anxious to get going. After an elaborate dinner, which the worker shared, Mr. Johnson got up just as coffee was being served and said that he was nervous and wanted to go. The worker got up with him and they began to put on their coats. Mrs. Johnson stopped them, saying to Mr. Johnson that it was not polite to drag people off before they had a chance to finish their coffee. Everybody sat down again until coffee was finished. Several other distractions were engineered by Mrs. Johnson, including the temporary loss of her house keys. The worker said later that he had expected some resistance on the wife's part but that he had not been prepared for such a dazzling display.

In the first days after Mr. Johnson came home from getting "dried out," he felt poorly, and his wife seemed especially remote and downcast. Efforts to plug him into Alcoholics Anonymous were not successful, and within a month he was back drinking again with his old cronies, who during his period of abstinence had begun to call him "The Preacher." However, he was much picked up in heart, was eating well for the first time in years, and had begun actively to look for work. The worker had to terminate the case at this point, after arranging for it to be taken over by another case worker. Subsequent developments were both hopeful and unhopeful.

On the unhopeful side, as Mr. Johnson began to act more self-assured, his wife was becoming more and more unhappy. At one point, she threatened to desert the family if Mr. Johnson did not stop drinking totally. There was a possibility that she might replace Mr. Johnson as the invalid; five years before she had been seeing a psychiatrist intensively, and had nearly been hospitalized at that time. However, she began to see the new social worker regularly, and this seemed to help her keep going.

Another unfortunate event was that the Housing Agent had expressed opposition to Mr. Johnson's working full-time again, telling him that if he did, the family would still have to leave their apartment. The original worker phoned the agent to check on this, and the agent, after trying to get him to agree that Mrs. Johnson was a terrible housekeeper (also grounds for ineligibility), said that it might be "more humane" to tell

Mr. Johnson that it was the end of the line as far as his ever working again was concerned, rather than let him get his hopes up. This was particularly discouraging from the worker's point of view. Even if some changes could be brought about in the family system, it was difficult to believe that much permanent good could be done when the systems outside the family remained so fixed.

However, Mr. Johnson turned the tables on those who had consigned him to the dust-bin. He found a summer job cooking for a camp. When he returned, the owner of the camp offered him another job in the city at a very good wage. His old employer was also asking him to come back, arranging for him to work in such a way that his income level would no longer be a problem. Mr. Johnson decided to accept the second alternative, but was faced with the task of turning down the first. The new social worker was prepared to do the task for Mr. Johnson, on the premise that it was so difficult that it might immobilize him and the downward spiral would begin all over again. But the next time Mr. Johnson came in, he told the worker that he had settled the matter himself and was already back at work.

The starring—and unexpected—development was that Gail, who had been doing marginally at college, was getting A's and B's at midterm. It would be encouraging to believe, and consistent with family theory, that the opening up of difficulties between husband and wife had the advantage of setting Gail free from the family triangle she seemed to have been caught in, thus allowing her to succeed on her own. It would also be encouraging to believe that the thirty operations described in the Appendix were not in vain.

This story has been told in some detail in order to show how an elaborate interplay of systems—social, familial, individual—contributed to the breakdown of a person, a breakdown which might otherwise seem to be the result of some disorganizing process within the person himself. We started with the paradoxical social situation, centering on housing, which Mr. Johnson was caught in. Peeling off this outer layer, we saw how the social dilemma was reflecting and reinforcing a long-standing marital dilemma which also contained contradictory elements, such as Mrs. Johnson objecting to her husband's drinking while supplying him with liquor. Getting down to the layer of biological health, we saw how the medical system was putting Mr. Johnson in another impossible position, mainly by giving him drugs which caused him to have dizzy spells for which it prescribed more drugs.

We also attempted to trace, through an analysis of recorded or observed communications between Mr. Johnson and the persons in the systems around him, the subtle ways in which a scapegoat is created. We saw that the communications were characterized by a confusion of benevolent/derogatory attitudes, intricately masked. There is no direct evidence that white persons in the helping agencies were influenced by the fact that Mr. Johnson was black, but some of their expressed attitudes resembled stereotyped white opinions about the "passive" or "shiftless" black male who is nevertheless treated in a kindly manner because he is not accountable. This study has not gone into the effect of national social issues, but the week that Mr. Johnson started drinking again was also the week that Dr. Martin Luther King was killed. How much the tensions sparked by this event were reflected in the life of any particular black family is open to conjecture, but this is another factor which cannot be pushed aside.

The Johnsons will probably continue to experience difficulties in their lives together. There is at least a hope that the oldest girl may continue to hold her own at college and get out of the vicious dependency cycles that have trapped her parents. The worker may also have prevented Mr. Johnson from getting fixed in the invalid position he was clearly headed for. It is equally possible that he will still fall back into that position, or that his wife or a daughter may have to fill a similar one.

Whatever its outcome, this case illustrates the breadth and complexity of the context the worker in a low-income area has to struggle with in his efforts to help an individual or a family. We began by saying that helping systems may inadvertently combine to cause harm to their mutual clients. If we have demonstrated that in at least one case this was so, then the question may properly be raised: How does one work in such a situation? And is this way of working, which we have here put into a "systems" framework, radically different from traditional or even newer models of social work? Our answer is yes, for reasons which we shall try to suggest below.

In working with the Johnsons, it was found necessary to add to individual or family "treatment" sessions, which are a standard part of social work procedure, a set of strategies directed toward the various systems which impinged on the family. The expectation for this approach was developed in the first home visit:

Worker said, You know, I haven't been sure that my role in this situation has been clear to you. People in our society have to deal with big organizations like the Housing Authority or the hospital. It's my job to see that they get what they need, and that they don't get stepped on or forgotten. . . . People can get pretty mad sometimes when they have to deal with the Housing Authority. Mrs. J. responded, Yes, you sure can. As a matter of fact, I understood that was what your role was.

The worker's role, as presented above, resembles in many ways the models of social casework involving systems intervention which Scott Briar calls "social broker" and "advocate" models (5). In these models, the worker becomes a super-authority who mediates between the family and the agencies, guiding his clients through the maze of services they are entitled to and fighting for their rights. In our story, the worker was attempting a very different kind of operation. Throughout his involvement, he found himself subverting the intrusions of the helping agencies into the family's life whenever these intrusions pushed the husband further into helplessness *vis à vis* the family, or the family further into helplessness *vis à vis* society. While attempting to equalize the skew in these concentric sets of relationships, the worker also tried not to become too much of an authority himself. Whenever he could, he turned the task of dealing with the agencies back to the family, using this tactic to resist becoming too omnipotent a figure in family affairs.

Why it is so important to attain an equity in the total balance of relationships—individual within family and family within society—is perhaps explained by Montague Ullman in his essay, "A Unifying Concept Linking Therapeutic and Community Process." Ullman has made an interesting bridge between a condition perceived as social: poverty, and a condition perceived as individual: mental illness, using the concept of power:

We are suggesting that poverty and mental illness are expressions of an inequity in power relationships. Poverty emerges as the material precipitate of an underlying insistent imbalance in economic opportunity, while neurosis may be defined as the internalized reflection of existing inequities in the day to day lives of people (6).

The writers would qualify Ullman's use of the term "power" by putting it in an ecological context. As an ecologist knows, if one species in an interdependent group becomes too successful—too powerful—it only invites its own demise. Power, in looking at such groupings, is a matter of total equilibration, not of strength of individual parts, because only when all parts are in balance, does each operate at an optimum level.

How to redress an imbalance of power when dealing with disturbed people in poor families *when the presence of powerful helpers is one of the factors contributing to the imbalance in the first place* is the problem as it is conceived by a "systems" worker. Specific tactics seem to fall naturally out of this way of putting the matter. Each intervention, the whole process in fact, serves a double purpose: a piece of help, a suggestion, or a task, is pursued not only for itself but because it also helps to equalize the balance of power in whatever arena is in question, or in several at once. For instance, if one looks at the Appendix, it will be clear that the worker initiated few of the contacts needed to raise the scholarship. Most of this work was done by Mrs. Johnson. Assigning this task to Mrs. Johnson was done not only to give her a chance to materially help her daughter, but to demonstrate her competence at a time when the family sessions, with their emphasis on re-establishing the husband's strength in relation to his wife, tended to plunge her into despair, and possibly into the same helpless state she was herself in five years before. It also, as explained above, prevented the worker from taking too much initiative.

This tack, applied to Mr. Johnson, was not quite so successful. He was given the task of applying to all the agencies which he thought might provide him with funds while he sank into dependency. In the visit described above, the worker tried to encourage him:

Mr. J. said that he intended to go over to the Veterans' office and the union today, but he had this dizzy spell. He didn't know if the Veterans' Aid applied. Worker said, It would be good to find that out. Mr. J. said, Would you want to find out about it? Worker said, Well, I really think it is better if people do for themselves where they can. Why don't you call tomorrow . . . and then Monday I'll check with you to see how far you have gone.

However, as Mr. Johnson went through the process of tackling these agencies—public welfare, the Veteran's Administration, and the like—it became clear that they took as much as they gave, especially the last symbol of a black man's financial independence (until recently): his insurance policy. The worker began to feel that this task was fatally untherapeutic for a man whose sense of worth he was trying to rebuild, even though he wanted to be sure that there would be some cushion in the event the worst happened. He took it upon himself to see that the demands of Workmen's Compensation were met, so that the family had funds to function with. But this taking over was done in the context of supporting Mr. Johnson in the family sessions, where a major goal was to reinforce his status as a husband and father.

Except for the contact with workmen's compensation and a few critical interventions to support Mrs. Johnson's scholarship efforts, the worker's own actions in regard to outer systems turned out to be mainly resistive. What he did was to block the confusing and doublebinding communications from social and medical authorities who insisted on placing Mr. Johnson in the invalid position. When the Housing Agent turned out to be extremely rigid in this regard, the worker blocked the agent's access to the medical system. The agent could not certify Mr. Johnson's helplessness without the medical system's cooperation. The worker would not return calls; he would deliver quite unsatisfactory written documents well beyond deadlines set by the agent. When it became necessary for the Johnsons to deal with the Housing Authority themselves, the worker referred them to a lawyer who specialized in housing matters.

The worker also had to frustrate his own system, the medical one, in its customary functioning. The psychiatrist had intervened directly with the physician to reverse the pattern of increasing Mr. Johnson's medication. This step had one consequence not reported in the body of this paper: when the doctor who had been prescribing the drugs saw Mr. Johnson again, he took the small reserve of pills Mr. Johnson had stored up against a panic and hurled them into a wastebasket. Fortunately, the worker was present and was able to support Mr. Johnson through this crisis. Nevertheless, such incidents underscore the need for training in greater skill in systems intervention. On this evidence, it seems that hell hath no fury like a helping system scorned.

The above discussion has highlighted some of the strategies that emerge when attempting to apply a "systems" approach to social work in poor communities. Perhaps the most obvious difference between traditional social work and the type of activity described herein is this: the more traditional model does not see the persons who are helpers of a given individual or family (and this includes the social worker himself) as part of the problem to be attacked. If reducing inequities of power within all the interlocking systems inhabited by a distressed person is the therapeutic task, the role of the helper is going to have to be re-cast. It will be increasingly harder to separate the specialist in "emotional" problems from the specialist in "community" problems. In fact, if these practitioners do not combine to produce a new type of helper, they may find themselves atrophied stubs on a form which has developed very different limbs.

For the time being, however, this form is still evolving. The worker in this study found himself doing combination-work for which there is as yet no training and only the beginnings of a theoretical base. Lacking this, it would seem best to present case stories such as this one in an interim attempt to document some of the perplexities the worker meets and has to deal with on this new frontier.

Appendix

Number of Operations Needed to Secure College Assistance Funds for Miss J., Nov. 28, 1967 to Feb. 12, 1968

a1. 11–28–67. Mrs. J. speaks to worker about problem of college assistance for daughter. Illness of Mr. J. has made it impossible for family to provide this money.

a2. 12–7–67. Worker calls Urban League for information. He is referred to College Assistance Program.

a3. Same date. Worker gives information to Mrs. J., who makes appointment with College Assistance Program for December 19. Persons in that office give her conflicting information about who to go to, but someone finally comes in and makes an appointment with the right person.

a4. 12–11–67. Mrs. J. calls Sam Arcaro, who used to work for Franklin Settlement House and who is in touch with a donor interested in Miss J.

a5. 12–12–67. Mr. J. and worker go to see Father Arcy at All Saints Parish. The family are members of that parish and Mr. J. is a well-known figure there.

a6. Same date. Fr. Arcy writes to President of Southern College, where Miss J. is a student. Fr. Arcy tells Mr. J. to get in touch with Mrs. Xavier, who is head of the Parish Scholarship Fund. Since Mr. J. and Mrs. Xavier have a feud going, the worker and the family decide that Mrs. J. might be the best one to approach her.

a7. The President of Southern College refers the matter to college loan officer, and writes Fr. Arcy to that effect.

a8. 12–18–67. Miss J. comes home from college. Worker talks with her; she is not particularly happy at school, but she wants to continue.

a9. 12–19–67. Miss J. and her mother go to College Assistance Program where she is given an application for a National Defense Loan.

a10. Same week. Miss J. goes to see Mr. Watson at Franklin Settlement.

a11. Same week. Miss J. goes to see Sam Arcaro.

a12. Miss J. goes to see Fr. Arcy too. She is sick with the flu during the last part of her vacation, and does not follow up on any of these appointments.

a13. Miss J. returns to college in South Carolina.

a14. 1–4–68. Mrs. J. calls Mr. Watson, finds that he is waiting for Miss J. to return.

a15. 1–5–68. Mrs. J. goes to see Mr. Watson, who says that Franklin Settlement will help with some money, but cannot give the whole amount.

a16. Same date. Mrs. J. contacts Sam Arcaro, who says that Miss J. gave him the impression that she wanted to transfer when she talked with him. He will not act until this is clarified.

a17. Same date. Mrs. J. writes to Miss J. at college, asking her to contact Mr. Arcaro.

a18. 1–14–68. Mrs. J. has been trying to reach Mrs. Xavier for weeks. Finally she succeeds, only to learn that Mrs. Xavier only raises money, she does not dispense it. Mrs. J. is referred to the Diocesan Scholarship Fund, represented by Father Chipworth and Mrs. York.

a19. Week of 1–14–68. Worker calls Mrs. York and finds that Miss J. must apply herself. They only have limited funds and cannot give the whole amount.

a20. 1–22–68. Worker calls Miss J. in South Carolina, asking her to respond to Mr. Arcaro and the Diocesan Scholarship Committee. Miss J. is not in; worker does not reach her.

a21. Same date. A letter arrives from Miss J. She very much wants to live off-campus, and has made arrangements to do so; her mother approves. Miss J. thinks this will solve the problem of her unhappiness at school.

a22. 1-23-68. Worker calls Father Chipworth, a friend, who also knows the family. He agrees to give $300.

a23. 1-23-68 to 1-26-68. Mrs. J. makes a number of attempts to reach the college business manager to get a postponement of the date when fees are due. He is never in when she calls.

a24. 1-24-68. Miss J. calls worker two days after his call. Worker tells her that the log-jam has been broken.

a25. 1-28-68. Diocesan Scholarship Committee votes the $300 that Fr. Chipworth had promised.

a26. 1-30-68. Fr. Borden, pastor of All Saints Parish, writes the $300 check and sends it to Miss J. at college. He sends it to the dormitory, which instead of forwarding it to her new address, returns it to her home address in New York.

a27. Same date. Mrs. J. contacts Franklin Settlement, which immediately comes through with the remaining funds.

a28. Same date. Worker writes to college business manager for delay in fee due date.

a29. 2-2-68. Returned scholarship check sent by Mrs. J. to Miss J. Fees are now paid.

a30. 2-12-68. Worker receives letter from college business manager, dated February 9, granting delay in due date for fees. (See step 29.)

(During this period the worker had twelve family interviews with the parents, parts of which were spent working out the next step in the above process. However, the worker's main business during this time was related to the health of Mr. J., and other issues arising from that. Our society expects low income, sometimes disorganized families, under stress from illness and other factors, to negotiate a complex assortment of systems in order to survive. It is a remarkable achievement that the members of the Johnson family were able to play such a significant part in this particular issue of raising scholarship funds.)

References

1. Auerswald, E. H., "Interdisciplinary vs. Ecological Approach," *Family Process,* 7, 202–215, 1968.

2. Ruesch, J. and Bateson, G., *Communication; the Social Matrix of Psychiatry,* New York, Norton, 1951. Pp. 194–195.

3. Bateson, G., Jackson, D., Haley, J. and Weakland, J., "A Note on the Double Bind—1962," *Family Process,* 2, 154–161, 1963.

4. Keniston, K., "How Community Mental Health Stamped Out the Riots (1968–1978)," *Transaction,* July/August, 21–29, 1968.

5. Briar, S., "The Current Crisis in Social Casework," *Soc. Wrk. Practice,* 19–33, 1967.

6. Ullman, M., "A Unifying Concept Linking Therapeutic and Community Process," a speech presented at the American Psychiatric Association meeting in Detroit, May, 1967.

The advocacy function in social work practice has not
been clearly defined for the practitioner. One reason is
the potential conflict for the practitioner when his own
organization is not responsive to the needs of its consumer population. Riley adds some clarity to this issue
with a discussion of the advocacy function with respect
to work with families. Case examples illustrate how
worker advocacy activities can change organizational
policies and programs to make them more responsive to
family needs.

Family Advocacy: Case to Cause and Back to Case

Patrick V. Riley

The word "advocacy" has come rather recently into the everyday
vocabulary of social work. It has long been a working word and concept
in law. Dictionary definitions speak primarily of pleading the cause of
another. The concept of family advocacy as developed by the Family
Service Association of America and its member agencies is not limited
to pleading, and in the long run the cause is always our own, though
at first glance it often may seem to be that of others. Our definition
reflects the times—it is written on Corrasable Bond, not cast in concrete.
It is developmental, which means it changes as we learn. Here is the
way we are stating it today, and it is this definition on which the
discussion following is based:

Family advocacy is a service designed to improve life conditions for
people by harnessing direct and expert knowledge of family needs with
the commitment to action and the application of skills to produce
community change. It deals with institutional systems rather than with
individuals. Its purpose is to assure that the systems and institutions
bearing most on families work for those families, rather than against
them. Wherever possible, the advocacy planning and implementation
are carried through in an alliance with the persons and groups who may
benefit most immediately and most directly from achieving the goals
of that particular advocacy effort. As soon as possible, in those situations in which the agency initiated or provided the leadership for the
advocacy action, the leadership and decision-making power is transferred to these "consumer" groups.

Reprinted with permission of the Child Welfare League of America from *Child Welfare,* Vol. 50
(7), 1971, pp. 374–383.

Family advocacy service is needed by families at all socioeconomic levels, since it is concerned with provision of a humane social environment for all and is related to problems common to all. The problems may be in any institutionalized services and conditions, such as housing, employment, welfare, education, health care, abuse of legal and civil rights, and special problem areas such as drug usage and alcoholism. Priority for advocacy service should go to families, neighborhoods, and communities in the greatest jeopardy, which have suffered most acutely from the impact of racism, dehumanization, poverty, injustice and inequality of opportunity.

Roots of the Program

The Family Service Association of America officially launched its family advocacy program on October 10, 1969, with a memorandum and a working paper distributed to the 340 member agencies. The working paper contained concepts and descriptions of family advocacy that had been developed within family service at that time. It had not sprung full grown from the soot-stained, far-from-ivory tower that houses the national headquarters of FSAA in New York. Its roots were firmly implanted in work in progress at that time in several member agencies, and best articulated by Family Service Association of Nassau County, New York. FSAA did, in fact, observe an approach in practice in a member agency, found it good, developed it further, and attempted to spread it throughout the membership. The reaction was mixed and, like mixed drinks, fairly strong. From within and outside the membership of FSAA, some said that this was nothing new, that it was "old wine in new bottles." (We were and are prepared to argue that, though we believe the test should be not whether it is old wine in new bottles, but whether it is good wine.) The greatest reaction, however, was the concern that, in advocating advocacy for Family Service agencies, we were abandoning our stock in trade, the area of our competence and excellence, family casework. We had, apparently, failed to make clear our concept that family advocacy depends heavily on casework for its knowledge base, draws its greatest vitality from casework and other direct service programs, and facilitates casework and other direct services by removing external barriers. Although the situation is greatly different today from what it was then, an inferred threat of family advocacy to individualized services of family and children's casework is still perhaps the greatest barrier to the adoption of family advocacy programs in agencies that have considered themselves "casework agencies." Because this is true, the "case to cause and back to case" aspect of family advocacy deserves emphasis.

"Case to cause and back to case" describes the situation exactly. It is that simple. A helping person and a client coming together on a problem constitute the case. A condition in the community, external to the client, neither caused by him nor subject to his· control, is a contributing cause to the problem and a barrier to its resolution. In case-to-cause advocacy, the helping person and the client direct corrective attention to the external condition identified as a contributing cause. When that cause is corrected, the helping person and client can then return to the case, where the client's strengths and the helping person's skills can now be utilized more effectively. That's it: case to cause and back to case.

This is, of course, a skeletal description, pure and oversimplified. It will give rise immediately to many questions, probably prefaced with such words as "Yes, but—," and "What if—," and probably also the question, "What's new or different about that?" In anticipation of such questions, let us examine the concept further.

An Example of the Process

First, neither the helping person nor the client necessarily, though he may, participates in the corrective action other than bringing the "cause" to the attention of appropriate persons or organizations and providing testimony or documentation as needed. Second, the corrective action has as its goal systems change, so that the benefit is "permanent" and affects all future users of that system. Third, the helping process—casework, child placement, legal aid, homemaker or Big Brother service—need not actually come to a halt or recess while the advocacy action is under way. A few case-to-cause examples may be helpful.[1]

Mrs. A. did not appear for her 11 o'clock appointment one morning at Family Service. She telephoned at 2:30 to explain why. She had an 8 o'clock appointment that morning for her 4-year-old orthopedically handicapped son at the public child hospital outpatient department. She had arrived promptly at 8 with her son, accompanied also by her 2-year-old daughter. After standing in line a while to check in and to identify herself, she was told to have a seat and her name would be called. After perhaps another 45 minutes, her name was called and she was directed to another section of the hospital, where she again checked in and was again told to wait. The wait was even longer there, the children were increasingly restless and uncomfortable, and Mrs. A.'s 11 o'clock appointment at Family Service came and went. The children's lunchtime had also come and gone before mother and children completed the clinic visit. By the time Mrs. A. and the two small children reached home, it was approaching 2 o'clock, and all three were in a state of near hysteria.

[1]The following agencies furnished the examples used: Family and Children's Service of Denver; Family Service of the Cincinnati Area; Family and Children's Service of Greater Lynn, Massachusetts; Family Service Association of San Diego County, California; Sunbeam Home and Family Service of Oklahoma City; Family Service Society, Buffalo, N.Y.

How would most social agencies have responded to this situation, at least during the 1950s and most of the '60s? My guess is that the caseworker or perhaps a supervisor or administrator of the agency would have telephoned the Social Service Department of the public hospital, spoken to the medical social worker colleague, perhaps known personally to the agency social worker, and said something like, "For Pete's sake, can't you see that Mrs. A. is taken care of on her appointments without her and the children having to wait all day?" The medical social worker would have explained the clinic's operating policies and procedures, proving beyond the shadow of a doubt that there was no other way the clinic could function and still get its work done. The medical social worker would find some way, however, to see that Mrs. A. got special treatment on her next appointment.

Mrs. A. would have an easier experience at the clinic next time, and would no longer miss her casework appointments for this reason. The hospital and clinic system would continue to operate in the same way, with hundreds or thousands of other families having experiences similar to that from which Mrs. A. was now saved. She was saved by the desire of one social worker to do a favor for a colleague, or perhaps out of respect for the agency, or perhaps because of the wish of a sensitive and sympathetic social worker to help another human being. She was not saved because her cause was acknowledged to be just, or because of respect for her rights, her dignity, or her power. There was case-oriented advocacy here; it helped Mrs. A. temporarily, and was accomplished by coupling good intentions with the limited use of power—of individual social workers—a degree of power not possessed by Mrs. A. herself.

This hypothetical reconstruction is advanced as a reasonable description of what might have happened before in a "typical" agency. Let us look at how the same case-to-cause situation was actually handled last year by a Family and Children's agency with a family advocacy orientation and commitment. First, the caseworker described the problem to the supervisor and agency administration. Second, the hospital was contacted, in this case by the family advocate, though it might have been by an agency administrative staff member, community worker, or board member. The hospital confirmed that this was the way it operated, explained its reasons, and agreed to talk about the matter with representatives of Family Service and other agencies. Third, other agencies were contacted and the experience of the effects of their hospital policy was documented. Fourth, a meeting was arranged with representatives of agencies and those hospital staff members having the power to modify the system in question. Fifth, after learning the effects of their policies on the very families they were attempting to help, and being challenged to modify the system in order to serve families better at the relatively low cost of some inconvenience to themselves, the hospital initiated and carried through a thorough revision of its clinic scheduling processes. As a result of the dialogue process, other by-products also came about, including more effective use of volunteers in the hospital, and the way in which the hospital waiting areas were organized and furnished.

The effects of successful advocacy can extend far beyond the precipitating cause. In this case, for instance, the hospital is a teaching center. Fledgling physicians and other trainees were being taught that this type of disregard for the time and dignity of patients is the approved way to operate. Now they are getting a different message that may influence them throughout their careers.

The differences between the hypothetical reconstruction and the actual case are both obvious and profound. In the actual case, there was a system change so that all families affected by the system will benefit both now and in the future. Change came about primarily because of recognition that the institution's own policies and practices were defeating its own goal of service to people. The effect of power and the desire to avoid a confrontation or unpleasant incident, or the desire to cooperate or to appear cooperative with community agencies, may also have constituted some part of the motivation for change, but that is irrelevant once the change has come about in the presence of a motivating factor that enhances the stature and functioning of all concerned. A basic principle of advocacy is always to use the positives of documentation, explanation, persuasion and appeal to the sense of fair play and moral justice of the system or institution from which change is desired, and to give credit generously both where it is earned and where giving credit will help achieve further advocacy action. Being given the name can motivate the game. Much can be accomplished without the naked use of power, although the presence of power in the background, never mentioned but known to all, is always a tremendous catalyst to the achievement of objectives.

The Use of Power

Nearly everyone has more power than he utilizes or perhaps realizes. Power, like muscles, requires exercising in a planned, controlled way to realize its potential, and, like muscles, can also be overstrained and used up. There is power in social work and social agencies. It must be used, used judiciously, and not thrown around; to let it lie fallow in the face of the needs of those with less power would be a betrayal of our basic purposes.

Perhaps several other examples will demonstrate both the kind and the scope of advocacy. Every family agency has a number of youth in its caseloads who are actual or potential dropouts from high school and junior high. In many of these cases, the school system's policies of using suspension for discipline contributes to the dropout process. The youth who at best may be poorly connected with school and perhaps barely keeping up with or falling behind his classes, is given another shove down the dropout road when he is suspended from those same classes for from 3 days to 2 weeks at a time for smoking at the wrong time and place, fighting or scuffling in the hall, being insubordinate to faculty, or other behavior calling for some corrective measures. One agency, reporting on this subject, stated: "In our Community Council, a monthly gathering of all professionals working in the area, we have begun a study of the problem in concert with the public school department, who are keenly aware of the problem, and are doing their utmost, with severe limitations of staff and money. We hope in several sessions of our council meeting to evaluate a plan for *inschool* suspension, and improve services for truant children." The advocacy efforts here are to support the schools in the development of corrective measures that will advance the school's goal of education rather than defeat that goal. This is another principle of advocacy: help the system to see how its own purposes are being thwarted by its own policies and practices, and then support the system in developing alternatives that will enhance rather than inhibit achieving the system's own goals.

Another example involving the educational system is the following, reported directly from a family and children's agency.

A 13-year-old boy was brought to our agency for counseling. He had been a disrupting element at home and school for many years and was an underachiever. A study of his social history and symptomatology indicated perceptual problems as a major underlying problem. A referral was made to a medical, diagnostic and evaluation clinic, which confirmed that he had a visual perceptual problem and recommended family counseling along with special schooling. A series of conferences was held with school personnel to help them understand the boy's perceptual problem and distinguish it from his emotional overlay. The teachers and administration began to recognize that this boy could be helped if special schooling, not available at this time, could be provided. Further conferences were set up between experts and school personnel to help them see the need for an educationally handicapped program. These conferences played a major role in stimulating the school system to get an E. H. program started. This boy was recently placed in the E. H. program just prior to his 16th birthday.

The casework with him and his family becomes much more effective, having gone from case to cause and now back to case.

Other thumbnail case-to-cause examples are as follows:

Advocacy action taken by a family service agency to encourage and support an 18-year-old black girl in filing suit with the local Fair Employment Practices

Commission resulted in changing the long-standing, discriminatory hiring practices of a major public utility firm.

The family service agency contacted the Department of Agriculture in Washington to point out that a particular ruling involving bankruptcy filings penalized families who attempted to pay their debts and favored those who did not. The Department of Agriculture has acknowledged this inequity, and has indicated that an effort will be made to modify this ruling.

A family and children's agency has many cases of children whose needs indicate institutional placement in their home communities near their parents. After exhausting all possibilities, the agency is sometimes forced to refer the case to the state, and placement may be made in a state school as far as 200 miles from the child's home. Such cases led the agency to pursue and, in 1969, to achieve the passage by the state legislature of amendments to the state's Children's Code, authorizing the public agency to utilize voluntary agencies for the placement of children through purchase-of-service agreements. This was followed by promoting an active interest of the State Children's Association in furthering this program. As a result, it is now possible for many children in the future to receive appropriate placements near their families.

Local family service workers presented to their agency's Community Action Committee documented evidence that recent changes in public welfare, which had been labeled as "progressive," were presenting increased hardships to many AFDC families. The committee invited the local welfare rights organization to send representatives to share with them their experiences and ideas about improvement. To the surprise of most agency members, the welfare recipients gave top priority to the need for changed public attitudes. Said one: "We don't drive that welfare Cadillac you've heard about, and until politicians and newspapers start telling the truth, nothing can really be done to help the welfare situation." Through the influence of an agency board member, a top newspaper reporter was assigned to cover the next meeting, with both the welfare rights organization and the welfare department represented. A full report of this 2½-hour meeting made the local paper, with the welfare department director affirming and illustrating the ways in which the "welfare" is constantly maligned and misrepresented.

This example illustrates another advocacy principle: When there is a difference in your perception of where the problem is and where advocacy should focus as compared with the consumer group's perception, go with the consumer group's perception. In this case the agency identified public welfare policies and practices as the problem and the advocacy target; the welfare rights representatives "gave top priority to the need for changed public attitudes." The agency wisely accepted this modification of agenda. If the welfare policies and practices continue to be a problem for welfare clients, the agency and the clients will later aim their "advocacy by coalition" in that direction. The person wearing the shoe knows best where the shoe pinches first and most, and will direct corrective action there first. If the agency has identified a more basic cause it wishes to remedy, it will be more successful in eventually achieving its longer-range goal by focusing on where the client says the shoe is pinching now.

These few examples are taken from a large and growing file of examples accumulating from the work of FSAA agencies across the country. Their file of advocacy work indicates that the most common targets of family service advocacy are the systems involving education, public welfare, health, housing and employment. The actions range from seeking changes in operating policies and practices that can be readily achieved at the local level, to seeking to influence public attitudes, to seeking to change state or federal legislation or administrative policies.

Advocacy may also take the form of the establishment of program services either by the agency itself or, as a result of agency advocacy, by another community group or agency. The example previously cited that led to the development in the schools of a program for the educationally handicapped is an illustration. In another city, the family service agency received a petition signed by more than 300 community residents requesting agency services in support of their own efforts at community service. The residents and the agency together developed a neighborhood services program called "Neighbor Know How." Self-determination, self-help, agency skills and resources, and United Fund financing cooperated to produce an effective program.

Research Needed

This "service program" type of family advocacy is not new. Family service agencies historically have responded to unmet needs in the community, and often by establishing the needed services themselves, such as homemaker, day care and legal aid. Often as these services have grown, they have been spun off to form separate specialized agencies. It is ironical that today there is a strong and widespread move in the opposite direction; that is, to merge specialized service agencies with the family and children's agencies. The field suffers from this kind of pendulum swinging, and research as to the most effective organizational model is badly needed.

Whether "family advocacy" is new or just a new name for something old is of importance to some people. At FSAA we care far less about whether it is new than about whether it is effective. We do believe that it is new in its emphasis, in its focus on systems change, and in its increasingly systematized body of knowledge of theory and technique. We are proud that it is not totally new and are glad that it encompasses the best of family service and social work advocacy efforts over the years. Frances Brisbane, director of the FSAA Family Advocacy Department, has said: "In some instances, of course, to do more of an old thing could be to accelerate irrelevant action. If, for instance, one has the old social work technique of 'manipulating the environment' as a frame of reference, then advocacy is new, since the goal in advocacy is to make manipulating the environment less necessary."[2] The commonly held concept of "manipulating the environment," as illustrated in the "hypothetical reconstruction" cited earlier, leads a worker to call a worker in another institution and arrange for a personal favor. The result is often paternalistic treatment for a client, because the other worker respects "us," not the client. In advocacy, the request is made or demanded because the person(s) or family(ies) has a right to the service. The request or demand is made and carried through on a policy-making level. As a result, other people, known and unknown to our agencies, present and future, can and will benefit.

As mentioned earlier, not everyone or every agency has rushed to embrace family advocacy as a major program. There are a hundred reasons why it cannot be done by the agency, and a thousand reasons why it cannot be done by "me" as an individual staff member, whether practitioner or executive. To state that there are risks in implementing family advocacy is to state the obvious; to state that there are no risks in operating a community agency today on a status quo basis and without an advocacy function is to state the ridiculous.

The executive director of a family service agency that is in the forefront of advocacy practice faces his own anxiety directly. At a recent conference he said:

I can understand why people resist advocacy. Everything about it makes me nervous. I like my job; I want everybody to like me. Politicians scare me; reporters too. I never know what board members will do, even the conservatives. The conservatives are conservative on some issues and lead the charge on others. You often don't know whether your actions result in the changes produced; you just know that the changes took place. Then why do it? Because these things are in the way of families, they get in the way of trying to help families with their emotional problems; things like slum rent gouging, school expulsions, welfare practices. The family service agency is an observation post about family problems.

If this agency director, with all of his experience, know-how, and success in advocacy, is still nervous about it, maybe we will just have to learn to live with our nervousness. We can do this by realistically cataloging the risks, learning everything that can be learned about them, taking steps to minimize them without sacrificing the advocacy cause, and being aware of what the risk is in not risking. A section in the *FSAA Advocacy Manual* deals with risks this way.

There are some encouraging indications. Although we do not yet have hard, quantified data, accumulating experience is demonstrating that the most vigorous advocate agencies, those that risk the most, even

<hr>

[2]Frances Brisbane, "Advocacy and the Family Service Agency," paper presented at Advocacy Forum of Central Regional Council of FSAA, Toledo, 1970.

in controversial areas that bring criticism and even retaliation on the agency from some quarters, seem to be not only surviving, but growing stronger.

Some of the Problems

Advocacy can be painful for some of us and is probably threatening to most of us. Reaching out to and making common cause with people who are not but may seem to be unlike ourselves, extending our boundaries of concern, functioning as a community service rather than "just an agency within a community," are not without problems, both internally and externally. To retreat after one encounter with difficulty or rejection is a temptation. It gives the opportunity to take the position, "Well, we tried. This shows what we have been saying all along, that our efforts are not wanted, not appreciated, and we should stick with what we know best." We should expect some rebuffs when we enter an area of concern in which our action role is new, but in which others have been living and risking a long time. To retreat after one, two or three rebuffs would be irresponsible and misguided. We should expect to have to establish our credibility among those who have already done so. Those who want the role of being on the side of the poor and on the side of making systems work for all of our families now must put their words and commitments into action, or abandon the field to those who really do have the commitment. More and more these are the people themselves, those who need and use the services and the systems and are determined to make them work better for themselves. These people will regard those social agencies that hold themselves aloof from the gut problems because "that's not our function" as a part of the problem rather than a part of the solution. No matter how prestigious or high the quality of their service, these agencies will themselves become the targets of advocacy action, because they do not use the knowledge and power they have on an advocacy basis, and therefore help the problems to continue.

The Black Caucus of FSAA, which first confronted FSAA in 1969 and has been doing so constructively ever since, has said:

In 1969, it was a popular belief that "middle-class organizations" that had not been confronted as a strategy for change at least once were considered totally irrelevant and beyond repair by minorities and many middle-class whites. Everyone, including people that needed the service but could not consume it in the way it was delivered, was saying: "Social workers are plotting to pull out from the poor." A strong feeling for the Seventies was building up rapidly in 1969—"Dismantle the social work system and build one capable and willing to serve the needs of all families." Dr. Andrew Billingsley, the author of *Black Families in White America* and an active Black Caucus participant, said about the FSAA confrontation: "The little minor skirmishes that seemed like struggles last night in order to alter the simple format of the program were painful indeed for lots of people. Yet that is nothing compared to the pain, the agony, and the suffering that we all must still go through if we are to do what is required to turn this around, to make room particularly in this society for all people, for black people, brown people, and other people who have been traditionally put down by the domination of the white Anglo-European system."[3]

All of this is a part of the internal advocacy process that has been and is continuing to go on within FSAA. Advocacy, like charity, begins at home. It means seeing that one's own organization plans *with* people rather than just *for* them, and is sufficiently representative of groups to be served that planning with them is possible. It means changing by-laws, scrapping policies, changing procedures that are a part of the problem rather than a part of the solution. It means orienting the service delivery to the consumers in terms of time, place, type of service, type of staff and attitude. It means using what power we have. It may mean altering or holding in abeyance the agenda of the agency in order to begin with the agenda of its client group. But that is social work principle, too—begin where the client is.

Internal advocacy obviously has its own risks. Any agency uses its constituency, bylaws, procedures, and staff as it does because these meet someone's needs. If they meet the client's needs, the community's needs, no changes are necessary. Every organization, however, has institutionalized some aspects of its functioning. This comes about to make things easier for the agency, but often at the expense of clientele and community. Many institutionalized aspects of social agencies need changing today. Such change will be threatening to those whose needs are met by the existing system, to those whom the system protects, and to those who have grown comfortable with it. The board of directors will be split to some degree. Experience indicates, however, that the board will become more vital rather than less so, and the same will be true for staff. After all, being a participant is more exciting than being a spectator. And the exercise of power has its own attractions and compensations. One compensation is that compared to the tough, painful, self-involved process of internal advocacy, external advocacy can seem a breeze.

Advocacy Agency Needed

The 1970 White House Conference on Children stated as a major recommendation the "establishment of a child advocacy agency fi-

---

[3]Black Caucus of FSAA, "The Minority Point of View," mimeographed statement, March 1970, 3.

nanced by the federal government and other sources, with all ethnic, cultural, racial and sexual representation." This prompted editorial comment in *Social Casework,* in the January 1971 issue: "It is a sad commentary on our 'child-centered society' that 61 years after the first White House Conference on Children . . . such a recommendation must still be made."[4] The recent *Report of the Joint Commission on Mental Health of Children* calls for a nationwide network of child advocacy councils. This report says white racism is the major mental health problem of the nation. The *Report of the National Advisory Commission on Civil Disorders,* in March 1968, declared white racism a barrier to the achievement of the goals of a free, democratic society. Social work's Eveline Burns commented in 1965: "It will take the social work profession a long time to live down the unhappy fact that it was not they but the economists and political journalists who awoke the nation to the urgency of the poverty problem."[5]

Poverty, white racism, the unresponsiveness of society, and the need for advocacy with regard to these are the themes we have been hearing. Many of us have been confronted dramatically by eloquent spokesmen for welfare rights groups and ethnic minorities, and have been both castigated and challenged. We have been told that social work, not religion, is the modern-day opiate of the people; that social workers, by providing some bare level of ameliorative funds or services to ease ever so slightly the plight of the most visible victims of unjust systems, have aided those unjust systems to continue to work against people rather than for them. It is alleged that we social workers, while masquerading as friends and benefactors of our clientele, have been part and parcel of oppressive systems. With our oil cans of inadequate financial assistance and services, reluctantly provided, we are pictured as the lubricators of the machinery of an exploitative and inhumane society. We have allegedly quieted the squeaking wheels, greased the bearings, and let the machinery continue to roll on its own mindless and heartless course.

Such is the indictment heard from some quarters. Much of social work rejects it totally and angrily. Some of us social workers accept it as true about the rest of social work, excluding ourselves and our particular sector of the field. Some of us may accept it totally and spend the rest of our careers in unproductive breast beating. Some of us, perhaps with a few old scars as mementos of previous efforts to improve or change what should be people-serving systems, will nevertheless recognize enough of ourselves in this indictment to cause us to listen,

[4]Editorial, *Social Casework,* LII, No. 1 (1971), 45.
[5]Statement by Eveline Burns cited in Alex's Rosen's "A Social Work Practitioner to Meet New Challenges," in *Social Welfare Forum* (New York: Columbia University Press, 1963), 226–227.

to attempt to understand, and to learn. To the extent that we do learn, we reassess our goals and our methods in the light of today's society and today's problems. We pledge that we will never again be the oilers of dehumanizing machinery without making every effort, matching all our professional skill and know-how with an unswerving commitment, to change that dehumanizing machinery into genuine and effective people-serving systems. That's what advocacy is all about.

Taber describes the use of an ecological systems approach as a framework for efforts to deal with the pathology of black ghetto life. Two natural systems are intervened with—an adult social network and a teenage gang. The pathology is shown to be the outcome of transactions between the individual ghetto dweller and his social system.

A Systems Approach to the Delivery of Mental Health Services in Black Ghettos

Richard H. Taber

In our attempt to develop new and more effective models for the delivery of mental health services to children in a black lower socioeconomic community, we have found the concept of the ecological systems approach extremely useful. Using this model, we have explored the ecology of our community in order to define naturally occurring systems of support within the community—systems which, when utilized as a target for special types of intervention, could maximize the impact of our work.

This paper will focus on the rationale for our selection of two small natural groups: a partial social network composed primarily of mothers of highly disorganized families with young children, and a peer subsystem of 14–17-year-old boys. The ecological framework provided significant direction to our attempts to approach and work with these indigenous systems in such a way that members of the natural groups were given mental health services without being required to perceive themselves as patients.

The Rebound Children and Youth Project is jointly sponsored by the Children's Hospital of Philadelphia and the Philadelphia Child Guid-

Reprinted with permission of the American Orthopsychiatric Association from *American Journal of Orthopsychiatry,* Vol. 40 (4), 1970, pp. 702–709. Copyright © 1970, the American Orthopsychiatric Association.

ance Clinic. It is charged with providing comprehensive health, dental, mental health, and social services to children in the area adjacent to these two institutions.

The community is a black ghetto in which 47% of the families have incomes below $3,000 and "only 38% of the 1,131 children covered in our survey are growing up within an intact family unit."[5] The project enjoys a positive image in the neighborhood because of the involvement of the community in on-going planning and the sensitive work of indigenous community workers as well as the provision of much-needed pediatric services on a family basis.

We began this project with the view that many children in the black ghetto live with several pervasive mental health problems, primarily poor self-image and the concomitant sense of powerlessness. There are three ways of conceptualizing this problem. One is the individual psychological approach, which would identify early maternal deprivation as a primary cause. This factor can be identified in numerous cases we see clinically. Many children in this population have experienced early separation, abandonment, or maternal depression.

A second is the sociopolitical point of view, which directs attention to the systematic oppression and exploitation of this population by a predominantly white power structure. It also identifies historical and current influences which have undermined the family structure in the black ghetto and points to white racism as the source of black feelings of inferiority.

The ecological systems approach, the third way, directs our attention to the transactions and communications which take place between individual members of the poor black population and the systems within and outside of their neighborhood—that is, what actually goes on between the individual and his family, the individual and the extended family, the individual and the school, the individual and his job, the individual and the welfare agency, etc. Our exploration of these transactions, or "interfaces between systems," shows that most of the transactions which take place are degrading and demoralizing, and are experienced by the ghetto resident as "put downs."

When the problems of poor self-image and sense of powerlessness are approached from the concept of ecological systems, pathology is seen as the outcome of transactions between the individual and his surrounding social systems. Because no one element of these systems can be moved or amplified without affecting other elements, the ecological approach to the delivery of services requires exploration of the ways in which "the symptom, the person, his family and his community interlock."[2]

As an example, to plan effective services for a 15-year-old boy we must explore not only the boy as an individual but also what takes place at the interfaces between the boy, his family, the school, and other formal institutions and at the interface with peers, adults, and other representatives of the larger society. Chances are that his family expects little of him that is positive except that he stay out of trouble. He may often hear that he is expected to turn out to be a no-good bum like his father. At the interface with adults in the neighborhood he meets with open distrust and hostility. If he should wander out of the ghetto into a white area, his blackness, speech, and dress quickly cause him to be labeled as a hoodlum and treated with suspicion. He sees the police or "man" as a source of harassment and abuse rather than protection. If he is still in school he has become used to not being expected to learn.[3] He may not know that the curriculum was designed with someone else in mind, but he is certainly aware that his style of life and the style of learning and behavior expected in school do not mesh.[8] If he is in contact with a social or recreational agency, chances are that its program is designed to "keep him off the streets" and control his behavior. Competence is not expected from him and cannot be demonstrated by him. However, his peer system, usually a gang, does give him an opportunity to demonstrate competence. He is needed by the gang in its struggle to maintain "rep" and fighting strength. Gang membership offers him structure, a clear set of behavioral norms, a role and opportunity for status—all essential elements in the struggle toward identity. He is, however, then caught up in a system of gang wars and alliances which he has little or no control over, and which limits the availability of role models.

Adults in the ghetto neighborhood have similarly limited opportunities for self-definition as persons of worth and competence. For reasons which have been dealt with elsewhere,[6] a mother may not perceive herself as able to control her children's behavior outside of her immediate presence; yet she is expected to do so by a whole series of people representing systems within her neighborhood—her neighbors and relatives, the school, etc.—and outside her neighborhood—the attendance officer, the police, etc. Her transactions with people representing formal social agencies and other social systems are usually experienced as destructive. In the interface with welfare, legal, medical, and other services, she receives attitudinal messages which are critical or punitive or, at best, patronizing. If she goes for therapy or counseling in a traditional psychiatric setting, she must accept another dependency role —that of patient. One of the conditions of receiving such help is usually that she admit to a problem within herself. She may also perceive the therapist's interpretations of her behavior as robbing her of any expertise about herself. What may hurt her most are the verbal and nonverbal attacks she receives from moralistic neighbors.

One source to which she can turn for acceptance and support in dealing with personal and interfamilial crises is her social network of friends, relatives, and neighbors. An important function of the network is to offer her guidance in her contacts with external systems. A friend or relative may accompany her to an appointment. Often after an unsuccessful encounter at an interface, the group will offer sympathy from collective experience and suggestions for avoiding or coping with the system the next time the need arises.

Having identified the existence of these two social groups in our community (the social network and the gang), we began to wonder how to utilize our knowledge so as to intervene in these systems in a way that would maximize their natural mental health functions. Unlike members of an artificial group, members of a natural group have day-to-day contacts and ongoing significance in each others lives. The effects of therapeutic intervention in them should be able to transcend a one-hour-a-week interview and reverberate through the ongoing system. Also, intervention with natural community groups fits with our point of view that the answer to the problems of ghetto residents must come from the emergence of self-help groups within the community. Sources outside the community will never be willing or able to pour enough resources into the ghetto to solve the problems there. And our recognition of the value of local self-help organization brings us to a point of substantial agreement at the interface between our project and emerging black awareness and black nationalism.

We sought to work with natural systems without requiring that the people perceive themselves as patients. The intervenor sought to define his role as that of advisor, rather than leader or therapist. We felt that this model would prove most effective for the promotion of indigenous leadership and help establish the self-help system on a permanent basis. Through successful task completion, people would have concrete reason to see themselves as worthwhile and competent.

In order to avoid making people patients we chose to focus attention on transaction and communications at strategic interfaces rather than on individual problems. We find that this focus is more syntonic with the point of view of our target population, because members of the disorganized lower socioeconomic population tend to see behavior as predominantly influenced by external events and circumstances rather than intrapsychic phenomena.[5, 8]

One advantage of an approach which does not require that people perceive themselves as patients is that the natural group and the intervenor's involvement are visible. This increases the potential of the group for having an impact on other individuals and systems in the community. And the individual, far from being shamed because he is a patient, feels the pride of being publicly identified as a member of a group which enjoys a positive image in and outside the community.

The "C" Street Network

The social network we choose to work with was one of highly disorganized family units which had been observed in the course of an anthropological study of families in the neighborhood.[4] The families which formed the core of this network lived on "C" Street, a street which has a reputation in the neighborhood as a center of wild drinking, promiscuous sexual and homosexual behavior, the numbers racket and gambling.

The approach to the "C" Street network was planned by a project team which included a pediatrician and two indigenous community workers. Our plan was to seek to improve child-rearing practices and parent-child communication by raising the self-esteem and effectiveness of the parents. The indigenous community workers played a key role in introducing the mental health intervenor to members of the network and have played important ongoing roles as linking persons in the interface between network members and the white middle-class social worker.

Our approach to the system was through one couple in the network who in response to a survey question had indicated interest in participating in a discussion group on neighborhood problems. The worker introduced himself as a person interested in working with neighborhood discussion groups. It was agreed that such a group might be most effective if it were limited to people who knew each other well or who were related. Despite the expressions of interest by the network members, it was several weeks before the group began meeting formally. Before the members could trust the intervenor and before they could feel that meeting together might really accomplish something, it was necessary for the social worker to have many contacts with the members in their homes or on the street. In addition to discussions of members' ideas of what could be accomplished by meeting together, these contacts were social in nature, since it was necessary for the members to see the intervenor as a person who was sincerely interested and was not turned off by clutter, roaches, etc.

Initially we wanted to let the network define itself, but we were also committed to including the men of the community in our intervention program. Because of the sex role separation in this group, however, we had limited success in including men in formal group meetings, although the intervenor did have other contacts with the men in the network.

One critical step in the development of this program was that the network members, assisted by the community workers, needed to help the intervenor unlearn some of the anti-organizational principles of group therapy and to recognize the importance of ordered, structured communications. In other words, the group itself had to push "to stop running our mouths and get down to business." Once officers had been elected and rules had been developed for conducting meetings and a dues structure set up, the group became task-oriented. The format was that of an evening meeting in the home of one of the members, the formal business meeting followed by a social time during which refreshments including punch and beer are served. The first main areas of concern were more adequate and safer recreation for the children and improvements in housing. Through group and individual activity, houses were fixed up and the street beautified. Recreation for the children included children's parties and bus trips, planned and executed by the mothers, and the sponsorship of a play-street program.

One of the community workers is now working more closely with the group as the social worker begins to step back. The group plans to run its own play-street program this summer, as they are convinced that they can do a better job than the community house that ran it last year.

The Nobleteens

The other natural group which we began to intervene with was a subsystem of the local gang. The boys initially contacted were still in school, although far behind; they did not have major police records. The intervenor discussed with them the idea of getting together with other boys to discuss what it's like to grow up black in a ghetto community. They were asked to bring their friends.

Letters and personal reminders were used for the first several weeks. The intervenor was frequently out on the street, available for informal encounters. Unlike the adult network, where almost all our contacts have continued to be in the group's neighborhood, the boys have had their meetings in the clinic from the outset. They still stop by almost daily to see their advisor.

The initial 10-meeting program was focused on current relationships with school, police, and community, on vocation and the development of black pride and awareness, on sex and parenthood. Use was made of movies such as the "Lonely One" and "Nothing But a Man" and dramatizations of written material such as *Manchild in the Promised Land.*

At an early meeting of the group one of the more articulate members referred to the tape recorder and asked if this was to be like a study of ghetto youth. The intervenor said that that was not the purpose but that one project that the boys might be interested in would be to make tape recordings about life in the ghetto to educate "dumb white people." The group picked this up enthusiastically as an opportunity of showing people outside the neighborhood some of the positive things about themselves, since they thought that the papers usually talked about the bad things. The passive process of having discussions that were tape recorded turned into the active process of making tape recordings. From his position as a learner from a white middle-class background, the intervenor could ask questions and promote reflections. It became possible to highlight and underline examples of positive coping. The group became for the boys a place in which they could express the most positive aspects of themselves.

After the initial period, the group decided to become a club and the intervenor's role was then defined as that of advisor. (One of the club president's functions is to be a "go-between" between members and advisor.) The group structured itself and took a more active task focus —throwing dances, starting a basketball team, starting an odd-job service (which has since involved contracts to move furniture), writing articles for the Rebound Newsletter. Carrying on their "thing" about educating people outside their system, the boys made presentations to the staff and agency board of directors, spoke on a "soul" radio station, and wrote articles about themselves. Maximum use of these experiences was made by the intervenor in promoting recognition and development of individual assets and skills.

As a result, new opportunities for role experimentation and contact with role models has been made available to the boys. Through successful completion of tasks the group has won a "rep" in the neighborhood and gets positive reinforcement from adults. One development is that the Nobleteens have "quit the corner." As they became involved in the Nobleteens and began to see themselves as valuable people with futures, the boys spent less time hanging out with the gang and reduced their delinquent activities. This affected the fighting strength of the gang in the balance of power with other gangs, and so it challenged the Nobleteens' existence, beating up several members. The next day, a member of the gang happened to be stabbed, but when a runner came to enlist the Nobleteens for revenge, they refused to fight.

A black male community worker is now co-advisor to the Nobleteens. His focus with the group will be to further promote positive black identity through involvement in activities such as a Black Holiday marking the date of the assassination of Malcolm X. He will also be helping the boys take on a business venture of benefit to the community. The present intervenor hopes to develop a program in which a subgroup of the club will be hired as big brothers to younger boys who have been clinically identified as needing a relationship with an older black male.

The Role of the
Intervenor

Because the intervenor or advisor is in frequent contact with group members, often on a social basis, he enters into and can influence the social context on their behalf. He also stands in a unique position in the group in that he is conversant with external systems. He can therefore provide a linking function by bringing the systems together, promoting what is hopefully a growth-producing transaction for the group member and an educational one for the representative of the external systems. In terms of communication he can act as a translator for both sides. Because accommodation has taken place between him and the group members, he is better able to use their language, and they, his.

Several examples here may illuminate the therapeutic possibilities of the intervenor's role in the interface between the natural group and the external system.

Example 1:

In the first several months of the Nobleteens, Rick, a 14-year-old boy, visited as a guest, a cousin of a member. He was known by the nickname "Crazy" because of his impulsivity and lack of judgment. He impressed the worker as a depressed, nonverbal youngster. He then stopped coming.

During the summer the advisor was approached by Rick's mother to act as a character witness. Rick had been arrested for breaking into a parking meter and she was panicky because he had already been sent away once. The advisor talked with Rick while they cleaned paint brushes. Rick convinced the advisor that he really didn't want to be sent away again and the advisor convinced Rick that it wasn't going to be as easy to stay out of trouble as Rick pretended it would be. They finally agreed that the advisor would recommend Rick's inclusion in the club and would report his impressions to the court.

Rick was known to the boys in the Nobleteens but usually hung out with a more delinquent subgroup. When the advisor recommended his inclusion in the club, one of the members (who happened to be retarded) questioned why Rick should have preference over the boys who were waiting to get in. He then recalled seeing the advisor coming down in the elevator with Rick's mother, realized that it was about the trouble Rick was in, and quickly withdrew his objection.

Beyond this there was no discussion of Rick's problem, but the message was clear. The club members included him in their leisure activities and protected him when trouble was brewing. Eventually the charge was dropped, and he has not been picked up for delinquent behavior since that time. He has responded positively to the feeling of group inclusion, appears noticeably less depressed, and is more verbal. The payoff came for Rick when he was unanimously elected captain of the basketball team.

Example 2:

A well-known child psychiatrist was brought to a Nobleteen meeting to consult with the boys in writing a speech for influential people in the health and welfare field. His goal was to argue for more flexibility on the part of youth-serving agencies. The intervenor's only role was to bring the two together. The psychiatrist was familiar with the boys' language, and they were experienced in discussing topics which focused on their relationships with external systems. Tape-recorded material from the meeting was included in the speech, and the boys gained a great sense of competence in verbalizing their concerns and points of view.

Example 3:

At one meeting of the "C" Street network club, two members informed the advisor that Mrs. White, the club president, was having an extremely severe asthma attack. The group discussed this informally and came to the conclusion that it was really her "nerves" and that she should go into the hospital. Mrs. White had been hospitalized several times previously and was diagnosed as a borderline schizophrenic. Mrs. White's main supports, her sister and her closest friend, were extremely anxious, their own fears of death and separation coming to the surface. This placed them in a real approach-avoidance bind. The advisor agreed to visit Mrs. White after the meeting.

Mrs. White was lying on the couch coughing in uncontrollable bursts. The advisor soon labeled the coughing (which was panicking her and the other two women) as a "good thing" and encouraged it. He sympathetically listened to Mrs. White recount her dramatic collapse on the hospital's emergency room floor and her subsequent hallucinations. While she talked, the two network members busied themselves cleaning up the house and attending to the children. Once the advisor had listened he began exploring areas of stress with her. The most recent crisis was that she was being threatened with eviction for nonpayment of rent. She had contacted her relief worker, who had promised to contact the landlord. The advisor promised to talk to the relief worker. He also learned that in desperation she had gone to a different hospital. She had confidence in the treatment she received there, but did not see how she could go back for an early morning clinic. The advisor agreed that Rebound could provide her with a cab voucher.

Then the three women and the advisor sat and discussed the events of the club meeting. Mrs. White's coughing subsided and she became calmer as she related to outside reality. The friend and the sister's anxiety was also reduced. They could then respond in ways which reduced rather then heightened Mrs. White's anxiety.

The significance of this intervention lies not so much in the availability of the professional to meet the immediate dependency needs and to manipulate external systems on the woman's behalf but in his being in a position to repair her system of significant supports. A member of her own system would thenceforth be able to remind her that her rent was due when she got her check and remind her about the attendance officer if she became lax in getting her children off to school. The program continued to meet her dependency needs and support her medical care through the cab vouchers. Initially the vouchers were obtained for her by the professional; later she took responsibility for reminding him about getting them; eventually she went to the clinic's business office to get them herself. She has not suffered a severe attack or psychotic episode since the intervention.

Our commitment was to develop models for the delivery of services which multiply our therapeutic impact by bringing about change in existing systems. By focusing on competence and mutual support rather than on pathology, we have experimented with a model for the delivery of services to people who do not wish to perceive themselves as patients.

References

1. Attneave, C. 1969. Therapy in tribal settings and urban network intervention. Fam. Proc. 8:192–211.

2. Auerswald, E. 1968. Interdisciplinary vs. ecological approach. Fam. Proc. 7:202–215.

3. Clark, K. 1965. The Dark Ghetto: Dilemmas Of Social Power. Harper and Row, New York.

4. Leopold, E. 1969. Hidden strengths in the disorganized family: discovery through extended home observations. Paper presented at meeting of Amer. Orthopsychiat. Assn.

5. Leopold, E. 1968. Rebound children and their families: a community survey conducted by the rebound children and youth project. Mimeo.

6. Malone, C. 1966. Safety first: comments on the influence of external danger in the lives of children of disorganized families. Amer. J. Orthopsychiat. 36:3–12.

7. Minuchin, S., et al. 1967. Families of the slums: An exploration of their structure and treatment. Basic Books, New York.

8. Minuchin, S. 1969. Family therapy: technique or theory. In Science and Psychoanalysis, J. Masserman, ed. 14:179–187. Grune & Stratton, New York.

9. Minuchin, S., and Montalvo, B. 1967. Techniques for working with disorganized low socioeconomic families. Amer. J. Orthopsychiat. 37:880–887.

10. Rabkin, J., et al. 1969. Delinquency and the lateral boundary of the family. In Children against the Schools, P. Graubard, ed. Follett Educational Corp., Chicago.

11. Speck, R. 1967. Psychotherapy of the social network of a schizophrenic family. Fam. Proc. 6:208–214.

12. U.S. Department of Health, Education and Welfare. 1968. Report of the President's Advisory Commission on Civil Disorders.

The school is the setting from which the worker's target becomes the *total* social service delivery system. The total system became a target as a result of the worker's perceptions of individual needs as a reflection of misconceptions between the individual and his immediate environment. Although the author does not identify it as such, the connections between various units and subsystems within a specified situation provide an illustration of an "ecological systems" way of thinking in operation. Case examples illustrate the need for social workers to become involved with their clients in the clients' own environment.

Preventive Intervention

Berta Fantl

The term "preventive intervention" may take on more specific meaning as those equipped with knowledge of individual psychodynamics move into an era in which sociocultural factors can be comprehended with pertinence and greater differentiation. Environment is no longer seen as restricted to what is accessible to immediate perception and open manipulation.[1] A new kind of awareness of the person-in-the-situation configuration is evolving which is significant for helping professions concerned with broad human issues.[2]

Conspicuous features of our time are the rapid changes in family and community life, the growth of bureaucratic structures, the professionalization of services, and the cultural and educational assimilation of different ethnic groups in urban centers. Along with these changes we are experiencing a new broadening of community responsibility for those in crisis or in a permanent dependent status—new at least in this country. It is not as if all the old patterns had vanished, but life has become complicated enough for the sophisticated and educated, let alone those whose earlier experiences have had little emotional enrichment and who have lacked opportunity to develop differential skills and competence for new kinds of social living.[3] The complexity of city life, the pattern of taking and sharing in new community structures, the

Reprinted with permission of the National Association of Social Workers from *Social Work,* Vol. 7, No. 3 (July 1962), pp. 41–47.
[1]Herman D. Stein, "The Concept of the Social Environment in Social Work Practice," *Smith College Studies in Social Work,* Vol. 30, No. 3 (June 1960), pp. 188–210.
[2]Bertram Beck, "Prevention and Treatment," based on the work of the Subcommittee on Trends, Issues, and Priorities of the NASW Commission on Social Work Practice, 1959. (Mimeographed.)
[3]Nelson N. Foote and Leonard S. Cottrell, *Identity and Interpersonal Competence* (Chicago: University of Chicago Press, 1955).

establishment of new and meaningful interpersonal relationships in family affairs and organizational systems, cannot be left to chance alone. Simpler tasks than these we do not expect to accomplish without support and guidance, and without margin for experimentation and error.

Concept of a Neighborhood

In the fall of 1958 a small unit of social workers left the centralized downtown school child guidance services in which they had been working to take up residence in a lower-lower-class district. Psychological testing and psychiatric consultation were provided from the central agency by request. This move reflected a growing sense that clients who normally would not flock in significant numbers to the doors of social agencies need to be studied and more fully understood in their natural setting, and that social workers and their agencies need to become part of the neighborhood in order to make services available which are physically as well as psychologically accessible, when crises arise that readily motivate clients to use help—if help can be offered in a style congenial to their spontaneous ways of expressing problems as well as solving them.

Concern soon shifted from the traditional one-to-one relationships and work with "collaterals" to a broad awareness of the daily life of clients, their immediate dilemmas and crises, their family ties or lack of them.[4] Once enmeshed in the human problems of the neighborhood, the consideration arose of how much or how little casework services for a few families would accomplish in view of the type and number of problems encountered and the over-all needs of the neighborhood. This is not meant to imply that there is not a crying need for more and better diagnostic and treatment facilities for clients with emotional problems. But with social problems as they increasingly exist, every social agency needs to take an honest look at how well it serves the population it thinks and says it is serving, and whether in our present knowledge and skills there is perhaps room for innovations of service that might benefit larger numbers of people, in different dimensions of human behavior and relations.

Once the major areas of strength and weakness of the neighborhood were identified as compared to the rest of the city, as well as major social institutions, the composition of ethnic groups, the neighborhood pattern, and ways in which people communicated and related to each

[4]Berta Fantl, "Casework in Lower Class Districts," *Mental Hygiene,* Vol. 45, No. 3 (July 1961), pp. 425–438.

other, a new conception evolved of the work to be done, which, despite gaps and imperfections, seemed more realistically related to the welfare needs of the total neighborhood than were the traditional clinical services. Casework services continued to be provided for a limited number of clients, and increasing time was spent in collaboration and consultation with some of the "caretaking agents" who exercise a profound influence on the lives of clients.[5]

A keen awareness developed of the existing social distance between clients and the caretaking agents, their prejudices about each other, and the breakdown of meaningful communication, which seemed to defy every effort and good intention of either party for a more positive interaction that might make full use of the meager number of services available in the neighborhood. One was aware not so much of lack of interactions as of opposing interaction and negative attitudes. Invariably prejudices and stereotyped perceptions were intensified by fear of "what people might think"—ignorance of another way of life and hopeless discouragement after repeated failure to establish rapport. People were often not sure what was expected of them, or how to act or what to say, or how to time their requests.

It is perhaps of interest to note that, as the social workers gradually became recognized and accepted by the client group as persons from whom one could "get help," the first few self-referrals were requests for help in conveying ideas and information to the schools, to public welfare officials, or to the police, or questions regarding them. It became apparent that not just the "doing of things" is important in initial relationships with multiproblem clients, but also ability to convey the feeling that we are not afraid to grapple with the complicated role relationships and interactions of their social environments.[6] These clients may not have had opportunity to develop the type of personality structure that fosters introspection and psychological awareness more commonly attributed to middle-class clients; be this as it may, most of them showed considerable awareness and discomfort about some of the more obvious social and cultural factors that interfere negatively with their social relationships and functioning.

Prejudices and stereotyped perceptions may have deep psychological roots; yet one gained the firm conviction that with patient, skillful, repeated intervention, and given a minimum of unfavorable attitudes, prejudices and stereotyped perceptions could be sufficiently modified to permit more satisfying behavior. One saw teachers become less

[5]Gerald Caplan, *Concepts of Mental Health and Consultation* (Washington, D.C.: U.S. Dept. of Health, Education, and Welfare, 1959).

[6]For a similar conceptualization of differential interventions see Ludwig Geismar, "Three Levels of Treatment for Multiproblem Families," *Social Casework,* Vol. 42, No. 3 (March 1961), pp. 124–128.

discouraged with their jobs, policemen discover that they and certain groups of children did not need to be enemies—or at least not all the time—and the school social worker feeling at home in situations which not long before had been incomprehensible and would therefore have resulted in closing a case through the withdrawal of either the client or the agency.

Emerging Focus

Although an effort was made in the same way to understand other social institutions, it seemed logical as a school agency to try especially to understand the social structure and position of the schools in the neighborhood.

Such questions were asked as: How, on the whole, do school people in our neighborhood view their pupils and their families? How do the various ethnic groups view education as a goal for their children? Are there conflicting aims in the over-all educational system which put unbearable pressure on administrators and teachers, making a favorable response to their pupils more difficult? At what points does the value system of the educator conflict with those to be educated? Why is there such great turnover of teachers, nurses, and social workers in a neighborhood like this? Why is the neighborhood so little challenge to anyone? When and at what points are expectations about each other not met? What is the status problem in working in this district?[7]

We were concerned with what the low self-concept of our clients might mean to their interpersonal relationships and interactions. Were they taking out social and emotional frustration on each other? Was the societal strain (poverty, unemployment, discrimination) so high that impulsive behavior was one way of releasing tensions—taking also into account that waiting for any kind of gratification was not the usual neighborhood pattern? Many Negro clients maintained that living in the South had not been "too bad." Was it so bad that they needed to use denial as a defense, or were role expectations fewer, more personal in nature, better defined, and thereby less confusing? Could one realistically expect less stealing and violence (which might reflect a change of values) so long as social conditions did not leave room for equal and useful opportunities and outdated laws did not "fit the crime"?[8] Not only individuals but whole neighborhoods need to find their identity

[7]Elizabeth D. de Losada and Berta Fantl, "Working Papers." Unpublished manuscript, 1958–1960. We wish to express our gratitude to Edmund H. Volkart, Ph.D., professor of sociology at Stanford University, California, for his sustaining interest in our work and for the opportunity to discuss this type of question with him.

[8]Richard A. Cloward and Lloyd E. Ohlin, *Delinquency and Opportunity* (Glencoe, Ill.: The Free Press, 1960); Erik H. Erikson, "On the Nature of Clinical Evidence," *Daedalus,* Proceedings of the American Academy of Arts and Sciences, Vol. 87, No. 4 (Fall 1958).

in society, and we need to understand the latent function performed by these "bad" neighborhoods in relation to the rest of the city.

By such questions one would not expect to find specific answers to problem situations in their own way as unique as individuals under close analysis. But the questioning broadened our psychological frame of reference to include the social systems, norms, values, and customs of the recipients of general welfare services and the helping professions; it provided a beginning for a more appropriate and flexible approach to mastering the environment while meeting inner personal needs.

Focus was on the problem situation, on the quality of interaction, on possible problems in communication. One tried to understand the inner and outer stresses to which people were responding and the expectations they had of themselves and of others. By disentangling, clarifying, and supporting complicated role relationships in the context of socio-cultural factors and personal needs, it was hoped to re-establish an equilibrium for better communication and social functioning, and more mutually satisfying relationships. Recognizing the gaps and limitations of our present conceptual frame, the ultimate goal was to create a more benign neighborhood climate for clients by widening understanding of psychological, cultural, and social factors in the light of recent knowledge.

Sometimes it seemed that the mere presence of the social workers, their desire to understand, and their frank appraisal of what could be done or what did not seem possible brought a lessening of tension. More often they were more than mere listeners and observers. While paying attention to the minute details of what was going on between people and the types of stresses they were reacting to, they often intervened carefully with words or actions, taking pains not to overdo and letting the client or consultee handle the situation the moment he seemed able to, yet leaving the door open for further intervention for the same or other problems.

Case Excerpt

The following case excerpt can illustrate only a few among several points which are the concern of this paper.

Tony

The counselor of a high school phoned the school social worker when she learned that the couple she had asked to come to school as Tony's parents were in fact foster parents, and that the public welfare department was planning to place Tony with his father, who had been released from prison a few months previously after serving a ten-year sentence for murdering Tony's mother, in Tony's presence, when the child was 3 years old. As distant relatives, and with their own children nearly grown, this couple had taken Tony into their home, showered him with affection and much later, when their finances were no longer sufficient, asked the public welfare department for financial assistance, to which they were entitled as foster parents.

The counselor, who also carried teaching responsibilities, was not only new in her position as "personal problems counselor"; she was also new to the district and not without anxiety and inner tension in meeting her professional obligations. She had asked Tony's "parents" (they had registered him as their child) to come to school, since she considered him emotionally disturbed and in need of professional help. Tony was just sitting, not learning, and was completely inarticulate when questioned by teachers, although seen talking a few times to his classmates. The foster parents presented their story in poorly spoken English, with many gestures and references to the Lord. The counselor, bewildered and upset, wavered between deep sympathy and utter disbelief that so much human tragedy could be possible, of which only the barest details are reported here.

The social worker went over to the school immediately; the foster parents, without really knowing who she was, repeated eagerly and helplessly some of their story. A few telephone calls to public welfare and the probation department confirmed what they had to say. In one department the case load had not been covered because of a long-standing job vacancy, while in the other the worker was new and unfamiliar with his case load; there had been no planning for co-ordination of services. Tony's father showed a long history of emotional outbursts and instability; living by himself and without a steady job, he was left without the support of a worker who might have helped him to get re-established in the community. The foster parents had sought physical protection from him because he was threatening them, but the police had not believed them "because people come with stories like this every day."

After this crisis was settled through appropriate interventions by the school social worker, when it had been clarified who was going to do what next, she noticed that the family had been repeatedly out of money and food and that the $70 they were receiving monthly from the public welfare department for Tony's care was their only steady source of income. (In order to save this amount the public welfare department had "considered" placing Tony with his father.) The foster mother was in need of an operation and unable to carry on with her job; the foster father had suffered two strokes several months earlier which disabled him. His social security payments had not come through. Dressed in his best suit, he had gone downtown several times to settle this matter. Again his limited ability to express himself in the situation and his lack of sophisticated know-how prevented him from dealing effectively with the bureaucratic structure of our social agencies. Because of complications in verifying his birth, it took the school social worker several weeks to locate his application and see that it was moved into the right channels.

Possible Lines of Intervention

One point about this case not unlike other cases is that there was a family in extreme despair, hanging on to each other and surrounded by agencies set up to protect and help people to function more adequately. Yet because of the complexity of structural processes inherent in any large-scale organization, agencies frequently create a climate that defeats much of their original intent. Frequently they are dealing with people who have never had opportunity to acquire the skills and competence to relate in the more impersonal and differential ways to the various officeholders of our growing bureaucratic structures. It is of no use to stay away from these situations and say, "If only the other agencies (police, court, public welfare, and so on) knew what they were doing!" and "We are the only ones who know what is right," since one must realize that all agencies, including our own, are interrelated in the client's social field. If structural or educational changes are necessary, we ourselves must become involved in this aspect of the client's life as one among several ways to bring about change.

1. The school social worker, in her dual role as a caseworker with clients and as a consultant to school personnel, saw several possible avenues for intervention. She could have "reached out" to this family, establishing a continued casework relationship and, with some awareness and attention to the social situation, focusing mainly on the psychological make-up of the clients. By "strengthening their ego" through primarily psychological means she might have hoped that eventually they would be able to deal more effectively with relationships in their environment.

In all probability this approach would have failed, since the worker very quickly recognized that "ego strength" was not lacking, but that these clients had never had the socializing experience to know how to handle themselves in these types of situations. It cannot be said too often or emphatically that not being able to make the right connection in our social systems (including social agencies and clinics), or not following the right societal track from our point of view, is *not necessarily* a sign of poor ego organization.

In this case the point is perhaps plain, but the same often holds true in less extreme situations. Recent studies of character disorders which elaborate on the individual's psychodynamics without looking at the elements in the environment pertinent to his problem miss important clues for psychological treatment, social intervention, or a combination of both. "More casework services" or even "selected case loads"—as a highly desirable and well-intended aim—will not meet our expectations without development of problem formulations and treatment approaches as appropriate for specific client groups as they are realistic for casework. Moreover, as we shoulder the heavy responsibility of being consultants and collaborators in other agencies, we need to clarify what conceptual framework to adopt when the behavior and problems of clients are defined and discussed and social issues are at stake—even when nontechnical language is used, and though the clients are in need of psychological treatment.

Social policy and casework practice with clients of lower classes operate under the same roof. The increasing interdependence of man in relation to man and man in relation to his wider environment, as well as his internal functioning, need the most careful and flexible exploration. The point is not that any one conceptualization is "right" while others are wrong; but to find the conceptualization that will provide us with the most helpful leads in looking at the total needs of clients.[9] It is of little comfort to know that other professions are searching for similar reformulations, differentiations, and refinements. Albert Cohen in recent writing has the following to say: "A major task before us is to get rid of the notion . . . that the deviant, the abnormal, the pathological and, in general, the deplorable always come wrapped in a single package."[10]

2. As a school consultant the social worker could have focused mainly on the conflict situation of the counselor as it related to her professional role. By recognizing her anxiety in being confronted with a perplexing situation and relieving some of her guilt for not being able to handle the situation more adequately—and, in general, through emotional support and some clarifying information—the counselor might have been enabled to deal more effectively with the clients. There were many other cases in which just this occurred.

In this instance the role of the counselor was extremely taxing, in a

---

[9]How can we think in the framework of "limited goals" for the neediest in our midst and for families burdened with a constellation of troublesome problems, when "expanding goals and sight" are needed? How is it that as social workers we need to be reminded that "constructive attitudes" are essential for working with certain client groups?

[10]Albert K. Cohen, "The Study of Social Disorganization and Deviant Behavior," in *Sociology Today* (New York: Basic Books, 1959), p. 463. This is not unlike what Fritz Redl has to say in more psychological terminology, describing delinquent types, in *New Perspectives for Research on Juvenile Delinquency* (Washington, D.C.: U.S. Dept. of Health, Education, and Welfare, Children's Bureau, 1955).

position new to her and a district quite different from her own background and previous professional experience. Her professional training had prepared her to meet parents who would recognize her as an educator and be concerned about the emotional aspects of their child's nonlearning. Instead she was presented with a family constellation and background she did not expect, while the foster parents in their personal way looked to her as a last resort for help, after telling their story to a number of people. It was not that the counselor was basically inflexible about her role or that she lacked emotional warmth. But it often happens in lower-lower-class districts that the social distance and discouragement between clients and the caretaking agents—whether teachers, social workers, or others—are very great, and the perception of each other becomes blurred. In addition, the types of problems encountered are often dramatically aggressive; they are differently handled and seemingly unrelated to one's own social and emotional world, so that one's defense system may become quite threatened. The fluid give-and-take of feelings and words urgently needed with these clients *could not be produced without more adequate understanding and genuine empathy* for the various aspects of the total situation.

3. By remaining centered on the clients' needs, but focusing on the problem situation in all its emotional, social, and cultural facets, the school social worker decided to relieve the counselor of a pressing task which was more than she could be expected to handle at the moment. By intervening at this point the social worker established immediate rapport, not only with the foster parents but also with the counselor, with whom she had worked before. Through the disentangling of role relationships, the clarification of tasks and responsibilities, the re-establishment of channels of communication, and a sensitive awareness of the spoken and unspoken feelings of all persons involved, the family received the help they needed most. After the counselor got a "feel" of the neighborhood and the particulars of Tony's situation, she established good rapport with the foster parents, who often came to see her to discuss informally various events of their life.

Since Tony was a fearful child with emotional problems, and no treatment facilities were available for this type of "unmotivated" family, the social worker saw him for diagnostic purposes while the counselor explored resources within the school which would give him some opportunity to develop academically, emotionally, socially, and physically. Frequent and increasingly frank discussions with the school social worker made it possible for the counselor to air some of her own feelings of professional disappointment, her high self-expectations, and her physical fears of the neighborhood. Clarification of some of her misconceptions as they related to particular situations of children and their families lent support to the positive concern of the counselor for her students. After she had experienced the satisfaction and security of handling a few cases well, her warm and spontaneous behavior reappeared and she became keenly interested in her students and an active participant in neighborhood affairs.

Conclusions

This case is not set down as a success story, and deals with only one aspect of the work.[11] The experience of finding and mobilizing potential resources in a neighborhood said to have few potentials was most rewarding. This mobilization occurred through social action, work on community committees, or—as has been suggested here—through work with caretaking agents and short-term contacts with clients during varied crisis situations.

With this broader conception of the work a different type of social worker evolved—one who saw himself as a part of the client's social field, who was ready to enter and deal with crisis situations in a new context and was perceived by others in that way. Being accused of "superficiality" and "lack of depth" in treatment became inadvertently a compliment, as the realization grew that casework sensibility, awareness, and skills can be used in more ways than one to enrich different dimensions of human behavior and help to unfold human relationships.

What emerged from this venture into social and cultural horizons was not the generality still attributed to social science theory, but the richness it added to a limited understanding and way of dealing with human problems. A more positive perspective was also gained on the inner strength of individuals and their drive for adaptation in an increasingly complex world.

[11]For other aspects see Fantl, "Casework in Lower Class Districts," *op. cit.*

The Mobilization For Youth project for juvenile delinquency, in New York City, was one of the more widely
publicized endeavors in recent years to use the generalist
approach to social work. Purcell and Specht illustrate that
individual patterns of response must be understood
within the context in which they occurred. Interventive
strategies are to be selected to meet individual needs
rather than to actualize preselected methods of practitioners or particular agency goals.

The House on Sixth
Street

Francis P. Purcell
Harry Specht

The extent to which social work can affect the course of social problems
has not received the full consideration it deserves.[1] For some time the
social work profession has taken account of social problems only as
they have become manifest in behavioral pathology. Yet it is becoming
increasingly apparent that, even allowing for this limitation, it is often
necessary for the same agency or worker to intervene by various methods at various points.

In this paper, the case history of a tenement house in New York City
is used to illustrate some of the factors that should be considered in
selecting intervention methods. Like all first attempts, the approach
described can be found wanting in conceptual clarity and systematiza-
tion. Yet the vital quality of the effort and its implications for social work
practice seem clear.

The case of "The House on Sixth Street" is taken from the files of
Mobilization For Youth (MFY), an action-research project that has been
in operation since 1962 on New York's Lower East Side.[2] MFY's programs are financed by grants from several public and private sources.
The central theoretical contention of MFY is that a major proportion

Reprinted with permission of the authors and the National Association of Social Workers from
Social Work, Vol. 10, No. 4 (October 1965), pp. 69–76.

[1]Social work practitioners sometimes use the term "social problem" to mean "environmental
problem." The sense in which it is used here corresponds to the definition developed by the social
sciences. That is, a social problem is a disturbance, deviation, or breakdown in social behavior that
(1) involves a considerable number of people and (2) is of serious concern to many in the society.
It is social in origin and effect, and is a social responsibility. It represents a discrepancy between social
standards and social reality. Also, such socially perceived variations must be viewed as corrigible.
See Robert K. Merton and Robert A. Nisbet, eds., *Contemporary Social Problems* (New York: Harcourt, Brace, and World, 1961), pp. 6, 701.

[2]A complete case record of the Sixth Street house will be included in a forthcoming publication
of Mobilization For Youth.

of juvenile delinquency occurs when adolescents from low-income families do not have access to legitimate opportunities by which they can fulfill the aspirations for success they share with all American youth. The action programs of MFY are designed to offer these youths concrete opportunities to offset the debilitating effects of poverty. For example, the employment program helps youngsters obtain jobs; other programs attempt to increase opportunities in public schools. In addition, there are group work and recreation programs. A wide variety of services to individuals and families is offered through Neighborhood Service Centers: a homemaking program, a program for released offenders, and a narcotics information center. Legal services, a housing services unit, a special referral unit, and a community development program are among other services that have been developed or made available. Thus, MFY has an unusually wide range of resources for dealing with social problems.

The Problem

"The House on Sixth Street" became a case when Mrs. Smith came to an MFY Neighborhood Service Center to complain that there had been no gas, electricity, heat, or hot water in her apartment house for more than four weeks. She asked the agency for help. Mrs. Smith was 23 years old, Negro, and the mother of four children, three of whom had been born out of wedlock. At the time she was unmarried and receiving Aid to Families with Dependent Children. She came to the center in desperation because she was unable to run her household without utilities. Her financial resources were exhausted—but not her courage. The Neighborhood Service Center worker decided that in this case the building—the tenants, the landlord, and circumstances affecting their relationships—was of central concern.

A social worker then visited the Sixth Street building with Mrs. Smith and a community worker. Community workers are members of the community organization staff in a program that attempts to encourage residents to take independent social action. Like many members in other MFY programs, community workers are residents of the particular neighborhood. Most of them have little formal education, their special contribution being their ability to relate to and communicate with other residents. Because some of the tenants were Puerto Rican, a Spanish-speaking community worker was chosen to accompany the social worker. His easy manner and knowledge of the neighborhood enabled him and the worker to become involved quickly with the tenants.

Their first visits confirmed Mrs. Smith's charge that the house had been without utilities for more than four weeks. Several months before, the city Rent and Rehabilitation Administration had reduced the rent for each apartment to one dollar a month because the landlord was not providing services. However, this agency was slow to take further action. Eleven families were still living in the building, which had twenty-eight apartments. The landlord owed the electric company several thousand dollars. Therefore, the meters had been removed from the house. Because most of the tenants were welfare clients, the Department of Welfare had "reimbursed" the landlord directly for much of the unpaid electric bill and refused to pay any more money to the electric company. The Department of Welfare was slow in meeting the emergency needs of the tenants. Most of the children (forty-eight from the eleven families in the building) had not been to school for a month because they were ill or lacked proper clothing.

The mothers were tired and demoralized. Dirt and disorganization were increasing daily. The tenants were afraid to sleep at night because the building was infested with rats. There was danger of fire because the tenants had to use candles for light. The seventeen abandoned apartments had been invaded by homeless men and drug addicts. Petty thievery is common in such situations. However, the mothers did not want to seek protection from the police for fear that they would chase away all men who were not part of the families in the building (some of the unmarried mothers had men living with them—one of the few means of protection from physical danger available to these women— even though mothers on public assistance are threatened with loss of income if they are not legally married). The anxiety created by these conditions was intense and disabling.

The workers noted that the mothers were not only anxious but "fighting mad"; not only did they seek immediate relief from their physical dangers and discomforts but they were eager to express their fury at the landlord and the public agencies, which they felt had let them down.

The circumstances described are by no means uncommon, at least not in New York City. Twenty percent of all housing in the city is still unfit, despite all the public and private residential building completed since World War II. At least 277,500 dwellings in New York City need major repairs if they are to become safe and adequate shelters. This means that approximately 500,000 people in the city live in inferior dwelling units and as many as 825,000 people in buildings that are considered unsafe.[3] In 1962 the New York City Bureau of Sanitary Inspections reported that 530 children were bitten by rats in their homes and 198 children were poisoned (nine of them fatally) by nibbling at peeling lead paint, even though the use of lead paint has been

[3]Facts About Low Income Housing (New York: Emergency Committee for More Low Income Housing, 1963).

illegal in the city for more than ten years. Given the difficulties involved in lodging formal complaints with city agencies, it is safe to assume that unreported incidents of rat bites and lead poisoning far exceed these figures.

The effect of such hardships on children is obvious. Of even greater significance is the sense of powerlessness generated when families go into these struggles barehanded. It is this sense of helplessness in the face of adversity that induces pathological anxiety, intergenerational alienation, and social retreatism. Actual physical impoverishment alone is not nearly so debilitating as poverty attended by a sense of unrelieved impotence that becomes generalized and internalized. The poor then regard much social learning as irrelevant, since they do not believe it can effect any environmental change.[4]

Intervention and the Social Systems

Selecting a point of intervention in dealing with this problem would have been simpler if the target of change were Mrs. Smith alone, or Mrs. Smith and her co-tenants, the clients in whose behalf intervention was planned. Too often, the client system presenting the problem becomes the major target for intervention, and the intervention method is limited to the one most suitable for that client system. However, Mrs. Smith and the other tenants had a multitude of problems emanating from many sources, any one of which would have warranted the attention of a social agency. The circumstantial fact is that in individual contacts an agency that offers services to individuals and families should not be a major factor in determining the method of intervention. Identification of the client merely helps the agency to define goals; other variables are involved in the selection of method. As Burns and Glasser have suggested: "It may be helpful to consider the primary target of change as distinct from the persons who may be the primary clients. . . . The primary target of change then becomes the human or physical environment toward which professional efforts via direct intervention are aimed in order to facilitate change."[5] The three major factors that determined MFY's approach to the problem were (1) knowledge of the various social systems within which the social problem was located (i.e., social systems assessment), (2) knowledge of the various methods (including non-social work methods) appropriate for intervention in

[4]Francis P. Purcell, "The Helping Professions and Problems of the Brief Contact," in Frank Riessman, Jerome Cohen, and Arthur Pearl, eds., *Mental Health of the Poor* (New York: Free Press of Glencoe, 1964), p. 432.

[5]Mary E. Burns and Paul H. Glasser, "Similarities and Differences in Casework and Group Work Practice," *Social Service Review,* Vol. 37, No. 4 (December 1963), p. 423.

these different social systems, and (3) the resources available to the agency.[6]

The difficulties of the families in the building were intricately connected with other elements of the social system related to the housing problem. For example, seven different public agencies were involved in maintenance of building services. Later other agencies were involved in relocating the tenants. There is no one agency in New York City that handles all housing problems. Therefore, tenants have little hope of getting help on their own. In order to redress a grievance relating to water supply (which was only one of the building's many problems) it is necessary to know precisely which city department to contact. The following is only a partial listing:

No water—Health Department
Not enough water—Department of Water Supply
No hot water—Buildings Department
Water leaks—Buildings Department
Large water leaks—Department of Water Supply
Water overflowing from apartment above—Police Department
Water sewage in the cellar—Sanitation Department

The task of determining which agencies are responsible for code enforcement in various areas is not simple, and in addition one must know that the benefits and services available for tenants and for the community vary with the course of action chosen. For example, if the building were taken over by the Rent and Rehabilitation Administration under the receivership law, it would be several weeks before services would be re-established, and the tenants would have to remain in the building during its rehabilitation. There would be, however, some compensations: tenants could remain in the neighborhood—indeed, in the same building—and their children would not have to change schools. If, on the other hand, the house were condemned by the Buildings Department, the tenants would have to move, but they would be moved quickly and would receive top relocation priorities and maximum relocation benefits. But once the tenants had been relocated—at city expense—the building could be renovated by the landlord as middle-income housing. In the Sixth Street house, it was suspected that this was the motivation behind the landlord's actions. If the building were condemned and renovated, there would be twenty-eight fewer low-income housing units in the neighborhood.

This is the fate of scores of tenements on the Lower East Side because

[6]Harry Specht and Frank Riessman, "Some Notes on a Model for an Integrated Social Work Approach to Social Problems" (New York: Mobilization For Youth, June 1963). (Mimeographed.)

much new middle-income housing is being built there. Basic services are withheld and tenants are forced to move so that buildings may be renovated for middle-income tenants. Still other buildings are allowed to deteriorate with the expectation that they will be bought by urban renewal agencies.

It is obvious, even limiting analysis to the social systems of one tenement, that the problem is enormous. Although the tenants were the clients in this case, Mrs. Smith, the tenant group, and other community groups were all served at one point or another. It is even conceivable that the landlord might have been selected as the most appropriate recipient of service. Rehabilitation of many slum tenements is at present nearly impossible. Many landlords regard such property purely as an investment. With profit the prime motive, needs of low-income tenants are often overlooked. Under present conditions it is financially impossible for many landlords to correct all the violations in their buildings even if they wanted to. If the social worker chose to intervene at this level of the problem, he might apply to the Municipal Loan Fund, make arrangements with unions for the use of non-union labor in limited rehabilitation projects, or provide expert consultants on reconstruction. These tasks would require social workers to have knowledge similar to that of city planners. If the problems of landlords were not selected as a major point of intervention, they would still have to be considered at some time since they are an integral part of the social context within which this problem exists.

A correct definition of interacting social systems or of the social worker's choice of methods and points of intervention is not the prime concern here. What is to be emphasized is what this case so clearly demonstrates: that although the needs of the client system enable the agency to define its goals, the points and methods of intervention cannot be selected properly without an awareness and substantial knowledge of the social systems within which the problem is rooted.

Dealing with the Problem

The social worker remained with the building throughout a four-month period. In order to deal effectively with the problem, he had to make use of all the social work methods as well as the special talents of a community worker, lawyer, city planner, and various civil rights organizations. The social worker and the community worker functioned as generalists with both individuals and families calling on caseworkers as needed for specialized services or at especially trying times, such as during the first week and when the families were relocated. Because of the division of labor in the agency, much of the social work with individuals was done with the help of a caseworker. Group work, administration, and community organization were handled by the social worker, who had been trained in community organization. In many instances he also dealt with the mothers as individuals, as they encountered one stressful situation after another. Agency caseworkers also provided immediate and concrete assistance to individual families, such as small financial grants, medical care, homemaking services, baby-sitting services, and transportation. This reduced the intensity of pressures on these families. Caseworkers were especially helpful in dealing with some of the knotty and highly technical problems connected with public agencies.

With a caseworker and a lawyer experienced in handling tenement cases, the social worker began to help the families organize their demands for the services and utilities to which they were legally entitled but which the public agencies had consistently failed to provide for them.

The ability of the mothers to take concerted group action was evident from the beginning, and Mrs. Smith proved to be a natural and competent leader. With support, encouragement, and assistance from the staff, the mothers became articulate and effective in negotiating with the various agencies involved. In turn, the interest and concern of the agencies increased markedly when the mothers began to visit them, make frequent telephone calls, and send letters and telegrams to them and to politicians demanding action.

With the lawyer and a city planner (an agency consultant), the mothers and staff members explored various possible solutions to the housing problem. For example, the Department of Welfare had offered to move the families to shelters or hotels. Neither alternative was acceptable to the mothers. Shelters were ruled out because they would not consider splitting up their families, and they rejected hotels because they had discovered from previous experience that many of the "hotels" selected were flop-houses or were inhabited by prostitutes.

The following is taken from the social worker's record during the first week:

Met with the remaining tenants, several Negro men from the block, and [the city planner]. . . . Three of the mothers said that they would sooner sleep out on the street than go to the Welfare shelter. If nothing else, they felt that this would be a way of protesting their plight. . . . One of the mothers said that they couldn't very well do this with most of the children having colds. Mrs. Brown thought that they might do better to ask Reverend Jones if they could move into the cellar of his church temporarily. . . . The other mothers got quite excited about this idea because they thought that the church basement would make excellent living quarters.

After a discussion as to whether the mothers would benefit from embarrassing the public agencies by dramatically exposing their inadequacies, the mothers decided to move into the nearby church. They asked the worker to attempt to have their building condemned. At another meeting, attended by tenants from neighboring buildings and representatives of other local groups, it was concluded that what had happened to the Sixth Street building was a result of discrimination against the tenants as Puerto Ricans and Negroes. The group—which had now become an organization—sent the following telegram to city, state, and federal officials:

We are voters and Puerto Rican and Negro mothers asking for equal rights, for decent housing and enough room. Building has broken windows, no gas or electricity for four weeks, no heat or hot water, holes in floors, loose wiring. Twelve of forty-eight children in building sick. Welfare doctors refuse to walk up dark stairs. Are we human or what? Should innocent children suffer for landlords' brutality and city and state neglect? We are tired of being told to wait with children ill and unable to attend school. Negro and Puerto Rican tenants are forced out while buildings next door are renovated at high rents. We are not being treated as human beings.

For the most part, the lawyer and city planner stayed in the background, acting only as consultants. But as the tenants and worker became more involved with the courts and as other organizations entered the fight, the lawyer and city planner played a more active and direct role.

Resultant Side-Effects

During this process, tenants in other buildings on the block became more alert to similar problems in their buildings. With the help of the community development staff and the housing consultant, local groups and organizations such as tenants' councils and the local chapter of the Congress of Racial Equality were enlisted to support and work with the mothers.

Some of the city agencies behaved as though MFY had engineered the entire scheme to embarrass them—steadfastly disregarding the fact that the building had been unlivable for many months. Needless to say, the public agencies are overloaded and have inadequate resources. As has been documented, many such bureaucracies develop an amazing insensitivity to the needs of their clients.[7] In this case, the MFY social

---

[7]See, for example, Reinhard Bendix, "Bureaucracy and the Problem of Power," in Robert K. Merton, Alisa Gray, Barbara Hockey, and Horan C. Sebrin, eds., *Reader in Bureaucracy* (Glencoe, Ill.: Free Press, 1952), pp. 114–134.

worker believed that the tenants—and other people in their plight—should make their needs known to the agencies and to the public at large. He knew that when these expressions of need are backed by power—either in numbers or in political knowledge—they are far more likely to have some effect.

Other movements in the city at this time gave encouragement and direction to the people in the community. The March on Washington and the Harlem rent strike are two such actions.

By the time the families had been relocated, several things had been accomplished. Some of the public agencies had been sufficiently moved by the actions of the families and the local organizations to provide better services for them. When the families refused to relocate in a shelter and moved into a neighborhood church instead, one of the television networks picked up their story. Officials in the housing agencies came to investigate and several local politicians lent the tenants their support. Most important, several weeks after the tenants moved into the church, a bill was passed by the city council designed to prevent some of the abuses that the landlord had practiced with impunity. The councilman who sponsored the new law referred to the house on Sixth Street to support his argument.

Nevertheless, the problems that remain far outweigh the accomplishments. A disappointing epilogue to the story is that in court, two months later, the tenants' case against the landlord was dismissed by the judge on a legal technicality. The judge ruled that because the electric company had removed the meters from the building it was impossible for the landlord to provide services.

Some of the tenants were relocated out of the neighborhood and some in housing almost as poor as that they had left. The organization that began to develop in the neighborhood has continued to grow, but it is a painstaking job. The fact that the poor have the strength to continue to struggle for better living conditions is something to wonder at and admire.

Implications for Practice

Social work helping methods as currently classified are so inextricably interwoven in practice that it no longer seems valid to think of a generic practice as consisting of the application of casework, group work, or community organization skills as the nature of the problem demands. Nor does it seem feasible to adapt group methods for traditional casework problems or to use group work skills in community organization or community organization method in casework. Such suggestions—when they appear in the literature—either reflect confusion or, what is worse, suggest that no clearcut method exists apart from the auspices that support it.

In this case it is a manifestation of a social problem—housing—that was the major point around which social services were organized. The social worker's major intellectual task was to select the points at which the agency could intervene in the problem and the appropriate methods to use. It seems abundantly clear that in order to select appropriate points of intervention the social worker need not only understand individual patterns of response, but the nature of the social conditions that are the context in which behavior occurs. As this case makes evident, the social system that might be called the "poverty system" is enduring and persistent. Its parts intermesh with precision and disturbing complementarity. Intentionally or not, a function is thereby maintained that produces severe social and economic deprivation. Certain groups profit enormously from the maintenance of this system, but larger groups suffer. Social welfare—and, in particular, its central profession, social work—must examine the part it plays in either maintaining or undermining this socially pernicious poverty system. It is important that the social work profession no longer regard social conditions as immutable and a social reality to be accommodated as service is provided to deprived persons with an ever increasing refinement of technique. Means should be developed whereby agencies can affect social problems more directly, especially through institutional (organizational) change.

The idea advanced by MFY is that the social worker should fulfill his professional function and agency responsibility by seeking a solution to social problems through institutional change rather than by focusing on individual problems in social functioning. This is not to say that individual expressions of a given social problem should be left unattended. On the contrary, this approach is predicated on the belief that individual problems in social functioning are to varying degrees both cause and effect. It rejects the notion that individuals are afflicted with social pathologies, holding, rather, that the same social environment that generates conformity makes payment by the deviance that emerges. As Nisbet points out ". . . socially prized arrangements and values in society can produce socially condemned results."[8] This should direct social work's attention to institutional arrangements and their consequences. This approach does not lose sight of the individual or group, since the social system is composed of various statuses, roles, and classes. It takes cognizance of the systemic relationship of the various parts of the social system, including the client. It recognizes that

[8]Merton and Nisbet, *op.cit.,* p. 7.

efforts to deal with one social problem frequently generate others with debilitating results.

Thus it is that such institutional arrangements as public assistance, state prisons, and state mental hospitals, or slum schools are regarded by many as social problems in their own right. The social problems of poverty, criminality, mental illness, and failure to learn that were to be solved or relieved remain, and the proposed solutions pose almost equally egregious problems.

This paper has presented a new approach to social work practice. The knowledge, values, attitudes, and skills were derived from a generalist approach to social work. Agencies that direct their energies to social problems by effecting institutional change will need professional workers whose skills cut across the broad spectrum of social work knowledge.

Selected Bibliography

Fraley, Yvonne L., "A Role Model for Practice," *Social Service* Review, 43(2), 1969, pp. 145–154. A social work practice model based on role theory is advanced to use in analyzing individual interactions common to direct service relationships, and the possible application to nonclient relationships such as colleagues, supervisors, community leaders, and agency personnel. Six different variables are included in the discussion.

Golan, Naomi, and Gruschka, Ruth, "Integrating the New Immigrant; A Model for Social Work Practice in Transitional States," *Social Work,* 16(2), 1971, pp. 82–87. As a result of rapid political and social change individuals and groups are often relocated in new communities and situations, placing stress on both the individuals and the community. A prevention–intervention framework is proposed as a model for resolving transitional crises that may occur in income management, health, housing, education, leisure activities, and citizenship.

Hartman, Ann, "To Think about the Unthinkable," *Social Casework,* 51(8), 1970, pp. 467–474. Systems theory is discussed as a conceptual framework for social work practice that may enable intervention to shift from nearly exclusive focus on individual characteristics to include complex interactions and relationships with and between various systems of which any individual is a part. General practice implications are discussed.

Minuchin, Salvador, "The Plight of the Poverty-Stricken Family in the United States," *Child Welfare,* 49(3), 1970, pp. 124–130. A pathology oriented approach to intervention is discussed in terms of its frequent misuse and inappropriateness. Instead an ecological approach is suggested which can provide better understanding for the planning, development, and delivery of services.

A major component involves allowing natural systems of support to function more effectively.

Segal, Brian, "The Politicalization of Deviance," *Social Work,* 17(4), 1972, pp. 40–46. The definition of social deviance has expanded into the political arena where marginal man has little involvement or identification with society's essential goals. Social work must expand its traditional treatment approach and direct interventions at systems change in helping marginal man gain entry into society's mainstream. The concept of advocacy is discussed as one approach.

Sunley, Robert, "Family Advocacy: From Case to Cause," *Social Casework,* 51(6), 1970, pp. 347–357. Family advocacy is examined as a way for social work agencies and professional staff to bridge the gap between the many instances of grievance against social institutions and the many-faceted actions needed to accomplish institutional change. The focus becomes one of attention to individual and family need within the context of improvement of the social environment.

Author Index